Okanagan College LRC

D0389829

H
62
.T59

63391

## DATE DUE

| DATE DUE | | |
|---|---|---|
| DEC 1 1 1981 | | |
| FEB 1 0 1982 | | |
| MAY 2 1990 | | |
| MAR 1 1 1992 | | |
| APR 1 7 1998 | | |
| | | |
| | | |
| | | |
| | | |
| | | |

MURIEL FFOULKES L.R.C.
OKANAGAN COLLEGE
British Columbia
V1Y 4X8

# Toward Reform of Program Evaluation

## Aims, Methods, and Institutional Arrangements

Lee J. Cronbach

Sueann Robinson Ambron

Sanford M. Dornbusch

Robert D. Hess

Robert C. Hornik

D. C. Phillips

Decker F. Walker

Stephen S. Weiner

OKANAGAN COLLEGE LIBRARY
BRITISH COLUMBIA

# Toward Reform of Program Evaluation

63391

 Jossey-Bass Publishers

San Francisco • Washington • London • 1980

TOWARD REFORM OF PROGRAM EVALUATION
*Aims, Methods, and Institutional Arrangements*
by Lee J. Cronbach, Sueann Robinson Ambron,
Sanford M. Dornbusch, Robert D. Hess, Robert C. Hornik,
D. C. Phillips, Decker F. Walker, and Stephen S. Weiner

Copyright © 1980 by:   Jossey-Bass Inc., Publishers
433 California Street
San Francisco, California 94104

&

Jossey-Bass Limited
28 Banner Street
London EC1Y 8QE

Copyright under International, Pan American, and
Universal Copyright Conventions. All rights
reserved. No part of this book may be reproduced
in any form—except for brief quotation (not to
exceed 1,000 words) in a review or professional
work—without permission in writing from the publishers.

**Library of Congress Cataloging in Publication Data**

Main entry under title:

Toward reform of program evaluation.

Bibliography: p. 384
Includes index.
1. Evaluation research (Social action programs)—
Addresses, essays, lectures.  I. Cronbach, Lee Joseph,
1916–
H62.T59     361.6'1'072     80–8013
ISBN 0-87589-471-2

Manufactured in the United States of America

JACKET DESIGN BY WILLI BAUM

FIRST EDITION

*CODE 8034*

■■■■■■■■■■■■■■■■■

A joint publication in
The Jossey-Bass Series
in Social and Behavioral Science
& in Higher Education

Special Advisor,
Methodology of Social and
Behavioral Research
DONALD W. FISKE
University of Chicago

■■■■■■■■■■■■■■■■■

# Preface

This book originated in the Stanford Evaluation Consortium, which was established at Stanford University in 1974 (directed first by Lee Cronbach and later by Denis Phillips) to provide a working place for scholars and students who wanted to stretch beyond their specialties. In each year from 1973 to 1979, approximately twenty faculty members and an equal number of doctoral students made up the consortium. Most were affiliated with the School of Education at Stanford, but others came from the departments of sociology, psychology, statistics, and communication research. Several members had at some time held posts in or worked with federal or state government, and others had directed programs of educational or social innovation. Most members had held responsibility in evaluation projects, either local, national, or international. The projects ranged widely: art education, mathematics education, daycare, school vouchers, instruction by satellite broadcast, and so on.

In routine tending of a disciplinary garden, an academic has little occasion for discussion with colleagues in another specialty. But consortium members did have the opportunity to exchange experiences about past and current projects. Visitors brought additional views from governmental agencies, from contracting organizations, and from evaluation teams in the field. Consortium teams took on assignments that provided an even better setting for mutual education. Some of the tasks were small-scale evaluations, some consisted of consultative service to evaluations carried out by others, and some were armchair tasks such as critical reviews of evaluation plans and reports. From 1974 to 1978 such activities, along with a number of scholarly efforts, including this book, received financial support from the Russell Sage Foundation.

Within the consortium, a perception of evaluation as a novel political institution began to emerge. The writers of the present work, self-selected members of the consortium, set out to develop that view and present some of its implications. The professional specialties of these writers are as follows: Sueann Robinson Ambron (child development, programs for young children); Lee J. Cronbach (instructional psychology, measurement); Sanford M. Dornbusch (sociology of organizations, evaluation of persons and of programs in school); Robert D. Hess (family life and social development, institutions affecting children and youth); Robert Hornik (communications research, use of broadcasts in national development); D. C. Phillips (philosophy of education, philosophy of science); Decker Walker (curriculum theory, curriculum development and implementation); and Stephen Weiner (organization theory, policy analysis). David Rubin, Karen Shapiro, and Nancy Sherman were student participants who contributed to the work in many ways.

Ideas evolved in consortium seminars and meetings over a period of two years. When members responded positively to a line of thought, someone produced a draft of it. After the draft had been savaged by the committee, someone produced a second draft. Once most of the manuscript had reached the second-draft stage, Cronbach retreated to London to turn the fragments into a more coherent manuscript. The department of social psychology at the London School of Economics provided greatly appreciated working conditions. The manuscript was modified and extended upon Cronbach's return from leave.

The writers agreed not to sacrifice pointedness to get unanimity, and moderate conflicts of view within the writing group are recognized by pro-and-con statements in the manuscript. Each member of the writing group was free to add a signed footnote wherever he or she could not accept the final statement, but in the end no such statements were submitted. Others both within and outside the consortium have criticized and advanced our thinking.

Those who conduct evaluations and those who give advice on them are only part of our intended audience. We write also for those who plan and manage social programs and for those who commission evaluations. We address scholars in the social sciences, social activists of most shades of opinion, and persons concerned with human service programs. The book should help them not only to understand evaluation as an institution and its possible contribution to their ends but to appreciate the complexities of the evaluative task. A scholarly work might attempt to advance a formal theory; more modestly, we offer only a perspective, plus some advice that should fit many important situations. We rely little on abstract statements of relationships, which are hard to apply to new cases. Instead, we use anecdotes from past evaluations and a few invented examples to develop concrete images of what is to be avoided and what is to be admired.

Few statements in this book are new; what is new is the integration. Views put forward by Aaron, Cohen, Coleman, Cook, Lindblom, Nelson, Patton, Rein, Stake, C. H. Weiss, and others fit easily into our argument. No one of them has covered all the topics in this book, especially as several of these writers have been concerned with large-scale planning and policy making rather than with the delimited topic of program evaluation. Since our first premise is that evaluation is part of governance, policies for evaluation should derive from the process by which social decisions are reached. The writers just named describe this process much as we do and we trust that each of them will agree generally with our characterization of evaluation, but any of the writers can be expected to disagree with our argument here and there. It will take much further discussion to consolidate the school of thought that is, nevertheless, clearly in the making.

*Stanford, California*                            LEE J. CRONBACH
*June 1980*

# Contents

xiii

# Contents

# Tables and Figures

## Tables

xvii

# Figures

# The Authors

LEE J. CRONBACH is Vida Jacks Professor of Education at
Stanford University. He received his B.A. degree (1934) from
Fresno State College in mathematics, his M. A. degree (1937)
from the University of California at Berkeley in education, and
his Ph.D degree (1940) from the University of Chicago in education.

Cronbach's main research activities have been in educational and psychological measurement and the related theory of
psychometrics and individual differences. His experience with
evaluation includes participation in Evaluation in the Eight-Year
Study, the National Assessment of Educational Progress, the research of the School Mathematics Study Group, and other projects. In 1979, he received the Gunnar and Alva Myrdal award
for scientific contributions to evaluation from the Evaluation
Research Society. Cronbach's books include *Essentials of Psychological Testing* (1970), *The Dependability of Behavioral
Measurements* (1972, with others), and *Aptitudes and Instructional Methods* (1977, with R. E. Snow).

SUEANN ROBINSON AMBRON is assistant professor of child
development and early education at Stanford University. She

earned her B.S. degree (1966) from the University of Maryland in education, her M.A. degree (1968) from Michigan State University in child development, and her Ed.D. degree (1973) from Columbia University in education and psychology.

Currently, Ambron is directing a large-scale study of the effects of daycare on infants. She has worked with state governments and the federal government on daycare projects and received an A. W. Mellon award for her work in California on infant daycare research. Her major research interests are in human development, evaluation, and public policy; she has written articles on these topics and is the author of *Child Development* (1978) and *Life Span Development* (1979).

SANFORD M. DORNBUSCH is Reed-Hodgson Professor of Human Biology and professor of sociology and education at Stanford University. He was awarded his B.S. degree (1948) from Syracuse University and his M.A. (1950) and Ph.D. degrees (1952) from the University of Chicago, all in sociology.

Dornbusch has served as chairman of the sections on social psychology and methodology of the American Sociological Association and as President of the Pacific Sociological Association. He has been a consultant to the directors of the National Institute for Child Health and Human Development and the National Institute of Mental Health, as well as the President's Commission on Mental Health. His research interests in social psychology and organizations led to his work on evaluation within organizations, *Evaluation and the Exercise of Authority* (1975, with W. R. Scott). Currently, Dornbusch is working on program evaluation of education and youth service agencies, linking program evaluation to issues of social control.

ROBERT D. HESS is Lee L. Jacks Professor of Child Education at Stanford University. He received his B.A. degree (1947) from the University of California at Berkeley in psychology and his Ph.D. degree (1950) from the University of Chicago in human development.

Hess has been a visiting scholar at the Center for Advanced Study in the Behavioral Sciences. He has a long-time interest in the relationship of culture and social institutions to learning in children. His research includes analysis of family interaction and transmission of behavior patterns in families, effects of divorce on the social and school performance of children, and family influences on school readiness in both American and cross-national settings.

ROBERT C. HORNIK is associate professor at the Annenberg School of Communications, University of Pennsylvania. He earned his B.A. degree (1968) from Dartmouth College in international relations and his M.A. (1970) and Ph.D. (1973) degrees from Stanford University in communication research.

In 1977 and 1978, Hornik was co-principal investigator for a major review of the U.S. Agency for International Development's policy in communication for development. His current work includes studies of the use of communication technology for purposes of education and information, and research on social effects of mass media, with emphasis on how these issues affect developing nations. Hornik is the author of *Educational Reform with Television: The El Salvador Experience* (1976, with J. Mayo and E. McAnany), among other publications.

D. C. PHILLIPS is professor of education and philosophy at Stanford University. He was awarded his B.Sc. degree (1958) in biological science, his B.Ed. degree (1962) in education, his M.Ed. degree (1964) in philosophy of education, and his Ph.D. degree (1968) in philosophy of education and philosophy of science, all from the University of Melbourne.

Phillips has been a visiting scholar at the London School of Economics and Politics and at the Research School of Social Sciences, Australian National University. At present, he is on the executive board of the Philosophy of Education Society. He approaches education, especially educational research, from the perspective of the philosophy of natural and social science. Phillips has written on the logic of stage theories in education and psychology, on structure of knowledge and the curriculum, and on evaluation. He is the author of *Holistic Thought in Social Science* (1976), *Theories, Values, and Education* (1971), and *From Locke to Spock: Models of the Child in Modern Western Thought* (1976, with J. Cleverley).

DECKER F. WALKER is associate professor of education at Stanford University. He received his B.S. degree (1963) in physics and his M.A. degree (1966) in natural sciences, both from the Carnegie Institute of Technology, and his Ph.D. degree (1971) from Stanford University in education.

Walker has served on several curriculum development projects, has studied the process of curriculum development, and has written extensively on the problems of policy making, planning, and evaluation in curriculum work. Currently, Walker is at work on a basic text on curriculum.

STEPHEN S. WEINER is associate dean of the Graduate School of Public Policy, University of California at Berkeley. He earned his B.S. (1961) and M.S. degrees (1963) from the University of California at Los Angeles in engineering and his Ph.D. degree (1973) from Stanford University in education.

Weiner is president of the California Community Colleges' board of governors and chairman of the Student Financial Aid Policy Study Group for the California state legislature. Formerly, he was associate director of the Stanford evaluation consortium, consultant to the Rand Corporation, special assistant for the National Advisory Commission on Civil Disorders, and administrative assistant to Congressman James C. Corman. Weiner is the author of *Organizing an Anarchy: Belief, Bureaucracy, and Politics in the National Institute of Education* (1978, with L. Sproull and others) and *A Public School Voucher Demonstration: The First Year at Alum Rock* (1974).

■■■■■■■■■■■■■■■■■

# Toward Reform of Program Evaluation

## Aims, Methods, and Institutional Arrangements

■■■■■■■■■■■■■■■■■

■■■■■■■■■■■■■■■■■

# Our Ninety-Five
# Theses

■■■■■■■■■■■■■■■■■

This book calls for a reformation in evaluation, a thoroughgoing transformation. Its priests and its patrons, as well as those who desire its benefits, have sought from evaluation what it cannot, probably should not, give. The proper mission of evaluation is not to eliminate the fallibility of authority or to bolster its credibility. Rather, its mission is to facilitate a democratic, pluralistic process by enlightening all the participants.

Evaluation has vital work to do, yet its institutions and its ruling conceptions are inadequate. Enamored of a vision that "right" decisions can replace political agreements, some who commission evaluations set evaluators on unrealistic quests. Others among them see evaluation chiefly as a means to strengthen the hand of the commissioning authority. Evaluators, eager to serve and even to manipulate those in power, lose sight of what they should be doing. Moreover, evaluators become enthralled by technique. Much that purports to be theory of evaluation is scholastic: evaluations are endlessly categorized, and chapels are dedicated to the glorification of particular styles. Latter-day theologians discuss how best to reify such chimeras

1

as "goals" and "benefits." The technicians debate over numerological derivations from artificial models—"How many angels. . . ?" all over again. All too rarely does discussion descend to earthy questions such as, "Is worthwhile information being collected?"

Budgets for evaluations have jumped to startling levels, but few individuals and organizations are prepared for the intricacies of evaluation research. The federal procurement machinery and timetables for delivery of results are inimical to reflective planning and interpretation. Organizations and individuals undertake tasks that are beyond their capabilities. Evaluation results are challenged and discredited because no adequate critical process precedes their release. Professional ideals can become casualties when everyone scrambles to keep in step with budgetary and legislative calendars. It is none too soon to reflect, to repent (a little), and to entertain bright visions of a wholesome marriage between social research and social action.

Perhaps the best way to bring about a change in thought is to provoke argument. Following Luther's precedent, we set forth our principal points in the form of ninety-five theses. Being removed from their context and stripped of qualifying phrases, the theses neglect subtleties; reading the theses is no substitute for reading the book. This section is intended to entice into reading the argument with care those who might otherwise ignore it or skim the surface. That should make them eager to join in the needed debate about fundamental issues.

## Ninety-Five Theses

1. Program evaluation is a process by which society learns about itself.
2. Program evaluations should contribute to enlightened discussion of alternative plans for social action.
3. Evaluation is a handmaiden to gradualism; it is both conservative and committed to change.
4. An evaluation of a particular program is only an episode in the continuing evolution of thought about a problem area.
5. The better and the more widely the workings of social programs are understood, the more rapidly policy will evolve

and the more the programs will contribute to a better quality of life.

6. Observations of social programs require a closer analysis than a lay interpreter can make, for unassisted judgment leads all too easily to false interpretations.

7. In debates over controversial programs, liars figure and figures often lie; the evaluator has a responsibility to protect his* clients from both types of deception.

\* \* \*

8. Ideally, every evaluation will inform the social system and improve its operations, but everyone agrees that evaluation is not rendering the service it should.

9. Commissioners of evaluations complain that the messages from evaluations are not useful, while evaluators complain that the messages are not used.

\* \* \*

10. The evaluator has political influence even when he does not aspire to it.

11. A theory of evaluation must be as much a theory of political interaction as it is a theory of how to determine facts.

12. The hope that an evaluation will provide unequivocal answers, convincing enough to extinguish controversy about the merits of a social program, is certain to be disappointed.

13. The evaluators' professional conclusions cannot substitute for the political process.

14. The distinction between evaluation and policy research is disappearing.

*Note:* Following Keeney and Raiffa (1976, p. 515), we use the masculine pronoun throughout this work for the evaluator or scientist. Other significant persons (decision makers, clients, citizens, and so on) are referred to by the feminine pronoun. Another convention: We frequently speak of "the evaluator" in this work. But the tasks of the evaluator are so multifarious that no one person is versatile enough to perform them all. Hence, the term *evaluator* often refers here to a team or cooperating set of teams. The team members are to be seen not as specialists working on distinct subtasks but as persons who share responsibilities for each judgment.

\* \* \*

15. Accountability emphasizes looking back in order to assign praise or blame; evaluation is better used to understand events and processes for the sake of guiding future activities.
16. Social renovations disappoint even their architects.
17. Time and again, political passion has been a driving spirit behind a call for rational analysis.
18. A demand for accountability is a sign of pathology in the political system.

\* \* \*

19. An open society becomes a closed society when only the officials know what is going on. Insofar as information is a source of power, evaluations carried out to inform a policy maker have a disenfranchising effect.
20. The ideal of efficiency in government is in tension with the ideal of democratic participation; rationalism is dangerously close to totalitarianism.

\* \* \*

21. The notion of the evaluator as a superman who will make all social choices easy and all programs efficient, turning public management into a technology, is a pipe dream.
22. A context of command, with a manager in firm control, has been assumed in nearly all previous theories of evaluation.
23. An image of pluralistic accommodation more truly represents how policy and programs are shaped than does the Platonic image of concentrated power and responsibility.
24. The evaluator must learn to serve in contexts of accomodation and not dream idly of serving a Platonic guardian.
25. In a context of accommodation, the evaluator cannot expect a "go/no-go" decision to turn on his assessment of outcomes.

\* \* \*

26. What is needed is information that supports negotiation rather than information calculated to point out the "correct" decision.

27. Events move forward by piecemeal adaptations.
28. It can scarcely be said that decisions about typical programs are "made"; rather, they emerge.
29. The policy-shaping community does not wait for a sure winner; it must act in the face of uncertainty, settling on plausible actions that are politically acceptable.

\*   \*   \*

30. It is unwise for evaluation to focus on whether a project has "attained its goals."
31. Goals are a necessary part of political rhetoric, but all social programs, even supposedly targeted ones, have broad aims.
32. Legislators who have sophisticated reasons for keeping goal statements lofty and nebulous unblushingly ask program administrators to state explicit goals.
33. Unfortunately, whatever the evaluator decides to measure tends to become a primary goal of program operators.

\*   \*   \*

34. Evaluators are not encouraged to ask the most trenchant questions about entrenched programs.
35. "Evaluate this program" is often a vague charge because a program or a system frequently has no clear boundaries.
36. Before the evaluator can plan data collection, he must find out a great deal about the project as it exists and as it is conceived.
37. A good evaluative question invites a differentiated answer instead of leaving the program plan, the delivery of the program, and the response of clients as unexamined elements within a closed black box.
38. Strictly honest data collection can generate a misleading picture unless questions are framed to expose both the facts useful to partisans of the program and the facts useful to its critics.

\*   \*   \*

39. Before laying out a design, the evaluator should do considerable homework. Pertinent questions should be identified by

examining the history of similar programs, the related
social theory, and the expectations of program advocates,
critics, and prospective clients.

40. Precise assessment of outcomes is sensible only after thorough pilot work has pinned down a highly appropriate form for an innovation under test.

41. When a prototype program is evaluated, the full range of realizations likely to occur in practice should be observed.

42. Flexibility and diversity are preferable to the rigidity written into many evaluation contracts.

\* \* \*

43. The evaluator who does not press for productive assignments and the freedom to carry them out takes the King's shilling for selfish reasons.

44. The evaluator's aspiration to benefit the larger community has to be reconciled—sometimes painfully—with commitments to a sponsor and to informants, with the evaluator's political convictions, and with his desire to stay in business.

45. Managers have many reasons for wishing to maintain control over evaluative information; the evaluator can respect all such reasons that fall within the sphere of management.

46. The crucial ethical problem appears to be freedom to communicate during and after the study, subject to legitimate concerns for privacy, national security, and faithfulness to contractual commitments.

47. With some hesitation, we advise the evaluator to release findings piecemeal and informally to the audiences that need them. The impotence that comes with delay may be a greater risk than the possibility that early returns will be misread.

\* \* \*

48. Nothing makes a larger difference in the use of evaluations than the personal factor—the interest of officials in learning from the evaluation and the desire of the evaluator to get attention for what he knows.

49. Communication overload is a common fault; many an evaluation is reported with self-defeating thoroughness.

50. Much of the most significant communication of findings is informal, and not all of it is deliberate; some of the most significant effects are indirect, affecting audiences far removed from the program under investigation.
51. An evaluation of a particular project has its greatest implications for projects that will be put in place in the future.
52. A program evaluation that gets attention is likely to affect the prevailing view of social purposes, whether or not it immediately affects the fate of the program studied.
53. Advice on evaluation typically speaks of an investigation as a stand-alone study that will draw its conclusions about a program in complete isolation from other sources of information.
54. It is better for an evaluative inquiry to launch a small fleet of studies than to put all its resources into a single approach.
55. Much that is written on evaluation recommends some one "scientifically rigorous" plan. Evaluations should, however, take many forms, and less rigorous approaches have value in many circumstances.
56. Results of a program evaluation are so dependent on the setting that replication is only a figure of speech; the evaluator is essentially an historian.

\*　\*　\*

57. An elegant study provides dangerously convincing evidence when it seems to answer a question that it did not in fact squarely address.
58. Merit lies not in form of inquiry but in relevance of information. The context of command or accommodation, the stage of program maturity, and the closeness of the evaluator to the probable users should all affect the style of an evaluation.
59. The evaluator will be wise not to declare allegiance to either a quantitative-scientific-summative methodology or a qualitative-naturalistic-descriptive methodology.
60. External validity—that is, the validity of inferences that go beyond the data—is the crux; increasing internal validity by elegant design often reduces relevance.

*   *   *

61. Adding a control costs something in dollars, in attention, and perhaps in quality of data; a control that fortifies the study in one respect is likely to weaken it in another.
62. A strictly representative sample may provide less information than a sample that overrepresents exceptional cases and deliberately varies realizations.
63. The symmetric, nonsequential designs familiar from laboratory research and survey research are rarely appropriate for evaluations.
64. Multiple indicators of outcomes reinforce one another logically as well as statistically. This is true for measures of adequacy of program implementation as well as for measures of changes in client behavior.

*   *   *

65. In project-by-project evaluation, each study analyzes a spoonful dipped from a sea of uncertainties.
66. In any primary statistical investigation, analyses by independent teams should be made before the report is distributed.
67. Evaluations of a program conducted in parallel by different teams can capitalize on disparate perspectives and technical skills.
68. The evaluator should allocate investigative resources by considering four criteria simultaneously: prior uncertainty about a question, costs of information, anticipated information yield, and leverage of the information on subsequent thinking and action.
69. A particular control is warranted if it can be installed at reasonable costs and if, in the absence of that control, a positive effect could be persuasively explained away.
70. The importance of comparative data depends on the nature of the comparison proposed and on the stage of program maturity.

71. When programs have multiple and perhaps dissimilar outcomes, comparison is invariably judgmental. No technology for comparing benefits will silence partisan discord.

*   *   *

72. Present institutional arrangements for evaluation make it
difficult or impossible to carry on the most useful kinds of
evaluation.
73. In typical federal contracting, many basic research decisions
are made without consulting the evaluators who will do the
work.
74. The personal scientific responsibility found in ordinary research grants is lacking in contract evaluation; the "principal
investigator" is a firm with interchangeable personnel.
75. Though the information from an evaluation is typically not
used at a foreseeable moment to make a foreseen choice, in
many evaluations a deadline set at the start of the study
dominates the effort.
76. Evaluation contracts are increasing in size, but tying many
strands into a single knot is rarely the best way to get useful information.
77. Large-scale evaluations are not necessarily better than smaller
ones.
78. Major evaluations should have multiple sponsorship by agencies with different perspectives.
79. Decentralizing much evaluation to the state level would be
a healthy development.

*   *   *

80. Society will obtain the assistance that evaluations can give
only when there is a strong evaluation profession, clear about
its social role and the nature of its work.
81. There is a boom town excitement in the evaluation community, but in constant dollars federal funding for evaluation research has regressed in the last few years.
82. It is inconceivable that evaluators will win their battle for
appropriate responsibilities if they remain unacquainted

with one another, insensitive to their common interests,
and fractionated intellectually.

* * *

83. For any suitably broad social problem, a "social problem
study group" should be set up. It would be charged to inform
itself by weighing, digesting, and interpreting what is known.
It would foster needed investigations and make the policy-
shaping community aware of what is and is not known.

* * *

84. Honesty and balance in program evaluation will be increased
by critical review of the performance of evaluators and
sponsors.
85. Oversight by peers is the most promising means of upholding professional standards and of precipitating debate about
strategic and tactical issues.
86. The best safeguard against prematurely frozen standards
for evaluative practice is multiple, independent sources
of criticism.
87. There is need for exchanges more energetic than the typical
academic discussion and more responsible than debate
among partisans.
88. Reviews of evaluation should be far more frequent than at
present, and reviews from diverse perspectives should appear
together.

* * *

89. For the prospective evaluator, basic training at the doctoral
level in a specific social science is preferable to training restricted to evaluation methods.
90. Training in evaluation is too often the stepchild of a department chiefly engaged in training academicians or providers
of service.
91. Case-study seminars scrutinizing diverse evaluative studies
provide a needed interdisciplinary perspective.

92. Internships with policy agencies that use evaluation sensitize future evaluators to the realities of evaluation use and nonuse. These realities are hard to convey in a classroom.

\* \* \*

93. The evaluator is an educator; his success is to be judged by what others learn.
94. Those who shape policy should reach decisions with their eyes open; it is the evaluator's task to illuminate the situation, not to dictate the decision.
95. Scientific quality is not the principal standard; an evaluation should aim to be comprehensible, correct and complete, and credible to partisans on all sides.

# 1

■■■■■■■■■■■■■■■■■■

# Where Evaluation
# Stands Today

■■■■■■■■■■■■■■■■■

In the twentieth century, social progress has become the public business. This is true especially in the United States, but the same concern is active throughout the world, in rich nations and in poor. The civic conscience has accepted responsibility for raising the quality of life of communities and of everyone in them. To this end, ambitious programs are launched in seemingly endless succession. Some are touted as highly promising ways to render a valuable service, while others are no more than the latest efforts to cope with perplexing problems that have resisted the best efforts of the past. Only experience with a new scheme can indicate whether it is moving in the right direction and what faults in it remain to be overcome. Society is constantly learning about its own procedures and the difficulties it is trying to overcome. And the process by which society learns is evaluation, whether personal and impressionistic or systematic and comparatively objective.

Systematic evaluation is increasingly sought to guide operations, to assure legislators and planners that they are proceeding on sound lines, and to make services responsive to their publics. Evaluation has thus become the liveliest frontier of American social science. It invites—even entices—members of traditional disciplines to leave their settled fields and migrate to a land where history is being made.

No one, however, is fully equipped for the pioneer's tasks. The political scientist and the economist find familiar the questions about social processes that evaluation confronts, but they lack preparation for field observation. Sociologists, psychologists, and anthropologists know ways to develop part of the data needed for evaluations, but they are not accustomed to drawing conclusions in fast-changing political contexts. The scale and uncontrollability of contemporary field studies tax the skills of statisticians. Even at their best, statistical summaries fall short, because evaluative inquiry is historical investigation more than it is a search for general laws and explanations.

Many evaluation reports receive little attention, and some observers think these reports deserve no more than they get. Technical critics and political partisans are likely to object to the way a study was performed or to the interpretation it was given. The intellectual and practical difficulties of completing a credible evaluation are painfully evident in such disputes, and in the smoke of battle the positive contributions that current evaluations make become obscured. This chapter reviews the origins of the demand for evaluation, and some difficulties that have reduced evaluation's social worth.

Evaluations are initiated for many purposes, sometimes conflicting ones: choosing a best prospect among several proposed lines of action, fine-tuning a program already in operation, maintaining quality control, forcing subordinates to comply with instructions, documenting that one's agency deserves its budget, creating support for a pet proposal, casting suspicion on a policy favored by political opponents, and so on. Even among the purposes that call for honest inquiry, the range is greater than any single study can fulfill. The team that has carried out one successful evaluation cannot expect the same style of work to succeed in its next undertaking, where the political context may be wholly different. The evidence to be sought in each instance is that which will produce the greatest difference in social thought and action.

We do not expect overnight reform of the institutions that control the fate of evaluations. We do not provide a blueprint for a new institutional structure, concepts and institutions will have to evolve. But once the suppliers of evaluation services and the customers for those services reach a common understanding, not only will evaluations be better, they will also be better used.

## A Concept of Program Evaluation

By the term *evaluation*, we mean systematic examination of events occurring in and consequent on a contemporary program—an examination conducted to assist in improving this program and other programs having the same general purpose. By the term *program*, we mean a standing arrangement that provides for a social service. Program evaluation is sometimes concerned with an established program, sometimes with a plan that could be established if found suitable.

Since we speak for the most part about evaluations of American social programs, our conclusions will not be equally appropriate outside the United States. Other polities have other ways of dividing authority, as well as other ways of resolving conflicts of interest and interpretation. The kind of information that can be used and the actors who can use it differ from nation to nation. Much that we say would apply, with amendments, in other countries that have elaborate social programs. As one moves away from the Western democratic tradition, however, the function or relevance of evaluation is likely to change. It also should be said that our thinking is in terms of the present, not of eternity. Our theses will have to be revised to fit the United States of the year 2000.

Even within the United States, of course, many social programs are exceedingly diverse, and their activities often differ greatly from site to site. An example would be state provisions to support local daycare centers that meet certain criteria.

Diverse though the centers are, however, the state agency is following a policy that is subject to evaluation, and the local center is carrying on an activity that is subject to evaluation. The state policy and the local activity are both aspects of the "program." (We are not distinguishing between "program" and "project" as government terminology does.)

A program may be under the control of a single administrative office—television's "Sesame Street," for example. When uncoordinated, independent units together supply a service, their combined activities can be reviewed as a program. A community's ambulance services provide an example of this. Similarly, a package of materials for teaching reading is a suitable subject for field evaluation, even though each teacher uses the materials in her own way.

Programs appearing as examples in this book are preponderantly educational, inasmuch as our experience has been mostly with education evaluations. Nonetheless, we intend our remarks to apply over the full range of human service programs. The services whose evaluations are described in just one source (Abert and Kamrass, 1974) range over transit, recreation, health, police, manpower, community development, income maintenance, and drug rehabilitation. We dare to consider so wide a range of activities for the very reason that we intend to warn against generalizing. The variety of programs and political contexts within any one of these fields is great, and there is no "right way" to do evaluations within any of them. The questions to be considered in planning evaluative work are much the same in all these fields, however. What we have to say is less pertinent for services that are highly technological (weather forecasting, for example, or sewage disposal), but the difference is that evaluators of a technology encounter the questions we discuss less often than do evaluators of other services, not that they never face them.

*Evaluations To Be Considered.* Our main concern is with complex, organized programs—those that affect many persons in many places. The discussion also applies, however, to the evaluation of a program confined within a single institution. We see no fundamental difference between evaluation of career education in one city with a dozen junior high schools and evaluation of career education in a sample drawn from fifty states. We speak primarily of dispersed programs, because evaluations of them take up more resources and are potentially more influential. We shall treat evaluations for local purposes only incidentally. Although the evaluations most often discussed are of services that a client receives for a year or more, much of what we say is also applicable to services of short duration. The plan for a one-hour film and discussion program on venereal disease is a target for serious evaluation; what we say should apply to it.

We are interested in program evaluations that contribute to enlightened discussion of alternative plans. Much that goes under the name of evaluation lacks the systematic and purposeful character we seek. Some work collects facts, giving hardly a thought to their possible relevance to action. Other collections of potentially significant facts lack the force of evaluations because the facts are not organized and interpreted for use. Still other would-be evaluations are strong on judgment but have no systematic investigation behind them.

An evaluative inquiry of the kind that this book seeks to encourage would have the features listed below. Only occasional comments will be made about investigations of a substantially different character.

1. The intention of the evaluation is to influence social thought and action during the investigation or in the years immediately following. (It is reasonable to hope for long-term influences as well.)
2. The evaluation is set up by an agency having responsibility for a program or by one taking responsibility for fostering other programs to meet the same need. We say more about government agencies than others, but we do not limit our thinking to them.
3. Evidence is collected on experience with an already existing program or one installed for research purposes. After the

analysis, the investigator sets forth just how he reached his conclusions. He documents his observations and reasoning so that readers can judge the plausibility of each conclusion.

4. The evaluator aims to give a comprehensive and disciplined interpretation. The account is intended to impress fair-minded persons, including those whose preconceptions or preferences run counter to the findings. Furthermore, the information collected is made available for others to scrutinize and interpret independently.

This list omits some features prominent in other conceptions of evaluation. We do not stress quantitative-statistical methods, or "goal attainment," or the intent to judge a program as good or bad. Such emphases block useful inquiries. (We shall amplify this assertion later.) Our list of features does not fit evaluations that stress "accountability." An accountability system looks back at what was done last month or last year with intent to apportion responsibility among the program's operators. This is both a limited view of the reasons for program success or failure and a limiting view of how evaluation can best be used to bring about improvement. Evaluation is not used, we think, to bring pressure on public servants, though it should assist in understanding why shortfalls occur.

In listing four features to identify the evaluations to be considered here, we by no means suggest that evaluations within that class should be similar in objectives or procedures. On the contrary, evaluation plans should be adapted to circumstances. The political and intellectual milieu of a newly hatched idea is very different from that of a program in regular, permanent operation. Emerging programs and established programs should be investigated differently.

Program evaluations vary in the intimacy of the evaluator's relationship to those who participate in the program and those who influence its future. The evaluator who works for an extended period with a school staff or a policy maker will, if adept, have frequent opportunity to communicate on a basis of frankness and mutual trust. In contrast, synoptic statements about a broad program or policy will be comparatively formal, and they will have to reach a distant audience through impersonal channels—reports, speeches, and the mass media. The likely balance between intimacy and formality in an evaluation will depend on the stage of program maturity, the nature of the evaluator's commission, the evaluator's preferred style, and other factors. We shall urge the evaluator to take advantage of the full range of opportunities open to him, from providing personal assistance to clients to broadcasting statements to all who care about the social problem under investigation.

Much has been made of the contrast between evaluation carried out within an agency and evaluation by outsiders. The evaluator who has no permanent tie to the agency that manages a program is supposed by some to be more impartial and more credible than the insider. Evaluators who develop close relations with program developers or other partisans are in danger of being co-opted, it is said, to the point where they cease to be properly cold-blooded scientists. The "in-house/out-house" distinction will have no place in this report. Insofar as co-optation derives from friendly relations between program participants and evaluator, the relations depend on the style of the evaluator more than on his locus of employment. We shall not advise the evaluator to avoid opportunities to be helpful; he is hired to improve public services, not to referee a basketball game.

Insofar as co-optation derives from the power of the official who pays the evaluation bill, the evaluator whose income depends on contracts and hence on the continuing good will of the sponsor is no less a peasant slave than the evaluator on the agency's payroll. Wholey (1973) makes the point that the evaluator engaged by a higher-level agency, one that oversees a program, is not subject to the pressures that bear on the evaluator engaged by a program manager. As we see it, however, the former evaluator is not independent or free from pressure; the pressures in the two cases are different only in kind (see Chapter Three).

The problems of probity in evaluation lie in the behavior of sponsors and evaluators; the solutions lie in the development of effective critical review to foster proper relations between them. At present, not many evaluation researchers have the freedom of the free-lance critic. Some arrangements for evaluation encourage full, free, and honest reporting, and the evaluation community—indeed, the entire polity—should be fighting to establish them (Coleman, 1980). Intimacy is no deterrent to frankness, nor is the formal status of contractor (as opposed to employee) a guarantee of frankness.

*Connections and Contrasts.* We see evaluation as an integral part of policy research, and we therefore blend ideas appearing in the policy-research literature with ideas about evaluation itself. The distinction between evaluation and policy-research activities is beginning to disappear, as members of one subcommunity come to appreciate the ideas springing up in the other.

Rivlin (1971), speaking of the potential and the limitations of policy analysis, embraced Campbell's (1969b) vision of an experimenting society, where preliminary tryout of a social action is an adjunct to planning. Quade's (1975) textbook devotes a chapter to "evaluation and experiment" as tools of policy analysis, stressing their function in forward planning and adaptation. Policy analysts, like evaluators, have become increasingly thoughtful about their interaction with decision makers and about the need to illuminate emerging questions rather than to hand down a verdict on what happened last year. The current hopes and discomforts of the policy-research community, which match those in the evaluation community, are well represented in the symposium edited by Beckman (1977).

Policy analysts project the meaning of interventions far into the future. In metropolitan planning, for example, a time horizon of twenty years or more is recommended (Boyce, Day, and McDonald, 1970). But estimates about uncertain matters are usually made from an armchair on the basis of experience and hunch (Dasgupta, Sen, and Marglin, 1972; Quade, 1975). Moreover, analysts rely on experience that is only indirectly related to the new plan; rarely can a realistic trial of a grand strategy be made (Rivlin, 1974). Time is usually too short for fresh field studies on the eve of a policy decision, so analysts draw heavily upon experience in past programs and innovative trials, that is, upon evaluations.

Policy analysis, like evaluation, goes beyond the provision of information about programs and consequences. As B. L. R. Smith (1977, pp. 256–257) warned his colleagues, "Policy analysis will . . . disappoint if it is assumed that information is the main idea. The provision of information is too mechanistic a concept. Data alone are more apt to clutter than to provide useful inputs into the policy process. If we view policy analysis more modestly, as the inheritor and codifier of the useful experience of the past decade with analysis, and as a close relative of plain old-fashioned good staff work, the future outlook would appear reasonably bright." Beckman's introduction notes that staff work "elucidates the value premises of all options and proponents and opponents of them" and that it "gives a more informed basis to the pluralism and processes of partisan conflict and compromise which are the hallmark of the legislative process" (1977, p. 222).

Program possibilities are by no means confined to the exemplars that were evaluated. The analyst limits himself unduly if he simply chooses whichever past program gave the best results (Nelson, 1977). Thus—and we shall say this over and over—evaluation of a program has its greatest use in pointing the way to better future programs. A particularly useful kind of evaluation activity in an established program is systematic, steady monitoring of the services delivered by each installation and of the needs in its catchment area that remain unmet. On the one hand, we wish to encourage this steady self-analysis as much as we wish to encourage well-conceived studies of generic programs. How to use monitoring, on the other hand, is a topic remote from the issues that we address in this book. To consider it, we would have to look closely at the economics of information and at the personal and organizational connections in the institutions using the data.

Fortunately, an impressive new book covers monitoring (that is, "information systems") thoroughly: *Evaluation of Human Service Programs* by Attkisson and others (1978). These authors restricted themselves to program evaluation defined "as a feedback process within ongoing program management" and set policy-oriented studies to one side (pp. xiv, 10). Thus our two teams have strung the fence wire to bound our respective ranges on just the same line—and then all unwittingly have taken the same name for our respective sides of the fence. We suspect that the world will continue to speak of the whole open range as "program evaluation." But we shall respect the fence. We have plenty of mavericks to corral on our side and can leave Attkisson and his team to advise the program managers. We protest only their suggestion that policy-related research is less committed to improving ongoing programs than are managers' evaluations.

As our definition of program evaluation indicates, we emphasize studies that center on a service or agency. This leaves to one side the studies that back away from services in order to survey needs of the population or the adequacy of services taken all together. Such investigations survey a sample of citizens or interview informants in sampled communities or institutions. They may compile routine statistics (road accidents, say), or they may turn to intensive study of specimen communities. A study of unemployment, for example, may describe the pool of unemployed workers, appraise the barriers to employment (lack of skill, local oversupply of labor, poor circulation of information about openings, and so on), go on to identify the services attempting to reduce these barriers, and then assess their adequacy. Another end product is the time series of a social indicator such as the unemployment index. This is a form of monitoring, but monitoring distant from any one program.

Synoptic investigations of this kind, conveniently but inelegantly referred to as "needs assessments," perform the same kind of service as program-centered evaluations. They are particularly well suited to draw attention to a need that has been overlooked or to identify a sector of the population that is receiving less adequate service than the other sectors are. Working at a greater distance from the deliverers of service, survey researchers are not as capable of explaining shortfalls as are evaluators of specific programs. But they have the countervailing advantage of considering simultaneously the patchwork of services related to a need, and they can thus identify areas in which agencies duplicate each other, pursue conflicting policies, or coordinate eligibility rules so poorly that deserving clients are left out in the cold.

As we shall not elaborate on the survey approach, it seems well to draw attention to two pertinent sources. The work by Katz and others (1975) subtitled "A Pilot Study in the Evaluation of Government Services" covers seven kinds of services, with the intention of examining problems in the large. Along with their conclusions, they discuss how needs assessments serve as a companion to program evaluations. Their point of view and recommendations about social research and its utilization appear to be wholly compatible with ours.

We shall mention just one conclusion about the seven services to illustrate how macroevaluation, comparing across services directs attention to generalized issues that program evaluation cannot reach. Having interviewed representative citizens about their experience with various offices in the early 1970s (after a decade of rising alienation), Katz and others reported (1975, p. 199): "In the 1960s, the buzz words of new service agencies were paraprofessionals, relevance, rapport, team approach, and nondirective leadership. The lack of these elements in social security and unemployment compensation offices has not had a negative effect on the satisfaction of clients. Our data suggest that these factors may be less important for client satisfaction than clear eligibility criteria."

We draw attention also to *Policy Issues and Research Design* by Coleman and others (1979). This volume is primarily a demonstration of how a survey with broad and multiple purposes should be designed in order to contribute to policies that touch many interests and are carried out through many agencies. The monograph offers a "conceptual design" for a national longitudinal study of young persons attending high school in the year 1980. The political theory of "pluralistic social research" that guided the Coleman team matches the theory of this volume, as later quotations from their book will attest.

## Historical Emergence of Evaluation

Today's policy-oriented research seems at first glance to be without precedent. It is true that the applied social research of earlier years was incomparably smaller in scale and more detached from the centers of power than policy research is today. However, both the ideal and the practice of "systematic thinking for social actions" have a long history.

For centuries, thinkers had visions of a science of society that could make truth the basis for social choice. Their aspirations are the foundation for today's aspirations—and disappointments. A review of highlights of the last three centuries will remind us that applied social research, like other human endeavors, develops not in a steady expansion but in spurts and slumps and changes of direction. Moreover, it will remind us that a social technology reflects a political theory: ideals for evaluation are rooted in ideals for governance.

We will speak of three periods: 1600 to 1900, 1900 to 1960, and 1960 to date. (The unequal time spans enable us to take a closer look at more recent events.) The ruling intellectual force in the first period was the Enlightenment, and the American political system is one of its lasting expressions. In reviewing the present century, we limit our attention to American events. The year 1900 marked the springtime of the Progressive movement, which can be seen as a further expression of Enlightment ideals, given added force by the optimism of Lester Frank Ward's Social Darwinism. For the Progressives, change was growth. They were citizen reformers: in their hands, evaluation was research for the sake of shaking up existing institutions. But Progressive zeal was replaced by academic propriety as the empirical social disciplines became established; the rest of the period down to 1960 was lit only occasionally by flickers of evaluative activity. The resurgence of political research and evaluation in the 1960s came at the initiative of government officials, and the urges of management have dominated evaluative efforts for two decades.

*From Enlightenment Philosophy to Reformist Research.* In the 1600s, natural science established itself as a powerful instrument for overturning traditional beliefs. Not coincidentally, philosophy had a rebirth; older images of man in his relation to external forces were called into question, as were all human institutions. The great intellectual theme was rationality, the *aqua regia* that could dissolve away tradition and superstition, leaving clarity and truth as building materials for a new order. For the construction of grand social theories, the method good enough for Aristotle was good enough for his latter-day admirers, and no premium was placed on direct observation.

But the beginnings were there. Thomas Hobbes was interested in the concrete matters that we would now call public administration: facts about people were needed to regulate human affairs. William Petty, possibly with Hobbes' personal encouragement (Cullen, 1975, p. 4), broke the ice with a research program he called "political arithmetic." Petty set out, he said, to rely on numbers and measures to assess social conditions in place of the words that others considered adequate. Moreover—in an echo of natural science—he would "consider only such Causes, as have visible foundations in Nature." Few investigators in those early days followed Petty's lead. From time to time scattered tabulations on population, mortality, and health did appear, but a century passed before empirical social research gained momentum.

In the late 1700s, the quest for orderly information leaped ahead in France, Belgium, Germany, and England. Local governments had begun to take responsibility for services once provided for neighborhoods by cooperating householders or patrons. Central governments were starting to take modest responsibility for domestic services that reached across local jurisdictions. A clearer picture of the magnitude of the various problems was needed. Thus, social research—the census—was written into the United States Constitution. In 1797, *Encyclopaedia Britannica* could speak of statistics—"state-istics," as it were—as a "word lately introduced to express a view or survey of any kingdom, county, or parish" (p. 731). Statistical offices were set up to compile summary tables from routine reports resting in scattered files.

Ad hoc surveys were launched by curious investigators or by partisans of new services. In many skirmishes in the campaign for better sanitation, the ammunition was data on environmental conditions and mortality rates. Likewise in the fight for public financing of elementary education, surveys of the extent and the judged quality of existing schools were used as weapons (Cullen, 1975, pp. 65–69). Increasingly as the century wore on, reformers seized upon statistics as a political pickax.

For Florence Nightingale, back from the Crimea and pursuing her second career as a reformer of health services, statistical study was the key to the cipher wherein legislators and administrators could read "the thoughts of God." In 1891 she pressed Francis Galton to throw his weight behind an expansion of social research. One example in her long list spoke of the:

> results of Forster's Act, now twenty years old. We sweep annually into our Elementary Schools hundreds of thousands of children, spending millions of money. Do we know:
>
> (i) What proportion of children forget their whole education after leaving school; whether all they have been taught is *waste*? The almost accidental statistics of Guards' recruits would point to a large proportion.
>
> (ii) What are the results upon the lives and conduct of children in after life who don't forget all they have been taught?
>
> (iii) What are the methods and what are the results, for example, in night schools and secondary schools, in preventing primary education from being a *waste*?
>
> If we know not what are the effects upon our national life of Forster's Act is not this a strange gap in reasonable England's knowledge? [Quoted in Pearson, 1924, pp. 416–417.]

After more examples Nightingale continued: "What is wanted is that so high an authority as Mr. Francis Galton should jot down other branches upon which he would wish for statistics, and for *some teaching how to use these statistics in order to legislate for and to administer our national life* with more precision and experience. . . .

"You remember what Quetelet wrote—and Sir J. Herschel enforced the advice—"Put down what you expect from such and such legislation; after_____ years, see where it has given you what you expected, and where it has failed. But you change your laws and your administering of them so fast, and without inquiry after other results past or present, that it is all experiment, seesaw, doctrinaire, a shuttlecock between two battledores" (quoted in Pearson, 1942, pp. 417–418). These sentiments, save for their grand style ("I have no time to make my letter any shorter") and transatlantic referents, would have seemed at home alongside the 1968–1970 Gaither lectures of Hitch, Schultze, and Rivlin.

*Activism and Passivity Among American Social Scientists.* In the United States, as in other countries, many of the early empirical social scientists began to see themselves as constituting a profession of specially qualified analysts. They were enchanted by the vision of the power they might claim by virtue of the superior evidence on which they could base their recommendations. Many early social scientists became activists (or vice versa), initiating studies of contemporary social conditions and institutions in order to win support for actions they favored.

Joseph Rice, an early leader of the Progressive movement, exemplifies this pioneering enterprise (Grinder and others, 1966). Originally a pediatrician, Rice became a liberal editor with a special interest in reforming education. In Rice's time the curriculum was bogged down, with most of the pupil's time going into drill on a few basic skills. In 1895, to prove that nothing would be lost if effort were redirected to richer subject matter, Rice appraised student achievement in schools and classified the data according to the time each school devoted to spelling drills. This survey was probably the very first tó use a standard test of ability.

Rice's evaluation influenced practice. But, ironically, its influence was just the opposite of what he intended. The spelling scores were not high. That finding made educators highly conscious of spelling results, and the subject came to receive undue prominence. The consequence was more drill in spelling, even though Rice established that the schools that had allocated more time to spelling drills had *not* produced better results. This instance of perversity is not unique; again and again in later decades, standardized tests produced similar distortions that tended to narrow the curriculum and to promote use of drill (Tyler and others, 1978, p. 9). Here we glimpse a significant generalization: whether an evaluation is launched to promote a cause or to report neutrally on events, the measurement procedures and reports can easily have a wholly unanticipated influence on what happens next.

Today's survey research originated in Rice's brand of social advocacy. Surveys were frequent around the turn of the century, and many of them were launched in the spirit of muckraking. A journal entitled *The Survey* was a forum for persons outside the government who thought that bringing shortcomings of society to light would motivate reform. The popular journals and books based on field studies did indeed support reforms; Jacob Riis' portrayal of slum conditions and Abraham Flexner's report on medical training are well-known examples. Stone and Stone (1975) see a 1906 episode as the turning point in the establishment of research on public affairs. Civic leaders in New York, financed by foundations, obtained a charter for a bureau to investigate local government, but Tammany shut the doors of city hall in their faces. The bureau then chose to do what it could out of doors. A survey of the condition of the streets, set alongside the funds reportedly spent on building and maintaining roadways, was *prima facie* evidence of misuse of funds. The ensuing battle reached the courts and the office of Governor Charles Evans Hughes before a borough president was removed for incompetence.

The business community of those days was impressed by the new efficiency experts who had appeared in industry, and business executives sitting on the governing boards of social services pressed for greater efficiency in those services. Callahan (1962) and Tyack (1974) document how in the early years of the century the public schools were pressed to find "the one best way" of conducting education. The methods that would speed up a factory's assembly line were expected to rationalize public services also.

At the height of this efficiency movement in education, evaluations for managerial purposes became commonplace. A school superintendent would invite a team of experienced administrators and scholars to look over the system she directed, to certify the respects in which it met certain contemporary standards and failed to meet others, and to suggest reforms (or budget increases). The surveys concentrated heavily on whatever could be counted or measured. As a notable example, Ayres (1908) cross-tabulated age against grade-in-school for a large population of pupils. He convinced educators that it was wasteful for a system to take six or more years to move a child through the first four grades. Statistics on attendance, promotion, and cost became prominent in the surveys. Once standard achievement tests became available, they too were emphasized.

Social scientists moved into government service, particularly during the Woodrow Wilson and Franklin Roosevelt administrations. Their role was typically that of the adviser who draws upon available knowledge and concepts rather than of the investigator who collects data for policy purposes (Merton and Lerner, 1951, pp. 290–292). After 1900, as the disciplines of the behavioral sciences became steadily stronger, social research became more academic. As Lyons (1969, p. 8) tells it in his history, academicians withdrew from social battles. In part "to acquit themselves of the accusation of reformism," they spent their time refining methodology for the study of safe topics. Most social scientists other than economists maintained a safe distance between their work and the tensions of management and politics. Between 1920 and 1940, few of them did research on institutions, and even fewer were interested in producing short-run changes in the settings they studied. Lynd's famous *Knowledge for What?* (1939) was a rebuke to social scientists for shrinking from policy debates.

This is not to say that no data were collected on social services. Many school districts established research offices to

monitor student progress; many cities established research bureaus in imitation of the New York model; and some social agencies arranged for in-house research. Faculty members within
schools of education, social work, and the like reported many
comparatively academic studies of institutions and their effects.
Glueck's 1936 plea for evaluation in social work gives us a glimpse
of research-linked-to-decisions as a professional activity struggl-
ing to be born. Not the least bold of Glueck's proposals was
a follow-up study to determine whether shotgun marriages are
a good idea. (She did not say how the decision maker holding
the shotgun was to be persuaded to base policy on the research.)

In scattered work in the 1920s and 1930s, close observations of institutions at work did change perceptions of them.
The Eight-Year Study of thirty high schools in the late 1930s
is noteworthy—the only early educational evaluation that "is
still noted with some respect," according to Munro (1977, p.
vi). As we shall see in Chapter Three, it encouraged new thinking about the ends and means of education, but it did not inform policy makers about the effects of the programs it studied.

A second example is the controlled experiments of Roethlisberger and Dickson (1939) on physical environments in a Western Electric plant at Hawthorne, Illinois. They wanted to know
which work environment led to greatest productivity; they concluded that social relationships and perceptions were far more
influential than ventilation and the other physical variables that
they had manipulated. The study is famous for the Hawthorne
effect: persons who know they are experimental subjects act
differently from the way they otherwise would. More important,
however, was the interest in group processes the report aroused,
paving the way for the "action research" of the period from
1935 to 1960.

In the forefront of action research were Kurt Lewin and
his students. They examined how the success of programs in
education, industry, and housing depended on interpersonal
interactions, and they demonstrated that group processes could
be deliberately altered. Experimental intervention in institutions and communities was a central method of Lewinian field
research. Lewin's students made many theoretical contributions,

OKANAGAN COLLEGE LIBRARY
BRITISH COLUMBIA

but social psychologists gravitated away from applied research after Lewin's death in 1947 (Deutsch, 1975, p. 2; Sanford, 1970).

Government organizations carried out some social research: routine activities such as the census and special studies such as the 1933 volumes on *Recent Social Trends* (see Lyons, 1969). Local social services arranged for limited reviews of their own operations. Down to the 1960s, however, almost all systematic *evaluative* studies were privately supported and pretty much in the spirit of basic research, or else they were carried out as part of the internal management of a governmental unit, safely insulated from political storms. For example, from 1941 on, military psychologists and sociologists worked in special offices and laboratories within the armed services, quietly evaluating and improving programs for training and programs for enhancing morale.

Evaluative studies of psychotherapy were so numerous between 1945 and 1960 (and so controversial) that the Children's Bureau (Herzog, 1959) issued guidelines for the use of administrators who were considering setting up evaluative research in their agencies. The bibliography for these guidelines is dominated by academic research, however; it includes few reports from service agencies, planning agencies, and professional conferences. The guidelines cover many problems discussed in today's literature; passage of twenty years has made the profession aware of additional difficulties, but it seems not to have eliminated any.

*Evaluation as Handmaiden to Political Leadership.* A great change came during the 1960s. Activists bent on increasing the federal role came to power; for them and for their fast-learning opponents, evaluation became politics continued by other means. Several leading figures, of whom Robert McNamara is the best known, were policy analysts by profession as well as by inclination. Planning and systems analysis did not reach far beyond the Department of Defense in the Kennedy years, but after the 1964 election President Johnson imposed program budgeting on the entire government. Offices charged with program evaluation sprang up, some at staff levels detached from any particular program and some under the control of specific programs (Williams, 1971, p. 108).

Evaluative studies were commissioned for immediate use to manage government business and to win political acceptance for new program proposals. The ostensible aims of tighter managerial review were to verify the worth of innovations and to promote them, to make sure that programs (old and new) operated efficiently, and to hold the line on program budgets. But perhaps the root motive was to press for reform. Top officials found it hard to interest old-line bureaus in new proposals; the chief desire of the agencies, they felt, was to get more money for more of the same old activities (O. Graham, 1976). Evaluative inquiries increased in number and in size; the typical study now commissioned by the federal government was on a vastly greater scale than anything seen before. The Westinghouse evaluation of Head Start, for example, reported data from a nationwide selection of more than 100 instructional centers.

Long before the massive studies of compensatory education and desegregation, educational evaluation had burgeoned as a side effect of curriculum reform. In the wake of Sputnik's launching in 1957, the National Science Foundation began to support development of new curricula in mathematics and science. These ventures started as creative activities guided by professional imagination and judgment, not as structured research. Before long, the foundation began to ask project directors for formal evaluations. In calling for evaluations, the foundation may have wished to assist schools in deciding whether to use the new curricula; surely it hoped also to support its future budget requests with evidence that past expenditures had paid off. The studies conducted were sometimes simple and rather informal, but a few were extensive and conformed to the canons of experimental design.

It seems fair to say that most curriculum makers in the post-Sputnik period resisted the idea of evaluation (Quarton, 1966) and kept evaluators walled off from day-to-day developmental work. If they wanted evaluative information at all, it was to impress sponsors, potential customers, and the scholarly community. The major studies made little difference in school decisions; the acceptance or rejection of the curricula in question had been determined by other events before the studies were finished. (See, for example, the history of evaluation in Harvard Project Physics in Cronbach, 1978.) But despite the limitations of the post-Sputnik evaluations, educators came increasingly to see evaluation as central to curriculum development. Indeed, Munro (1977, p. ii) has said that "most innovators are now prepared to accept evaluation of their products and many regard favorable evaluation as a necessary prerequisite to the acceptance or introduction of their work."

During the Kennedy-Johnson period, Congress came to see evaluation as a possible means of control. Money passes through many hands when Congress authorizes a federal bureau to make grants to states, which in turn make grants to community agencies. The Elementary and Secondary Education Act (ESEA) of 1965, for example, funded additional school services for children of the poor. To be eligible for funds, a local educational agency had to offer an evaluation plan and the state agency had to promise a summary report. The language is significant; the report was not merely to describe how the money was spent but to set forth "the effectiveness of payments under this title and of particular programs assisted under it in improving the educational attainment of educationally deprived children." Moreover, the data were to include "appropriate objective measures of educational achievement." This requirement reaches far beyond the traditional report as to where funds were spent. It demands data rather than reassuring testimonials.

Whether to evaluate and how to evaluate are political decisions, and the legislative history of ESEA offers a nice example of this. Local school officials wanted federal aid that they could allocate as they chose. Congress rejected that concept but was prepared to give categorical aid. Congress, however, suspected that categorical aid would be diverted or used to maintain school practices that had been producing unacceptable results. Senator Robert Kennedy proposed evaluation as a control. As McLaughlin (1975, p. 4) tells the story, "Kennedy remarked in the Senate Subcommittee hearings on ESEA: 'I just question whether they [school administrators] have, No. 1, focused attention on where the real problems are and, secondly, whether they have the ability to really perform the functions.' He thought that the parents had a right to know what was taking place in the schools and how Title I dollars were being spent. He expected that the evaluation mandate would provide a new source of political power that parents could use as a 'whip' or a 'spur.' Kennedy hoped a Title I project reporting requirement would force local schools to reform their practices in light of the priorities expressed by parents and focus on solving the 'real problem'—the failure of disadvantaged children."

Kennedy proposed a much tougher evaluation requirement than the one that ultimately came into being. School officials objected to Kennedy's plan; for the federal government to specify educational objectives and measuring procedures was, they said, intrusive and inappropriate. The head-on collision threatened passage of the bill, and Francis Keppel, as Commissioner of Education, persuaded Kennedy to accept broad language. This language, in turn, was given a least-restrictive interpretation by guideline writers in the Office of Education, who saw local officials and state officials as a constituency to appease (McLaughlin, 1975, pp. 19–20). The local schools were thus left free to report any kind of "objective" data regarding "needs" of their own choosing. The evaluation reports were chaotically diverse and could not be aggregated in a way useful for policy review. Not until 1978 was a more systematic reporting procedure imposed on local districts (Tallmadge and Wood, 1978).

Some studies of this period had the aim of altering political sentiment. Congress mandated the study entitled *Equality of Educational Opportunity*, the so-called Coleman Report of 1966. Seemingly, the intent of this study was to document that children of ethnic minorities were receiving inferior school services and thus to generate pressure for more equal treatment in schools. Similarly, the National Assessment of Educational Progress had a political mission (Greenbaum, Garet, and Solomon, 1977). Just as statistics on disease rates maintain public interest in appropriations for health services, so, according to those who started the National Assessment Project, periodic reports on educational accomplishments and shortcomings would make it easier to obtain more generous appropriations for schooling.

*Themes of the 1970s.* The hopes held for program evaluation a decade ago can be seen in a strong recommendation from a committee of the National Academy of Sciences (Advisory Committee..., 1968, pp. 57–58): "Program evaluation requires major increases of social and economic information as a basis for measuring the effectiveness of public policies and programs. Increased information brings on increased problems of analysis and of developing conceptual schemes that relate information to the goals and responsibilities of the department or agency. Thus, questions about facts and what they mean become broadened into questions about applying knowledge or finding out something that is not yet known or is little understood. The need for information thus brings with it a need for research, a need for understanding of research by top administrators, and a need for behavioral scientists in government service; a need, in sum, for strengthening the conditions for the effective use of the knowledge and methods of the behavioral sciences."

The main development in concepts of program evaluation from 1969 to date can be summarized briefly. First, the policy-analysis community came to realize that field research could give it a better basis for planning. Second, criticisms of the first large evaluations led to attempts to promote an experimental methodology whose results would supposedly be less open to challenge. Thus the Social Science Research Council enlisted a group of experienced field investigators to write the work entitled *Social Experimentation*, which is both guidebook and manifesto (Riecken and Boruch, 1974; see also Boruch and Riecken, 1975).

The best example of sophisticated field methodology comes from the bold New Jersey negative income tax experiment mounted by the Office of Economic Opportunity. Eligible households in four cities were divided randomly among seven welfare plans and a control group. Each welfare plan guaranteed a minimum income; when recipients raised their income above that level by direct earnings, the payments were reduced by some fraction. The seven experimental formulas ranged over plausible guarantee levels and reduction rates. The principal dependent variable was the extent to which recipients remained in the labor force, as workers or seekers after work. The difficulties that the study encountered (Rossi and Lyall, 1976), along with its artificial character (Rivlin, 1974), made it clear that scientific care and control will not eliminate controversy about evaluation procedures and results.

Indeed, the third main development of the past decade has been the growing but belated recognition that politics and science are both integral aspects of evaluation. Looking back, we can see that time and again political passion has been a driving spirit behind the call for rational analysis. On the one hand, rationalists advocated bringing to social affairs the neutrality and detachment that have served natural science and technology so well. And, on the other hand, the very call for value-free inquiry was politically motivated, generally by discontent. The savants of the Enlightenment were fighting traditions entrenched in royal and ecclesiastical power. The Progressives wanted social initiatives to which the legislators and mayors of the time were indifferent. The policy makers of the 1960s sought to use analytical methods to break up bureaucratic hardpan so that new programs could take root. But many a political contestant seems to have said, "Let us ask the oracle: Minerva can be counted on to support our side." The contestants might have asked, more humbly, "What message does Minerva have for us?"

## Demand and Supply in Evaluation

In this generation American government has become more ambitious than ever before. Social programs are costlier and more complex. Consequently, demand has grown for a technology of government. Systematic planning and quality control, it is hoped, will replace patchwork initiatives and chaotic operations.

The federal expansion is most conspicuous, but lower levels of government also have increased their efforts to cope

with social needs, and all are searching for system in government. The same can be said of other nations. Programs on the
grand scale are rare in developing nations, but the fruitfulness
of programs is a vital concern there also—their problems are urgent and their resources scanty.

   *The New Need for Information.* Public services have conferred conspicuous benefits. In this century, the United States
has improved public health and the distribution of health services; Americans are receiving schooling to a greater extent than
in any other generation; the distress of old people is reduced by
regular payments from the Social Security system and by local
services never before available. Even though continuing unemployment is viewed with unease, more American adults now
hold jobs than in any previous period. With each step forward,
however, aspirations rise, and rising aspirations breed discontent
as well as further progress.

   The mere fact that persons are being kept alive longer
calls for new health services, new educational services, and useful
social roles for the elderly. Not as much hard manual labor is
required to produce goods today as in the past. Although this
speaks of a better quality of life for breadwinners, it means that
more of the young and the less educated are left with no work.
Each advance in living conditions and opportunities for minority citizens heightens distress over the disparities that remain.

   Publics everywhere hold the optimistic conviction that
there can be still greater advances: whatever social gains were
made in the last generation can be equaled in the next. Perhaps
something can be accomplished just by expanding existing programs, but many services are close to the point of diminishing
returns. The communities and individuals who lag behind the
standard of normal well-being are those for whom the existing
institutions and services are poorly suited (Glennan, 1972).
Thus, optimists continue to press for innovative programs that
will reach the hard cases.

   Social programs are not adopted without question. The
same public that cherishes governmental services and protec-
tions doubts that the agencies are efficient and honest (Katz and
others, 1975; Aaron, 1978, p. 159). Moreover, a service that

promises to benefit some citizens may be of no benefit to others or even contrary to their interests. Legislators and administrators constantly face painful choices, given the fact that every proposal has both critics and defenders. And, of course, programs often have disappointing results. Some programs fail because the assumptions underlying them do not match prevailing social conditions. Others "fail" because the service is not delivered as the planners intended. Either result increases skepticism about the next proposal.

Social renovations disappoint even their architects—that is the iron law of social change. The abandonment of nationwide Prohibition is perhaps the most dramatic acknowledgment of the limits of government in American history, but retreats from untenable positions have been required in many other policy areas. The Social Security program is unmatched in popular appeal and perhaps in the wisdom of its conception, yet it now requires new sources of funds to stave off bankruptcy. A strategy of economic interventions intended to prevent inflation and deflation enjoyed a few years of encouraging success, only to contribute in the end to a once-inconceivable world in which unemployment and inflation rise simultaneously. Educational reforms are abandoned even when apparently successful. The new math, for example, came in with prestigious backing as the answer to fossilization and triviality in the prevailing curriculum. The instructional materials did what was intended reasonably well. Yet the movement had a life-span of less than twenty years, fading out when marketable skills came to have higher priority than intellectual excellence. This history of disappointment increases the uncertainties of those who seek constructive courses of action.

Choices rest on beliefs, the more trustworthy the better. The government official, pained by conflicting pressures and hard choices, hopes that better information will reduce her uncertainties. Everyday observations and conversations may equip village leaders to resolve whatever dilemmas they face, but the official in a big city is necessarily out of touch. Daily experience and conversations give her only a sketchy representation of the urban scene. Uncertainties increase rapidly as a program spreads over a larger area and over a larger population, and as it comes to be operated through more layers of organization. The citizen is left in an even poorer position than the official to pass judgment on the worth of programs.

The need for systematic and often subtle information to supplant or confirm casual observations is what generates the call for evaluation. Only rarely does an intervention produce an abrupt change. A significant trend can be masked by the ebb and flow of daily incidents. It is not to be hoped, for instance, that the participation of policemen in community-betterment activities will quickly dispel the hostility and mistrust of ghetto dwellers. Furthermore, carefully chosen anecdotes can give the impression that mistrust is still rampant, or, if selected with the opposite bias, the goodwill toward officers now prevails. Such information has no credibility for those who do not wish to credit it. A systematic observer using professional controls to guard against bias can better determine whether progress is being made.

A closer analysis of the observations is required than a lay interpreter can make. Unassisted judgment leaps all too easily to false interpretations. When American high school students score much below their European counterparts on a comprehensive test in mathematics, for example, a large part of the difference can be attributed to the fact that American schools serve a cross section of the whole population. American high school students are thus not comparable with the student bodies of the more selective European schools. In debates over controversial programs, liars figure and figures often lie; the evaluator has a responsibility to protect his clients from both types of deception.

*Consequence of Government Sponsorship.* Evaluations seem to become larger year by year, partly because they are being initiated by bodies that command large resources. Most of the massive evaluations are planned with the U.S. Congress as the primary audience. Indeed, Congress has, with some frequency, included a mandate for evaluative reports when authorizing an innovation. For many years, it has attached to the program authorizations of some agencies a "set aside" that earmarks a standard percentage of the appropriation for evaluation of the program. In the Legislative Reorganization Act of 1970 and the Congressional Budget Act of 1974, Congress gave the General Accounting Office (GAO) sweeping orders to conduct its own evaluations. The GAO has pushed the process along by offering a draft section that can be attached to any authorizing legislation. The section calls for a statement of detailed objectives, a report on effectiveness in achieving them, and a listing of the evidence for those conclusions (Marvin and Hedrick, 1974).

State and local governments also have become avid consumers of evaluative services (Chadwin, 1975; Beckman, 1977). In the state of California, for example, agency after agency is adding an evaluation staff. Not all such staffs are concentrated in the state capital; subunits are set up in major population centers to be nearer the sources of data and to detect unique local problems. California's legislature has provided itself with its own small social research unit, whose functions, like those of the GAO in Washington, can only grow. What is happening in California is happening in other states, and the movement spreads with every exchange of experience among governors or top officials.

The requirements for large-scale evaluations have created a social research industry. Executive agencies can build up staffs for a steady kind of data collection, but a special, intensive study generally has to be contracted out. In response to this demand, firms such as the Rand Corporation, SRI International, and American Institutes for Research have assembled staffs of social scientists, networks of field observers and interviewers, and stables of consultants. The contracted studies have become larger and larger, and expenditures of one million dollars a year are not uncommon for a single major study. (In the largest budgets, however, much goes into costs of trial services—welfare payments, for example, or a staff to provide family counseling. Only a fraction of the budget is for data collection, analysis, and other costs of actual evaluation.)

The evaluation industry does not consist wholly of giant firms. In every section of the country are tiny local outfits, some of them headed by apprentice social scientists who have not yet finished their graduate training or even—one hears—by English majors who have found too little demand for their services as experts on *Beowulf*. Most of these firms assist local agencies in preparing the evaluative reports required by state and federal offices. But not all their work is so routine. More challenging tasks come when a local official or city council seeks guidance from a study of local provisions for daycare or for rehabilitation of drug users.

Evaluation activities have mushroomed without plan, and evaluators are being asked to do an astonishing variety of things. There is a "boom town" excitement in the evaluation community. One well-known tabulation showed that federal expenditures in 1974 for program evaluation were six times those in 1969; when cited by enthusiasts, that figure gives the impression of endless expansion to come. The cold facts, however, appear to be that federal expenditures for evaluation have been nearly level in the last few years. Moreover, congressional committees have begun to lower the "set asides" that tithed program appropriations to support an evaluation component.

A painstaking analysis of expenditures for social research and development appeared late in 1978 (Study Project on Social Research and Development, 1978). No reading of the data can deny that federal funding for evaluation research has regressed when measured in constant dollars. This freeze set in before political writers began to talk of a tax revolt, and long before government spending became the pivotal issue of the 1978 elections.

Expansion has not yet stopped, however. If expenditures from state, local, and private funds were known, they would almost certainly show that there was real expansion down to 1978, and one suspects that more is to come. The so-called Sunset Act or Program Evaluation Act—which some have dubbed the Evaluator's Full-Employment Act (Elisburg, 1977, p. 68)— has in some of its versions called for overwhelming amounts of evaluative activity. The version that passed one house of Congress just before adjournment in 1978 was toned down nearly to the point of reasonableness; but whichever of its successors is ultimately enacted may greatly intensify evaluation activity.

Table 1. Obligations of Federal Agencies for Four Categories
of Social Research and Development in Three Fiscal Years
(in Millions of Dollars)

|  | 1975 | 1976 | 1977 |
|---|---|---|---|
| *All Agencies** |  |  |  |
| Program evaluations | 52.5 | 61.7 | 63.6 |
| Demonstrations: policy oriented | 209.7 | 204.0 | 199.4 |
| Demonstrations: promotion oriented | 152.4 | 183.2 | 178.9 |
| Research | 585.6 | 655.3 | 701.1 |
| Total | 1000.2 | 1104.2 | 1142.9 |
| *Department of Health, Education,* |  |  |  |
| *and Welfare (HEW)* |  |  |  |
| Program evaluations | 33.0 | 38.4 | 38.0 |
| Demonstrations: policy oriented | 165.3 | 155.3 | 144.2 |
| Demonstrations: promotion oriented | 107.0 | 130.0 | 120.5 |
| Research | 230.3 | 242.7 | 242.5 |
| Total | 535.6 | 566.7 | 545.2 |
| *Department of Housing and* |  |  |  |
| *Urban Development (HUD)* |  |  |  |
| Program evaluations | 2.5 | 3.6 | 4.0 |
| Demonstrations: policy oriented | 18.8 | 18.9 | 19.4 |
| Demonstrations: promotion oriented | 7.3 | 6.8 | 9.4 |
| Research | 6.9 | 9.9 | 14.6 |
| Total | 35.5 | 39.2 | 47.4 |
| *Department of Justice (DOJ)* |  |  |  |
| Program evaluations | 3.4 | 4.8 | 4.3 |
| Demonstrations: policy oriented | — | 0.4 | 0.3 |
| Demonstrations: promotion oriented | 2.0 | 11.6 | 8.7 |
| Research | 23.2 | 28.3 | 25.0 |
| Total | 28.6 | 45.1 | 38.3 |

* *Note:* Includes all departments and independent agencies, not merely HEW, HUD,
and DOJ.
*Source:* Abramson (1978), pp. 30, 134, 276, and 309.

Evaluators may benefit, but they may also find themselves
pushed into building spurious facades instead of being supported in inquiries likely to improve programs.

Table 1 displays some of the facts that document the
standstill in federal funding. Interpretation is rendered difficult
by the unorthodox categories that the survey adopted. The survey looked at all "social knowledge production and utilization,"

including collection of routine statistics and dissemination activities. However, it probably failed to count dollars spent by state and local units on locally managed evaluations out of federal appropriations for programs.

Of the seven categories of the survey, we attend to the four most likely to include the evaluations that concern us:

- Program evaluations. These are summative appraisals of established programs.
- Demonstrations for policy formulation. These include pilot studies and field tests of prototypes where the emphasis was laying a groundwork for future recommendations. "Social experiments" were placed under this rubric.
- Demonstrations for policy implementation. A program in this category was accepted as desirable by some agency, and the field trial was intended as a means of debugging and as a showcase. Some part of the funds went to assessing outcomes in the hope that the data would encourage adoption of the program demonstrated.
- Research. This category includes attempts to understand the effects of programs and policies on persons and institutions. But it also includes whatever more fundamental research an agency supported.

In the last three categories, then, a large and unknown fraction of funds went into nonevaluative work. In the demonstrations, it may be that nearly all the money went into providing and administering the service rather than into observation and interpretation. What fraction of the expenditures in the research category related directly to present programs and initiatives contemplated for the near future cannot be estimated without a fresh survey.

Even so, Table 1 is easily read. Funds obligated for these four research categories showed only local variations over the three-year period. Agencies varied greatly in their distribution of funds over the categories, but agency strategies changed hardly at all. The fact that a pause in spending for evaluations is upon us gives even greater point to the main concern of this book, namely, increasing the benefit from each evaluation dollar. Now may be the ideal time to develop new strategies and to amass professional opinion in support of work that is worth doing.

As evaluations become more central to policy, they inevitably become more and more an object of evaluation themselves. The Congressional Budget Act of 1974 directed the GAO specifically to analyze program evaluations prepared by and for any federal agency. The GAO's increasingly active role is certain to have a profound influence on the practice of evaluation.

In making recommendations, the executive branch refers to conclusions from evaluations, and the GAO undertakes to verify those conclusions. It feels called upon to audit or cross-check every step in the research—insofar as its resources permit —much as it would cross-check an agency's financial accounts. Marvin (1977, p. 7), associate director of GAO's Program Analysis Division, points out that this brings the office, representing the public, into judging matters "previously thought to be solely the province of the experimental community." He refers specifically to the GAO's intent to judge whether an appropriate range of hypotheses was considered and to audit experimental data as the study proceeds.

*Our* argument in later chapters will point out some inadequacies of existing review mechanisms for evaluations, and in Chapter Six we shall recommend new arrangements for timely review by qualified groups outside the contracting agency and the evaluation team. But from the GAO perspective "the profession policing itself" is not enough: "Auditing represents the public interest and thus the participation of the audit discipline symbolizes the need for broader public involvement in social experimentation intended to influence public policy. If policy making is to be expanded to include the results of social experimentation, then appropriate citizens need to be involved in a public process starting in the early planning stages of a social experiment, and throughout the different phases of the experiment itself" (Marvin, 1977, p. 6). Inasmuch as the GAO is strongly backed by Congress, we see no point in asking whether the GAO *should* take this awesome responsibility. The GAO has gotten into the act, and evaluation will be much affected as a result.

## Disappointment with Evaluations

Complaint has accompanied the expansion of evaluation. Everyone seems to think that evaluation is not rendering the service it should. While the major complaint is that evaluations are not affecting decisions, this is by no means the only source of distress.

*Have Evaluations Pulled Their Weight in Policy?* The gloom and variety of criticisms are illustrated by some of Timpane's (1976) comments on the evaluations of Title I of ESEA. Under the heading "A Wave of Failures" (of evaluation, not of the program), Timpane (1976, pp. 417–418) said:

> [Study A found few] effects and was widely (and wrongly) cited . . . as proof that Title I did not yet work and should be held down in size.
>
> [Study B was] conducted largely as an intergovernmental bureaucratic intrigue, with a hidden agenda [and] foundered . . . on the states' unwillingness to report achievement data honestly and fully. . . .
>
> State and local evaluations required by the federal statute were of little use for federal program decisions. [Italics removed.]
>
> There is plenty of reason for dismay in reviewing these results. At the end of all these studies [far more than are mentioned in the excerpts above], the effectiveness of Title I as an educational program is still unknown.

Only a small fraction of the criticisms of evaluation can be discounted as coming from partisans who disliked the finding of a particular study. A surprisingly large part of the criticism comes from those who advocate greater reliance on evaluation and from persons who earn their living as evaluators. Thus, Mark Thompson (1975) could quote negative assessments of evaluative activities from the GAO, from Wildavsky, from Suchman, from Rivlin, and from Wholey and go on to say that "the consensus inherent in these statements is that evaluation and policy analysis have not had great impact upon governmental decisions" (p. 2). Thompson continued: "On an absolute scale— weighing the costs of evaluation against its benefits—there seems to be no escaping recognition of the general failure of evaluation despite its occasional moments of success. Policy analysis, within which evaluation plays a major role, was touted a decade ago as a panacea for myriad woes of governmental management. The remedy was purchased but the diseases have not been cured or substantially alleviated" (p. 4).

In each of the recent symposia that brought together representatives of the evaluation-sponsoring and evaluation-conducting communities, similar disparagement of work to date appears, mixed in with positive reports on particular efforts and a general enthusiasm for trying to do the evaluative job better. In one symposium (Chelimsky, 1977b), nine federal agencies responsible for vastly different kinds of social services were heard from. All but one said that, on balance, evaluation studies had not been helping their agencies as much as could reasonably be expected. The ninth agency is not a noteworthy exception; it would be easy to cite attacks on the evaluations that it has arranged. At Chelimsky's meeting, however, the agency representative chose to look on the bright side.

Just why have evaluations not had great impact on decisions? Various explanations are offered. First, evaluators rarely come out with strong recommendations and often report that given social services have no measurable effect on their clients. The typical formal comparison of services reports small, if not negligible, average differences in outcomes of old and new programs. No wonder, then, that the statistical results fail to change program proponents into skeptics or vice versa. All they do is make the evaluation seem pointless. When a horse race ends in a dead heat, bettors on both sides remain convinced that, another day, their favorite will win.

Second, evaluative information has seemed to lack political punch. When an expensive innovation is not bringing observable benefits, terminating it might seem to be the logical response to the report. But almost always the program "proven ineffective" continues, so critics feel that evaluations do not carry the weight they should. No matter how excellent a study is technically, its facts will not sweep political sentiment and power aside. The backers and operators of a program can find many bases for rejecting a negative evaluation, starting with the suggestion that the evaluation came before the program was adequately shaken down. Or perhaps they will say that the evaluation measured the wrong outcomes or paid too little attention to sites where the program worked well. Instead of ending controversies, evaluations seem to fuel the fire. This was the case with the Follow Through study which attempted a horse-race comparison of a variety of plans for compensatory education in the early grades. An interpretation that emphasized the average performance of students on certain posttests covering a limited range of content was unsatisfactory to sponsors of wide-ranging programs. See, for example, the temperate but distressed response from one sponsoring group (Weikart and Banet, 1975).

A third explanation offered is that evaluation will not become influential until studies are carried out properly. Evaluators and policy makers, it is said, are only now learning how to do high-stakes investigations; once the craft is worked out somewhat better, evaluations will have more impact. This cheerful note was struck by Timpane (1976), by Mosteller and Moynihan (1972), and by several commentators in Rivlin and Timpane, 1975b). According to this view, a great many mistakes were made during the evaluations of 1965–1975, but everyone is wiser today. Evaluators and those who commission evaluations, statisticians and economists, legislators and agency managers, all have learned something about the pitfalls to be expected in evaluating broad-aim human resource programs—pitfalls of question definition, threats to validity, implementation, instrumentation, analysis, timing, communication, and so on.

Many social scientists with a methodological interest insist that most evaluations have been technically inept, unworthy to be a basis for decision. They object that designs have been insufficiently rigorous or that analysis has been insufficiently sophisticated; that is why, it is argued, evaluation reports do

not permit a "correct," unhedged verdict that the program itself was or was not worthwhile (Rieckep and Boruch, 1974;
Bentler and Woodward, 1979).

A very different note of criticism-joined-with-optimism
has been sounded in the most recent commentaries. According
to this view, instead of promoting single definitive studies that
promise unquestionable guidance on a narrow issue of policy,
evaluators should be contributing to the slow, continuous,
cumulative understanding of a problem or an intervention. This
is our own position, and we shall elaborate on it as we go. It is
akin to the methodological critiques in expressing discontent
with past uses of research funds—a discontent evident, for example, in the remark of the Study Project on Social Research
and Development of the National Research Council (1978, p.
76) about "poorly motivated, and largely noncumulative studies
of social problems."

*Dissatisfaction Among Evaluators.* Whereas persons who
commission evaluations complain that the messages from the
evaluations are not useful, evaluators complain that the messages
are not used. Evaluators who see themselves as fearless seekers
after truth come to feel that they have been assigned walk-on
parts in a political pageant. Indeed some evaluations are "shows"
set in motion to make the sponsoring agency or elected official
look good or to discomfit an opponent. It is asserted—by members of the potential audience as well as in the private talk of
evaluators—that some sponsors do not want an honest inquiry.
Rather, they steer the evaluator so that his conclusion will score
a point for the sponsoring agency (for example, Bernstein, 1977;
Wurzburg, 1979).

The evaluator's second complaint has to do with the sponsor's ineptness. Those who commission evaluations often specify
the work to be performed in such a way that no worthwhile
study could be carried out, at least within the time allowed and
budget provided. Rossi (1979, p. 21), on the basis of a scrutiny
of several hundred government announcements calling for bids
on evaluation studies (requests for proposals or "rfp's"), notes
that "in most cases it seemed to me that one would have to be

methodologically naive, on the verge of slipping below the poverty line, a scientific hypocrite, or a combination of the above to have responded to most of the rfp's we reviewed."

An evaluator who thought that his inquiry was worthwhile and honestly sought when he began it may find, after his study is completed, that he is dealing with a fresh set of officials who have no interest in the study. For that and other reasons, an evaluator may derive little of the satisfaction from his work that other professionals get. Note this plaint (Davis and Salasin, 1975a, p. 625):

> An evaluator, who has been responsible for nearly $3 million worth of contract evaluations and who has engaged in intensive evaluation of his own, lamented to us recently that he was finding little professional satisfaction in his current work. His primary frustration stemmed from the futility of his efforts; there seemed to be so little response to the findings he supplied. As is the case with many evaluators, "Dr. A" came into the field of evaluation from research. He had gained wide respect through his many publications on the topic of personality development of a specific age group. His decision to dedicate himself to program evaluation was based upon the understandable belief that even more professional significance would be realized in that pursuit. But things turned out differently: his [basic] research studies bore theoretical relevance and accommodated his creative concepts; by contrast, his evaluation studies deal with largely ungeneralizable matters, directed by policy makers rather than, by contrast, his own creativity. Results of his research studies were readily publishable; results of his evaluation studies seldom find open doors to publication. On reporting his research findings, he received accolades from his colleagues; by contrast, on reporting evaluation studies, he is apt to draw captious attacks on his methods. His research findings were used by other scientists: by contrast, he feels his evaluation findings rarely are

used by anybody. In general, as he experiences it, the response to his dedicated endeavors has changed from approbation to opprobrium.

*Inconsistency of Complaints.* The myriad complaints about evaluation are, as a set, mutually contradictory. One person complains that evaluations take too long to come up with findings; another complains that studies are conducted too hastily. One critic says that personal and institutional values intrude into the findings; another objects that evaluators concentrate on facts to the exclusion of values. Do those who sponsor evaluations tie the evaluator's hands so that he cannot exercise appropriate judgment? Or is the fatal error the failure of policy makers to define just what they want to know from the evaluation? And so it goes.

But such criticism, however widespread, does not necessarily indicate that evaluation is at fault. The critics themselves may be at fault. Each critic may, in good faith, be representing the partial view suited to her role in the evaluation enterprise, to her professional affiliation, or to her personal and professional commitments. Even within a single agency that commissions an evaluation, the hopes and fears of any one officer regarding its practical consequences will differ from those of her superior at the policy level and her subordinates close to field operations (Chelimsky, 1977; Pedersen, 1977). Congress, with its urge to show results by the next election, is in step neither with the career bureaucrat nor with the academic thinker. Academics see social interventions as complex activities to be evolved through cycles of planning and modest tryout. For bureaucrats, affairs creep on in their weary pace, while the enthusiasms of elected officials strut their brief hour upon the stage and vanish.

Even among evaluators the cacophony of criticisms may be a symptom of varied backgrounds and training, as well as of the unfamiliar demands made by the evaluation task. Evaluators and those who write about evaluation have come from many backgrounds. What we might call the generalist—ready to attack any problem—was perhaps trained in economics, sociology, systems analysis, psychology, or statistics. There are also substantive specialists, familiar with past interventions and with related research on delinquency or mental health or higher education.

Each field has had its own tradition in evaluation, its own criteria of proper procedure, and its own respected sources (Nelson, 1977). As a result, each field provided narrow preparation. Economists and systems analysts were accustomed to large compilations of data, but they had little background in instrumentation and data collection. Psychologists knew a great deal about observing and questioning individuals, but they lacked experience with institutions. Those trained in the laboratory were ill prepared to deal with the fluid field setting, where even the meaning of a measuring instrument can change from one site to another. Similar difficulties were faced by statisticians, sociologists, and others new to evaluation. Investigators who had previously collected data in social institutions were somewhat better able to appreciate the requirements of an evaluation. But to them also, the intellectual, logistical, and gladiatorial complexity of evaluating a nationwide program was new.

Rare is the individual who has been acquainted with investigative traditions other than his own discipline or field of practice. This is readily seen in several works used for training in educational evaluation that were published in the early 1970s, each a compilation of articles setting forth general recommendations or reviewing the experience of particular projects. The authors of the articles were drawn from the limited circle of psychologists, statisticians, and measurement technicians whose careers were in educational research or who were specialists in reading, teaching of science, educational administration, or the like. The book edited by Worthen and Sanders (1973) will serve as an example; it featured writings by Bloom, Cronbach, Guba, Provus, Scriven, Stufflebeam, Stake, and Tyler—all prominent in educational circles. Sociologists and economists were largely ignored: Rivlin and Suchman did not appear in the index, Coleman and Campbell were barely referenced. Nor has education been unique in its insularity. The Rossi-Williams (1972) compendium of articles presented sociologists and economists aplenty but cited only three of the eight persons who were salient for Worthen and Sanders.

No matter what their prior experience, evaluators were unprepared for the tasks of recent years. For one thing, evaluations were being done in real time, as an adjunct to an ongoing examination of policy or to the installation of a program. The evaluator was exposed to scorching political winds, sometimes from the moment the study began. The few real-time evaluations made in earlier days had usually checked on stable activities in a temperate climate; a recommendation for technical adjustment could be accepted (or passed over) without political conflict. Another great change, as we noted earlier, was the unprecedented size of inquiries—an enormous number of units observed on a preposterously cramped time scale. Once the computer had made such studies possible, the quantity of evidence began to take priority over its quality and pertinence; concomitantly, promptness of reporting began to take priority over thorough study of meaning. Many of the studies received wide publicity, often of a kind that simplified findings to the point of distortion and thereby stirred up unnecessary controversy. Evaluators found themselves under pressure to compromise principles and standards that their training had taught them to value highly. These tensions have heightened the criticism of evaluation from within the evaluation community itself.

*Toward Realistic Shared Expectations.* The criticism that pours down on program evaluation as an institution (even as it is handed ever larger tasks) may be justified by evaluation's showing to date; or, instead, it may reflect an underappreciation of evaluation's benefits; or it may be that the expectations placed on evaluation have been inappropriate. We find some truth in all three explanations, but the third one expresses the most fundamental problem.

If any single intellectual sin is to be blamed for the present chaos, it is the readiness to make general assertions that supposedly apply to all evaluations. The reader is told that the evaluator should be present from the earliest days of program planning—or, contrariwise, that it is useless to start evaluating until the program has stabilized. Again the reader is told by one writer that the evaluator has to be insulated from program managers, who might seduce him from objectivity; he is then told by another that evaluators cannot communicate with and influence program managers unless they interact with them informally from the outset. Writers begin with different notions about the kinds of programs that it is fruitful to evaluate and about the kinds of questions an evaluation should try to answer. Some seem not to realize that their premises are restrictive; each one seems to think that he is describing what everyone else means by "evaluation." Consequently, statements sensible enough in the restricted context that a writer has in mind are remembered by the reader as assertions about all evaluations.

Helter-skelter diversity of practice and conflicting recommendations evidence the need for clearer thought. We are in full accord with Thompson's assessment (1975, p. 6): "Many of the problems evaluation faces stem from a fundamental misapprehension of what evaluation is and of what it can and should do. . . . [M]ost of the accepted definitions focus myopically upon limited aspects of evaluative operations and . . . few cast an eye to the basic purpose of improving decisions. . . . Abounding dicta . . . have been uncritically accepted as axioms."

The hope that an evaluation will provide unequivocal answers, convincing enough to extinguish controversy about the merits of a social program, is inevitably disappointed. A more appropriate conception of what evaluations should do—and what a good many of them are doing even now—would change the questions investigated and the research plan, the way in which the evaluator interacts with the political community, and the way in which findings are used.

In the 1970s awareness has grown that academic, rationalist, and scientific ideals do not take into account many of the intricacies of politically significant decisions. Only under special circumstances is the decision likely to turn solely on the empirical evidence (Ezrahi, in press). The scientist gazes at a colony of experimental subjects from the remote end of a microscope. In the reality of a program evaluation, the evaluator swims in the same ocean as his subjects and is buffeted by the same cross-currents. Perhaps it was the Williams-Evans (1969) review of the Head Start evaluation that first said emphatically that a theory of evaluation must be as much a theory of political interaction as it is a theory of how knowledge is constructed. Acceptance of this view has come slowly.

The current evaluation literature is markedly different from that of 1970 and earlier. For one thing, the interface between social research and social change has been directly studied, notably by Caplan and Patton but also by several others represented in Weiss' collection of papers (1977). The consensus is that evaluations and other social inquiries do matter. Their role is not to produce authoritative truths but to clarify, to document, to raise new questions, and to create new perceptions (Lindblom and Cohen, 1979).

Second, evaluators from the several disciplines and program specialties have been coming together in conferences with policy makers and program managers (Abert and Kamrass, 1974; Abt, 1976; Chelimsky, 1977). The conference papers form a kaleidoscopic pattern, not a coherent image, but at least it can no longer be said that most evaluators are out of touch with persons in other roles and disciplines. The same is to be said of the massive *Handbook of Evaluation Research* (Guttentag and Streuning, 1975; see also Ross and Cronbach, 1976). The participants talk past one another, but getting all voices into the same conversation—however jumbled—is a move toward convergence.

Generalist evaluators are increasingly aware that they cannot deal intelligently with a social problem without becoming thoroughly acquainted with the problem and the institutions related to it (Nelson, 1977, pp. 31–32). Working closely with substantive specialists is only a partial substitute for personal familiarity. For their part, specialist evaluators have long suspected generalists, believing that only specialists in the pertinent substantive field are likely to ask appropriate evaluative questions (Stake, 1976, p. 11). That suspicion is fading; interaction between the two types of evaluators is promoting mutual respect.

The time for a synthesis of views in evaluation has clearly arrived, and an evaluation community is in fact beginning to form. Several organizations of evaluators have sprung up, and it is significant that the Evaluation Research Society and the Council for Applied Social Research are moving toward a merger at this writing. Half a dozen journals now supplement the pioneer *Evaluation*, now retitled *Evaluation and Change*. A forum has developed; a broad group is now poised to reconsider the foundations of practice in evaluation.

## A Preliminary Criticism of Conventional Thinking

Some evaluations are carried out with large budgets and some with small; some follow formal procedures and some are casual; some extend over a nation and some stay within a single building. Evaluations, then, are exceedingly varied. Nonetheless, most works in the literature on evaluation set forth a stereotypic description of the "proper" plan. Those putting forward the stereotypic description acknowledge that compromises with the ideal are inevitable. But when the evaluation takes a form quite different from the stereotype, these writers speak of the departures as signs of incompetence, lack of serious intent, or political interference. The job of evaluation is said to be scientific appraisal, and the conventional presentation tells the evaluator and the purchaser of evaluative services to judge evaluations by their rigor. In one set of papers, the scornful phrase "fooling around with people" has been used to dismiss evaluations that do not closely approximate the stereotypic ideal (see, for example, Gilbert, Light, and Mosteller, 1974).

Our view is quite different: evaluative investigation ought to serve those who are discussing or regulating social actions. It is therefore highly appropriate for the form and style of evaluations to differ. We see a place for evaluations that fit the stereotype; evaluations do have a scientific element, and sometimes appraisal *is* the job. In the main, however, we find the stereotypic approach off target.

We intend continually to contrast our view with the conventional view and its working assumptions, although in the present section we do no more than remind the reader of the main elements in the conventional view and say as briefly as possible why it is not appropriate for all evaluative tasks. The ensuing section will develop succinctly our own orientation, setting the stage for its elaboration in later chapters.

*Evaluation Defined as Scientific Appraisal.* In the conventional view, evaluation is a scientific or technological task. Skillful, impartial investigation is to provide "a firm assessment" of the program or institution (Rossi, Freeman, and Wright, 1979, p. 21).

At the start, it is said, an official or official body foresees that a decision about a program is going to be required by a date we will call Decision Day. The form of the decision will depend on the maturity of the program; judging the potential of a brand-new proposal is a different matter from passing judgment on a service that has been in operation for ten years. Still, the conventional view thinks of the decision as primarily an allocation of resources. Which initiatives will be backed by hard cash? Which old programs will be given resources for expansion? Which ones throttled down? Which eliminated altogether?

The individual or body passing on these matters is presumed to be rational in the sense of emphasizing value for money. When rationality takes over from political considerations—so goes the stereotype—resources will be spent where greatest benefits can realistically be expected. Each decision is seen as an isolated decision about a distinct and separate program. Reference is made to the "go/no-go" decision to proceed with a proposed program or discard it, as well as to a survey of existing programs as a first step toward eliminating any whose payoff is not demonstrated. Reference is made to the survey among competing programs designed to achieve the same ends (which makes direct comparison possible). It is presumed that the proper course of action will be unmistakable, once dependable facts about the programs are assembled.

To abbreviate the description of the stereotypic model, we confine attention to an innovation that is to be adopted if it proves better than no program at all or better than an existing program that it could supplant. Moreover, we speak of arrangements for collecting data on the new program without elaborating on the similar study of the contrasting ("control") program.

The decision maker, uncertain as to what the innovation can accomplish, calls for a trial run. She judges that Decision Day is far enough away to allow a worthwhile field trial. She sets Deadline Day for the study just prior to Decision Day and sits back to await the report.

A program director is named to set the trial in motion so that it can be observed. The proposal at this point, of course, is only an outline on paper. Actions by staff members in the various sites turn the proposal into the realizations that can then be field tested. Under ideal circumstances, the evaluator would play a large role in discussions about the form that the trial realizations are to take and where they are to be installed. Ordinarily, however, the new activity is embedded in or attached to an ongoing institution, and this circumstance means that many matters are not open for consideration. Even when the program is new and independent, the treatment specifications are likely to be more or less complete before the evaluator comes along.

Whatever the realization, the same arrangement is to be kept in place from the start of the study to the end. The evaluation is to appraise a particular program, not a shifting target. Freeman (1964, p. 194) expressed the ideal in memorable words: "Once [the impact model] is formulated, [the researcher] must continue to remain within the environment, like a snarling watchdog ready to fight alterations in program and procedures that would render his evaluation efforts useless." This says flatly that the evaluation is spoiled if the program manager changes the rules to render better service to clients. What the program operators or observers learn from experience is not to be used; the program is to "play statue" while the evaluator's slow film records its picture.

The decision maker began with a comparatively vague question: "How well does the innovative idea work?" The evaluator has responsibility for reshaping this question to fit into research techniques. He translates "How well does it work?" into "How thoroughly does the realization achieve the intended outcomes, the goals?" He will therefore extract from the advocates of the program a clear statement of the changes they expect to produce. Then he can measure accomplishment against claim. Attention usually centers on aspects of the clients' behavior or conditions of life: crime, housing, education, health, and so on. Sometimes the variables characterize the community served rather than persons or families. Transforming the vague initial question into hypotheses stated operationally will enable the investigator in the end to attach a statistical confidence level to a statement such as "the new program brought results on this variable to a satisfactory level."

Many practical considerations enter into the choice of subjects. The most common recommendation is that the experimental social programs and a contrasting service be set up in companion sites—as many of each as can be managed—and that the evaluator make a maximum effort to control which persons go into each treatment group. The plan can take many forms, depending on the constraints on the study. One device that finds favor is to split the sample at random, promising control-group members that they will receive the experimental service as soon as the first wave of appraisal is over.

Some writings give the impression that the evaluator should set up his investigation and then take a slow boat around the world while the program does its work. On the date the "effects" are ripe for measurement, he returns to port. Many writers are indeed reluctant to have the investigator come near the program site. They fear that he will lose objectivity—becoming enthusiastic about what he sees, wanting to ingratiate himself with the staff, or feeling such sympathy for the clients that he wants service to them to continue—and slant his report accordingly. The practical evaluator is unlikely to remain so remote. For example, since the questions for his final questionnaire must be accepted as reasonable by respondents, he must negotiate with program participants. If he wants to test schoolchildren, he will have to negotiate for class time and perhaps parental consent. But the evaluator is advised by the conventional writers to hold contacts to a minimum and to avoid intimacy at all costs.

When the time span allowed for the treatment ends, the camera shutter snaps. Marks someone put onto paper are coded into numbers for the computer to think about. It is told to average the data from all the experimental cases and to lay the average alongside the benchmark that the control group provided. Out of the statistical mill pops the conclusion: Significant difference! (or No effect!). Preferably, the investigator will have sufficient confidence in the formal logic of his design to say what *caused* any differences that appeared. (The economist evaluator would perhaps process the data to state the benefit [expressed on a numerical scale] that would result from operating the program at each of several expenditure levels.) The evaluator now writes a report, much as a laboratory investigator reports to a journal. What he writes goes to the decision maker. Having a numerical estimate of the benefits to be expected from each of the alternatives, she presumably knows what action is right to take—and she takes it.

The evaluation just described is what Frank Baker (1967) called a stand-alone study. It has a beginning date and a scheduled ending date. It draws its conclusion in splendid isolation, strictly from its own data. A stroke or two of caricature appears here because the guidebooks on evaluation themselves caricature the research process. In later chapters, however, we shall mention investigators who behaved adaptively within this model, and we shall also quote with considerable approval the appraisal-oriented writers who have warned that a field study is altogether less tidy than a laboratory study.

*Timetable of the Stand-Alone Summative Study.* The conventional study has four successive phases—planning, execution, interpretation, and reporting. The timing of phases is usually awkward, primarily because the work is to be ready on Decision Day. Planning usually moves fast; the study is launched hurriedly to take advantage of favorable political winds and the availability of funds. The planning may be a collaboration among decisions in the agency, amplifications in the field, alterations to disarm critics at the site, revisions to cope with unforseen obstacles, and so on to convergence. The program realizations, as well as the plan for inquiry, are likely to change. The final compromise design examines fewer variables than enter into the politically relevant questions about outcomes, and it examines them with less control than the first plan called for.

The execution phase receives the majority of the evaluator's attention, time, skill, and funds. Systematic observation of people who may feel threatened by the study, carried out under deadline pressure, requires first-rate diplomacy, logistics, and quality control—all this in addition to scientific skill in ob-, serving elusive social variables. Fieldwork is extended as long as possible, so that the program has a chance to produce results. As a consequence, interpretation is crowded into a very short time. The data are hustled through the computer, and the tables slapped into final report. On Deadline Day the report is likely to be delivered in incomplete form. Sometimes even the minimal report is so far behind schedule as to produce agonies of embarrassment for the sponsor, who must stall off her superiors when Decision Day has come and gone. (Sometimes, no doubt, the full report is ready, and the master copy reaches the sponsor on schedule.)

Some reports remain as private communications to the manager who ordered them. Others are transmuted into an "executive summary" that gives to higher authority whatever message the sponsor of the evaluation chooses to emphasize. The evaluator's full report sometimes becomes openly available, months or years later, in an archive or a published document. The time pattern of the stand-alone summative study consistent with the stereotypic recommendation looks something like that represented in Figure 1.

This schedule is not at all like that of true science. A scientific study does not stand alone. Instead of originating on the instant, when the politics are ripe for the study, the plan for a particular scientific probe often grows out of months and years of prior inquiry by this investigator and others. Baker (1967) pointed out that the Fisherian stand-alone study was invented for fieldwork in agriculture and might be appropriate there. But Finney (1956), writing as an expert on field experiments in agriculture, disparages stand-alone efforts in much the same terms as Baker's. Moreover, Fisher himself did not rely only on stand-alone experiments in his fieldwork but in seeking explanations looked at survey data, historical records, and experiments all at once (see Edwards and Cronbach, 1952).

In a scientific study, the elements of the design—the instruments, the specifics of the treatment realizations, and so on—will be pretested by miniature trials, perhaps of small seg-

Figure 1. Timetable for the Conventional Summative Evaluation

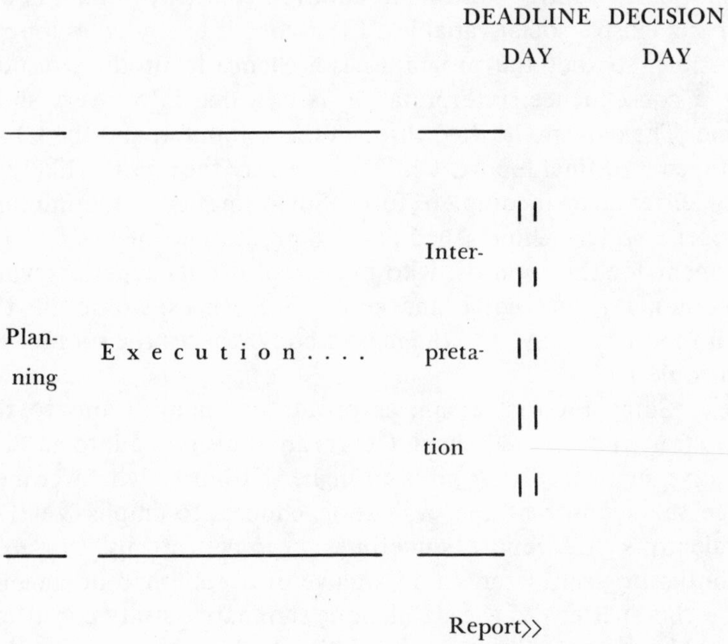

DEADLINE   DECISION
DAY           DAY

Plan-     E x e c u t i o n . . . .    preta-   ||
ning                                            ||

Inter-  ||
||

tion   ||
||

Report>>

ments of the basic plan. The hypothesis, and sometimes the perception of the central research issue, may be modified. Planning is interaction between scientist and nature as much as the formal study is, and ordinarily more time is given to it than to the "execution" run that an ultimate publication summarizes.

Unless the funds come from an obsessively bureaucratic source, there is no contract to deliver a preconceived product. The only deadlines are those deriving from the investigator's need to make a case for academic tenure or for further funding. Interpretation receives a major share of effort (though publication may come promptly when the initial hypotheses have been so ripened by previous research that the new facts speak for themselves). Reports are given formal publication "when they are ready." They are exposed to competent criticism before they are made final, and they emerge from the scientist's pen, not from the institution studied or from a special-interest group or from the elders of the tribe.

These contrasts between scientific inquiry and evaluation are not necessarily grounds for criticism of either. But recognizing fundamental differences between the two styles of investigation gives some sense of the pressures that make it impossible for evaluations to conform to the stereotypic ideal.

*Reservations About the Conventional Ideal.* We agree with the rationalists that evaluation should contribute to wiser social actions. We do not agree that the one best action will be made crystal clear by a factual study. The conventional view embodies a theory that society is as lawful as other aspects of nature. Whatever causes discontent is a problem that detached and impersonal inquiry can resolve. This theory leads to unrealistic expectations from evaluation. The line of criticism to be developed in Chapter Two can be adequately foreshadowed in these words of Rein and White (1977, pp. 269–270): "The problem-solving image is a kind of long-standing fantasy in which the games and the roles of science and politics are not in conflict. On the scientific side, it expresses the hope that participation in political activities is, or can be made to be, a matter of value-neutral decision making. . . . On the political side, the fantasy expresses the hope that contributory science can retain its authority, while remaining employable for the settlement of political value questions."

A decade ago, it seemed sensible to draw a line between conclusion-oriented and decision-oriented research (Cronbach and Suppes, 1969). Evaluation fell into the latter category; the research worker was commissioned to answer the definite question the sponsor posed, so that the sponsor could act. But this statement oversimplified. Social agendas cannot be reduced to a single sharp question that remains fixed during the period of the research. Evaluation does not and cannot end political dispute by reducing the merits and demerits of a proposal to "facts." As our argument develops, we shall join other current writers who see evaluation as contributing to conclusions or fresh perceptions that can influence a variety of plans and actions. Only a minority of evaluations are to be judged primarily by their service to whoever commissioned them.

The formal study of outcomes is almost never sufficient in itself. The evaluator should inspect program workings from many angles. Even the evaluator who minimizes his contact with program operators forms a great many impressions about the program realizations. He hears, for example, that the instructional materials were delivered late. He hears that when the regular teacher was ill for six weeks a substitute teacher took over without a briefing on the new materials. He finds out that a dozen children in one class were excused from taking the post-test because their command of English was judged inadequate. The developers who originated the innovation tell him that they bitterly resent the sponsor's decision to inquire into only a few of the effects they intended to produce. He learns that the program is positively regarded in some communities and viewed with suspicion in others. The stereotyped summative appraisal makes no provision for taking all the evaluator's knowledge into account. That is why sensible evaluators do not "go by the book." (And if the book is out of touch with reality, a new book is needed.)

The distinction between studies that ask how good a service is and those that ask how the service can be improved has been around for decades. Cronbach (1963), addressing the National Science Foundation and those who directed the large curriculum projects that it funded, argued for shifting evaluation resources from the first kind of study to the second. A rejoinder by Scriven (1967) defended the emphasis on getting one's money's worth. To polarize the discussion, Scriven coined the now-famous terms *summative* and *formative*. These handy terms are not adequate for today's discussions. As we see it, evaluations are used almost entirely in a formative manner when they *are* used. This is true even of studies that confine themselves to measuring outcomes. Scriven would not agree with us entirely, but a current paper of his (1978b) sees as much virtue in studies of process and program detail as we do. An either-or question has been turned into a question of resource allocation; how much of the evaluation effort goes into outcome measurement depends on the case in hand (see Chapter Four).

A social agenda almost never calls for a choice between fixed alternatives. Only rarely are "go/no-go" decisions made; rather, there is a continual search for alternatives more acceptable than those in sight when the study began. The questions that were in the mind of whoever commissioned the study will not match those that enter the political discussion later; hence, a study limited to the original narrow questions ignores much that is important. An accurate report on poor results from a program initiated in Year 1 will be of doubtful relevance in Year 3 because the program managers will have made changes that render posttest scores obsolete on the day they are collected. Or, if Freeman's snarling evaluator were able to prevent managers from improving the service, the managers would then insist that this year's posttest data do not indicate the merits of the revised program they will operate next year. In problematic areas, each year brings new issues, new social goals, and new proposals (Rivlin and Timpane, 1975b). The community is at least as well served by the discovery of new possibilities for action as by the definitive appraisal of a program fixed upon in the past.

We intend particularly to take issue with the time perspective of the stereotypic approach. One of the most frequent complaints about evaluations is that reports come in late and so perform no function—research and interpretation are compressed in time for the sake of delivering the report to a waiting decision maker as early as possible. But recent studies of utilization (Weiss, 1977) indicate that timeliness is a much-overrated concern. Evaluators have effects through short, informal feedback loops long before any final report is ready. And the final report has ramifications stretching over a long future. The contribution to thinking about the problem area and to shaping future programs is a larger contribution than the short-run impact on the program studied. Although evaluations study current events, inquiry is a continuing social process. In that process a particular evaluation is only an episode and its reporting date or stopping date only a passing incident.

Whether the emphasis is to be on what to do next or on rethinking the entire social problem, one wants considerable description of events. To speak more generally, one wants varied information collected by various techniques. The stand-alone study is not a good way to get the understanding that would permit better attacks on social problems. In the best of cases, where program outcomes are good, the evaluator should be in a position to point to possibilities for better outcomes in the future. When outcomes are disappointing, those who set policy ought to be told where things went wrong so that they can judge whether a modification of the program is worth trying. If attempts to patch up a program seem doomed to fail, one wants the research to spot faulty original assumptions so that future initiatives can avoid them.

Many of the observations on which the evaluator bases his suggestions are impressionistic rather than objective and statistical. They are conjectural, since they deal with possible futures. But the aspiration of social science is to make the future better. Far more is to be learned from evaluation than a precise answer to an obsolete question.

## A Standard for Judging Evaluations

In this book we offer a unified conception of evaluation. We start at a fundamental level: what function should evaluation perform in a society, particularly in the United States of the present day? An evaluative study of a social program is justified to the extent that it facilitates the work of the polity. It therefore is to be judged primarily by its contribution to public thinking and to the quality of service provided subsequent to the evaluation.

*Excellence as Service to the Social System.* If evaluations are not to be judged by the solidity of the answers they give to narrowly defined questions, what is an appropriate criterion? Nelson's words (1977, p. 30) about policy studies apply equally to program evaluations since both tasks are political, not purely scientific:

> Policy analysis now is well understood to be a much less neutral, much more active, aspect of the steering process than policy analysts originally liked to tell themselves. With the development of this self-understanding, it has been increasingly apparent to members of the profession that it is important to know how policy is actually made, the forces that bear on the process, and the parts that

cannot be moved, to know where the movable
levers are and how they can be maneuvered. Political scientists, virtually absent in the early ranks of
those who were considered part of the policy analysis community, are now playing a growing role.
Their original absence is worthy of note here. One
would have thought that political science, not economics, would have been the home discipline of
policy analysis. The reason it was not was that the
normative structure of political science tended to
be squishy, while economics possessed a sharply
articulated structure for thinking about what policy ought to be.

We would add the comment that, whereas economics and operations research have inspired most policy analysts, it was experimental psychologists and survey researchers from sociology
who offered "a sharply articulated structure" for most program evaluation.

To return to Nelson (1977): "[T]here are many problems that are not adequately characterized as involving a central
steersman controlling a well-working rudder . . . (p. 33). Policies
bubble up as actions taken or proposals generated from below,
only a few of which can be subjected to executive scrutiny. . . .
Even for those cases where policy is deliberated and decided at
a high level, it has become apparent that the steering wheel often
is but loosely connected to the rudder. The impact of policies
depends in good part on the performance or reaction of people
not under the direct control of the policy maker . . . (p. 34).
No one really believes any more that most of our problems
could be solved if only a good systems analyst had the czar's
(or the president's) ear" (p. 36).

Excellence ought to be judged against how evaluation
could serve a society. A society is an arrangement for making
lives more satisfactory. Evaluations can improve the welfare
of citizens only by contributing to the political process that
shapes social actions. An evaluation pays off to the extent that
it offers ideas pertinent to pending actions and people think
more clearly as a result. To enlighten, it must do more than
amass good data. Timely communications—generally not "final"

ones—should distribute information to the persons rightfully concerned, and those hearers should take the information into their thinking. To speak broadly, an evaluation ought *to inform and improve the operations of the social system*.

We do not assume that a rational decision maker will start, stop, or amend a program as soon as reliable information reaches her. Although something close to rational choice by a single actor occurs at times, most allocation decisions are worked out in a pluralistic community. The process is not one of choosing among a few alternatives but of negotiating a next forward step. The evaluator's customers form a policy-shaping community of greater or lesser breadth which works out an accommodation among divergent beliefs and values.

Proposals for action are reshaped as experience is gained and as more participants become concerned about a particular cost or benefit. As we said earlier, the program that the evaluator studies will change as his investigation goes on, and audience members will come up with program variants or proposals that he did not directly investigate. Moreover, the ideas that a study offers will reach far beyond the program. Information about one program—whether it comes from formal evaluation or other sources—often modifies the community's view of such large issues as the reasons for joblessness, the fairness of the system of justice, or the priority to be given childcare services.

This conception makes the evaluator far more than a technician or a detached recorder of events. His function is like that of a teacher who amasses knowledge so that students will benefit from it. In other words, the evaluator's function is to help each person who holds a stake in social and institutional actions to understand a proposed action just as well as stakeholders with competing interests do. A citizen who makes faulty assumptions is in danger of bringing about results she does not want. The report from an evaluation can (and ideally it would) spur the citizen to reconsider any questionable assumptions. An evaluation can show that goals of proposed actions are inconsistent or it can suggest new goals. It can alter the way the servers and the served perceive their own roles. That is to say, evaluation can change the system. At its best, it helps the system live up to its own principles.

Even though social priorities are determined by many factors besides information (Lindblom and Cohen, 1979), evaluations do contribute to basic social thought. They challenge accepted propositions, they introduce new concepts, they provide empirical facts that theories must fit. Traditional research works toward a better picture of man and society, but it moves slowly so as to minimize risks from ill-grounded theory. Society has to act each year on the basis of its best present picture, risky though that process is. Evaluation checks on the contending beliefs rapidly and thus can reduce the short-run risks of ill-conceived action.

The evaluator has a political influence even when he does not aspire to it. He can be an arm of those in power, but he loses most of his value in that role if he does not think independently and critically. He can put himself in the service of some partisan interest outside the center of power, but there again his unique contribution is a critical, scholarly habit of mind. He can, we assert, render greatest service if he becomes an informant to and educator of all parties to a decision, making available to them the lessons of experience and critical thinking. Since information provides power, such diffusion of information is power equalizing.

This consciously assumed role can easily be misinterpreted as a grab for power, career opportunity, or political influence. Large responsibilities, however, should induce humility. The techniques available to evaluators are limited, and so are the allowable resources. In a busy world evaluative reports receive limited attention, and many forces besides the evaluation influence decisions. The evaluator is like the educator in that both fall short of the influence they would like to have. Their knowledge is limited. Those they serve are slow to revise long-standing views and reluctant to think hard. The evaluator is not a superman who will make all social choices easy and all programs efficient, turning public management into a technology. Everyone will be better off when that pipe dream is abandoned.

In describing a role for evaluators, we are proposing a direction of movement, not a goal ever to be fully attained. We ask only that evaluators, singly and as a profession, be aware of the actions and choices that are appropriately under their own control, or could be.

*Directions for Reform.* Even if one allows for the inescapable limitations of the art, evaluation today is rendering less service than it could. We place much of the blame on the defective institutions and norms of the evaluation enterprise. The stereotyped evaluation wastes talent on studies that teach little. The present arrangements of procuring evaluations and communicating findings are calculated for a mythical world where problems break up into neat packages and a single bureau can take effective action by considering only the package assigned to it. In the real world, social problems are interconnected, and the policy-shaping community does not leave controversial matters to be settled by bureaus of limited scope. Thus, new institutional arrangements will be required if evaluation is to serve the system well.

The stand-alone summative study, we have said, is severely limited, but we do not intend to erect some other single ideal in its place. Rather, we advocate flexible attack. Any one program should be studied in diverse ways, and the studies should be scheduled so that appreciation of the program develops steadily. As Figure 2 suggests, interpretation should be a continuing process, not one linked to deadlines for specific actions.

Moreover, thinking about social action should break away from concern with specific programs and agencies to consider a social problem as a whole and the multiple lines of attack on it. Social actions are motivated and constrained by widely held beliefs about a problem and about the potency of certain kinds of intervention. These views are a by-product of the work of program staffs, journalists, academic investigators, evaluators, and others. The by-product, having the pervasive influence it does, may have more to do with whether social actions are sterile or fertile than do the direct, ad hoc conclusions of an evaluator.

A mechanism is required to help social thought develop somewhat as scientific thinking develops. A theory in science gains acceptance through the intensive exchange and mutual criticism of a specially interested "college" that digests all that becomes known about a particular topic. In Chapter Six we shall suggest forming a "social problem study group" for review, interpretation, and guidance of both investigation and policy.

Figure 2. Concurrent and Sequential Activities in Flexible Evaluations

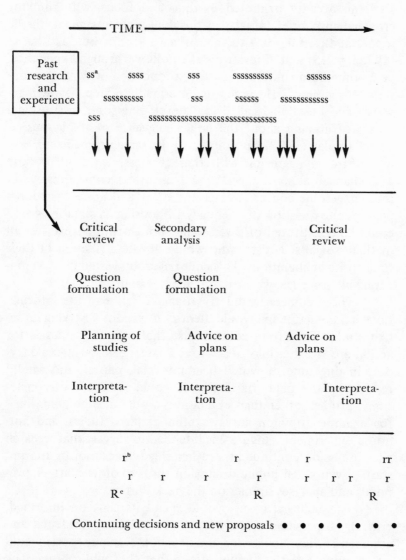

The diagram of the stand-alone study (Figure 1) emphasized an activity delimited in time and focus, with thinking crowded into brief initial and terminal segments and with the report at the end going to the official sponsor. But, as Elmore (1975a, p. 45) said in reviewing the Follow Through experience, "experiments do not necessarily produce self-evident prescriptions for policy." He urged an intermediate step between research and "use" and called for "developing some institutional means of arguing about the policy relevance of ambiguous results." Caplan (1977) has pointed to the same urgent need.

Strongly agreeing with these writers, we shall propose a mechanism along the following lines. Informed persons would recognize some concern as ripe for study and possible action—perhaps the question of adequacy in housing. A standing group could be constituted of diverse and thoughtful persons—not all of them social scientists—who would devote a fraction of their time to its deliberations. This collegial group would have a comparatively long life, with rotating membership.

The members would try to make sense of the information that comes in and would identify questions deserving intensive study. The group could advise that certain proposals for action are worth a pilot test or, at a later stage, a full-scale tryout. In due time, it would hear informal, partial, and candid reports on the field trial. Later, it would see drafts of conclusions. Studies other than evaluations would also be going on— for example, opinion surveys, ethnographic studies, and hothouse experiments. Figure 2 is intended to suggest that research and discussion continue at a rather steady pace, not by fits and starts. Even when public discussion turns to other matters, proposals and analyses simmer on the back burner.

The collegial group would spend its time on informed, critical, dispassionate analysis of contradictory evidence and arguments. Then undigested and question-begging reports would not dominate the communications that the public hears. The panel itself would issue reports rarely. Members informed by the collegial discussions would be encouraged to render reasoned, but not necessarily impartial, accounts to the public.

Social actions are worked out through accommodation. The community that influences a decision may be large or small, depending on the issues and the publicity it has received. Neither policy-making officials, pundits, legislators, nor lobbyists for special interests can alone determine the action to be taken. Rather, they play a negotiating game in which it is discovered that certain lines of action have widespread support and that others have little backing. Information enters into this struggle in various ways. Better digested information, one hopes, will lead to more mature action than raw gobbets of fact and opinion snatched on the run. (And that characterization does apply to information from evaluations released as they are at present, without peer review.)

Without carrying this complex topic further here, we need only say that partisan thrust and counterthrust, massed pressure and stubborn resistance, "standpattism" and creative statesmanship will continue to forge actions in the future as they have in the past. But a quieter milieu for discussion is required *in addition* to these. The collegial group is to act as buffer between observers and political actors. It is not to censor communications but to ripen them. The public should continue to hear many voices carrying discordant messages, but it would benefit if more speakers were disciplined by collegial discourse as happens now with respect to economic issues (Johnson, 1976). Once advocates of divergent policies have restated positions to make them seem reasonable to professional colleagues, the differences that remain are worth taking to the public.

Another major institutional need is for a strong professional community of evaluators who share a common vision of their work. It takes a coherent profession to develop an art and the necessary working arrangements, as well as to think through proper standards and uphold them. The evaluator venturing into the political arena can no longer be guided solely by the habits of thought of the scientist (Frankel, 1976). The political sensitivity he acquires ought to be used in addition to, and not in place of, his training in impartiality. He should remain a voice for reason.

In a volatile political situation, powerful parties contend for high stakes; on occasion, coercion or other improper influence is exerted. The individual evaluator is among the least powerful actors in the drama and he needs protection, especially when a finding threatens powerful interests. Strong professional supports are needed if the evaluator is to live up to professional ideals.

We are defining a professional role in which evaluators consider themselves responsible to the larger social interest. They should exercise independent judgment as best they can but should not attempt to substitute that judgment for the political process. The evaluator has a counterpart in, for example, the consulting engineer who reports on all relevant aspects of a potential mine site, including tonnage and quality of ore, risks from flooding or earthquake, consequences for the ecology, and so on but who does not himself try to settle whether the hole will be dug.

Even this self-restrained role implies a significant expansion of the evaluator's responsibilities. We are asking him to act as something of a social philosopher. We urge evaluation teams to raise questions that others neglect and to make sense of what is perplexing. The evaluator we have told to think deeply is not to see himself as a philosopher-king; in the same breath we advise him to respect the citizen's right to decide. A mission to educate is not a warrant to convert others to one's political views. We tell the evaluator to struggle (as any educator struggles) to help the client work out a consistent and realistic view of her own. The evaluator is almost uniquely in a position to collect, learn from, and communicate the perceptions about a program and about social goals that various sectors of society have. He thus facilitates dialogue and accommodation.

The reformation we call for has already begun. Several writers—most conspicuously C. H. Weiss and J. S. Coleman—have described the problems of evaluation in language similar to ours and have proposed changes in designs and procedures to fit political reality. More significant, many of the proposals are being adopted here and there. We have urged, for example, that commissioners move away from stand-alone evaluations of programs and toward a more synoptic view of the numerous programs that address the same social problems. That argument was pressed on Congress when it developed "sunset" legislation. (See the testimony of the comptroller general, Elmer Staats, and the director of the Congressional Budget Office, Alice Rivlin, in Subcommittee on Intergovernmental Relations, 1977b.) As a result, the legislative proposal moved a long way toward a problem orientation. Equally desirable, a longer time horizon was built into the review plan.

We have also urged that an evaluative effort employ a bundle of studies that use different techniques to examine subquestions and that the plan be adapted as the studies expose uncertainties more clearly. Examples of this approach can now be found. One is the congressionally mandated evaluation of services to handicapped children under Public Law 94–142. This evaluation is extraordinarily difficult because the children served are heterogeneous, program directives filter through several layers of government, the relevant psychological theory is weak, and the concerned constituencies are well organized for political action. We understand that some members of Congress originally entertained totally unrealistic notions of what evaluation could accomplish. With the best of intentions, some of them proposed that the individual remedial plan worked out for each handicapped child in a local school district be copied and sent to Washington, where an evaluator would decide, one by one, whether the plans were sound or unsound. Then Congress could be assured that the money was benefiting all the children.

After the law was passed with a strong but less specific evaluation mandate, the specialists given primary responsibility (Mary Kennedy and Garry McDaniels) negotiated with the relevant congressional group and with other interested parties. This process shaped a plan that makes possible an inquiry rather than simply an administrative gesture; it chooses samples of various kinds and sizes, each suitable for investigating particular questions (Bureau of Education for the Handicapped, 1978; also, McDaniels, personal communication). Intensive studies of operations in a handful of school districts were given a place alongside the gross census figures on children served. Summative appraisal was not dropped from consideration, but it was recast into a program of methodological development and pilot research, on the grounds that valid appraisal of benefits from these programs is beyond the state of the art.

Another example of realistic, politically astute evaluation is the massive strategic plan worked out by Cook and others (1977) for Peace Corps programs in health and agriculture. Not only is every kind of research method given a place, but the plan recognizes that the methods to be used—in what places and for what questions and with what investment—are to be determined in the light of the usefulness of the information to the relevant policy-shaping communities in the United States and the host country.

Among those whose writings five years ago seemed to say that quantitative, unbiased appraisal of treatment effects is the only worthwhile way to spend evaluation funds, many now express a far more catholic view (for example, Cook and Campbell, 1979). For some of them, this is no more than clarification. Though they held a balanced view ten years ago, they overemphasized "internal validity" when trying to encourage social experiments. For others, the better balance of recent statements represents belated recognition that highly controlled summative studies are useful under specialized circumstances but that, in the absence of those circumstances, evaluations in other styles are advisable.

Our call for reform, then, is not a lone cry. We hope that our general position, if not all our specific recommendations, will be acceptable to the majority of members of the profession and also to those operating programs and making policy. In this book we consider the evaluation process as a whole in the light of political theory, statistical theory, and—especially—experience with evaluations. This enables us, we think, to offer a rationale for reshaping the entire enterprise, placing hitherto scattered proposals in a consistent framework. At least, that is our ambition.

For all the recent progress, the battle for reform has barely been joined. Many of the most recent textbooks in evaluation still take the stereotypic line. Summative appraisal that tells the decision maker which alternative action to take is held out as the aim of real evaluation. And the draft guidelines for federal evaluations that the GAO has circulated, while accepting the importance of fitting the evaluation plan to the political and administration context, nonetheless place heavy emphasis on controlled experiments to assess impact (Comptroller General, 1978; also see Chapter Four).

This book makes a try at setting down some first principles for the profession that is to come. We offer visions, not blueprints, of a ship that can deliver a cargo through waters roiled by political storm—not a punt for the tranquil backwaters of an academy, not a Charon's barge destined to freight baled-up reports to oblivion.

# 2

■■■■■■■■■■■■■■■■

# Evaluation and the
# Shaping of Policy

■■■■■■■■■■■■■■■■

Political and organizational realities determine what evaluation
can do. Misunderstandings of the policy-making process are
a source of both faulty evaluation practices and criticisms of
sound practices. Recommendations for evaluation should derive
from a sound understanding of how actions are taken. This
chapter on the process of governance sets the stage for the questions, "Where does evaluation fit in?" and "What service can it
render?" Most of the chapter speaks generally about how the
system uses information. Administrative and personal connections among key actors, as well as the political forces to which
the actors are sensitive, strongly influence the use of information. Those forces themselves arise out of belief systems built
up from past and recent experience.

Many of the themes of this chapter are anticipated in
a statement on how social research contributes to social action
from the Behavioral and Social Sciences Survey Committee
(1969, p. 96):

*Negotiating*, rather than seeking to reach an unequivocally "best" solution, is invariably involved, either explicitly or implicitly [in framing policy]. Usually, when those with one set of interests are benefited, some others suffer frustration or setback.

The solutions do not arise directly out of the alternatives emerging from research; therefore, the task is not that of choosing between readily available alternatives but of *inventing* or *designing* a viable course of action that may blend several of the originally formulated alternatives.

The *phrasing* or *rephrasing* of proposed courses of action in terms that are meaningful to the participants is of great importance. If these statements of intended action prove unacceptable, new courses of action may be invented.

Finally, in a real-life situation the policy issue is embedded in a context of other issues, is *competing* for the time and attention of the persons involved, and has higher or lower priorities, depending on the character of its relation to those other issues.

This description is significant for the conduct and reporting of evaluations. The process described is far more complex than is suggested by the stereotype of a single official who makes a crisp decision as soon as the facts come in. Since a comparatively abstract discussion will be required to develop this contrast, we preface that discussion with a concrete example of government in action.

## From Research to Action and Inaction: An Example

How information from research is used, and some of the reasons why it is used or ignored, can be inferred from a tale of school busing. The story is told with rare candor by Menges (1978), who observed events related to desegregation as a planner in the Department of Health, Education, and Welfare (HEW) under Secretary Elliot Richardson from 1970 to 1972.

*An Investigation of School Busing.* The ever-changing political background is an important part of the story. In 1970, when HEW set up the study, de facto segregation was under severe pressure. Courts were requiring many school systems to institute busing. Some courts insisted that every school in the district have the same racial mixture. Meanwhile, Congress had appropriated special funds to help schools adjust to desegregation. Only schools making "a reasonable effort" to desegregate were eligible, and HEW had to judge applications for funds in that light.

For all the force behind desegregation, antibusing sentiment also was strong; there was even a push for a constitutional amendment prohibiting the use of busing to achieve desegregation. The Nixon administration was considering which forces to align itself with, what further legislation to propose, and what guidelines to adopt for administering existing laws. Officials in school districts were under pressure from law enforcement agencies, from advocates for minorities, and from vocal opponents of busing. When the evaluation of alternative plans for busing started, the controversial issues were "How much busing?" and "How far must children ride?" The evaluation directed attention to a question that should have caused participants to think quite differently: "Where are the lines on the map?"—that is to say, "*Who* rides?"

This particular piece of policy research sponsored by HEW was unlike the usual evaluation in that it was largely a computer simulation. However, as busing practice also was reviewed, the study did evaluate local plans both individually and in the aggregate. Here is the line of reasoning used in the study. Start with two working assumptions presumed to be politically acceptable: (1) a child can walk three quarters of a mile to school; (2) bus rides of thirty-five minutes are tolerable. (The technique could, of course, be used with other limits.) On a map of any school district, show where the pupils live, identifying each one by ethnicity. Superimpose lines to bound the attendance zones, proposed or actual, of individual schools. Measure off how much busing that zoning plan requires and

Table 2. Ethnic Mixture Obtained with Various Busing Plans
in One School District

|  | Percentage of Children Bused | Ethnic Mixture* |
|---|---|---|
| Minimum transportation allowed by the geography | 22 | 57 |
| Same minimum, distributed to maximize desegregation | 22 | 68 |
| Maximum desegregation with slight increase in busing | 23 | 86 |
| ACTUAL PRESENT ARRANGEMENTS | 34 | 44 |

* *Note:* This index is related to the percentage of "majority" classmates in schools attended by the average minority child. It could in principle rise to 100 if busing were extended to an unrealistic extreme.

tally the ethnic composition of each school's student body. By feeding one plan after another into the computer, identify the boundaries that achieve the greatest degree of ethnic mixing for a particular amount of busing.

Illustrative results for one large metropolitan county are shown in Table 1. A similar analysis was made for each of forty-four urban areas. It was found that substantial desegregation could be achieved without additional busing: simply shifting the boundaries and bus routes would do the trick. Increasing the amount of busing *very slightly*—using carefully chosen boundaries—would considerably increase ethnic mixture. Prevailing zonal patterns were open to severe criticism, as they were not promoting desegregation.

*Response of School Officials.* The findings received little publicity, too little to affect public sentiment. At one point in 1972, after administration policy had been worked out, the staff of HEW did talk to the press. News stories and columns were written, but apparently the political participants who would have found the evidence congenial missed the point of the findings.

HEW was unsuccessful also in influencing local decisions. Communications to school administrators carried the message that "traditional small-town" ways of laying out attendance zones do not fit the urban scene, are too expensive, and bus more children than necessary. Although HEW prepared a "simple and explicit handbook" to guide local mapping studies, school officials paid no attention—"traditional methods were entrenched," says Menges (1978, p. 35). The procedures were technical enough to repel superintendents. Worse, they promised political headaches. "Who gets bused?" is a politically loaded question. The HEW report and the handbook properly left those considerations to one side, but a local decision maker ignores the political question at her peril. As a general rule, public officials rarely run far ahead of popular sentiment and usually shun action that could stir up fresh controversy.

If controversy is already rocking the boat, however, the official has to consider alternative actions. Had local partisans of desegregation heard of the report and pressed for the new method (or had Washington used the mapping analysis as a standard for funding), local administrators would have studied it. With local mapping studies in hand, the communities could have worked out new plans. No doubt the departure from existing zones would have been modest; the zones called optimal by the single-minded computer would surely not have been accepted. But neither would the analysis have been ignored, at least in communities where the desegregation cause had a voice.

The failures of HEW to interest local officials in the mapping technique can easily be overgeneralized; systematic procedures can contribute to local conflict resolution. Keen and Morton (1978, pp. 152–158) describe how computer mapping was used to everyone's satisfaction in negotiating new school-attendance boundaries in several communities. What set the stage for success, first of all, was that the district had to remap because of declining enrollments and so everyone was prepared to face a disruptive issue. Second, the technical specialist worked personally with the school officials as a missionary for the research approach. Although the questions and ideas of school officials were incorporated into the analysis, they never had to engage the alien machinery directly. Third, the computer offered a starting map and, during open hearings, prepared instant modifications for inspection. When a parent spoke up for moving a boundary three blocks to the east, the computer could quickly tell the audience what the consequences would be for minority enrollment, distances traveled by children, and so on. The technology did not impose a solution. Rather, it moved the negotiation toward equilibrium. Both citizens and officials became more sophisticated about the process as trade-offs took concrete form before their eyes.

*Federal Response.* Now let us turn to Washington. Did the HEW study make a difference there? Yes, in that it educated leaders; no, in that the mapping procedures were not written into administrative rules.

The research team handed Menges a preliminary report at the end of 1971. In January of 1972, Menges briefed Secretary Richardson on the main findings, the rationale of the study, and its limitations. The policy that emerged at high levels in HEW was to defend busing in moderation. On the one hand, officials recognized that some busing proposals were creating unreasonable hardships; such complaints were seen as calling for procedural remedies, not for a retreat from the busing principle. On the other hand, the courts had been imposing a strict standard of "proportional racial balance" for want of other guidance. HEW policy makers saw this as overkill and were determined to oppose it, understanding that far more modest busing would achieve very nearly as much integration. In the county used earlier as an example, not even busing one third of the children could achieve proportional balance, but it could bring the index within 2 percent of the reasonable limit. In Menges' words, "the prospects of reconciling the social benefits of attending neighborhood schools [with] desegregation were opened up by the analysis results" (1978, pp. 31–32).

The circle that discussed the results at this time was small: a few persons from the executive office of the president, a few from the Department of Justice, and a few from HEW. Calls for a constitutional amendment had faded (not because of the study). The Justice Department had been instructed to prepare standards for busing to indicate the conditions under which it would bring legal action (and hence to tell schools whether their present plans were acceptable). It put forward draft standards on which HEW was asked to comment. Though the standards, according to Menges, were another example of overkill, they might well have been promulgated if the policy study had not been in hand.

Armed with the mapping technique, Menges wrote a critique of the Justice Department standards and sent it through Secretary Richardson to the White House. A presidential message consistent with this criticism went to Congress in March 1972 as a supplement to the next piece of relevant legislation. Note the timing. All this action took place within a few months after Menges had received the preliminary report. If the analysts had made no report save a final one at the end of their work many months later, the evaluator would very likely have been playing to an empty hall. The moving finger writes. . . .

To Menges' distress, President Nixon proposed a moratorium on busing for desegregation, retreating from the original plan to issue standards under his authority and instead asking Congress to "fashion a standard"; the motivation for pushing the monkey onto the back of Congress is easy to see. Menges felt that some of his effort was wasted, but the policy adviser obviously does not call the plays. He is off to one side, pushing forward his analysis as a referee rolls a football into a rugby scrum. The main difference is that the political scrum is in action even without the ball.

One official within HEW did act directly on the basis of the research, namely, the office responsible for negotiating voluntary desegregation agreements with local education agencies. In districts where this office was negotiating, the mapping technique became a basis for deciding what agreement was within reasonable bounds.

In contrast, a second office did not make use of the research. Its charge was to decide which districts were making a reasonable effort to desegregate and were thus qualified for funding. That agency's staff chose to stay with their old rules for deciding what was reasonable; change would have drawn unwelcome complaints from districts likely to lose funds. The central staff that had sponsored the evaluation and developed policy implications was too busy to do battle; by default, matters came to rest. As the Behavioral and Social Sciences Survey Committee noted, issues compete for time and attention. It is not that Secretary Richardson lacked the power to direct the lower office; it is just that no commander can attend to everything.

The study, then, illustrates what is almost inevitable: the educative and administrative potential of an evaluation will be only partially realized. But the evaluation did offer a fresh conception of how to set up a busing plan in a locality, how to judge its efficiency, and how much busing is enough. Officials in close communication with the policy adviser took from his report a broad message: *moderate* busing is justifiable. The technology of mapping, being an administrative detail, did not interest policy officials, even though it was a potent way to define an enforceable policy. Potential audiences more distant from the staff that commissioned the research seem to have ignored the message, if it reached them at all.

An administration willing to be perceived as "pro busing" could have done more to promote racial mixture by efficient busing, but that essentially political choice was for the president to make. It is interesting to speculate how much additional forward motion a *pro bono publico* evaluator might have produced if he had developed similar evidence using private funds and then had done his best to make its significance apparent to the public advocates of desegregation.

## Rational Management or Enlightened Accommodation?

The Platonic image of concentrated power and responsibility is one of two long-standing ideals of governance. The second image—of pluralist accommodation—is truer to most governance of social programs and most shaping of policy. It is convenient to speak of a context of command and a context of accommodation. Both images are realistic and each has its philosophical base. At any given time, some elements of public affairs are under the authority of an official or body that has full command, while active roles in governing other public affairs are scattered among the various ranks of society. The terms will be clarified as we proceed, and it will become evident that command and accommodation are both present in most situations. The mixture varies over time within a single program or institution, as the agenda or the degree of public concern changes.

The theory of evaluation, however, has been developed almost wholly around the image of command. It is supposed that information flows to a manager or policy official who has a firm grasp on the controls. She can reach a "correct" decision and act on it. Once her decision is made, subordinates follow orders; the action that she wants, she gets. Hence she bears full responsibility.

Actually, however, most action is determined by a pluralistic community, not by a lone decision maker. Parties having divergent perceptions and aims bear down on lawmakers and administrators. Information can change perceptions but is unlikely to bring all parties to agree on which facts are relevant or even on what the facts are. If the term *decision* is understood to mean a formal choice at a particular time between discrete alternatives, decision making is rarely to be observed. When there are multiple participants with multiple views, it is meaningless to speak of one action as the rational or correct action. The active parties jockey toward a politically acceptable accommodation.

Political theorists do not agree on how to make government judicious and efficient. Some would concentrate power and information so as to concentrate responsibility. In a society such as Plato's Republic, faithful stewards determine policies that serve the public interest. The contrasting conception— a heritage particularly of the French Enlightenment—assigns responsibility to the citizenry collectively. Rousseau, Condorcet, Burke, and other developers of the modern democratic ideal did not intend to substitute brute electoral power for the judgment of anointed officials. Rather, they sought to capitalize on collective intelligence (K. M. Baker, 1975). In this vision, members of the public or their representatives weigh alternative policies and plans in the light of their beliefs. Citizens exchange views and come to a working agreement. Collectively, they decide what services they want and then pass judgment on the services delivered.

*Command and Its Requirements.* The Platonic concept of governance calls upon officials to make plans and execute them. It allocates to public officials the kind of responsibility ordinarily assigned to managers in corporations, save that the public officials' priorities are set by the public interest. The decision maker is to determine the most rational course of action or at least one that promises to be satisfactory.

A decision theorist would say that this policy maker is engaged in a "game against Nature." Nature's pieces on the board are facts and factual relationships. The more the policy maker knows about where Nature's pieces are placed, the better she can forecast the consequence of any action open to her. Weighing the forecasts on a scale of values leads to a rational solution, or so the theory goes. A "rational" decision is said to be apolitical. One team of decision makers, it is supposed, would make the same choice as another having the same facts (including facts about the sentiments of the populace).

Many an administrator who thinks of herself as a decision maker has little effective control over events. Horst and others (1974) uncharitably refer to such a figure as a "pseudomanager." Many decisions that become official when ratified by the managers assembled in one room are the result of a collective process that has taken place in many rooms. And, after the "manager" has spoken, many voices in many other rooms will determine what happens. Truman's remark about Eisenhower, newly installed in the Oval Office, is apposite: "Poor Ike! He'll sit there and say do this and do that and nothing will *happen*. He'll find it's not like the army" (Self, 1975, p. 104). Kennedy's discovery of the same truth played a dismaying part in the Cuban missile crisis (G. Allison, 1971).

Effective command is probably more prevalent in industry than in government. Decisions affecting production are often tangible, and in such cases compliance is readily monitored. Command may be assigned to a staff or executive committee whose members are expected to have divergent beliefs—indeed, that is the point of having a group. Though no single person is the decision maker, the context is nonetheless one of command when a managing group is committed to preserving its corporate authority. After debate reaches a conclusion, the participants close ranks and carry out the decision.

Among public agencies, the U.S. Forest Service offers an instructive example of effective command. Its operating decisions have to be delegated to the ranger who knows the local scene, and that ranger is a proud professional. Even so, rangers remain faithful to regional and national policies. Command decisions stick, though the relations of higher to lower officers are far from authoritarian. Kaufman's classic study (1960) explained how this climate, ideal for rational decision making, was brought about and maintained. We mention only a few points, doing less than full justice to his story.

The Forest Service got off to a healthy start. It was founded at the turn of the century on the crest of a wave of popular sentiment for conservation. Congressional committees favorable to conservation took jurisdication, and the popular conservation movement maintained support for the agency. In contrast, the business interests that might have constituted an opposition were disunited.

An offshoot of the Progressive movement, the Forest Service was founded on the belief that public business could be scientifically managed. A research arm was established to collect facts relevant to policies—to learn, for example, how changes in density of grazing affect various types of range. A factual finding of this kind has definite implications for policy, and on such physical matters it is easy to detect whether a ruling is being obeyed.

A shelfful of detailed directiveness or guidelines from headquarters make service policy explicit. But the rules do not, for example, try to set rates of grazing or logging. Instead, they specify what to weigh into a current local decision in the light of past experience in such terrain. New rulings are added from time to time, and old ones amended. Rangers are invited to send in opinions on such matters, and they believe that what they say carries weight. While these and other procedures manifest the administrators' respect for rangers, the ranger's acts are minutely supervised. The visitor from headquarters inspects the log of day-to-day activity—fences checked, laborers hired, timber yield estimated, grazing rights granted. Any violation or misunderstanding of policy, or any action thought to be inefficient, is noted in the supervisor's written report, along with remarks on what has gone well.

Kaufman found the morale of the rangers to be high. They believed in the ideals of the Forest Service, including the ideal of basing policies on evidence. All members of the service had similar knowledge about forest cultivation. The superiors had risen from the ranks and were trusted. Internal harmony regarding principles and values, together with favorable public sentiment, may have done more to maintain a context of command than the administrative devices. The research carried out by the service was relevant and it was put to use because the questions asked were insiders' questions, in tune with the ideology of officials at all levels.

The foregoing characterization remained true when Nienaber and Wildavsky (1973) looked at the Forest Service in the late 1960s, although tensions between the local level and the top level had become apparent. This was traceable not to a change in internal management, but to two kinds of budgetary pressure. First and more painful, funds were increasing slowly while recreational demands and the accompanying costs were rising sharply. Second, Congress and the Bureau of the Budget had begun to demand elaborate justification of budgetary details; this led to greater reliance on outdated formulas, limited the flexibility of operations, and soured the old harmony of outlook. Rangers became increasingly alienated from "the bureaucracy."

These tensions were eroding the power of command. The central officers, having allocated funds within program categories to win approval for the budget, feared a congressional reproof if expenditures did not conform to the fiscal blueprint. The fieldworkers, unable to stretch the funds to match the promises, used their own judgment in cutting back activities ("reprogramming"). Nienaber and Wildavsky (1973, pp. 61–62) commented: "[T] he agency has to decide between one of two options: either to fund the base more realistically . . . or to limit visitor use of recreation areas. As it is now, the local administration is making those decisions by reprogramming funds and turning away visitors when areas are full. What appears to be desired, at least by local personnel, is an agency-wide policy on these questions. Actually, there is a policy but they do not like it. So they try to get around it. The result is that Washington gets its way in the budget, and local officials get part of theirs back through reprogramming."

We shall have further occasions to comment on the fragility of command. Pressures from external authorities and constituencies, or pressures arising from operating personnel, inevitably make command a sometime thing. What is a matter for command decision this year may have to be resolved next year by accommodation.

*How Accommodation Operates.* The features that mark a context of command are reversed in a context of accommodation. Instead of being a game against Nature, the pluralistic process is a multiparty game; Nature is only one of the players (von Neumann and Morgenstern, 1953). The stakeholders play their cards and tally their separate winnings and losses. Each one foresees consequences that follow each possible action, but with many sets of values in play there is no "best" result. Almost never can a player get everything she wants; hence, a label "mutual accommodation" or simply "accommodation" becomes appropriate. Participants representing many interests throw weight on the tiller. The course at each moment is determined in a political manner, that is, by exchange of views, exertion of pressure, individual acts of noncompliance, and compromise—all leading to a *modus vivendi.* Participants may or may not know what next action they favor, but they recognize that they have something at stake and do not trust officials to represent their interests.

Under conditions of accommodation, it can scarcely be said that decisions are "made." Rather, they emerge (Orlans, 1973). A lone decision maker is able to zero in on a restricted topic, compare definite plans for action, and choose one of them. In the context of command, the major questions identified by the manager at the start of an evaluative study are likely still to be the salient questions when the study is finished; in the context of accommodation, however, new issues are introduced whenever a partisan feels that she can gain ground thereby.

Rarely does a vote dispose of the agenda. Sometimes there is a "great debate"—as on the Panama Canal treaties—but the eventual vote usually settles only a subissue. The debate serves as symbol of a struggle that the parties intend to continue. Some decisions are reached after noisy political contention; many are resolved by quiet exchanges. A "drift toward decision" is more usual than high-keyed debate (March and Olsen, 1976). And, as Lindblom and Cohen (1979) emphasize, the weight of separate actions of consumers and seekers of services, as well as administrators, moves policies forward—or halts them—perhaps in the absence of conscious policy analysis.

Events move forward by piecemeal local adaptations. No one action represents a new policy; rather, the various steps have a cumulative effect. The broad outline of new policy is shaped as a sandbar is shaped—by the intermittent but never-ending pushes and pulls of crosscurrents. Members of the community know something about social needs and present services. As individuals they are well aware of the public servants they meet face to face and vaguely aware of the others. Through private exchanges and mass media, views spread and proposals for action are heard. As participants gain information, they come to recognize the limits of what proposed actions might accomplish and of what others can be persuaded to accept. Leaders piece together a limited plan of action that is compatible with a number of interpretations present in the community.

Even a politicized struggle rarely comes down to a massing of forces behind this or that fixed alternative. The attention of a policy-shaping community is scattered. The discussion of a single topic wanders over numerous themes, complaints, and proposals for action. As discussion proceeds, new possibilities for action are entertained, and individuals reexamine their conceptions. The process converges; it settles on a law or operating procedure that leaves few persons perfectly content, and few unwilling to live with the outcome.

The market process, also pluralistic, contrasts with accommodation through discussion. Many innovations are like commodities in that their fate is determined by innumerable separate "purchasing" decisions. This family buys a Ford while that one buys a Datsun. Similarly, when a package of instructional materials is placed on the market, one school staff buys it, but another opts for a competing product. A student chooses among colleges or between college and another kind of training. The individual decisions determine which offerings will survive (Lindblom and Cohen, 1979).

For the evaluator, these scattered decisions need information much like that suitable in a context of accommodation, as is made evident in Lindblom's book on markets (1977). The members of a large audience apply their several values to translate the information that they can use into action. Diverse communications shape the ideas on which action is based. In view of its similarity to the context of accommodation, we shall not treat the "market" context separately.

The American system is designed to operate by accommodation, according to the pluralist school of political scientists (Dahl, 1967; Lindblom, 1965, 1968, 1972; Braybrooke and Lindblom, 1963; Fesler, 1975). But even those who admire pluralism as a form of political organization are likely to speak of it as if it were irrational. Lindblom (1972) writes of "muddling through," and March and Olsen (1976) speak of the system as a "garbage can." For Justice Brandeis the purpose of democracy was "not to promote efficiency but to preclude the exercise of arbitrary power." And Tocqueville ([1835] 1945, pp. 251–252), despite his enthusiasm about what he saw in America, qualified his praise: "When the opponents of democracy assert that a single man performs what he undertakes better than the government of all, it appears to me that they are right. The government of an individual, supposing an equality of knowledge on either side, is more consistent . . . and more accurate in details than that of a multitude. . . . Democratic liberty is far from accomplishing all its projects with the skill of an adroit despotism. . . . Democracy does not give people the most skillful government, but it produces . . . an all-pervading and restless activity, a superabundant force, and an energy which [may] produce wonders."

Lindblom (1972) would not deny that a single mind can be more attentive to details than a group can, but he points out that when any large problem is faced the volume of potentially relevant detail is overwhelming. Moreover, many of the essential ingredients for a decision can be known only so vaguely that precision is unattainable. Lindblom made a specific rejoinder to those who object to piecemeal adjustment of the social machinery as nonrational: "A skillful practitioner of muddling through is by no means muddled; he is instead an extremely shrewd, sensitive, and skillful decision maker. Nor is the mind of a practitioner of disjointed incrementalism disjointed" (p. 4). (The reference to *a* decision maker seems to suggest a departure from pluralism. But in context it is clear that Lindblom's "decision maker" advances a policy for consideration with the expectation of being confronted by proposals from others.)

The two categories of command and accommodation are sufficient for our argument, but we note an elaboration that others have found useful. Problems or issues may be classified along the following dimension: the degree to which there is agreement about values in the relevant community, and the degree to which there is agreement about causality or, more generally, about facts and working hypotheses. These dimensions in turn define four cells; how policies will be determined and how large a role research will play depend on which cell describes the situation at hand (March and Simon, 1958; J. Thompson and Tuden, 1959; Pedersen, 1977; Delbecq and Gill, 1979; Ezrahi, in press). Figure 1 presents a paraphrase of the Thompson-Tuden version.

Figure 3. Rationality of Policy Making as a Function
of Community Agreement

With regard to values

| | | Consensus | Disagreement |
|---|---|---|---|
| With regard to facts | Consensus | Rational analysis | Compromise |
| | Disagreement | Judgment | Inspiration |

In the upper-left cell there is general agreement on the pertinent values and on the relevant technology; hence, quick agreement can be reached. A manager is charged to work out means toward the agreed end. In a case where malaria is the problem, for example, a program to drain swamps is almost certain to remain in the context of command. Expert testimony is sought and trusted; evidence from evaluation of alternative techniques is likely to determine future practice. In this cell, the polity wants rational analysis and is prepared to delegate matters to specialists.

When unemployment or discrimination or mental health is at issue, however, agreement on the broad aim leaves room for much disagreement regarding priorities. A certain action will help more in a big city than in rural areas. Another action will increase the power of one group of leaders at the expense of others. To complicate matters, one of these actions is expected to reduce economic deprivation but to make clients more dependent. So "expert opinion" settles nothing.

Nor, when experts contradict one another, will the public be content to leave matters to managers and technicians. Nuclear power and solar power provide a nice contrast. Using solar power may or may not be economically feasible, but the uncertainties are clearly subject to research and none of them has threatened a widely held value. Nuclear power is said by some specialists to be a threat to life and the ecology and is endorsed as safe by others. So nuclear power is politicized while solar power is turned back to the managers, the engineers, and the cost-benefit analysts.

Thompson and Tuden distinguish between the upper-right cell in Figure 3, where they expect disputes to be best resolved by a legislature, council, or other representative body, and the lower-left cell, where they see the appropriate mechanism to be a collegial organization of the "wise and knowing." The judiciary plays just such a role with regard to certain disputes, and some recent writers think that a "science court" could be equally useful.

It is difficult for responsible officials, including legislative bodies, to act when confronted by contentious experts. Synthesis by a collegial group is especially desirable to help the polity utilize information from evaluations. Chapter Six will make proposals toward this end, but we expect the "wise and knowing" to facilitate political settlements, not to substitute expert judgment for them. As the controversy over recombinant DNA shows, disturbed citizens are unlikely to accept a vote of experts as decisive (Graubard, 1978). Representatives (who may or may not be part of a formal body) play a large role in deciding which facts will be treated as relevant and which experts as qualified. Both of these cells, then, require accommodation.

The fourth cell (lower right in Figure 3) is the "organized anarchy" of March and Olsen (1976). Thompson and Tuden see this situation as ripe for a charismatic leader; March and Olsen use milder language to emphasize the large influence of whichever individuals persistently give personal attention to the matter. But the shift is from sheer personal influence toward accommodative mechanisms whenever an issue or proposal is formulated sufficiently to become the subject of research.

Our contrast between command and accommodation follows the path of March and Simon (1958), who long ago examined a four-cell scheme and collapsed it into two strategies for reaching settlements, namely, analysis and bargaining. Perhaps the most important message the four-cell scheme adds to their dichotomy is that, as closer collegial study brings experts into agreement, organizational actions become increasingly rational.

## Elitism and Participation: A Historic Tension

The urge to make governmental operations efficient (and the accompanying distaste for the working out of the popular will) has a long history. According to Locke and other British social theorists of the seventeenth century, neither tradition nor divine will could justify the form of a government. Nor could proper actions be deduced from *a priori* principles. Only from experience could a society learn what practices are sound. Twentieth-century American pragmatism speaks in this same empiricist voice: new programs are to be tried and judged by their results. Nothing is good or bad, save as consequences make it so.

In this view, a social problem is best resolved by rational analysis. The ideal process, as described by a prominent figure in the Kennedy administration, would go like this (Sorensen, 1963, pp. 18–19):

first: agreement on the facts;
second: agreement on the overall policy objective;
third: a precise definition of the problem;
fourth: a canvassing of all possible solutions. . . ;
fifth: a list of all possible consequences that would flow from
　　　each solution;
sixth: a recommendation and final choice of one alternative;
seventh: the communication of that selection; and
eighth: provision for its execution.

All the strings are thus in the hands of the decision maker. She is to know all, to integrate all, and to settle on the one best course of action. It is true that a decision maker supported by an analytic staff can reason systematically and synoptically in a way that a community-wide group cannot. However, even Sorensen adds that the case in which the decision process matches the ideal "is the exception."

The rationalist ideal of efficiency is in tension with the ideal of democratic participation. Rationalism is dangerously close to totalitarianism (Talmon, 1960; Jouvenel, 1963; Popper, 1966). When the stakes are large, whoever does not acknowledge the rightness of an authority's "solution" is seen by the rationalist as "fractious, mischievous, self-centered and evil-minded" and hence is to be put down (Jouvenel, p. 205). The danger is not hypothetical; recall the presidential reactions to protests regarding Vietnam.

Concentrating information and, therefore, power in the hands of central management is seen as the sovereign remedy at some moments in history, yet, at those very times, some observers of the system have warned that the "efficiency" so achieved is illusory (Egger, 1975, p. 79). The larger the role of experts in governance, the more difficult it becomes for ordinary citizens to give direction to action (Durand Maillane, 1792, quoted by K. M. Baker, 1975, p. 317; MacRae, 1973). When information is closely held, what reaches the public is filtered so that it supports policies that the authorities favor. Insofar as information is a source of power, evaluations carried out to inform a policy maker have a disenfranchising effect (Wiles, 1971). An open society becomes a closed society when only the officials know what is going on.

*Experts as Reformers.* The earliest attempts to bring systematic social research to bear on American government had an elitist spirit. Sympathy for the plight of urban masses motivated the Progressive movement (see Chapter One); but, as Josiah Royce put it, reform was to be brought about by the "leadership of the wisest and best." In the West, populism mingled with Progressivism; in the urban East, however, "Progressivism was a mild and judicious movement, whose goal was not a sharp change in the social structure, but rather the formation of a responsible elite, which was to take charge of the popular impulse toward change and direct it into moderate and, as they would have said, 'constructive' channels"—a leadership occupying, as

Brandeis so aptly put it, 'a position of independence between
the wealthy and the people, prepared to curb the excesses of
either'" (Hofstadter, 1955, pp. 163–164). Social scientists were
happy to volunteer for the elite, confident that they were proper
trustees of power.

These "new radicals" (Lasch, 1967) were bent on using
rational planning to ward off the dangers of reforms arising out
of popular sentiment and agitation. For example, Albion Small,
a leading sociologist of the University of Chicago, wanted to
establish an institute of social science that would examine not
only the factual arguments for programs but also decide on the
pertinent values and advise the polity on the proper course of
action (Christakes, 1978). Public management was seen as
a technical specialty, beyond the grasp of popular understanding. Nicholas Murray Butler, the politically prominent president
of Columbia University, "could confidently assert, to the ap-
plause of the Merchant's Club of Chicago, that he should 'as
soon think of talking about the democratization of the treatment of appendicitis' as to speak of 'the democratization of the
schools. . . . The fundamental confusion is this: Democracy is
a principle of government; the schools belong to the administration; and a democracy is as much entitled as a monarchy to
have its business well done.' A common school run for the people but not by the people. . . ." (Tyack, 1974, p. 77).

Sentiments of similar force are heard even today. Here is
an economist writing in a bicentennial review of American civic
affairs: "Given the pandering of economically undertrained
legislators . . . to the self-serving demands of special-interest
groups . . . and the shortsighted demands of ill-informed voters,
economists cannot contribute greatly to the nature of life in the
United States. . . . Perhaps were all elective personnel chosen by
lot, . . . out of a universe of persons with at least bachelor's degrees. . . , few legislators would have time and opportunity to
become effective errand boys for special interests, and the role
of the economist in government could become more effective.
Politics then could no longer swamp economics as it does today,
relevant expertise could become effective, and economists, confronted by economically subversive political demands. . . , could

resign with salutary effect" (Spengler, 1976, pp. 67–68). A similar arrogance was to be found in the Kennedy-Johnson administrations, so David Halberstam's ironic title *The Best and the Brightest* (1972) reminds us. Nisbet, writing in 1975 in the *New York Times Magazine*, alleged that social scientists arrogantly claimed the role of Comtean priests in the "new church of knowledge." Whether they did make that claim, whether they had much influence, and whether that influence had been for good or bad was the subject of a resounding, inconclusive battle in the *American Scholar* (*Social Science*, 1976).

*Ambivalence at the Top.* Aligned with experts though they were, the Kennedy-Johnson administrations were also the ones that introduced the slogan "maximum feasible participation." The development of the evaluation requirement of the Elementary and Secondary Education Act's (ESEA) Title I illustrates this tension especially well. Senator Robert Kennedy and Commissioner of Education Francis Keppel supported the requirement as a means of forcing local school officials to do what the policy makers in Washington thought they should be doing (McLaughlin, 1975). William Gorham of the Office of the Assistant Secretary for Planning and Evaluation of HEW wanted the evaluation data to guide policy making; in the future, the officials thus informed could better advise communities on effective practices. Both views favored reform from the top. But Kennedy was also backing the evaluation as a means of giving local parents more power in relation to local officials (see Chapter One). Kennedy hoped that a Title I project reporting requirement would force local schools to reform their practices in the light of the priorities expressed.

Kennedy was thus pursuing contradictory objectives, unless it could be assumed that needs and aspirations are the same wherever poor children are found. If collecting uniform data on questions generated in Washington could force superintendents to focus on what the planners considered important, the superintendents would for that very reason be less able to spend resources on what local citizens valued. There were and are divergent views regarding educational objectives for children of minority backgrounds. The rallying cries of those days—"black

English," "deficit or difference?," "maintaining the culture," and "imposing middle-class values"—recall some of the disputes. In the end, because of superintendents' resistance to controls rather than because of their passion for democracy, standardized evaluation was supplanted by a weak requirement. At least in the first ten years of ESEA, evaluation served neither elitist management nor enlightened local participation.

Something of the same ambivalence set the stage for a story worth retelling as an example of how unrealistic rationalists can be. An attack on delinquency in Philadelphia was to be launched by enlisting the widest possible community participation and interest. Support came from an agency in the Kennedy administration and from the Ford Foundation, and academic planners from Temple University were put onto the job. As Marris and Rein (1973) have told the story, militant politicians and dozens of community agencies already had fingers in the pie; a power struggle had begun even before the planners came in. The sponsors, wearing their rationalist hats for the moment, decided that the planning group was to be independent of the local institutions that their planning was to reshape.

The planners were happy with their assignment: "As the Temple staff conceived it, planning was to be based solely on dispassionate empirical studies, carried out with scientific rigor. First, basic information must be collected for the target community and interpreted according to a theoretical rationale. From this analysis, programs would evolve, which were then to be carefully evaluated and reassessed. Step by step, the accumulation of research findings would determine viable solutions to social problems, which could be replicated in other communities" (Marris and Rein, 1973, p. 108). A planning memorandum included these statements: "[I]t is critical that all program activities of the [agency] be integrally related to the assumptions of the conceptual scheme."

"In any rationally structured organization of this type, [behavioral scientists] hold the prime responsibility and prerogative for 'making the diagnosis' and suggesting a series of alternate courses of action for 'treatment'" (pp. 108-109).

As Marris and Rein commented (p. 108), "This conception frankly repudiated the right of politicians or agency staff to obtrude their opinions upon the planning procedure." Such ingenousness invited a rude response. By the end of the year the social scientists were out of the picture, and all efforts at planning had been dropped.

Elitism is politically out of fashion today, while pluralism and direct action are in. Many forces, some of them ideological, have combined to make citizens more active in recent years. "The expectation that basic rights will be equally afforded, that equality of treatment, opportunity, freedom of movement, [and] participation and of influence within the framework of a democratic, open, responsive, political system will effectively be enjoyed by all, apparently became vastly more widespread and [came to be] taken much more literally by most segments of the American population after World War II" (Inkeles, 1976, p. 35). Inkeles supports his assessment with data from public-opinion polls.

The civil rights struggle figured importantly in this change, in part by making the votes of minorities more potent, in part by showing how much demonstrations and protests could accomplish. A direct causal chain runs from the "Freedom Riders" in the South to student protests against the war in Vietnam, alternative life-styles, and local mobilization on environmental issues. Another force has been the attempt to give local groups, especially in cities, a formal place in the control of federally funded services. This spreading of authority was intended to overcome feelings of impotence and alienation among poor and minority voters.

Movements toward grass-roots influence, along with the disenchantment that sprang from Vietnam and Watergate, have brought steadily increasing demands for public knowledge of public affairs. Alongside the lobbies for propertied interests, which have resources for assembling their own information, there have grown up citizens' lobbies—"open up the system" became the slogan of Common Cause. The Freedom of Information Act unlocked closed files. Neighborhood groups, ethnic groups, and organizations representing operating personnel are now quickly mobilized when an issue touches their interests. For example, in addition to using their power for economic advantage, teachers' organizations have begun to press for or against educational plans. It is this volatile, fragmented community that today exercises power on any issue it chooses for attention. And it is for this reason that evaluation must learn to serve in the context of accommodation and not dream idly of serving a Platonic guardian.

Coleman and others (1979, p. 6) take the same position: the present-day need is for "pluralistic policy research," not for research that aims to advise the Princess. According to them, "The policy researcher is not the servant of the government official. He, like the official, is the agent of the people—the people not as a mass, but through their various roles, activities, and interests. In this conception, policy is the outcome of a clash of interests, not the product of a governmental policy maker. The proper function of social policy research is to inform those interests—not a particular subset of those interests, not government, but the interests themselves—so that they may be better informed about their interests and thus press more rationally for them" (p. 6).

## The Policy-Shaping Community

The community that plays an active role in shaping policy is of course far less extensive than the electorate, and in the present section we consider factors that make for greater or less participation. We speak of this audience as a policy-shaping community (PSC) to emphasize the communication that exists between citizens and those who speak for constituencies or agencies. Even in the market context, as noted earlier, individuals respond to many of the same communications, and their actions cumulate into a message for the supplier. First it will be useful to categorize members of the audience for an evaluation.

*Major Roles.* The scheme of Table 3 applies to communities of many kinds and sizes, but it oversimplifies drastically. Abt (1979) estimates that a given program will have from ten to

Table 3. Roles Within the Policy-Shaping Community

Public servants
  Responsible officials
    Policy level
    Program level
  Operating personnel
The public
  Constituents
  Illuminators

twenty major constituencies. What members of a PSC have in common is a concern with certain social agendas, not geographical or organizational affinity. How active the persons from the several categories become will vary with the program and the action under consideration.

Table 3 conveniently divides the public from its servants. The term *public servants* usually refers to those who hold government posts, but for our purpose the category is also to include private firms that render services. We have in mind not only private hospitals, private universities, individual physicians, and the like but also commercial enterprises such as firms supplying transportation in a metropolitan area.

Among public servants it is convenient, though artificial, to separate officials from operating personnel. Officials are particularly active in initiating evaluations and in considering evaluation results, but operating personnel at lower levels influence decisions too. They have interests to be taken into account, and a program plan can rarely be carried out without their understanding and consent.

We follow Pedersen (1977) and Weiss (1974a) in distinguishing officials responsible for policy from those directing operations. The term *policy* is to be understood in this context as representing broad plans, general principles, and priorities from which programs stem. The questions before the policy officials have to do with authorization and allocation. Policy officials include legislators and school board members, as well as administrative officers. Congressional aides and policy analysts fall into this category, even though their authority is slight.

Having broad and numerous responsibilities, policy officials attend to large questions and care little about specifications. Every individual carrying responsibility decides to neglect some of the proposals on her desk to save time for more urgent ones. Policy is blocked out with broad brushstrokes, and operational planning is left to lower levels. Thus we observed earlier that the policy officials considering busing had to decide whether to intensify pressures for busing or to try to hold them off, but the mapping technique itself they shunted off to the program officials.

As Pedersen (1977) comments, the questions reaching the policy official (and that includes nearly all the questions that arouse a large PSC) depend heavily on value judgments. Facts about the probable social effects of a service are of interest to the policy maker. But the benefits and nonmonetary costs of competing programs differ in character; hence, judgments are neither easy nor mechanical.

In contrast, the program officer has little interest in comparisons across programs. She wants to keep her own program going and preferably growing. She is interested in what Pedersen calls out*put* as distinct from out*come*; for her the test of program operations is how many clients were served, not how clients' lives were altered. This is again a response to pressing responsibilities, not indifference to outcomes. The manager took up her position with the understanding that the program was worthwhile in principle. Delivery is her main responsibility.

The responsibility resting on those who carry out a program plan differs from that of the planners. We class among operating personnel the teachers, social workers, principals, and local office managers—in general, those on the firing line. According to Weiss (1974a), program managers focus on strategies of operation, on finding a regular procedure for resolving recurring difficulties; tactics for treating specific instances they leave to operators near the scene. But Weiss' distinction among policy, strategy, and tactics is a little too neat. After all, President Kennedy or at least his executive committee thought through what *tactic* to use in stopping the first Soviet freighter to approach Cuba with missiles. And the ranger who makes today's tactical decision about particular grazing land has a strong interest in any proposed directive about strategy. Nonetheless, Weiss' tripartite division indicates which kinds of issues and which kinds of information are most certain to be on the minds of persons at the three levels.

We turn now to the second main rubric of Table 3. Some issues are put to a referendum of the whole citizenry. Far more often, however, members of the public exert influence through constituencies. One kind of constituency is the program clientele. Labor unions, taxpayers leagues, and other interest groups are also potential audiences for evaluations.

A special role within the public category is that of the illuminator, who reflects on public affairs and offers interpretations. The influential persons we have in mind include reporters and commentators, academic social scientists and philosophers, gadflies such as Hyman Rickover and Ralph Nader, and some novelists and dramatists. Illuminators are important in shaping policy because they frame and reassess broad issues. They are the ones most likely to spread a new social philosophy or to make large parts of the population aware of emerging values. The evaluator can play the illuminator's role, but we have chosen to pretend that evaluators do not enter the PSC, in order to speak more easily about communications to and from the evaluator and to and from the community.

*Activation of the PSC.* Some issues excite nearly everyone at a certain moment; at such times the PSC includes an enormous number of persons. Some are intent on the issues and strive to become well informed. Some follow the action passively but still constitute a significant presence. However, actions affecting a program are usually taken quietly, with comparatively few participants and most of them from the program staff. And even within a program that is controversial as a whole, some decisions remain command decisions. It is therefore pertinent to consider both the factors that broaden the PSC and the factors that permit an action to be taken by a single decision maker.

Among the innumerable matters about which a community might be concerned, only a few ripen at any one time into political agendas. Topics are brought to center stage by events

or by an appeal from some illuminator. Pollution and despolia-
tion of the environment, for example, were potentially significant for decades, but it was Rachel Carson's powerful *Silent
Spring* that turned the spotlight on them. Similarly, Aaron
(1978) documents that down to 1963 "poverty" was not a significant problem in the eyes of the public or of the academic
social scientists. Heightened consciousness does not by itself
move a matter from the context of command to the context of
accommodation. Someone must generate proposals for action so
that members of the community can perceive potential threats
or benefits. That perception is what triggers political activity.

The spotlight flares and fades (Blumer, 1972; Downs,
1971). For decades or centuries a social shortcoming is taken as
"the way things are." At some point, however, it comes to be
consciously accepted as a problem. A service to deal with it is
set up. The service is delegated to a manager in one decade, is
pulled and hauled by public controversy in the next. As public
concern diminishes, it ceases to be seen as a problem and slips
back under managerial control. Thus, in the years before 1957,
decisions about science education were made by thousands of
individuals, each pretty much in command of her own situation—a textbook writer, a publisher, a local committee deciding
which book to purchase. Almost no decision was intended to
affect a large fraction of the nation's students until Sputnik
made the quality of science education a recognized problem.
Vigorous discussion, legislation, well-budgeted experimental
projects, and evaluations followed for ten years; then interest
waned.

Legislators and citizens no longer have science education
on their minds (except for a few isolated agendas such as crea-
tionism). Even the finding (National Assessment, 1978) that the
competence of seventeen-year-olds in science subjects declined
from 1970 to 1973 and again from 1973 to 1977 could not
make the public view science education as a problem again. Science education is today an open market of ideas. Within the
wide limits set by state guidelines, each school district can go its
own way, and most of the decisions are left to the teacher or
the local group of teachers (Stake and others, 1978).

The arousal and nonarousal of potential participants is one of the mysteries of political life. Among the perplexities that could be the stuff of political drama, few play to large houses. On others, the curtain never rises. Constituencies, interest groups, and individual stakeholders throw quite different fractions of their potential weight onto the political scales (Almond, 1950; March and Olsen, 1976). Those who remain devoted to the same cause year in and year out, no matter what new distraction the headlines offer, tend to have a great cumulative influence—just because of their influence during the years when that cause is out of the limelight. In contrast, individuals and demographic groups whose interests could foreseeably be affected by a proposal remain strangely silent (as in the failure of the desegregation forces to pick up on the implications of the mapping analysis discussed earlier). We shall return to this subject, since one of the major potential contributions of evaluation is to help those with a legitimate interest in a given issue to recognize what is at stake for them.

*Accommodation and Command Within a Program Staff.* So far, we have spoken of public participation and nonparticipation. The staff of a program is also a potentially active PSC. Program operators often have strong and conflicting convictions. And, unless the operators feel unusually powerless, they will influence the accommodation. For example, a proposal that each hospital bed should serve more patients implies that patients should be discharged earlier. Because their professional values differ, administrators and physicians can be expected to disagree regarding the proper balance between use of facilities and length of patient stays. Tensions of these kinds, and therefore maneuvers and tacit bargaining, are present even in the purest context of command, as long as humans and not material objects are being "commanded." Any number of novels about the military life make this point. And so does the success story of the Forest Service, where concordance of values was the key to effective command.

Institutional tradition plays a large role in determining the range of participation. Some institutions have a tradition of centralization; their constituencies and fieldworkers do not expect to be consulted. In such cases the active PSC is small. In other institutions, the workers at lower echelons consider themselves autonomous professionals who are to be consulted when a widely applicable decision is made. The restaurant business provides examples of both extremes. The autonomy of the chef is legendary. A proposal to use microwave ovens, say, influences what happens in the kitchen only if the chef agrees to it. The manager of a hotel chain might purchase the ovens, but tradition denies her the power to "decide" that chefs will use them. The chef will decide. In contrast, the fast-food chain is dedicated to standardization. Headquarters determines the cooking time for the potatoes, and the fry cook is hired with the understanding that she will follow orders. In a fast-food chain the only decision makers who count occupy rooms at the top.

A significant qualifying remark must be added, however. Command is always subject to overthrow, tradition or no. Labor unions now put their weight into decisions that were once the exclusive province of management; indeed, in European countries legislation has institutionalized that once-unthinkable influence. Physicians could once expect their advice regarding treatment to be accepted very nearly as a command; today, they go to great lengths to inform the patient so that she can take most of the responsibility for the choice. Authority depends on faith. If the commander is to remain a Platonic steward, the political community has to believe her concern for the general interest. When that faith is weak, allocation decisions are drawn into the context of accommodation, and command authority is restricted to regulatory detail.

In a federal system, more and more programs come under plural jurisdictions. That means that more and more officials, each with a different power base, have interests at stake and also have a certain amount of power. Moreover, with more points where some control is exercised, there are more opportunities for public constituencies to exert pressure. Accommodation is the only possibility, and sometimes it is a remote one. One famous historical account expressed this frustration with pluralism in a title of surpassing length and poignancy: *Implementation: How Great Expectations in Washington Are Dashed in Oakland: or, Why It's Amazing That Federal Programs Work at*

*All, This Being a Saga of the Economic Development Administration as Told by Two Sympathetic Observers Who Seek to Build Morale on a Foundation of Ruined Hope* (Pressman and Wildavsky, 1973).

Education is a particularly clear example of a service shaped by mutual accommodation. It is a game any number can play. In theory, the common school has always been under the "local control" of a school board. But the board must be mindful of factions within the community that keep an eye on this or that program of special interest: athletics, notably, or perhaps multicultural education. And regardless of the central decision, when the classroom door closes, the teacher is free to emphasize one kind of learning or another.

Voters, meanwhile, reject bond issues and leave the local administrators to juggle the fragments of a budget. State officials try to influence local priorities and standards. At desks in Washington, congressional staff members and bureaucratic guideline writers try to plant certain features in every realization of a federally supported program. But then the guidelines are reinterpreted locally to turn the edge of any unpalatable directive. And if someone who dislikes a local practice can find a legal handle, a judge stands ready to prescribe administrative practices from the bench.

With respect to bureaucratic control, we draw attention to the entertaining article by Cohen and Farrar (1977). Their subject is the trial of a school-voucher plan in Alum Rock, California. The underlying idea was to provide a menu of distinctive educational offerings in the form of "schools within schools," as well as to allow parents to shift a child into whichever curriculum they found most appealing, without regard to neighborhood boundaries. In the history of this venture Cohen and Farrar find evidence for a general allegation about professional reforms: "[T]he only way to get anything done is to let the locals do what they like—as long as they say they are doing what the reformers like. The reformers are really at the mercy of those they are reforming" (p. 82).

*Stages of Program Maturity.* The political world of the emerging program is distinctly different from that of the fully mature program, and it will be useful to distinguish among stages of maturity. This will offset any hint of overgeneralization in the preceding sections and will introduce terminology for later use. We adapt the scheme of four stages described by Suchman (1970), altering his terminology and perhaps some of his ideas. We shall speak of the so-called breadboard stage, the superrealization, the prototype, and the established program.

First, a warning. Used in discussing the development of social entities, the biological metaphor of stages can mislead. Stages may be marked off by some technical criterion or rite, but the developing entity does not change abruptly. Neither does the way others regard the entity. At most, certain avenues of action are opened or closed off. It follows that, during "stage three," for example, characteristics of earlier and later stages may be observed from time to time. Sometime a stage may be "skipped." Moreover, some facets of activity may appear for the first time and hence be at the earliest stage when others seem to have reached their final form. The stages are a convenient metaphor within which both truth and convenient fiction can be discerned.

A program or program modification has to start as a gleam in someone's eye. Almost always, the new idea is speculative and indefinite. Even if the initiator does have a sharply etched proposal, the individuals she interests in it will speculate enough about alternatives to cause the proposal to become more or less indefinite. Indeed, this is a first accommodation; only by acknowledging that details are open to modification is the developer likely to attract supporters.

Ideally, the first phase consists of developmental trials in which variants of the proposal are observed in action. Engineers call this the "breadboard stage." Temporary hookups of components are readily modified with each day's new test result or suggestion. This stage goes beyond the pencil sketch and the computer simulation to a genuine empirical trial, but the work involves daily tinkering, not definitive measurement of yesterday's version. Breadboard activity turns a bright idea into a proposal for action. Alternatively, the developer can decide, after a minimal investment, to cancel the venture. Some piloting and developmental work remains to be done even after a social program has moved far along toward adoption and many of its components have been bolted into position.

The trial of a superrealization, which logically would come second, is a painstaking assessment of what the proposal can accomplish at its best. The specifications recommended at the end of the breadboard activity are strictly followed. Third would come a substantial field trial. While its conditions are realistic, such a trial is limited in scope and in time. This trial of a prototype attempts to preview what will happen if the practice is made fully operational. Finally, the program becomes established with a permanent budget and an organizational niche.

Breadboard, superrealization, prototype, and established stages are to be seen in the history of "Sesame Street." Details of program segments were tested on laboratory audiences. Later, in a superrealization, children in preschools viewed taped segments; their regular, attentive viewing gave the lessons every chance to teach. The first year of broadcasting on a full scale was a prototype, inasmuch as no financial commitment to the future of the program or to the producing workshop had been made.

Not every program has such a nicely paced evolution. When Congress senses a public demand for action, it may authorize an untested program or even one whose activities no one has clearly visualized. Follow Through exemplifies how commitment may precede planning and development inquiry (Elmore, 1975; Haney, 1977). In 1967 the Johnson administration proposed Follow Through as an operational program. Congress passed the authorization but appropriated a meager $30 million instead of the $120 million anticipated by the planners. The simplest act of administration would have been to divide up the kitty—a few paltry dollars to every eligible community. But bright minds in the executive branch refused to treat the legislation so frivolously. Congress, they said, had appropriated only enough money for a trial, and a trial it should have.

Educational inventors who had worked out instructional proposals applicable to poor children were invited to install their plans as competing prototypes. The comparative study continued for seven years. The innovators carrying plans into the schools quickly found that their plans were not adequate for widespread application (Rivlin and Timpane, 1975b). Revisions (which probably could have been done better, more easily, and more cheaply on a breadboard scale) continued while the supposed prototype study moved forward. It remains to be seen whether the Follow Through report (Stebbins and others, 1977) will influence direct action to establish a new program. (Discussion apparently *is* weaving it into the new enthusiasm for "basic," three R's, education.) It is possible that Follow Through will remain forever in Congress' deep freeze, as a program some long-ago vote authorized without providing resources.

To speak of "phases" implies that a proposal comes due for a vote or decision only at the end of each phase of trial. That may be true when the innovation is an isolated product. A new surgical operation is evolved warily, operations on animals preceding circumspect trials on humans, which in turn may give warrant for a clinical trial under the best of hospital conditions. If that trial produces good results, the procedure is disseminated gradually. Trials in a second or third hospital check results in more typical circumstances. This record encourages medical practitioners, one by one, to accept the proposal as a standard procedure (or to distrust it). The prospective patient who ultimately hears of the procedure and learns enough to judge that the risks of the operation are acceptable (or are not) is also a decision maker.

The audience for information widens as the program moves toward maturity. When controversy surfaces, the PSC tends to become larger. At the breadboard stage, however, the proponent of a proposal is not ready to persuade others. She may be working entirely on her own, with no more help than the acquiescence of the local guinea pigs. Or perhaps an agency has given support without commitment to see what can be made of a hopeful idea. The same can be said of the superrealization. Very few persons are aware of the proposal at this stage, barring some freak of media attention. These quiet backroom stages are important if social prospecting is to venture more than a few yards off the beaten path and come up with plans thoughtful enough to be worth a political debate. Political commitment to an idea increases at the later stages. More and more people have something at stake, and the PSC increases accordingly. Once the program is established, promises have been made to staff, clients, and communities. Even to launch a prototype is to increase the number of interests to be accommodated.

The four stages are most distinct when the community attending to the program differs from stage to stage. In developing a new educational or medical product, a single entrepreneur may direct the breadboard work and deal with (or be) the evaluator. The developer and a small nucleus of coplanners exercise effective command, however hard the developer works to maintain the enthusiastic collaboration of the staff. The superrealization is, by definition, strongly controlled. The prime audience is composed of the few decision makers who control funds for a prototype trial. If their decision is negative, the program proponent may be able to build a political constituency (as now and then happens with a purported cure for cancer). But such occurrences are rare.

If the funds for the prototype trial are allocated—and that decision often moves forward with little controversy and hence a tiny PSC—there is still the problem of finding test sites. Those wishing to test public health interventions have sometimes had to go abroad to find sites for their trials. Likewise, much as local school officials want additional money, they not infrequently refuse funds offered for an activity out of tune with local thinking. Hence an accommodative process goes on in arranging for a prototype trial; it usually is a community-by-community negotiation, and the larger polity is rarely alerted. Obviously, positive reports from breadboard runs and from the superrealization (if any) play some part in negotiating successfully for a prototype trial.

Once a prototype is launched, a proposal tends to gain a larger and larger audience, and political interests mobilize. A prototype is large enough to be visible, and its very existence hints that the innovation is close to being adopted as policy. Illuminators give it their attention, and a hazy public notion of a problem consolidates into more specific views of the particular intervention. Tension grows, unless the plan happens to be one everybody is enamored of. In fact, it is hard to find examples of policy proposals (as distinct from proposed technical procedures) that go through without significant opposition.

It is during the move toward establishment of the program and the determination of its authorized form that controversy becomes most apparent and that the opportunity for command is least. This struggle begins when a PSC becomes aroused, a situation that may occur before the prototype trial (if any). Completion of the trial is not needed to signal the kickoff of the political season.

For some programs, all stages serve about the same audience, and the "stages" are then much the same in character. This would be true of a proposal arising in a context of command and also of a thoroughly politicized proposal. When a rule for allocating money or power is being developed, the process is politically charged from the outset. Even breadboard trials will foment political struggle and (at best) accommodation. Throughout the Alum Rock trial of school vouchers, for example, political conflict was present within the school system and across the city. The trial of the New Jersey negative income tax proposal was under continual scrutiny, if not harassment, from elected officials in Trenton and Washington.

We have said that political activity grows and that the PSC widens with maturity, but now it is necessary to speak of the reversal that occurs as the program takes root. Once the program is in operation and the roles of participants are sorted out and stabilized, the large issues have been settled semipermanently. The PSC has agreed that certain services will be rendered, that managerial responsibility will be divided along certain lines, and so on. Almost all the decisions that remain to be made are decisions within the program. These are left to subcommunities or to managers granted command authority.

Recall that a grant of power can be revoked. In one year, a decision is a factory manager's sole responsibility. In another year, she may have to make the policy plausible to a congressional committee. But grants of authority once made are not often unmade. Issues are myriad, and only a few can crowd onto the same political playing field at one time. So the management of a typical institution remains steady, working out small accommodations within the program staff, testing modifications of procedures that create no political tensions, and starting occasional breadboard trials of new program elements that fit within its general charter.

Most of the time, the fully established, mature program is allowed to go its own way. The rare moments of attention from the external PSC are concentrated on limited issues. The public view of the military, for example, has certainly become more negative down to 1980, but this has had little effect on the conduct of military affairs. Perhaps the one major policy change forced on the military from outside during the last dozen years has been the abandonment of the draft, and this did not constitute a major change in the defense mandate.

Existing programs become entrenched. The trenches are defended by vested interests in government and among the clientele, as well as by those who believe that erratic changes of course would destroy the political system. Therefore, to increase a budget or to hold it steady is the usual option for allocative action with regard to the established program. Politicians often call for budget reductions. But budget officers, legislators, and voters who make allocative decisions do not have a free hand. In an established program, the political and psychological investments of managers, staff, and recipients of services loom large. Moreover, the plan for a service of a certain approximate kind and magnitude is often a hard-won accommodation. Overturning such a settlement would—if seen as a threatening precedent—destabilize the whole system that now makes antagonists willing to settle for a plan that gives them *some* of what they want.

## How Social Action Evolves

"God eternally geometrizes," said Plato, and belief in natural order was expressed in his social theory. Rationalists like to think that choosing a course of action can be reduced to a formal problem. Benefits can be optimized, a particular treatment can be shown by experiment to be better than its alternatives, or a program can be abandoned because it has proved to pay out less than its cost.

Unlike a social "problem," a problem in geometry has an indisputable solution, as Jouvenel (1963) points out. Even the student of geometry who cannot reach the solution can recognize its excellence when the schoolmaster writes it on the blackboard: The answer "is no less our own than if we had reached it alone. We are just as ready to champion the answer against any doubter, we have no doubt that he will be brought to see its rightness and be grateful to us for his own acquired conviction" (p. 204).

A geometric problem is bounded. The elements to be combined are known. They can be described in a few words or equations. And the standards by which a would-be solution is judged are few and consistent. To quote Jouvenel further: "A 'solution' is an answer which fully satisfied all the requirements laid down: when such a solution is found by anyone, everyone also acknowledges it. When, however, all the requirements cannot be met, then only a 'settlement' is possible, which does not meet the requirements of some parties and therefore leaves them . . . psychologically dissatisfied" (p. 189).

*Accommodation as Piecemeal Adjustment.* The settlement or accommodation reached in a round of political bargaining is what participants are willing to settle for. The action may not match any player's ideal, but it is within the acceptable range. The equilibrium is unstable, because the settlement is "right" only in a political sense. A limited shift in beliefs or political alliances, or perhaps a newly devised proposal for action, will make reopening the discussion worthwhile. Therefore, says Lindblom (1965, p. 217), "the decision-making process is never finished and never can be."

In an apolitical context of engineering or command, optimization is more a theoretical conception than an everyday practice. In Simon's (1957) characterization of the manager's work, "satisficing" replaces "optimizing." The manager tacitly sets a tolerance level for each aspect of the efficiency of operations—production, spoilage, turnover, grievances, and so on. So long as these variables seem to be within tolerance, the manager lets present arrangements stand. This enables her to devote energy to problems and opportunities of greater salience. It would be callous to suggest that the manager is satisfied when worker grievances average no more than three per month, but she is "prepared to live with" some such level. Her policy, then, is to seek an acceptable rather than an optimal state of affairs.

The same is to be said of engineering design. To check out all possible alternatives in pursuit of the optimum one would be unreasonably costly and even theoretically impossible, insofar as future uses of the product are to some degree unknown. So the engineer uses successive approximations to bring the design into the range of acceptable efficiency. Either the manager or the engineer may experiment to determine an approximate best value for some aspect of the operation. But costs of information and control can devour the profits from modest improvements in production (Arrow, 1974; Lindblom, 1972; Cyert and March, 1963).

Formal evidence and analysis obviously can feed into conflict arousal or conflict resolution; that is, they can play a part in the politics of accommodation. Recall once again that computer mapping could be used by local partisans of desegregation to challenge existing school attendance areas. When such techniques worked in school districts, they offered a means of compromise for setting the most acceptable boundary. And recall that, for the Washington agency challenging local plans, the mapping technique was a starting point in negotiating a compromise.

Even in management, the hope that an adequate flow of information can reduce a decision to an automatic choice among courses of action is now recognized as simpleminded. Elaborate "management information systems" that would substitute technology for judgment were proposed a decade ago. But comparatively few internal decisions are now seen as "programmable" in the sense that Simon (1960) used the term. Managerial tasks "are performed in an organizational context that is political and resists being programmed," according to Keen and Morton (1978, p. 11); also see Keen and Gerson (1977). By way of example, Keen and Morton spoke of production scheduling in a firm where one manager directs the production of washing machines while another of equal rank directs marketing. Their priorities conflict, since unsold inventory creates problems for one and relieves problems for the other. Consequently, what is needed is information that will facilitate negotiation of a compromise rather than information that can be cranked into a decision rule.

Working out a social program or regulating a complex organization is almost inevitably a process of successive modest changes. This process is conservative in Burke's sense of that term (1970, p. 249): "By a slow but well-sustained progress the effect of each step is watched; the good or ill success of the first gives light to us in the second; and so, from light to light, we are conducted with safety through the whole series. We see that the parts of the system do not clash. The evils latent in the most promising contrivances are provided for as they arise. One advantage is as little as possible sacrificed to another. We compensate, we reconcile, we balance."

The phrase *adjustment at the margins* sums up the character of most of the actions taken in a context of accommodation. Participants who wish to take a large step in a certain direction find few allies, but some small step will be welcomed by many interest groups, even groups with conflicting motives. The proposals themselves are trimmed to fit the players' assessment of the political situation. As a consequence, most social change is gradual. Still, successive small repairs and added fixtures do accumulate over time to create a different edifice.

Some critics object to the acceptance of gradualism by social scientists and government officials (Schultze, 1968; Best and Connolly, 1975). Piecemeal adjustment is undeniably a fact, but these critics favor bolder initiatives. Unless large visions are put forward, they say, institutions will improve much too slowly. If the power balance in the PSC determines which plans are accepted, individual and corporate interests will not be held in check by attention to the common interest.

This criticism surely is not to be read as a call for a government that takes actions contrary to the popular will. It must, then, be a call for arousing public opinion so that stronger action will be taken. This is the traditional role of illuminators and statesmen. A leader can win sympathy for a new social objective and (as in the politics of ecology) can push externalities reflecting a public interest ahead of private interests. Sometimes she can amass a coalition and put through a dramatic change. But a sharp distinction is to be made between leading the public to a new accommodation and taking action that runs counter to public beliefs.

*Prevailing Views as the Basis for Accommodation.* An individual copes with each day's events by making reasonable choices in the light of the situation as she interprets it. This interpretation is partial: it attends only to certain aspects of the situation and considers most of those aspects superficially. Interpretations, and even choices of what to attend to and interpret, are governed by a belief system. Beliefs come partly from personal experience, partly from education, partly from the influences of home, church, and advertisement. Some beliefs are deeply entrenched, others are subject to easy alteration; some are well warranted, others are contrary to fact or even inconsistent with one another. Just as a person has beliefs about how much sleep is normal, whether a trip to China would be enjoyable, and how much one can trust used-car salesmen, she holds beliefs about the causes underlying crime in the streets and about the system for administering justice.

For example, the prevailing view of poverty at the time that the War on Poverty began is captured succinctly by Aaron (1978, p. 20): "[T]he poor person was viewed as poor because of shortcomings of his own that may themselves be traceable to his own or his parents' poverty. . . . [H]e could emerge from poverty only if he changed, or was changed." Aaron documents the prevalence of this view by quoting writers whose sympathies and proposals differed markedly. The view had emerged in part from cross-sectional social surveys. Once research turned to "panel" surveys that looked at the same persons year after year, the premise was contradicted. Poor families did not represent a permanent class; many families cross the poverty line in any given year. "[T]he simple snapshot of poverty that many people carelessly adopted a decade ago has become a complex moving picture" (Aaron, 1978, p. 37). The subtler conception has not yet entered the prevailing view, however, and so is not yet the basis of policy.

The views of a person working in or served by a program are more specific than the views of a legislator or average citizen. If the parole system comes under discussion, for example, the prison official thinks of particular rules for administering paroles that might be amended, whereas a citizen calls to mind some pros and cons of a generous policy, along with a vague impression of the current practice. The perceptions of individuals and subgroups, shared through communication, blend into a prevailing view of a program or institution. Many times such impressions command a near-consensus.

As noted earlier, citizens have common views about what constitutes a social problem. Some conditions that are less than satisfactory are thought to be private rather than public business. Some conditions are thought to be incurable, or there is no confidence that government intervention would make them better. In other areas of social distress, the public believes strongly in the efficacy of a particular institution.

Since what makes headlines is disagreement, the reader may doubt that there is nearly universal agreement on *any* social topic. A backward glance should remove that doubt. Think back to the 1930s, when Glueck (see Chapter One) was raising a mild question about shotgun marriages. Surely, in those years, very few people doubted that pregnancy was grounds for marriage, that—in a case of divorce—custody of the child should go to the mother, and that only true economic hardship justified both mother and father taking regular jobs.

These examples bring us to a point that has not been raised thus far. When a near-universal belief is seriously questioned, the climate of opinion comes to be dominated by a modified number of alternative beliefs, each having its own adherents. That is to say, sectors of the PSC that share common interests or social background have their own prevailing views. The views of two sectors match in some respects and are diametrically opposed in others. The similarities cause them to center attention on certain concerns they share, and the agreements bound the field within which action proposals are likely to be taken seriously. The differences in beliefs of sectors create the polarities that accommodation has to balance.

Look again to the Elementary and Secondary Education Act (ESEA) for an example. In the 1960s it was generally agreed that poor and minority youths were badly educated. The black community in New York City believed that the educational bureaucracy was unsympathetic to its children and unlikely to make a constructive effort to help them if given federal money. No doubt similar views permeated the national black community, but it was the New York electorate that counted because Robert Kennedy was a senator from New York. Knowing of the black community's concern, he proposed an evaluation requirement for ESEA in order to put pressure on local administrators. This ran counter to some equally forceful beliefs of state and local school officials and of the National Education Association; namely, that the federal government eternally seeks to intrude into local management, that each such move is an entering wedge for a national curriculum, and that central controls will in time strip teachers of proper professional functions. The reader can understand why these beliefs were popular in the respective camps; even if they were "myths," they provided useful arguments. Statements for and against social proposals continually invoke widely shared beliefs. Speeches and press releases favorable to a proposal present it as a natural working out of accepted principles. The opposing statements make much of whatever beliefs seem contrary to the program's assumptions.

To go about its work, Congress has to learn about existing services and the political heat that a new proposal will generate. Popular views are their principal source. Citizens complain to their representatives about services that do not meet their expectations. If citizens believe that not much can be done about some problem, however, they complain much less frequently about the shortcomings of the relevant service. Elisburg (1977, pp. 67–68) makes it clear that any formal research is added onto a belief structure to which other sources are also bringing bricks and straw:

The Congress differs markedly from the administrative agencies. . . . It is a body responsive to the wishes of multiple, sometimes conflicting, sometimes shifting constituencies. [It] functions in a milieu which, by its very nature, is heavily politicized.

By politicized, I mean that the Congress listens carefully and continuously to its broad array of constituencies. I think that this listening is the members' first and most basic source of evaluation: it is a very finely tuned antenna. Sometimes the listening is carried out scientifically through the use of sample surveys. Sometimes it is carried out intuitively, as when rumblings and grumblings, wishes and preferences are brought to awareness by the delegations to the offices of the senators, representatives, or committees. The unrelenting deluge of mail and the representatives of special-interest groups bringing their clients' wishes and complaints to congressional attention are two additional sources of evaluation playing a role in the assessment of policies and programs.

This is probably the method of evaluation prescribed or implied in the constitution. It is the means by which our system of government has worked for two hundred years. It is not a perfect system as everyone knows, but it has been, on the whole, a successful device to balance overwhelming societal concerns with individual liberty and rights. . . .

While growing recognition of professionally based, expertly conducted program evaluation has been evident in recent years in the Congress, legislators and their staffs view this important secondary evaluation [as a] supplement within the political framework constitutionally required of them. . . .

It cannot be stressed too strenuously that scientific program evaluation is itself evaluated by the Congress in terms of its utility to promote the effectiveness and precision of legislative judgments in a political milieu.

Rein (1976) spoke of prevailing views as similar to the scientific paradigms that Kuhn (1962) has discussed. Kuhn pointed out how slow scientists are to abandon a theory after evidence that conflicts with it appears. Rein (1976, p. 103) made a similar comment about evidence on social processes: "New information is assimilated into a paradigm that is remarkably persistent and resistant to change. Policy paradigms are a curious mixture of psychological assumptions, scientific concepts, value commitments, social aspirations, personal beliefs, and administrative constraint. They are not able to organize disparate evidence and predict future patterns. They are more like personal belief systems, not entirely manifest, encompassing various contradictions rather than seeking to eliminate them."

Statements in line with generally held beliefs tend to be incorporated into the structure, according to Rein, and action is based on them. Thus an evaluator's report that a worrisome side effect did not in fact occur increases confidence in the workability of the belief system out of which the program grew. (An example might be a report that there seem to be few violations of an honor system used for administering university examinations.) Also, a report that suggests how minor adjustments will improve results is likely to be easily accepted since it is basically a supportive remark.

Information from research does not normally carry greater weight than other kinds of information. Speaking especially of cost-benefit analyses that purport to show citizens what they personally stand to gain or lose, Allen and Sears (1979, p. 175) cite diverse evidence that "symbolic political attitudes, acquired at an earlier age, continue to exert considerably more impact on adult policy positions than do the relevant, current, more situation-specific self-interest variables."

What contradicts the prevailing view may carry no weight at all, at least in the short run (Lindblom and Cohen, 1979). The psychologist Albert Poffenberger used to delight in warning the advertising community: "The truth may be too startling to be believed!" He would then tell the story about a maker of steamer trunks who could not sell his superstrong product, despite strenuous advertising efforts. To prove how sturdy the trunk was, the advertisements showed a photograph of the trunk with a circus elephant standing on it. No sale. The potential customers believed that trunks could not take such a weight and dismissed the advertisement as fakery.

## Reinterpretations and Social Change

As we have illustrated, remarkably sweeping changes in social views occur even within a single generation, and social institutions change accordingly. The process is one of slow extension of a new interpretation from a few believers to a wider segment of the community and ultimately, perhaps, to nearly everyone. Many new interpretations are hatched, but few survive, and not many of those attract enough adherents to affect contemporary action. Perceptions are continually being altered by observation and communication. Communications, for example, have a cumulative impact: the new *Zeitgeist* embraces ideas that have been on the fringe of the social conversation and make them part of the prevailing doctrine. Contrariwise, practices that once prevailed (routine use of group mental tests in schools, for example) become centers of controversy and in time lose all but die-hard support.

*Impact of Evaluation.* Evaluations have a substantial influence on policy, but that influence is "indirect," "long term," "secondary," or "conceptual," to quote investigators such as Caplan, Cohen, Knorr, Patton, and Rich (collected in Weiss, 1977), along with Alkin, Daillah, and White (1979). Much of the disappointment regarding evaluations that was summarized in Chapter One arises because the summative evidence about outcomes of a program has little direct effect on the priorities and budgets it is assigned. "Direct" effects are frequently unacceptable to the workings of the political system, and at the end of this chapter we shall consider why. Further, in Chapter Three we shall describe how evaluations do affect the program studied. These effects, we shall see, tend to be largest when the evaluator is intimately engaged with the program operators, not surveying them from a lofty perch. An evaluation concentrates on a particular present program, but we shall emphasize that studies of prototypes and established programs have their greatest implications for programs that differ—perhaps radically—from the one actually surveyed.

Rich's distinction between "instrumental" and "conceptual" uses of social research, including evaluations, captures a theme of all recent studies of utilization; we also like the term *enlightenment* as a description of the end use of inquiry (Biderman, 1970; Weiss, 1977; Lindblom and Cohen, 1979, pp. 73–81). The rational model calls for "instrumental use." A policy maker has a pointed question. She wants the evaluator to indicate what to do in the months immediately following his report (Weiss, 1977; Rich, 1977). In contrast, a member of the PSC makes "conceptual" use of a study when it causes her to think differently about a program, or a category of program, or a social need. That is to say, the study alters her map of the terrain. If enough others hear of the finding or its reverberations, the view prevailing in the PSC is changed.

So far, evidence on the impact of social research has come largely from interviews with responsible officials, particularly policy-level officials. Other sectors of the PSC have been neglected, though one exception is Almond's study (1950) of public thinking about foreign policy. The study of the public-as-client by Katz and others (1975) is only tangentially relevant. Still, if conceptual use outweighs instrumental use of research results among central policy makers, we can be certain that this is even more true of illuminators and constituencies.

One major survey (Caplan, Morrison, and Stambaugh, 1975) pointed up the degree to which evidence is amalgamated with less scientific news and with the beliefs that the listener already holds. As Caplan summarized the findings (1977, pp. 187–188):

> An important characteristic of the more frequent users of social research is a quality of mind or what might be called a "social perspective". . . : They react as if what is happening in the larger society were indistinguishable from what is happening within themselves.

[M] any respondents failed to distinguish between objective social science information and sub-
jective social sensitivity. Thus, most of the examples
they offered to illustrate knowledge applications
really involved the application of secondary source
information, organized common sense, and social
sensitivity. . . .

Further, regardless of whether or not the relevant information was "hard" or "soft" [with respect to degree of technical refinement], these respondents were eclectic in their use of information
sources and relied on newspapers, television, and
popular magazines as well as scientific government
research reports and scientific journals [as] sources.
In fact, one gets the overall impression that social
science knowledge, "hard" or "soft," is treated as
news by these respondents—allowing its users to
feel that their awareness does not lag behind.

Patton and others (1977, p. 151) support Caplan in arguing that technical quality does not increase utilization. Weiss
and Bucuvalas (1977, p. 223) seemed to reach a contrary conclusion by a different technique, but they had to take considerable pains to rationalize inconsistency in their data. But to return to Caplan (1977, p. 192): "[E] xamples in research on
criminal justice, welfare, work satisfaction, and education could
be cited to illustrate the fact that officials are willing to accept
findings that coincide with their beliefs, but unwilling to accept
findings that are counterintuitive to their beliefs, quite apart
from the issues of scientific objectivity and political feasibility."

A Widening Audience. It now becomes obvious that the
illuminators are particularly important in shaping the prevailing
view. A reported observation that challenges the prevailing view
(whether from an investigator or a casual bystander) gains its
influence by catching the ear of "students of the problem":
professionals, administrators, journalists, and so on. Aaron
(1978, p. 77) draws attention to the paradox that a decade of
"devastating criticisms" of the Coleman report served to spread
its skepticism about the effects of schooling and gave it more

influence than it would have had if not criticized. When a new perception commands attention, it is relayed to a wider, less specialized circle of communication. Here again, it may reverberate or die out.

But if its audience does widen, the message becomes generalized. Even among officials, Weiss and Bucuvalas (1977, p. 228) found that discussion proceeds at an abstract level, with little or no reference to the specific program from which the original observation came. Almost never is a specific evaluative study either the main support of an emerging proposal or the main source of doubts about an established one. Accounts of personal experience, journalistic analyses, recollections of history, and possibly echoes of scholarly theory orchestrate the new themes.

Many forces create readiness for change and shape the change itself. To quote Rein (1976), "In the long run, research and theory [including program evaluations] contribute to alterations in the framework... [p. 111]. Dominant policy paradigms ... evolve over time. And social science ideas, together with social, political, and economic changes, play a role. . . . The influence of research is often diffuse, oblique, and always embedded in the changes it reflects. . . . [I]t is difficult, if not impossible, to isolate the unique role of research" (p. 117).

To give one example, the prevailing view of mental illness in the first half of this century was that treatment had to be a one-on-one process; that is, a highly trained psychotherapist had to carry the patient through countless intensive treatment sessions. However, this psychological conception was challenged by a sociological argument that a person's behavior is a function of social contexts. Rein (1976) has described how a single piece of research by Stanton and Schwartz (1954) altered the balance of views. They studied a private hospital, Chestnut Lodge, where accepted psychotherapeutic methods were in use. But the evaluation showed that the hospital environment and the contacts of the patient with staff and fellow inmates influenced the course of therapy, often for the worse. The report urged reorganizing the hospital to provide for "milieu therapy." This criticism was at odds with the central beliefs of the staff of Chestnut Lodge. They did not assimilate it and took no action.

For the professional audience at a distance, however, the Stanton-Schwartz book documented what many of them had begun to believe. Advocates used the book to popularize the concept of therapy as a social process. The listeners most strongly affected were newcomers to the profession. They encountered the idea during their initial training, because faculty members in departments of psychiatry found the view appealing and made the evaluative report one of their textbooks.

That newcomers are especially open to new ideas is not surprising. Arrow (1974) has commented on the significant role this plays in institutional self-renewal. Corporations hire junior executives from graduate schools of business, expecting them to be valuable disturbing influences. Their attaché cases smuggle in newly hatched concepts, as well as techniques that conflict with those the corporation has used comfortably for years. No doubt the corporate community rejects ten ideas for every one it accepts, but change does occur. Perhaps—as with social practices—one must describe changes in a belief system as "adjustments at the margin." The point is that the successive small changes move the center of accommodation.

## How Important Are Program Results?

Of course everyone wants her health care providers to keep her vigorous to a ripe age, wants the public school to make the children of other families as admirable as her own, and wants highways safe for drivers like herself who *never* drive more than fifteen miles per hour over the legal speed limit. So mortality statistics, educational surveys, and highway accident figures are important in everybody's value scheme. But the question of this section is not whether people prefer to get more value for their money but just how much weight information on outcomes carries. Is the fate of an established program determined by its results? Does the action on an emerging proposal depend on the evidence from trials?

Only under very special circumstances does the PSC hang back until it is sure that it has a winner to put its money on. That remark is not cynical; it simply recognizes that action must go on in the face of uncertainty. No political leader can build a record by refusing to act during the eternity that elapses while a sure cure for a problem is being discovered and tested (Edelman, 1964). Leaders come out for plausible actions that are within the range of political acceptability. The intent in the pages that follow is to consider how goals and results figure in the decision-making process, whether the perception of results comes from evaluation or other sources.

From 1967 onward, many social scientists complained that the Westinghouse evaluation of Head Start had given the program an undeserved black eye and thus had undercut its opportunity to serve. The study is indubitably open to criticism, and press accounts gave the impression that the program had failed even though change in the IQ of its participants was an incomplete and rather unhappy criterion for judging it. A by-product of the professional mutterings was some correspondence between one of us and Daniel P. Moynihan in June 1975. Some of his points should interest our readers. (The sentences were assembled from the letters and from a statement drafted for publication that did not see print.) Moynihan wrote:

> I think evaluators would do well to keep in mind the degree of skepticism at the political levels of government. It is the people who believe.
>
> Most of the presidents for whom I have worked, and many of their cabinet officers, have come to their tasks with a well-developed sense of the limits of government and the frailties of human beings, especially of human beings in the role of advisers. They assume that most advice is self-interested and only intermittently accurate.
>
> They assume that most government action is symbolic. They expect that almost as many battles will be lost as won. In a word, they are people who know something of human conflict and competi-

tion. When news drifts up to such persons that a particular program is evidently not doing very well, be it a weapons system, a compensatory education program, or a scheme to flatten out the corn-hog cycle, this is most often half-expected. The temptation, more likely than not, is to hope the news is not too widely disseminated, as this endangers the symbolic purposes of the program. When the experts-turned-lobbyists for any of these causes respond that the evaluation was statistically flawed, it will frequently be the case that this comes as no surprise either to the politician.

The programs [nevertheless] go on. . . .

[With regard to Head Start the problem was that] the press—the media—responded to the projected fears of the professionals, and began reporting huge cuts in these programs, which were in fact in the process of huge increases. On [last] Thursday night . . . a senior editor of *Newsweek* responded with amazement to a statement by me that Head Start had not been abolished by the Nixon administration.

The general problem of government in the experimental mode is that experiments [innovative trials] create interests which make for the perpetuation of all manner of activities.

The response to the Head Start evaluation was fundamentally an accommodative one. On the one hand, the program had a clientele and the backing of leading scholars; on the other hand, everyone agreed that it had not operated as magically as promised. It is ironic that Timpane (1976), in discussing the "failure" of this and related evaluations, pointed out that as a "side effect" (!) much had been learned about the difficulties in designing effective compensatory education and about how to make it more effective. Changes included abandoning the rashly optimistic summer programs in favor of the year-long versions and bringing parents into active participation. Program changes occurred when evaluations altered the prevailing view of cause and cure.

Moreover, slippage between plan and delivery was observed in this and other programs (Gramlich and Koshel, 1975; Rivlin and Timpane, 1975b). This observation shifted the attention of policy makers from the theory underlying new program proposals to the practicality of carrying out the plan, and it also shifted the attention of evaluators and policy analysts increasingly to the study of implementation. Schick (1977, p. 262) calls this "a Copernican revolution in analytic thinking." We see all this as evaluation helping society to learn and to get better results—not at all as a "failure."

*Goals: Rhetoric and Reality.* References to the attainment of goals pervade discussion of social programs and their evaluation. Here, for example, is one book's lead sentence on "the state of the art": "We know that useful evaluation cannot proceed without consensus on program goals" (Attkisson and others, 1978, p. 465). We have considerable sympathy with the Attkisson book as a whole, but this remark seems rationalist to the point of unreality. Consensus on ends and priorities is mostly absent from a context of accommodation.

For rationalists, all thinking starts with a specified goal or purpose. To find a means to the stated end is what it means to "solve a problem," but that is not how social action is taken. The statement quoted above seems to imply that evaluation is worthwhile only in the context of command. In such a context, of course, to announce an objective is a constructive act. The goal can be interpreted as an aspiration rather than as a promise. Committing resources to a do-or-die attempt is what command is all about. Also in internal program management, settling on priorities among possible investments of effort is a proper way of leading a staff. But what function do goals have in the political activities that lead to accommodation? With a picture of this before us, we will be able to consider the political conditions that make it useful to focus on whether a program attained its goals. We will also be able to put calls for "accountability" into their political context, since they are closely linked to the rhetoric of goal attainment.

The goals or objectives stated for a program are almost always vague. Rationalists see this vagueness as an evasion. The

policy analyst is told to overcome it, either by extracting unequivocal statements from program supporters or by himself
framing a list of the goals. Students of the political process,
however, say that this very vagueness of goals is the key to
accommodation.

Goals are a necessary part of political rhetoric. An advocate has to appeal to values to make her claim on tax money or
to gain a hearing for an institutional change. But those who
send proposals to the legislature or make speeches of advocacy
almost never commit themselves to a specified goal. Only the
lofty goal evades challenge. "Justice," "freedom from want,"
and "opportunity" win support, or at least they legitimize advocacy. If a speaker were to say that a certain proposal is intended
to redistribute wealth, the words would ignite a fire storm of
controversy over who will take what from whom (Aaron, 1978,
p. 28).

Parties having different interests and political philosophies
can form a coalition, whereas one member of a party cannot endorse the goals peculiar to the next member's constituency.
Schultze's (1968) remarks have often been quoted: "The first
rule of the successful political process is, 'Don't force a specification of goals or ends'" (p. 47). Schultze took ESEA as an example; for some advocates it was a way to help church schools,
for some a way to help the poor, and for some a way to increase
public school budgets and also an entering wedge for broad federal financing. Schultze continued: "If there had been any attempt to secure advance agreement on a set of long-run objectives, important elements of support for the bill would have
been lost, and its defeat assured" (p. 48). (See also Rein and
White, 1977; Weiner, 1976.) But rationalists think quite differently about these matters. Witness Rossi's complaint about ob-
scurity in legislative statements of purpose; in his view, evaluators "need to bring to the attention of legislators and other
policy makers that current practices lead down the path to self-
destruction" (1979, p. 25).

Legislators who are quite sophisticated about their own
reasons for keeping "goals" lofty and nebulous unblushingly ask
program administrators to make goals explicit. As could be

anticipated, only conflict ensues. A 1974 amendment to the General Education Provision Act, directed at officials in the Department of Health, Education, and Welfare, (HEW), required evaluation reports. As the first step, officials were to "set forth goals and specific objectives in qualitative and quantitative terms for all programs concerned and relate those goals and objectives to the purposes of such program." (Comptroller General, 1977, p. 2). In due time, the General Accounting Office (GAO) found that no such procedure had been followed, and it wrote a highly critical report.

HEW tartly replied that legislation left program purposes unclear for the very purpose of getting the legislation passed. Nor, said HEW, was it prudent for an administrative agency to invent a list of the objectives that Congress might have had in mind. As the Office of Education, a unit within HEW, had been particularly criticized, the rebuttal went on: "The Office of Education proceeds at considerable peril in trying to further specify legislation. It has in fact been criticized on several occasions for going further than the Congress intended and of 'trying to legislate by means of regulation.' Furthermore, in many cases it has been the Congress' specific intention to avoid specifications of program objectives and to leave such judgments and decisions up to state and local officials" (statement reproduced in Comptroller General, 1977, p. 119). There follow quotations from House and Senate documents on just this unwillingness to have federally set goals.

*Mixed Motives.* Central figures in a context of accommodation usually exhibit a peculiar mixture of postures or motives. First, a political figure wants to show her serious intent to produce results. What better way than to come out strongly for "accountability"?

Second, discords are to be held to a minimum. But a directive that seems to impose standards on program staffs invites contention. The issues are multiple—"local control," "disguised speedup," "arbitrary emphasis on what is most measurable," "infringement of professional judgment," and so on. Hence no experienced administrator or legislator—save in a context of command—tries to set operational goals unless she is prepared to invest much energy in negotiating goal statements (and deliberately blurring them in the process).

Third, she must not be trapped between constituencies. In education, there is an obvious tension regarding proper standards for a high school certificate. Employers want a diploma to guarantee a comparatively high level of literacy and computation and spelling ability. But minority groups, committed as they are to the development of skills of their young people, are concerned for the future of the youngsters who do not earn a diploma and, hence, a meal ticket. They must press for lower certifying standards when their members pay the price for a shortfall in outcomes.

Negotiation over every goal that might be set would exact an unacceptable toll in energy and patience. And it defeats everyone's purposes to pretend that the goals negotiated cover all the outcomes that matter. In our view, the issue is what variables to measure—a main topic of Chapter Four. Agreement on that is not nearly so hard to attain as agreement on the *levels* a program or unit must attain if it is not to be branded a failure.

Deutscher (1976) hit it on the head when he advised evaluation planners to avoid "the goal trap." "Goals" seem to be as indispensable to political theatre as, on the puppet stage, are the air bladders with which the policeman belabors Punch. In both settings there are audiences who must not be disappointed, but sound and fury is beside the point for serious inquiry. Worse, there is some truth in Scriven's (1978b) charge that goal-based evaluation is "massively biased toward the management point of view." At best, such evaluation covers only a fraction of what should count in decisions.

Robert Weiss and Martin Rein (1969) pointed out, in what has become a classic paper, that the major initiatives of the 1960s were programs with broad aims: compensatory education, community mental health, Model Cities, and so on. Each initiative sought to ameliorate a distressing condition that had diverse origins and uncertain causes. Some of the desired outcomes, such as increased employment, were highly tangible. But others that were equally genuine and perhaps more fundamental to the social order could not be "defined operationally" without loss in translation—reducing alienation and anomie, for example.

We would go further. All social programs have broad aims, even supposedly targeted programs. Any "narrow-aim" program is potentially broad in its effects. It must have the unstated goal of not making other matters worse; it must not interfere with accepted policies or lower the quality of life. An appropriate example comes from attempts to reduce the importation of marijuana from Mexico. The federal intervention beginning in 1977 had this readily perceived and single-minded goal. But *not* threatening the health of Americans is an unvoiced aim of any program, and the spraying of paraquat on Mexican fields proved damaging to those who smoked the sprayed weed. Moreover, the spraying threatened the Mexican environment. The broader aims were not created by events; they were only highlighted by events.

## Accountability: Managerial and Political Uses

"Accountability" is a battle cry in today's politics, and it is one of the slogans most used in arguing for more and better evaluation. Left undefined, and with its consequences for the system unexamined, accountability is perceived as good. Who could oppose it? Dare anyone bearing responsibility say that she should be left "unaccountable"? But we are uneasy about the close association of evaluation with accountability. In many of its usages the word becomes an incantation, and one that can cast a malign spell. We will therefore be at pains to distinguish between appropriate and questionable demands for accounting. In this section we discuss primarily established programs, though a few young programs are also used as examples.

Accountability has a legitimate and historic role. The chief complaint of the American colonists against George III and his ministers was that they were not accountable, and the deliberations of the Constitutional Convention were much concerned with giving officials sufficient power to function without surrendering to them the sovereignty of the people. An official who has been given stewardship (whether in private enterprise or in government) is expected to take responsibility for what subordinates do. To ward off possible criticism, she requires reports from subordinates, and those who made her the steward retain the right to require reports from her. A steward, in the literal sense of that word, keeps accounts of property handled, and these are open to inspection. In social programs the public is concerned with services rendered as well as with property handled. But it is only in the context of command that an official has true control over subordinates and so can reasonably be expected to take responsibility.

If an official has been given control over certain activities, if she has the power to impose penalties on those who deviate from the instructions she gives, if the activities are of such a character that deviations from the instructions can be detected, and if the costs of monitoring are not too great—then indeed the manager can *manage*. And it is then fair to ask whether the manager was diligent and honest, used good judgment, and required subordinates to do as expected.

It will be recalled that the U.S. Forest Service met the conditions for command by making instructions definite (to the extent that acts could be specified in advance) and by reviewing most of the judgments of the ranger regarding specific local applications. The focus of attention was consistently on compliance and judgment, not on results. Thus, if a certain forest were severely damaged by an infestation of insects, the results would be a source of distress. But the Forest Service would not automatically call the results a "failure" of the ranger. The ranger would be blamed only if a study indicated that the ranger could probably have reduced the damage by applying available knowledge within the rules. The system itself failed if, in retrospect, it is seen that a different set of rules would have made better use of available knowledge. If the knowledge at hand was insufficient to stop the damage, the devastation was not a failure of stewardship.

A steward is responsible for acting as well as she can; it is not reasonable to demand that she produce good results unless the situation is actually controllable. In applying technology, much is under control. Standard ways of coping with troubles have been devised. The operatives can reasonably be expected to meet a high standard. Appropriate quality control should detect troubles promptly, and the approved technological remedy should be applied. The manager of a public water system is responsible for the quality of the water insofar as the technology for keeping the water free from contamination applies to the present conditions.

In contrast, the results from the usual social service cannot be regarded as a test of the manager's or practitioner's diligence and skill. A marriage-counseling service may aspire to hold the number of separations among its clients to a minimum, but the service is only one of many influences that determine whether a couple separates. The separation index is important information, but it would be unjust to blame the counseling service for a high incidence of separations.

A shortfall in results should be an occasion for an explanatory investigation—an investigation that might sometimes warrant assignment of blame to individuals or service units. In the absence of that explanatory study, the only reports that justify blame are reports of procedural negligence. We stress this because evaluation centered on accountability often damages the institutions trying to serve clients.

Accounts are, first of all, a record of actions taken. They are an instrument for verifying that system operations occurred as planned and for making changes if (1) operations violated directives or (2) operations consistent with the directives produced recurring bad results. A manager in command can know what facts about operations are relevant and should be able to obtain them. These procedures, when used to enforce compliance with an injunction, constitute proper personnel evaluation. Evaluation becomes improper when individuals are condemned for a shortfall over which they could not have full control. All too often, assignment of blame to individuals becomes the prime use of the accounts, while system improvement is forgotten.

Let us illustrate. Robert Bolt's play *State of Revolution* is set in the Russia of 1917–1924. The following scene occurs at a time when the Soviet regime under Lenin is embroiled in civil war. On stage are the robotlike head of the Cheka, Felix Dzerzhinsky, and his Revolutionary comrade Anatol Lunacharsky, the humane commissar for education (Bolt, 1977, p. 74–75):

Dzerzhinsky:    Comrade Lunacharsky, certain serious short-
                comings in your work have been drawn to the
                attention of the Cheka. . . . In January 1920
                your Commissariat indented for nine million
                pairs of children's shoes. This figure was unreal-
                istic but—

Lunacharsky:    It was not unrealistic. It was minimal.

Dzerzhinsky:    It was judged to be unrealistic by the Politburo
                of the Party. Which did however authorize you
                to obtain five hundred and fifty thousand pairs.
                But by January 1921 you had secured less than
                half that number. Why?

Lunacharsky:    What?

Dzerzhinsky:    You failed in your assignment, Comrade. Why?

Lunacharsky:    I failed, my dear Edmundovich, because those
                few remaining factories which are producing
                shoes are not producing children's shoes—but
                boots for the Red Army! . . . You have a nice
                pair of boots yourself I noticed.

Dzerzhinsky:    I need them. Someone in your Commissariat
                seems to have his feet up.

Lunacharsky:    Do you mean myself?

Dzerzhinsky:    I don't yet know the culprit.

Lunacharsky:    "Culprit"?

Dzerzhinsky:    When there is a failure there is either negligence
                or sabotage.

Lunacharsky:    What utter and disgusting rubbish. . . . There
                are no culprits in my Commissariat, and no one
                will be punished.

Dzerzhinsky:    You are satisfied by failure?

Lunacharsky:    I am satisfied by effort!

Dzerzhinsky:    By insufficient effort.

Lunacharsky:    By maximum effort!

Dzerzhinsky:    If your people are making a maximum effort,
                your people are incompetent and you are the
                culprit.

Lunacharsky:    They are people most of whom it is a privilege
                to work with; most of them are working four-

                              teen hours a day—in conditions that defy de-
                              scription.
Dzerzhinsky:     And yet they failed.
Lunacharsky:    And yet they failed. Precisely.
Dzerzhinsky:     The failure should have been reported.


Few social programs meet the conditions under which a manager can exercise command, and there is not much hope that stubborn problems with multiple causes will be greatly reduced by any one effort (Aaron, 1978). Yet accountability is most demanded of those public servants condemned to farm rocky ground, under capricious weather conditions. Why should this be?

We repeat, first, what was said about the demand for explicit goals: it is a righteous pose. The political leader who loudly calls for evidence that every dollar appropriated is well spent has merely said what voters want to hear. Accountability requirements are, moreover, a power play. They are a device for "making commands stick" even when one does not have full authority. In the tug-of-war that leads to accommodation, each participant exerts any available force to make the accommodation come out more nearly to her satisfaction. An accommodation, written into the ground rules for a program, invariably leaves latitude for local operators of community groups to modify the program through noncompliance or through shifting the balance of activities. That is entirely natural when effective hierarchical command has not been agreed on. Accountability mechanisms are restraints placed on lower-level participants by higher-ups. Command without the consent of the commanded makes gamesmanship the order of the day, as long as the commanded are too weak for outright rebellion (see Chapter Three).

The use of accountability for control—and its untoward effects—is nowhere better illustrated than in the scheme of "payment by results." The idea recurs in many forms, the most distinctive example being the attempt of the British Parliament to spend tax money efficiently on education. In the years around 1860, there was no British "school system." Children and youths received both general education and vocational training from independent schools. Where these schools existed, they had been set up by a lone proprietor, a church, or perhaps a charitable foundation. Poor children might receive no schooling at all, and the quality of what they did get was questionable. Better education was wanted as a foundation for the kind of technical education that would enable British goods to compete in world markets and also as a means of creating informed citizens.

The Newcastle Commission was asked in 1858 to propose plans for extending "sound and cheap" elementary education to all. Its 1861 report favored national grants to support service to the poor. The commission had been told that existing education was quite unequal. The brighter, more responsive pupils who could be counted on to remain past the age of eleven were the focus of the schoolmaster's attention. The remainder were allowed to absent themselves and to fritter away their time when present. With the twin aims of supporting only the effective schools and of equalizing educational opportunity within those schools, Parliament turned to per capita payments (Simon, 1970).

A test was given at each of six grade levels in reading, writing, and ciphering. The schoolmaster received two shillings and eightpence for each pupil who passed the test in one of these subjects. Whereas the Newcastle Commission had recommended this plan as a supplement to unconditional payments, Parliament made it the sole basis for distributing funds. (Duke, 1965, sees the action as the result of an accommodative process and as perhaps the only achievable action in a matter where church versus state, local versus central control, and service versus economy were all at issue.)

The consequences were not what anyone had intended. To be sure, the system was comparatively cheap, and the basic subjects were better taught. But schools drawing scholars of low aptitude were severely penalized (though they were most likely the ones serving poor neighborhoods). Teachers now neglected the school subjects omitted from the payment formula. And, in their effort to cram the weaklings to the point of payoff, they neglected the able students. Simon (1970) has spoken of the scheme as the origin of the system of segregation by ability ("streaming") that has distressed British social critics to this day.

Complaints about the schools under the acountability system were vehement. Matthew Arnold (1867) wrote of "a deadness, a slackness, and a discouragement . . . a lack of intelligent life." Because the reading examination was to consist of selections from a named book, all class time went into reading and rereading that book. The test score on which everything depended was an illusion, said Arnold, because it showed that children had memorized, not whether they could read. Complaints were widespread, but Parliament's only accommodation was to extend the system to additional subjects. It took thirty years for a weight of opinion to amass that was sufficient to kill the system itself.

Accountability schemes can indeed force those who deliver service into line. This makes sense when there is a single aim or full agreement on priorities—the condition for command. When there are multiple outcomes, however, dramatizing any one standard of judgment simply adds to the priority of whatever outcomes that standard takes into account. Whatever outcomes do not enter the scoring formula tend to be neglected. This would not be a ground for complaint if there were community-wide agreement that these outcomes should be neglected, but with broad-aim programs that is never the case (see Chapter Three).

What distinguishes "accountability-for-results" from other forms of outcome evaluation is that it compacts the data into a simple judgment of probity. The provider of services acted either correctly or irresponsibly. To describe a complex end state, some of whose aspects are measured and some unmeasured, in a single payoff formula imposes on everyone the priorities of whoever created the formula. Only in those instances when the formula is a thoughtful accommodation, worked out by a PSC conscious of what the formula omits and thereby proposes to sacrifice, does government by formula have any likelihood of faithfully representing the accommodative process.

"A demand for accountability is a sign of pathology in the social system," March (1972) has commented. Such a demand, each time it has occurred during the past century, has been a sign of discontent: those in charge of services are believed to be inefficient, insufficiently honest, or not self-critical. The demand may be colored by an idealist's distrust of elected officials and the party system, by a technocrat's distrust of ordinary human judgment, or by a businessman's skepticism about governmental efficiency. The antagonism is nowhere more clearly expressed than in Butler's previously quoted speech to Chicago businessmen about schools: "[I]f we can secure appointment [of those taking actions] by a responsible and conspicuous officer, we can hold him if we choose severely responsible, and commend him for the good and punish him for the bad. The advantage is that we then have somebody whom we can get at. The great difficulty is that we don't get at them often enough" (1906, p. 42).

Evaluation serves a democratic ideal insofar as it (1) improves performance so that there is no warrant for distrust and (2) dispels unwarranted distrust. Thus evaluation can on occasion cure pathology. Accountability was a prominent theme in the 1977 symposium of evaluators and federal officials that was cited earlier. Representative remarks were made by Donald Elisburg (Chelimsky, 1977a, p. 68) from the congressional staff when he spoke of congressional action to have money set aside for evaluations and to require impact assessments: "Both forms of congressionally mandated evaluation have the same purpose: to delegate to the executive branch a duty to determine what, if anything, happened as a consequence of the policies or programs tagged for special review."

Agency managers wanted help in their managerial tasks, and evaluators wanted to gain and communicate a better understanding of programs and problems. As Chelimsky (1977b, pp. 7–8) summarized the discussion:

> Not one of the agency representatives participating in the symposium espoused this perspective [Elisburg's], however; neither did the great majority of program planners, researchers, and practitioners (federal, state, or local) who were present. Whatever they may think about the importance of managerial accountability, agency speakers pointed out that program managers feel threatened by eval-

uations (and tend to fight both their implementation and the use of their findings) insofar as they
think that negative assessments of their programs
can be made public. These speakers, therefore,
considered it infeasible to perform accountability
evaluations in the face of opposition by program
managers and thought it unlikely that the findings
of such evaluations could ever be used. . . .

Agency representatives repeated over and
over at the symposium that program managers fear
for their programs and that they can be expected
to fight effectively against evaluation in the service
of accountability. A Department of Commerce representative had, in fact, discussed precisely this
situation in a presymposium interview: "OMB is
interested in having evaluations conducted *for
them* and in getting the results of those evaluations.
Why does OMB want the results of those evaluations? Because they are under pressure to reallo-
cate resources; they need excuses, reasons, to remove funds from the federal budget. So there's
really only one way to go and that is to lose by
providing OMB with information appropriate to
allow them to justify a reduction in funds for
a program."

(The extract is based on an interview with Thomas E. Kelly
and Robert A. Knisely that appears in Chelimsky, 1977a, pp.
170–178.)

## Do Ineffective Programs Die?

The *threat* of an adverse reaction at budget time disturbs
the sleep of program managers, even though the outcome is almost never worse than a standstill appropriation. But what impresses us is the slight attention paid to program outcomes in
decisions about program renewal.

A clear example came up in the 1977 hearings on the title
of ESEA providing for bilingual education. (See Subcommittee
on Elementary, Secondary, and Vocational Education, 1977a,

pp. 141–145.) A major evaluative study had drawn several conclusions: (1) Only in mathematics was achievement of students
in the program measurably better than that of similar students
outside the program, and there was a hint of worse achievement
in some subjects. (2) The program was intended to serve children
having better command of Spanish (or some other language)
than English, but in fact a large fraction of the children assigned
to bilingual instruction had better command of English than
Spanish. (3) The program was intended as transitional, as a stop-
gap until the child's English was sufficiently developed to enable him or her to participate in the regular English-language instruction. In actuality, many sites operated a program designed
to maintain Hispanic identity and language, with no effort to
return the child to the mainstream as Congress had instructed.

The criticisms of the program received attention if only
because a *Washington Post* writer prepared a major story on the
program just as hearings on the renewal legislation began. The
test results were included—but only in the twelfth paragraph of
the story, subordinated to the reporter's quotations from partisans and specialists he had talked to (Subcommittee on Elementary, Secondary, and Vocational Education, 1977a, pp. 649–
652). The outcome evaluation, which had been sponsored and
endorsed by the evaluation section of the Office of Education
(OE), was formally attacked at the hearings in a critique solic-
ited by the section of OE responsible for the program.

What was the impact of the findings and the challenge?
The congressional audience expressed great distress that the program, as realized, defied their intent to promote assimilation of
Hispanic and other minority children into the mainstream. At
the time of this writing, the executive branch is moving on several fronts to enforce the will of Congress. It expects to impose
testing requirements to make certain in the future that the children are better suited to be taught in the alternative language
than in English, both at the time they enter that instruction and
during each successive year they remain in the program.

From the outset of the fieldwork, it was apparent that
the program was far out of line with the intent of Congress and
might be precisely the wrong way to teach many of the children
assigned to it. One might well ask why the administrative agency

did not abandon outcome evaluation until a program was in place that reflected the plan? The answer seems to be that, after Congress mandates an evaluation, administrative agencies rarely dare ask it to reconsider. And why had the administrative agency not acted earlier to pull program operations back into line? Almost certainly, the explanation is the usual one for administrative inaction: "Don't start an argument." The so-called maintenance programs were popular with political leaders trying to capture ethnic constituencies. Moreover, enrolling the largest possible number of children in the program ensured a maximum number of positions (for example, as teaching aides) for fluent speakers of the minority language. These political aims far outweighed instructional aims. When Congress finally got the word and made its ire felt, action followed.

The evidence on the outcomes of the instruction, as distinct from the assignment policies, was passed over quickly. The legislators seemed courteously bored by the report on test scores and the dispute about their meaning. The members of Congress attending the hearings did not cross-examine the evaluator and his adversary to determine how weighty the criticisms were. Nor did anyone seem to care that the evaluator's final report, appearing a year later, left unresolved those factual disputes that the data might have clarified. Congress knew very well that it wished to continue the program. The program was strongly backed by only a minor fraction of the electorate but those voters constituted a major fraction in certain electoral districts. Also, the program had no organized political opposition.

Evaluators are not encouraged to ask the most trenchant questions about entrenched programs. Some traditional policies are nearly untouchable. We spoke earlier of the Forest Service as an exemplar of firm command, where accountability for stewardship can be enforced through close observation of practices and results. Nienaber and Wildavsky (1973, pp. 144–159) have pointed out, however, that the large questions about Forest Service policy have been and will continue to be decided by political accommodation. Consequently, disturbing questions are not faced. To open public lands for livestock grazing, for example, subsidizes ranchers; the fees they pay are small in proportion to their gains. The costs to the public are huge, in deterioration of the land and watershed, not to mention in direct costs for fences, reseeding, and so on. A 1969 memorandum by Robert Marty cited some of the pertinent facts and noted that appropriations are unlikely to increase sufficiently to offset the damage from overgrazing. Nor is the service able to turn aside the demands of the ranchers. Marty emphasized that this kind of dilemma could not be directly faced by the then-regnant (PPBS) control system.

After quoting Marty at length, Nienaber and Wildavsky (1973, p. 147) comment: "It is not surprising that program memoranda do not raise the basic question—should there be forage or range improvement programs at all?—because the relevant political men do not want to hear the answer. In order for evaluation to be worthwhile in this field, the initial steps would have to be taken by other political leaders. These men would have either to signify their willingness to abandon the programs or, more likely, to set out the terms within which they would be interested in analysis."

Within such a context of command, evaluators are free only to report on the execution of the policy handed down from the political community. To evaluate the policy would be far outside their commission. The policy could be overthrown, but only by a campaign sufficiently vigorous to put western members of Congress on the defensive and therefore ready to negotiate significant departures from the past practice. Once upon a time the climate of opinion enabled Gifford Pinchot and Theodore Roosevelt to take up arms in defense of the public lands; that was how the Forest Service began. The day may come when another leader can attack grazing policy with some hope of success. An established program is sometimes vulnerable to a single-issue campaign with daring leadership and an aroused constituency. It is not vulnerable to routine evaluation that perforce lets long-standing accommodations circumscribe the issues.

A time for budget trimming always comes. Do not measured outcomes count then? It is our impression that major reductions are almost always across the board, applicable to a whole agency rather than to specific programs in disfavor. Those who favor "sunset" laws would, if they could, overturn the habit of business-as-usual and initiate an equally serious review of every program in government. But it seems safe to predict that this drastic policy will not be enforced (Behn, 1977). Elimination of an established service and even of the bureau that operates it has been known to happen, but that is proof of a weak constituency.

Though not directly concerned with specific programs, Kaufman's *Are Government Organizations Immortal?* (1976) gives pertinent evidence. Kaufman set out to determine how many of the federal agencies that were alive in 1923 had disappeared in 1973. Of 175 agencies in the 1923 roster, only 27 had disappeared. Five of the 27 deaths were at the hand of a single new-broom secretary of agriculture, who came in with the first Republican administration in decades. Deaths of agencies did not imply deaths of programs; in most instances, functions were merged into those of an existing agency or a newly created structure. (Occasionally, a task deriving from the First World War was recognized to be finished, and then the program was terminated.) Formal appraisals of agency performance are never mentioned in Kaufman's review of the causes and instrumentalities of death. Ironically, however, the very first cadaver in his list is a reorganization inspired by Frederick Taylor that was intended to bring rationality and efficiency to the Department of Agriculture in the 1920s.

California's Proposition 13 of 1978 forced large cuts in school spending, but the specific cuts worked out by district officers are not being defended by cost-benefit criteria (Kirst, 1978). Counseling services, for example, are being cut. That is not because they are judged unhelpful to young people but because such services are at the margin. Instruction in reading has been the subject of vociferous public complaint, and this disaffection may even have contributed to the vote for reduction of taxes. But indications to date are that reading programs will be the last to suffer. They are at the core of the agreed-upon tasks of the school, and proposals to cut them would mobilize both teachers' unions and parents.

The position of officials who allocate budgets is awkward. Their mission is to accomplish what everyone else in government, and everyone in the public, stands ready to impede: reduction of expenditure. Every program has a clientele and a staff committed to maintaining it. Citizens who would like a service to be cut back or eliminated speak out, to be sure, but they always attack a service that benefits someone else. The operating personnel and clients of a program have no place on *their* agenda for budget cuts, and they are represented by bureaucrats and leaders of interest groups who know how to cultivate sentiment in Congress. A pluralistic and political community is only in rare instances dragged to the crossroads of a decision on termination (Behn, 1977).

Moreover, a program has ready defenses even when its measured outcomes appear to be unimpressive. Evaluation results are rarely clear cut. The defense can always say that the evaluator asked the wrong questions, collected inadequate data, or misinterpreted results. A multifaceted program is likely to have a favorable record in some respects even if the main hopes were not fulfilled, and its partisans can always advertise these successes—it is never too late to claim that the original priorities should be reversed.

It is true that the public, its representatives, and top policy makers become disenchanted with programs and institutions—the postal service and the military draft provide two recent instances. The former underwent no more than adjustments at the margin, whereas the latter was replaced by a radically different plan (the all-volunteer armed services). But in neither case did formal evaluation enter the picture. The public did not need formal evidence to arrive at a negative judgment in these instances, and it is hard to believe that positive evidence could have turned the tide of opinion. Those who are beginning to study the rare instances when a policy is reversed or a program terminated suggest that at least two factors are critical for a successful campaign: (1) a committed political leader who concentrates his fire on one target, and (2) a credible claim that the program does positive harm (Bardach, 1976; Behn, 1978). To charge that the program is ineffectual is not enough.

*Evaluative Challenges Appropriate to Established Programs.* Only two kinds of evaluation are likely to affect an established program. One is the study that helps a manager to retool.

The other is the development of an alternative program, so that those who lose faith in the old one have someplace to go.

American legislators who want evidence of program effectiveness are not out for the scalps of individuals; they are trying to hold up their end in a system of checks and balances. Their request for assurance that programs are paying off sounds to them like appropriate follow-through. But the request is perhaps primarily a symptom of the frustration inherent in the legislative role. Legislators are promised that a program will solve a social problem. They appropriate money, the money is spent, and the problem remains. A legislature can only authorize in broad language, leaving the program to be defined by regulations and operating decisions worked out at the numerous levels of the executive branch. When the results of an optimistic effort disappoint, the legislature is likely to think that the executive branch has failed.

It is understandable that a legislature would press a question about results: "We gave you all this money to spend. What have you to show for it?" The legislator will be well within her role if she erupts when told that she should not ask such a question because bureaucrats don't like it. Let us, then, look more closely: When is the question a fruitful one? When not?

The question about results could mean many things.

1. How much service was rendered? "How many shoes did you distribute? And how many in my district?"
2. How close did service and results come to the stated goals?
3. Has the underlying problem been relieved? By how much? This is needs assessment: "How many children still have frostbitten toes? Where are they located?"
4. Where in the chain of actions and reactions did results fall short of (or surpass) expectations? Any unexpected effects, good or bad? Under what circumstances were shortfalls common or uncommon?

Question number one is a significant question about stewardship. Moreover, since a positive answer to this question is politically useful, it is of interest to legislators. The agency head should be interested too, services being her stock in trade (Pedersen, 1977). Further, she should be able to assemble the facts at little cost. All in all, a fair question.

Question number two is a less suitable one; it reeks of readiness to find fault. Poor, dedicated Lunacharsky in Robert Bolt's play strained toward a goal no one could have reached. It is fair to ask whether a program is finding a worthwhile response or is reaching a significant fraction of those in need. It is fair to ask if a program is overstaffed, given the number of children for which it actually produces shoes. But these judgments can be made without reference to the stated goals and should not be distorted when that statement was unreasonably ambitious or unreasonably timid.

Question number three as stated does not make the mistake of confusing energetic delivery with relief given. Politically the question is realistic in not pressing for proof that the program *caused* whatever improvement occurred. A program associated with improvement has political merit no matter how flimsy the logical support for a causal claim. A positive answer to question number three—as to any of the others—has one important virtue. It gives legislators something to brag about to constituents. No *decision* can be based on a simple positive answer, however; more subtle analysis is needed to say whether the program will do further good if continued, and still more good if expanded. Program operators are nevertheless right in seeing question number three as a trap. Any unsatisfactory result can easily make the program staff the target of hostile criticism and punitive action, and by demoralizing them can make the service worse (Tyler and others, 1978, pp. 13-14). Criticism may be wholly unjust. Even when the program staff did all they could, other social forces or the nature of the problem may have prevented major progress.

Question number four is a *good* question. It starts with the understanding that shortfall is human yet leaves the door open for the pleasant surprise of success. By distinguishing between expectations and promises, it reduces the scope for blame. It invites a differentiated answer instead of leaving the program plan, delivery, and response of clients as unexamined elements within a closed black box. It recognizes the role of circumstances

Evaluation and the Shaping of Policy

149

external to the program. Therefore, it allows for the discussion of myriad alterations in the program rather than a choice between "thumbs up" and "off with someone's head." This question is especially suitable for broad-aim programs. It does not evade the concern with receiving value for money, but it points toward reinterpretations and options. It can modify assumptions about the delivery process or about the way clients respond to the service. It may suggest a change in goals. The attempt at understanding is based on the optimistic assumption that the program can be made to work. That ought to be consistent with the wishes of those who press for accountability *and* of those who believe in public services.

*Summative Evaluation and the Emerging Program.* The chief justification offered for stand-alone summative evaluations is that they permit a sound decision about adoption of a proposed program or a sound choice among competing proposals. In principle, such judgments might depend primarily upon evidence of program benefits and costs. Judgments take rather different forms at different stages of maturity of a proposal, and it is instructive to consider these differences.

To begin with, one must take into account the strong motivation to adopt some program to cope with a generally recognized problem. For all that is said about the excessive intrusion of government into all aspects of life, citizens do want more and more services, including regulatory services, if the price in tax money, costs of merchandise, and sacrifice of freedom is not too great. Consequently, the dice are loaded in favor of "go" decisions as soon as anyone has a proposal to offer. The limited elasticity of the overall budget is the chief deterrent.

The developer who embarks on a breadboard attempt at reform is strongly motivated to come up with a workable program. Negative results do not signal "no go." The signal is rather that she should overcome some faults of theory or operation. A decision to drop the effort comes only with despair; at the breadboard stage, "Back to the drawing board" is a "Go!" decision.

The eager developer may not wait for ironclad results before she begins to promote the program. Indeed, she may push for widespread adoption of the scheme prior to any hard test.

The untried development, however, is not likely to win much political backing. In a field such as medicine, with its tough-minded tradition in regard to the acceptance of new therapies, it is most unlikely that a proposed new therapy will move beyond the breadboard stage until there are suggestive (though no doubt limited) positive findings. Where there is no strong tradition of product testing, notably in the sale of textbooks and other curriculum materials, a developer can probably find a substantial market for materials that had no breadboard trial. However, even educational buyers are becoming more and more sophisticated, and they increasingly ask for evidence of effectiveness when a large instructional package is to be purchased. Those buyers will be far more interested in the results of a prototype trial than in breadboard findings.

At the superrealization stage almost nothing but the outcomes is of interest. In this we concur with Suchman (1970) and Weiss (1974a). A careful trial under optimum conditions is set up only when a select audience has to be convinced that the proposal is based on sound principles. The primary audience for a superrealization is either informed professionals or a policy staff long ago taught that the most enthusiastic proposal may fail under impartial test. The superrealization is almost always a quiet trial, and the use of the results is comparatively free from political pressure. If benefits are marginal or lacking or there are worrisome side effects, forward movement of the proposal is normally blocked. (Sometimes, mixed results lead to a positive but modified action. For example, when average outcomes of a new surgical technique are unsatisfactory, it may move into further trials with a restricted category of patients.)

Superrealizations are not often set up for social programs, because impatient policy makers are quick to put an appealing idea into practice on a substantial scale. They may, however, see the virtue of testing the prototype. Therefore, those who advocate superrealization trials of social interventions generally suggest imbedding them within the prototype, just to prevent a basically good idea from being discarded when the prototype test gives a "no-go" signal. That, however, seems to exaggerate the probability that poor results from a prototype test will put an end to a proposal.

Setting up a prototype trial is ostensibly an indication that policy makers intend to be guided by results. But while they obviously will find a realistic estimate of costs of a new service helpful, it is not at all clear that the magnitude of benefits will have a large influence on decisions. For some innovations the prototype is seen by all concerned as a last shakedown before a centralized decision to adopt is consummated. Sometimes, indeed, the "go" decision has been made official, and the trial takes place in the first sites to commence operations. Under these circumstances the test of the prototype is almost as restricted in influence as the test of an established program. Nevertheless, fewer aspects of the program are frozen: "How?" and "How much?" are still live questions.

In a context of accommodation, the evaluator cannot expect a "go/no-go" decision to turn on his assessment of outcomes, whereas information on outcomes is influential in a context of command—a decision all but made can still be unmade. And in the market situation where adoption decisions are made by local institutions or by individuals, prototype findings, widely disseminated, can strongly affect the offering's fate.

# 3

■■■■■■■■■■■■■■■■

# What Is Learned as
# Evaluation Proceeds

■■■■■■■■■■■■■■■■

An evaluation ought to inform and improve the operations of the social system. That is the standard suggested at the end of Chapter One as a basis for identifying when evaluations are not as useful as they should be and for deriving suggestions for better practice. The policy-shaping community (PSC) works in a complex manner as it takes up new proposals, modifies its institutions, and regulates the character and quality of services. Chapter Two showed that social agendas are always changing and that the political contexts in which issues are discussed are also in flux. The evaluator has many opportunities to help the community in its thinking, but these come at unpredictable times and through relationships both formal and informal.

This chapter describes how evaluations could affect the system. The evaluator will be portrayed as far more than an investigator who simply brings technical skills to a circumscribed problem, communicates a traditional scientific report, and leaves the scene. Our evaluator plays an active role in political events, preferably as a multipartisan who serves the general interest.

Having discussed evaluation and the political system abstractly in the two preceding chapters, we now turn to the evaluator's personal activities. The evaluator, we think, should engage others in a collaborative attempt to understand social events and take appropriate action. Influence comes from engagement, not detachment. According to studies of evaluation use (Weiss, 1977; Anderson and Ball, 1978; Alkin, Daillah, and White, 1979), nothing makes a greater difference than the personal factor. What counts is the interest of one or more officials in learning from the evaluation and the interest of the evaluator in getting attention for what he knows. Patton and others offer this summary (1977, p. 158): "The specifics vary from study to study but the pattern is markedly clear: Where the personal factor emerges, where some person takes direct personal responsibility for getting the information to the right people, evaluations have an impact. Where the personal factor is absent, there is a marked absence of impact. Utilization is not simply determined by some configuration of abstract factors; it is determined in large part by real, live, caring human beings."

## How Evaluation Can Influence the System

After an evaluation has been completed and used (or ignored), a historian can make a reasonable judgment as to whether the system is better off than it would have been without the evaluation. The planner who takes proper advantage of history should be able to judge the probable utility of a proposed evaluation. But the judgment will go awry if utility is defined narrowly.

*What It Means to Help the System.* The "system" to which the evaluative standard refers is broad; it consists of systems within systems. A society or the polity always falls far short of the dictionary specification of an "organized and integrated whole." Yet the polity is a whole in that an evaluation can affect not only the program evaluated but also the respect that citizens have for all officials. Failures in a limited sector can destroy trust in the machinery itself, and it then becomes impossible to govern.

The whole society is a system; so are second-level systems that cope with particular problems or services. The "system" that builds highways in the United States includes governmental offices, engineering firms, and construction companies. Better functioning of that system might mean no more than highways that are safer, less expensive, and less damaging to the physical ecology. But an eye surveying the larger system would also range over demographic effects and over the fairness of decisions that locate highways. Even a small activity would be judged from a lofty vantage point. Is the cumulative effect of evaluations such as this one good for the larger system?

Our standard refers to the effect of the evaluation on the polity in the large and in the small. To consider a polity as "an iland entire unto itself" is a convenient fiction, no more. We count local effects of the evaluation and those distant in time and space, those deriving from communications of the evaluator and those deriving from the very decision to evaluate. Social arrangements work well to the degree that the political ideals on which the governing machinery is based are achieved. In the intended scheme of American governance, citizens formulate and express their interests. By orderly processes they negotiate priorities. Citizens have confidence in the integrity of their institutions, and institutions merit that confidence. Restrictions placed on liberty are justified by the end result: there is a higher quality of life, more fairly distributed. Evaluation can work toward that end, or it can work against it.

Some writers, notably Scriven (1967), call upon the evaluator to *value* the program, that is, to tell the public whether the program is good enough. Our position is more in line with that of an international group of evaluators who met in England in 1972 (Macdonald and Parlett, 1973): "It is the reader's task [in digesting the report] to 'evaluate' in the literal sense of the concept, and the evaluator's task to provide the reader with information which he may wish to take into account in forming his judgment." Although the Cambridge group, having a populist orientation, saw the rank and file as the evaluator's chief audience, the identical statement could have been made by Pedersen in his analysis of the evaluator's service to a policy-making officer (see Chapter Two). Of course the evaluator draws attention to consequences someone cares strongly about, but affairs are rarely so simple that every reader would place the same valuation on the facts or favor the same action.

Decision making is proceeding well if participants reach decisions with their eyes open. Something is wrong when they support choices they would reject if they saw the likely consequences clearly. Not knowing what each program will accomplish, a citizen may support an attractive option that has little genuine promise. This is wasteful. Worse, it permits the illusion that, because "something has been done," the problem has been vanquished. Those who settle for a glittering promise lose their momentum and their influence. In W. W. Jacobs' story "The Monkey's Paw," a humble man and woman were granted three wishes—with a curse that after each wish was fulfilled they would be sorry they had made it. Regret, less dramatic but ever present, is the lot of participants in a democratic process who throw their weight behind proposals whose workings they misconceive. It is too much to ask for twenty-twenty foresight, but it is the role of evaluation to supply spectacles for every nose, to bring as much into focus as possible.

Some writers suggest a standard more limited than ours: Did the evaluation lead to sounder decisions about the program? The historian can ask that question, second-guessing the accommodation process. A soundly conducted and well-communicated evaluation is not to be downgraded, however, when the program to which it gave a high cost-benefit rating is not the one adopted. Even if reports from a trial are distinctly favorable, that finding rarely should be decisive. Almost always, uncertainties remain. Causal interpretations of the facts can reasonably vary, and so can value judgments. It is the evaluator's task to illuminate, not to dictate, the decision.

The same is to be said when the reports from the trial are unfavorable. When an elected official continues an ineffectual program dear to an electoral bloc, the evaluation played its role if it simply reduced expectations to a reasonable level. The official could not be expected to lay her personal future and her entire policy agenda on the line by killing the program unless it had distressing effects. Nevertheless, the evaluation did aid her in coming to a decision. Thanks to it, the official knew what she was settling for.

Under some circumstances, it makes excellent sense to keep in place a program that has no demonstrable benefits. Setting up a social program has symbolic significance; it implies that the system intends to cope with whatever troubles a certain clientele. Canceling the program seems to abandon the commitment unless a successor program is put in place.

Decisions get made with or without evaluation. Not uncommonly, support for a proposal coalesces and picks up momentum before the facts are in. Not uncommonly, the massive inertia of existing institutions stops an innovation dead. Any one evaluation is simply unlucky if its information goes for nought for such a reason. Those who launch evaluations have inadequate political insight, however, if *most* of their evaluations never come to influence social thought. Whoever plans evaluations adopts criteria for deciding when to evaluate and when not, and adopts a style of going about the work. That strategy ought to be judged not by any one instance but by its average success over many applications.

The cumulative and indirect contributions of an evaluation can be as important as the effects on the program studied. The Hawthorne investigation mentioned in Chapter One provides a sufficient example. It was intended to tell Western Electric's management how to regulate the physical conditions of work to achieve efficiency. The experiments proved this quest for a solution to be a forlorn hope. By bringing the social conditions of work prominently to attention, however, the report broadened the concept of working conditions and contributed to the evaluation of new arrangements. A program evaluation that gets attention, whether or not it affects the immediate fate of the program studied, is likely to modify the prevailing view of social purposes, of attainable goals, and of appropriate means of action (Rein, 1976, pp. 111–124; Weiss, 1977; Lindblom and Cohen, 1979).

*Accommodation, not Revolution.* Evaluation at its best assists in a smooth accommodation of social activities and structures to changing conditions and ideals. A system that functions better is less likely to be overthrown. A continuing, successful evaluation mechanism thus acts to preserve the system. Assisting in gradual accommodation, evaluation is both conservative and committed to change (see Aaron, 1978, p. 158). Evaluation is undertaken so that society will improve its services or their costs will become less burdensome. This is the stance of a friendly critic, not of a person who sees the system as either beyond reproach or beyond repair. Undertaking to serve the polity, the evaluator sets out to make a difference in social operations if he can. If convinced that a program is rigid and unresponsive to evidence, he is wasting his time in evaluating; only aggressive political action is likely to alter it. If convinced that the system as a whole is unresponsive, he must either become a radical or accept impotence.

The evaluator is like the lawyer and journalist in accepting the premises of the system as the basis for his work. Each does professional work in the faith that (if he or she is lucid) the system will use the message legitimately. The evaluator's alliance with the established order does not remove him from the historic "adversary role of American intellectuals" (Lipset and Dobson, 1972, p. 138). Evaluators accept principles but not things as they are. An evaluation is worth the effort for one of two reasons: (1) there is considerable likelihood that faults in the program and perhaps in its underlying conception will show up; or (2) documentation of the benefits of a program that works will encourage its wider application. If neither of these results is to be expected, the direct products of the evaluation will not repay the investment. The evaluator expects to stimulate change. Some observers lament that refined and technical social research can produce "only meliorist criticism" of institutions and programs. But to be meliorist is the evaluator's calling. Rarely or never will evaluative work bring a 180-degree turn in social thought.

Evaluation assists in piecemeal adaptations; perhaps it does tend to keep the *status* very nearly *quo*. Social research in Holland that had been intended to affect social decisions was surveyed by van de Vall (1975). His evidence supports the view of evaluation as handmaiden to gradualism. Many of the studies had no detectable consequence. The ones that were influential accelerated a change that already was winning acceptance. They characteristically disposed of a contention opponents were making about some minor uncertainty, showed how to overcome a practical difficulty, or gave proponents a talking point—worthwhile, but modest, contributions.

It is puzzling that van de Vall saw evaluations as providing only positive feedback since evaluations in America have had braking effects as well. An unfavorable report rarely deals a deathblow to a program, but it reduces the chances for expansion. Aaron (1978, p. 33) speaks of the summative evaluation's "profoundly conservative tendency," its "powerful biases toward showing no effects." Rivlin (1974) uses even stronger language. The so-called black box experiment, which pits a grand strategy (vouchers, say, or performance contracting) against control conditions, is very effective when the main purpose is to knock down a new proposal. The results, if not negative, are likely to differ from site to site, and this uncertainty is bound to suggest that intervention be delayed until matters become clear. "Only if one feels passionately that a problem is so urgent that some answer, even though it may be wrong, is better than none, will this effect be overcome." So says Aaron (1978, p. 158).

Coleman (1978, p. 79) draws a different moral from much the same kind of observation. "[R]esearch results, when they show defects of policy, legitimate opposition to the policy. Policy makers have already the legitimation provided by political authority, and have little need for additional legitimation. But opponents, lacking the power of political authority, gain the legitimacy of . . . 'scientific evidence,' . . . an important weapon in the political struggle." Evaluations in recent times have been more useful to outsiders than to insiders, Coleman believes. Thus in his view evaluation strengthens pluralism and distributes power.

Though we agree with Coleman, the fact remains that the revolutionary, formative, accommodative mode makes for slow redistribution of privileges. To the extent that gradual reform appeases citizens with rising expectations, it reduces their interest in radical proposals. The radical has a valid point in saying that the attempt to make the established order function slightly better postpones overthrow of the system. Evaluation can have no place in the radical's scheme of things. Karl Marx put it succinctly: "Anyone who makes plans for after the Revolution is a counterrevolutionary." Iconoclasts and revolutionaries have to deal in inspiration and passion; harsh caricatures of current operations and visionary claims for the world they will build support their message.

*Noninformational Effects.* Throughout this book we emphasize the contribution of evaluation to understanding. But evaluation, which is one part of the social machinery, affects how other parts of the machinery mesh or clash and thus affects the ultimate contribution of the system to the general welfare. The following story from *Newsweek* ("Support Your Local Detector," 1978) will help make the point: "The manufacturer of a controversial device for eluding police radar traps is about to launch an unusual advertising campaign—in a police magazine. Dale T. Smith, head of an Ohio firm that makes the Fuzzbuster radar detector, has placed a series of ads in *Law and Order* magazine in an effort to get policemen to soften their hostility toward the detectors and stop confiscating them. The ads will take the form of columns by Smith in which he argues that the purpose of police radar is to make drivers slow down, and that a driver with a radar detector does just that when the device is triggered."

The police officers hostile to Fuzzbusters have perceived their task as holding drivers accountable—the more speeders they catch, the more service they have rendered. A perhaps more sophisticated view is that police are to promote safety— a function they fulfill very well by proceeding down the highway at a safe speed in an easily recognized patrol car. In other words, the visibility of the evaluation mechanism changes behavior. And in principle, then, Smith's device combined with monitoring by the police helps "make command stick," since the speed limit is an accommodation grudgingly accepted.

Evaluation has numerous noninformational effects (Rein and White, 1977; Knorr, 1977). Sometimes an evaluation or monitoring procedure has only a ritual or symbolic purpose. To use these labels scornfully is to misperceive the utility of symbolic acts. Rituals and symbols remind participants of agreements and communal understandings. They reinforce the commitment to reach a further accommodation even as antagonists struggle over its details.

The very existence of evaluation as part of a system makes a difference. Van de Vall (1975) makes the perceptive remark that public services tend to be monopolies and do not receive the feedback from their customers that is normal in open markets. He continues: "The chasm between needs and policies, which results from this dearth of feedback, explains the recent proliferation of such 'substitute' feedback mechanisms as action groups, rent strikes, protest demonstrations, ombudsmen, classified data disclosures, ghetto riots, and student unrest" (p. 16). Program evaluation (along with needs assessment and other kinds of studies) provides feedback. To the extent that the existence of evaluation convinces citizens that the system intends to be responsive, the disruptive substitute mechanisms are unlikely to be used. The U.S. Forest Service gains such a benefit by making it easy for the rancher to complain when a request for a grazing permit is denied. The fact that the rancher's grievance is promptly reviewed prevents irritations from festering and, in time, threatening the system. Grievances disposed of one by one are unlikely to amass into a *cause célèbre*.

The instrumental function of the grievance system in settling particular cases is obvious. What is too easily overlooked is the symbolic function; the fact that every rancher with a grievance has an open door to a hearing forces the next one to assess how serious the complaint is. A grievance not worthy of being taken to court is not one around which mass resentment can coalesce. Hence the black-and-white option—to appeal or not to appeal—is significant with respect to the cases not heard as well as to those heard.

*The Evaluator as Educator.* The evaluator, holding the mirror up to events, is an educator. The success of an evaluation is to be judged as in any other educational effort by what it does to develop the learner's potential. This statement amplifies the preceding section's standard for evaluation by characterizing the evaluator's direct service to other persons; it is through their learning that the system changes (Lindblom and Cohen, 1979, p. 18).

The term *educator* can be given too limited a meaning. To be sure, most educators have thought long and hard about the topics that they discuss with their clients, and ordinarily they have a great deal of factual information. But communicating simple lessons is a small part of the work of a true educator, and we would say the same of the evaluator. The educator knows that it is not his place to make decisions for the student. It is the educator's responsibility to liberate the student, that is, to prepare the student to understand her situation and thus to be able to make intelligent choices. An important part of education is helping students to understand their particular aims and the values behind them; they must raise their sights to consider long-term possibilities as well as short-run advantages.

The educator seeks to awaken the student's appreciation of the complexity of phenomena, so that she does not give a fixed response in situations that are similar only on the surface. Also, the educator encourages questioning in order to make the student more tentative in her judgments and more aware when she is relying on debatable assumptions. Beyond that, the student is taught to consider how others see a situation. The respect for others instilled in this way supports accommodation.

All these statements about an educator apply to the evaluator who is attempting to help members of the policy-shaping community deepen their understanding of a program, a social problem, or the decision-making machinery itself. The evaluator settles for too little if he simply gives the best answers he can to simple and one-sided questions from his clients. He is neglecting ways in which he could lead the clients to an ultimately more productive understanding.

The concept of evaluator as educator has not been prominent in the literature, though it lies beneath the historic work of Ralph Tyler and his students and the "responsive evaluation" advocated by Stake (1974). Writers on policy analysis have generally ignored the educative process, as if arriving at a recommendation were all that counted. Quade's text barely mentions that the analyst must educate the client if his work is to be used, and he adds that such education is difficult (Quade, 1975, pp. 257-259).

Archibald's (1970) argument for a "clinical" systems analysis is, however, close to our position, and the educational function is also emphasized by writers on metropolitan planning (Boyce, Day, and McDonald, 1970; Lichfield, Kettle, and Whitbread, 1975). That views of these writers should resemble ours is not surprising—urban plans have political features similar to those of educational programs. In a metropolitan area, multiple agencies with distinct political bases provide intricately related services. Plans have to be updated continually, not merely set in place.

Writers formerly described metropolitan plans as if planning were a purely rational choice among a few structured alternatives. After reviewing ten years of work in that style, Day, Boyce, and McDonald (1970, p. 119) argued for a fundamentally different orientation that would involve a continuous process of convergent research and communication with interested parties: "Throughout this recommended process, evaluation is a learning, probing, testing, exploring kind of activity for both the professional planners and the decision makers. It begins with only a vague notion of development problems and several tentative, but specific, sets of objectives. The detail of the policies considered proceeds from gross to more precise as the range of policies is narrowed and as agreement is reached about objectives. Likewise, the precision of the evaluation should be at first coarse and then increasingly fine, as the policies and plans themselves become more precise. Only rarely is an initial specific policy [ultimately] selected. [Rather, comprehensive alternatives emerge.] Once these alternatives are evaluated [judgmentally], a reformulation or compromise of policy generally occurs."

Those who see evaluation as chiefly scientific make quality of information the principal standard. That standard is relevant; a cracked or warped mirror gives a false image. The evaluator does have to acquire knowledge; if a teacher has a misconception, her teaching will mislead the student. But the teaching activity has point only to the extent that the student's ideas become sounder and more complete. So knowledge should be made comprehensible and credible in addition to being correct and as comprehensive as possible. As Coleman (1972, p. 6) says, "If they are to affect action, research results must be assimilated by those upon whom the action depends. . . . Recent years have provided many cases . . . in which a client responsible for policy was presented with a single grand research report, which he was unable to digest. Such indigestion . . . means that the research was a failure."

Evaluation is often wasted because the message is lost from sight. Consider education for the mentally and physically handicapped, an arena haunted by the ghosts of disappointed hope. Over much of this century, parents' disappointment with the available services most often was heard politically as a demand for more of the same services. Quite a few evaluations looked at the educational results and were unable to show that the slow-paced and sometimes vacuous "special" programs made for better learning or better mental health.

Only in the 1970s was there a major reversal—in the direction of "mainstreaming." It is now said that all children should share the same classroom and activities to the fullest extent possible. Some part of the school day is to be set aside for lessons specially fitted to individual children (not just the handicapped ones). This new policy may or may not work out well; the term *mainstreaming* is capable of so many interpretations that results are sure to be mixed. What is significant for us is that perceptions of the old ineffective policy were extremely slow to shift. No new data came to the attention of those who finally spearheaded the change (Hobbs, 1975); in fact, negative findings on the old segregative special education had surfaced twenty years earlier. The data helped, ultimately, to make the case for change. But the failure to attend to them earlier bespeaks a failure in the system.

## Learning from the Decision to Evaluate

The very proposal to evaluate has political impact. To ask about the virtue of Caesar's wife is to suggest that she is not above suspicion. To single out an established program for evaluation signals that someone considers the program vulnerable (see Chapter Two). Its staff and constituents perceive a hostile political force in the making. They may then act more diligently or more circumspectly. They may also mobilize to resist change.

The opposite also occurs. A policy maker's decision to try out a proposed program may signal that the proposal has healthy prospects of ultimate adoption. The New Jersey negative income tax proposal described in Chapter One, for example, was only one of four possible lines of action that welfare reformers had been discussing in the 1960s. In choosing to set up a field trial of this proposal, the Office of Economic Opportunity signaled that it considered this approach especially worth refining and hinted that the negative income tax foreshadowed the operating programs of the future (Pedersen, 1978). To develop an idea "with no commitment" is a long step toward commitment.

The preemptive power of a staged "demonstration" is well recognized in Washington. In 1970, for example, Congress would not approve housing allowances for the poor, but Senator Edward Brooke was able to push through an authorization for experiments on such a plan. The experimental program was ostensibly an attempt to learn about costs, potential demand, and effects; but one of Brooke's staff candidly labeled the action an entering wedge to make the program an accomplished fact—however modest its initial scale (Lynn, 1977). Taking seriously the concept of an experiment, planners in the Department of Housing and Urban Development designed randomized field trials. In its role as opponent of spending, however, the Office of Management and Budget (OMB) delayed the experiments for two years.

A full-scale program would have required federal funds at a level OMB did not believe coming administrations would favor. Budget Director George Schultz blocked the experiments—until overcome in the political struggle—because he feared that the trials, as a display case, would create sufficient backing to establish the program without orderly legislative consideration.

Schultz stated: "[M]y immediate concern is that the scale of the demonstration program, together with the extent to which it deals with technical issues, will leave many with the impression that a decision has been made to go in the direction of housing allowances, when no such decision has actually been made" (Committee on Evaluation Research, 1978, app. 2, p. 2).

This kind of evaluation, ostensibly scientific in form and purpose, would have to be regarded as damaging the system—if Brooke's hopes and Schultz's fears were born out. Even an evaluator who, as a citizen, strongly favored housing allowances should condemn using evaluation as a hidden-ball play to smuggle a policy past the expressed judgment of Congress and the administration. This would only create suspicion and foreclose opportunities for constructive social experimentation in the future. But one cannot blame Brooke for trying to win a benefit for his constituency.

*Probing for a Sensible Charter.* To help others decide what inquiries are most worth pursuing is a major opportunity and responsibility for the evaluator. Often his knowledge of the art and of past research enables him to point out several alternative, pertinent inquiries. In the discussions that he thus stimulates, it may be agreed that possibilities he has suggested will be of far greater value than those that the inquiry originally proposed. Chapters Four and Five will consider the choice of questions for evaluative studies and the working out of informative designs. Here we demonstrate that the planning process itself affects the program and perhaps the larger system by what it teaches those the evaluator works with.

The evaluator starts to learn and to teach when he first comes on the scene. The first task is to mark out the target: "What is the program?" Those he talks with are likely to be vague and inconsistent in their thinking. Consider an evaluation of psychoanalytic therapy. A committee was once appointed by the American Psychoanalytic Association to mount definitive research on the effectiveness of psychoanalytic therapy (Cushing, 1952). As no two members could agree on what to count as psychoanalysis, the committee conducted a survey to find out what therapists do when they *say* they are doing psychoanalysis. The committee then found that the questionnaire response often did not correspond to the therapist's actual practice.

When confusion of this character surfaces, the evaluator is wise to provoke discussion and, if possible, accommodation. The educational evaluator will talk to teachers and district officials. They may want to block a threatening inquiry, or they may have recommendations they would like the evaluation to support. The evaluator finds himself bringing groups with conflicting interests into a discussion. Each can come to see more clearly its true concern and to perceive which political objectives it can possibly achieve.

Evaluation should not proceed without proper, informed political support. If the ambiguities hide beneath a general label until the evaluation is complete, pertinent questions are bound to be neglected. Moreover, if the potential users of the evaluation are in such conflict that they cannot agree on the target or range of targets, this is a strong hint that the evaluation will mean nothing to them (Brickell, 1976).

"Evaluate this program" is often a vague charge because its boundaries are unclear. Bounding the program is a significant early task, as Gardner (1975, p. 233) points out. In the mental health and welfare fields, the same clientele is the target of many different programs; it is next to impossible to tease out the effects or shortcomings of any one program. Gardner illustrates by referring to methadone treatment in an urban area. During the planning for evaluation, the evaluator should raise questions such as these: Do other drug abuse services need to be brought into the review? Is the concern with persons fully treated or with all those referred to the service? The answers elicited from those who will use its results also help to clarify the purpose of an evaluation.

Evaluations that originate in legislatures are especially hard to focus. California legislators have been known to ask, for example, "Is the Miller-Unruh Act working?" That act provides funds to augment reading instruction in schools where performance has been below a certain standard. Handed such a question, the evaluator has to point out that activities "under Miller-Unruh funds" can rarely be located. A district in which one school qualifies for Miller-Unruh money mingles that with money from other sources and spreads the whole fund over the district. The fund finances books, personnel, individualized sessions, field trips, and other activities expected to promote language development. Some schools in the district do not qualify for Miller-Unruh funds because reading failures, though equally serious, are less numerous. Yet they have almost the same resources and teaching activities as "Miller-Unruh schools" do. There is no distinctive program. It is not that the Miller-Unruh funds were "diverted" from the target schools but that more fluid moneys were used to give other schools similar facilities.

The evaluator, then, finds himself searching for an answerable question. Perhaps legislators want general assurance that with increased funding from several sources schools are rendering better service. To appraise a total reading program is not easy, and to tease out the consequences flowing from any one appropriation is impossible. Even a total appraisal would not be likely to point legislators toward any particular action. Perhaps the evaluator then concludes that the legislators really mean to ask, "Where can we save some money?" If so, then a study of the costs and benefits of specific activities might have some value. To start with the thought of a cutback in Miller-Unruh funds, however, directs attention to no particular activity. It only suggests that a readily identified class of districts or schools—the present beneficiaries—could get by with less money. That proposal is intensely political, sure to be settled by political forces and not by data on outcomes. At any rate, it is this kind of groping, inchoate activity that the evaluator must engage in to elicit a potentially productive charter.

Close analysis of the intent of an evaluation sometimes justifies aborting it. For example, the evaluator may persuade the would-be sponsor that the facts that could be found would make no difference (for political or intellectual reasons). If the decision to drop the evaluative study is a reasoned one, the evaluator has rendered a greater professional service than his costly, action-delaying inquiry would have. He has served as an educator, helping officials to perceive more clearly the action alternatives and their own political aims.

The Civil Rights Commission, for example, once contemplated a mammoth study of school desegregation. It hoped to demonstrate that desegregation proceeds smoothly and beneficially under proper conditions and to suggest how to set up such conditions. The evaluators proceeded enthusiastically to spell out a complex design (Crain and others, 1974). One important feature was an attempt to measure student performance and motivation both in schools that had not desegregated and in schools that had adopted particular arrangements for desegregation and for teaching the new student mixture.

The plan was sent for review to social scientists and to spokesmen for minority concerns. Features of the plan that one reviewer praised, another condemned. Much of the dispute centered on a technical issue: Could "types of arrangement" for desegregation be separated from community, pupil, and teacher characteristics sufficiently to show interpretable effects? While this technical question could have been resolved one way or the other by further discussion, a much weightier criticism bore on the political price of carrying out the evaluation. Several critics felt that, because educational effects have innumerable causes, any superiority in achievement of desegregated schools would be tiny at best and that such evidence would encourage opponents of desegregation. Moreover, the average test scores of minority students would presumably fall behind those of the majority, leading once again to disparaging, defeatist headlines. Thus many reviewers argued against conducting the study because of potential damage to the very cause that the Civil Rights Commission sought to advance. The study was abandoned. (Our information on the reviews and related action comes from personal communication with, and documents supplied by, Robert Crain of the Rand Corporation and Gregg Jackson of the staff of the Civil Rights Commission.)

It is not for us to say that the net benefit of the information from parts of the study would or would not have been worth the risk. Our point is that instructive discussion of the probable effects of the evaluation on the system took place *before* the evaluation was launched. The exchange of views among social scientists, representatives of political constituencies, and administrative officers itself had an educational effect. Some participants were reminded of the political risks of honest inquiry. Others were reminded of the difficulty of answering questions that on the surface seem straightforward.

The interchange could have had a further valuable effect on the evaluation community itself if the criticisms had been circulated. The file of reviews reveals how little agreement there is among eminent and experienced social scientists on matters of design and measurement. The file also tells more about the state of the art in evaluation in the 1970s than any published document. Interchanges that occur in private during the planning stages of many other evaluations would have great educative value if written up as candid case studies. What is learned about the process of evaluation may have as much payoff over the long haul as what is learned about the program being evaluated.

*Choosing Variables to Observe.* Before the evaluator can lay specific plans for collecting data, he must find out a great deal about the project as it exists and as it is conceived. Asking many questions of many people, he often comes to see the program in a new light.

Most basically, he has to find out what to measure in order to trace how the program works. The stated aims of program planners and operators suggest investigative targets, but the evaluator would be unwise to set out "to determine whether the project has attained its goals." That tends to circumscribe the evaluation and perhaps to misdirect it (Etzioni, 1960; Atkin, 1963; Scriven, 1972; Weiss, 1972b; Cook, 1974). At best, only a subset of program effects acquire the status of official goals. Program managers, wanting to make a good showing, may list just the tangible short-run outcomes that are most likely to be reached. At the other extreme, the rhetorical goals used to win support for the program may be so grandiose or so distant in time as to be beyond the grasp of the evaluation. Some relevant outcomes and associated opportunity costs are noticed only after the program and its evaluation have been in progress for some time.

Where goals are stated, the evaluator still is left with much probing to do. Rein (1976) has devoted an entire book to a forceful recommendation: Subject the stated goals to critical analysis. The objectives stated for some programs are ill considered and shortsighted (Quade, 1975, pp. 2, 87, 236, and 307). An obvious example would be to judge a social service by the material help and guidance it provides, while leaving out of account the danger that those served will become more dependent. To raise such questions is to add another dimension to the evaluation.

Coleman and others (1979) devote a book to the description of a research plan to "discover the structure of interests . . . and to learn what kinds of information are relevant to the interests" (p. 12). Their techniques included the study of legislative history and hearings, interviews with legislative aides, and interviews with representatives of all interest groups that had communicated with legislators. Additional informants were tracked down by other means.

The evaluator, then, should be far more than a passive notetaker trying to locate variables to study. From his own knowledge or from his consultation with experts he should come to understand the problem area and the history of similar programs well enough to suggest likely points of breakdown and possible unfortunate side effects. He can reasonably become devil's advocate, imagining the complaints that opponents might voice about the program. The evaluator can also suggest outcome variables that others have failed to mention, so that his clientele can decide whether data are wanted on these.

A valuable tactic is to ask informants about the chain of events they foresee. The evaluator planning a methadone study, says Gardner (1975), should ask informed persons about the biological and social mechanisms that are expected to produce effects—that is, about the working hypotheses of the program. He should ask planners and local operators what consequences they see as most important. Moreover, he should ask prospective clients what they hope to gain from the service and what possible consequences worry them. Mitroff, Emshoff, and Kilmann (1979) review the already extensive literature on this rather new concept of "stakeholder analysis." They apparently hope that it will be refined into a technology for achieving accommodation; our hopes for the approach are more modest.

Eliciting statements from informants does bring to light potential outcomes, impediments, and losses that may be of greater importance than those on an initial list (Boyce, Day, and McDonald, 1970, p. 128). A second value of the activity is its educative impact on the informant. At the very least she learns what is in her own mind—if, indeed, she does not change her mind as she reflects on her priorities. During this questioning, informants as well as the evaluator become aware of implicit assumptions. Further, when members of the Policy-Shaping Community (PSC) become conscious of the whole chain of events between initiation of a program and its end results, they come to think of a wider range of alternative actions than the "thumbs up/thumbs down" decision.

The evaluator "cross-polinates." All sectors of the PSC do not want or expect the same things from a particular program, and they are likely to conceive of it in diverse ways. As Coleman has pointed out (1972, pp. 8-9), the sponsor of an evaluation lists the questions high on *her* agenda, yet she cannot defend the program without answers to questions that concern other members of the community. The evaluator, telling the sponsor what concerns the interested parties, increases the political sophistication of a political figure (Dahlgren and Lindkvist, 1976).

Sometimes the evaluator, pinning down a vague directive, clarifies the social agenda itself; that is, he redefines the problem. Coleman (1972, p. 7) takes his famous Equality of Educational Opportunity survey as an example. When the Coleman team set to work, it judged that the survey commissioned by Congress could not be launched without decoding the congressional phrase "inequality of educational opportunity." When the team sought the help of informants from various groups, it discovered that segments of the population did indeed read different meanings into the phrase. There were those who saw racial mixture as the chief concern, others who looked at teacher quality, still others who emphasized the morale and intellectual tone of the school, and, finally, there were those who argued that only the end result of pupil progress mattered. In the ultimate study, data relevant to each of these political orientations were collected. The staff reasoned that only through the interplay of political interests could a policy be established. If it had let one ideology dominate the survey, the study could have advanced the interests of one group while shortchanging all the others.

Coleman (1972) argues that a major social contribution of the Equality study came in the planning—in the decision to compare performance of students of different backgrounds rather than to look at resource allocation alone. Mosteller and Moynihan (1972, p. 27) are emphatic on the educative impact this extended definition had. The report was "a watershed. . . . Henceforth no study of equality of education or equality of educational opportunity can hope to be taken seriously unless it deals with educational achievement or other accomplishments as the principal measure of educational quality. [Outcomes and neither input nor output of services] must henceforth be the central issue."

In itself, there is nothing either good or bad in having influence. One can speak with enthusiasm or alarm about the fact that what the evaluator and his advisers decide to measure tends to *become* the goals of a program. As this is one of the most significant influences of the evaluator, it is appropriate to drive home the point with further examples. A word will suffice to recall the "payment by results" story (see Chapter Two). Donald Campbell has pointed out a modern equivalent: "The imposition of a body count in Vietnam in an effort to overcome the typically inflated estimates of enemy dead. The result of this neat quantitative index was to encourage the creation of bodies. . . . Lt. Calley was engaged in the legitimized military goal of getting bodies to count. Measures of success can and do become reified" (Deutscher, 1976, p. 255).

Datta (1976) points to the effect of a planning decision in the original Head Start evaluation. The program had been installed with a dozen different motivations and hoped-for effects. The evaluators, trying for an unequivocal experimental/control comparison, were therefore frustrated in their attempt to get the sponsor to specify a dependent variable representing the program goal. The evaluators settled the matter for themselves by measuring IQ, and the rest is history. Many of those who heard about the evaluation came to perceive Head Start as an effort whose *sole* purpose was to raise children's aptitude. When the results on aptitude variables were unimpressive, the word went out that compensatory education had failed.

The work of Ralph Tyler and his students illustrates how the evaluator can deliberately bring to the surface goals that participants believe in but neglect. The evaluation work in their Eight-Year Study (Smith and Tyler, 1942) set for thirty years the pattern for thinking about educational evaluation, emphasizing as it did that data on student performance are appropriate for judging a program only if the measures truly represent the variables that the instruction is intended to change.

Setting definite goals to guide daily instruction was considered to be the teacher's responsibility, so Tyler's evaluators spent a long time asking teachers in the thirty experimental schools about their aims. The process was active rather than passive, though the evaluators did not see themselves as imposing goals. Rather, they hoped to probe beneath commonplaces to uncover goals that the teachers believed in but had not been fully conscious of. As matters turned out, no matter what a school's initial list of goals, each of the thirty local discussions ended with agreement on very nearly the same comprehensive set of objectives (Echols, 1973).

A teacher who came to a meeting prepared to list the *topics* of her chemistry course—oxidation, equilibrium, the halogens—was not allowed to stop there. Was she perhaps also concerned with her students' progress in the use and understanding of scientific method? Did her goals stop with proper use of the metric system and with successful reproduction in the laboratory of results described in the textbook? Or would she also want students to keep good records of observations? to find loopholes in arguments? to formulate scientific proposi- tions in testable form? Yes, all those, and the end was not yet. The chemistry teacher found herself led to confess concern that students develop socially while in her charge, that they broaden their interests, and so on. The list was further refined as test instruments were constructed. In the end, the chemistry teacher had redefined for herself what it means to teach chemistry. The evaluators proceeded this way because they believed that, sub- sequent to such an analysis, the teacher would bring her teach- ing more fully into line with *her* ideals.

## Learning from the Evaluator's Communications

It is natural to think of the formal report as the principal or the only communication from the evaluator and to look to its reception for the evidence of his influence. But the preceding section of this chapter demonstrated that the evaluator com- municates with members of the policy-shaping community (PSC) as he goes about the investigation, and those communica- tions make a difference. Even communications that present "findings" can be and usually are spaced out in time. Much of the most significant communication is informal, not all of it is deliberate, and some of the largest effects are indirect.

Wanting evaluation to have as much influence as the qual- ity of the observations warrant, we—like Anderson and Ball (1978) and Meltsner (1979)—advise the evaluator to seek out opportunities for communication to and with the PSC. This en- tails risks, however. Before this chapter ends, we shall look close- ly at the need for self-restraint and at the conditions under which an evaluator is justified in releasing independent statements.

*Opportunities for Communication.* One obligation of the evaluator is to make sure that his story gets to those who have the greatest power to act on it. Various studies of managers and officials have led to some conclusions on which Sproull and Larkey (1979) comment. "More information," they say (p. 95), "is often the last thing the decision maker wants, needs, or will use." Many claims impinge on the manager's time, and consequently she gets most of her information through short, informal, haphazard conversations. The informants most heard are persons close by; a few trusted informants are heard far more often than those who, by virtue of their formal positions, might seem to be more appropriate sources. Communication is rarely preplanned, and what one informant says is rarely checked systematically with other sources. It follows that the evaluator's official audience is unlikely to study a report. Most likely, unless the evaluator finds his own informal channels, high authority will hear of the work only from contacts who read the report and extracted a message to their own liking.

The Sproull-Larkey (1979) recommendations for the evaluator who wants to reach such an audience derive from the difficulty of capturing attention and the near impossibility of holding it.

> *Be around.* . . . [M]anagers exchange information mostly with "insiders." An evaluator may never actually become an "insider," but the benefits . . . can be approximated simply by being present and available.
> *Talk briefly and often.*
> *Tell stories.* The evaluator should always be prepared with a stock of performance anecdotes to illustrate the points.
> *Talk to the manager's sources* . . . those people the manager relies upon [p. 100].
> *Use multiple models.* . . . [P]resent the same findings from a number of different perspectives. . . .
> *Provide publicly defensible justifications for any recommended programmatic changes.* . . . Justificatory arguments . . . are apt to be very different than scientific arguments. If all else fails, employ lawyers, politicians, and rhetorical social scientists as consultants. Tell them what makes sense scientifically and ask them to justify it [pp. 100–101].

Much more can be learned from an evaluation than the specific facts about the sites investigated. An evaluator will often turn up messages significant for audiences far removed from the program under investigation. The Metropole County story (Weiner, Rubin, and Sachse, 1978) provides a nice example of this phenomenon, especially because the evaluation was carried out in a context of command—a context in which the evaluator is collecting information for a sole user. The Metropole evaluators performed that service and as a bonus educated a wider audience.

The prosecutor's office of the sprawling urban county of Metropole had widely scattered branch offices. A newly elected prosecutor commissioned an outside evaluation of them, and the evaluator found marked differences in how quickly criminal cases were disposed of. Moreover, some branches pressed for severe sentences whereas others were lenient. The prosecutor acted promptly to impose a uniform standard of practice. The prosecutor had suspected that operations were not in accord with agreed-upon values; the evaluation showed where action was needed, and later monitoring made it possible to hold subordinates to the standard.

These are the conditions under which fact-finding by itself is likely to cause an agency to function better: a stable situation, not a theatre of controversy; an agreed-upon definition of good performance; an official with clear authority and responsibility; an official new to the scene and hence with no vested interest in existing practices; subordinates lacking the political clout that would enable them to resist change. The information made the chief officer more powerful *within* the framework of what the community expected of the office. Those who lost power were the local managers who had previously not been supervised.

What is of special interest is the service that the evaluators provided to other localities. After reporting to the prosecutor who commissioned them, the Metropole evaluators chose to hold a press conference. Their tale of shortcomings in Metropole received nationwide coverage, sometimes on the front page. The report prompted citizens in many places to question officials who administered justice. Managers of law enforcement everywhere were put on notice that if *they* did not collect relevant local facts and correct deficiencies, they might soon be deposed. As the jargon has it, consciousness was raised.

To program managers and operators, the evaluator communicates useful messages that neither the general public nor the policy makers care about. The agency manager can make use of a highly differentiated picture. She learns, for example, which units have low morale and why. Her antennae may have given her a sense of the general level of morale, all units considered. The fresh information, even if not directly related to any pending managerial decision, suggests where managerial energy could well be directed. The managers and operators have much less use for summary statistics, except when the same information is collected repeatedly as a monitoring operation. Unanticipated changes in an indicator suggest where the manager can profitably focus attention, whereas one-shot statistics rarely advance her thinking.

A pointed observation can provoke thought among program operators as well as among managers. As an example of a kind of opportunity that is usually present, consider an evaluator's report on a set of college courses. He may relay students' comments that a course gave too much time to certain computations and too little to explaining how those formulas could be applied in the real world. This deadpan transmission by the evaluator—he endorses neither the factual content nor the value judgment implied in the comments—gives pause to the instructor. Even if her course was not included in the survey, she asks herself whether her students would respond similarly. By raising questions, the evaluator teaches.

In suggesting that the evaluator provide differentiated information, we also note the risks. Fine-grained information comes closer to gossip than to the fruit of systematic inquiry, just because of its idiosyncratic character. Still, anecdotes and quotations from unnamed informants, when representative of what the evaluator has seen, are legitimate information. The evaluator must be mindful of the risk of exposing individuals to criticism or punishment. Where clients or program operators come to feel that evaluators are acting as undercover agents for higher authority, evaluators find it increasingly difficult to function.

*Early Warnings.* The evaluation inevitably turns up information as to how well the program is going. Therefore, continual choices have to be made as to how much to say informally, before all the data are in and all the statistics double-checked. The positive case for informing program planners and managers of comparatively tentative findings is a strong one. The evaluator is going to discover failures of program delivery, great or small. If they are not repaired, the immediate clients may continue to be badly served. Thus, the sooner the program planners or administrators can come to grips with the difficulty, the sooner a genuinely beneficial service will be developed. A manager naturally wants the evaluator to call attention to trouble spots as soon as they are identified. Even the manager who already has located the trouble spots benefits when a formal evaluation documents them; his corrective action is now seen as impersonal rather than punitive (Patton and others, 1977).

Even the General Accounting Office (GAO), congressional watchdog though it is, makes criticisms early and quietly to program managers, before it barks loud enough to alert Congress. John Harper of the GAO has commented (Chelimsky, 1977a, p. 64): "[T]he *process* of doing our work often achieves whatever objectives we might have hoped to achieve by producing a report because, at the point of time when the agency gets the opportunity to comment on the drafts of our report, my experience is that the agency likes to say, 'We have already instituted action to correct whatever it is you have found.'"

We can further illustrate the virtue of early releases by referring to a program of a rather special nature (Cronbach, 1979). As part of their recruiting effort, the armed services give the Armed Services Vocational Aptitude Battery (ASVAB) test in high schools. At no charge the schools obtain scores to employ in vocational counseling of students. In return, the recruiters obtain names of young people who are likely to qualify for various military specialties. Most tests for schools are reviewed publicly so that counselors can judge their suitability, the reviews traditionally appearing in the *Mental Measurements Yearbook*. A review of a new test, once written, is normally held in confidence until this massive compilation is printed, sometimes two years after the review was prepared.

A critic asked to evaluate ASVAB in 1976 found radical defects in the then-current form. Among other defects, certain career recommendations to students rested entirely on chance differences in scores. With a million or more students tested each year, and presumably receiving bad advice as a result, the evaluator turned to forms of communications much more rapid than the *Yearbook* (which ultimately came out in 1979). He alerted the customers and some politically active persons by press releases, a few letters to members of Congress, and an interview given to a professional newsletter. At the same time, a copy of the critique went to the Pentagon office in overall charge of the program. That office accepted much of the criticism as valid and, aware that the criticism had been sent to Congress, responded almost instantly. The office was able to repair many defects prior to the start of the next school year— and was quick to tell both Congress and the customers that it had done so.

The ASVAB test continues to evolve. In his later communications, the evaluator recognized problems overcome and problems remaining, and the officials continue to make further repairs. An individual critical letter might ordinarily have no effect. In this instance, however, the letter had leverage because the program was controversial: both pacifists and civil libertarians object to recruiting in high schools. The program seems unlikely to be discontinued, but the Pentagon must accommodate to keep criticism in check. By using several channels to activate counterpressures, the evaluator hoped to bring about constructive change. Traditional publication might have had the same effect, but only much later.

An evaluator would want to be sure of his ground before acting so aggressively. The impotence that comes with delay, however, can be a greater cost than the consequences of a misjudgment. The political process is accustomed to vigorous advocacy from journalists, consumer advocates, economic commentators, and the like; the PSC is not going to be swept off its feet by an ill-considered assertion even from an evaluator.

Another argument for early warnings is that a summative evaluation may be worse than useless when carried to completion if the program assessed does not represent the plan. (An obvious example of this is the Performance Contracting experiment discussed in Chapter Five.) How the evaluator should act when asked to evaluate a spurious realization could be debated endlessly. Surely, however, postponing the evaluation for another year should be considered. Not until the trial program has stabilized do extensive measurements have any point. At the minimum, for the evaluator to say promptly that the program is not being realized as envisioned warns its proponents not to accept the evaluation as an assessment of the underlying idea.

The evaluator is frequently tempted or pressed to make preliminary reports to the public. Hazardous though release of less-than-final information may be, the risks are often worth running. The prevailing view of the program evolves while the evaluation goes on. The community moves toward tacit decisions even when a particular policy maker is prepared to await the evaluator's finished report. And, apart from the program under study, other proposals may come up for action to which the evaluator's observations will be relevant. The PSC, then, has good use for information long in advance of the date set for the final report.

Note, for example, that the congressional review of the Elementary and Secondary Education Act's provisions for bilingual education, and almost all the public attention, centered on an interim report. The contractor filed it a year in advance of the report that completed the project. The interim report had been scheduled by the sponsor with an eye to the congressional timetable; that is to say, the sponsor judged that an early transmission, incompletely analyzed and incompletely cross-checked, was more to the point than a report of better quality released after Congress had framed its bill. In other instances, when the evaluator notes the pertinence of what he already knows to the current political debates, he may be the one to suggest an unscheduled partial report.

Sometimes members of the PSC drag the evaluator into the limelight when he would prefer to stay invisible in his think tank, piecing his story together. There are two notable stories about this, the first of which involves the intervention of the White House in the early release of Head Start findings. Staff members inclined toward conflicting interpretations had not yet sorted out their disagreements, and the draft of the analysis had not yet been vetted by the staff's consultants. But President Nixon requested a summary to use in a major policy speech. How was the agency head to deny the White House? The president's speech was based on a superficial summary of not-yet-digested findings. Moreover, a few weeks later, with the analysis and review still in process, a House committee was demanding copies of the unfinished manuscript and invoking the Freedom of Information Act to get them (Williams, 1971).

The Nixon administration figures also in the second story (Kershaw and Small, 1972). When the negative income tax experiment started in New Jersey in 1968, the sponsor had judged that possible action on such legislation was years down the road. The very next year, however, saw the new Nixon administration proposing a family assistance plan that had some similarity to the negative income tax plan. Naturally, Congress asked for the early returns from New Jersey, and the investigators reported the tabulations to date, adding that the report was preliminary, limited, and inadequately checked. As always in a complex study, errors crept into the analysis—errors that normal procedures for report preparation would have caught. The misfortune here was that it was the GAO that discovered the errors, in the course of checking facts that interested Congress. Washington gossip forgets nothing discreditable. Years later, when the negative income tax study was issuing considered and verified reports, the whispers ran, "There was a GAO inquiry into one of their earlier reports, and the outfit didn't look very good."

The closer in time the evaluator's releases are to the moment when the observations were made, the greater the risk of error, exposure, and loss of credibility. If this risk could not be

tolerated at all, no evaluative information would be released
save as ancient history. The evaluator who reports on schedule
risks blind spots and inappropriate analysis. The earlier the reporting, the less the evaluator's security. But the evaluator who
takes no risk with report quality takes other risks. He risks that
political resolution will reach a point of no return without benefit of the information that he is processing. He risks having the
hearing for his genuine report preempted by leaks or by meretricious and partisan evaluative reports. With some hesitation,
we advise the evaluator to release findings piecemeal and informally to the audiences that need them. General release invites
larger risks of misinterpretation, and greater caution is required
(McDaniels, 1975b, p. 57). What is good for the system has to
be judged afresh in each case.

    *Opportunities to Foster Accommodation.* The evaluator's
work sometimes contributes to the accommodative process
simply by providing an occasion for cross talk among sectors of
the PSC. We have in mind here not the grand movement of policy but the reconciliation of perceptions about specific and perhaps local issues. For example, evaluators are ordinarily told to
identify program goals at the outset of their work. But as Said
(1974) points out, when feedback on accomplishments begins
to come in, goals become the subject of a fresh accommodative
struggle. This is to be seen in some of the current efforts to install "competency" examinations as a state requirement for
high school graduation. The powers that set the system in motion may have defined the performance standard in no uncertain
terms. "The passing score will be 70 percent on a test covering
the following subject matter," a mandate may say. But such
mandates often have an unhappy fate when it is found that the
number of students failing to reach the standard is politically
unacceptable (Tyler and others, 1978, pp. 7-12).

    The evaluator in such a circumstance has an opportunity
to precipitate a review of performance standards as soon as he
has begun preliminary trials of possible test items. He might do
well to assemble a group of advisers from sectors of the PSC
having different political concerns and let them look over the
data with him and make suggestions. Perhaps the data project

that a quarter of the students in a particular demographic group will fail an examination made up of items like these. The conflict that will inevitably break out among the advisers seems almost certain to precipitate a review and renegotiation of the mandate before the first operational test is put in place. Such a review would have been certain to follow the first *operational* test if the evaluator had done nothing but prepare the test as instructed. But since operational use of the severe standard would have hurt the life chances of many of the young people tested, provoking the negotiation at an earlier date was a proper service to the system.

The fact that the evaluator can make some claim to be a neutral scientist helps him in fostering negotiation. If the investigator can keep the image of a reflective and disinterested observer, those with whom he interacts are under some pressure to speak reasonably themselves (Ezrahi, 1978).

The history of the Three-on-Two Study in Hawaii illustrates how an evaluation can bring about a shift from contention to accommodation. The state of Hawaii began to assign teams of three teachers to elementary school classes of a size formerly handled by a team of two. Critics proposed to abolish the program, arguing that it had no benefit to offset its cost. The teachers union insisted that the program was valuable; also, understandably, the union was worried about the potential loss of teaching positions.

The state government initiated an adversary evaluation. Professional evaluators from other states were convened to jointly plan the process of collecting evaluative data. Teams—balanced on various factors—were formed before plans were discussed. When the plans were complete and the instruments ready, a coin was flipped to determine which side of the issue each team would defend. Representatives from the teams collaborated in interviewing personnel and conducting hearings. Once the data were in hand, each team set out to organize the data into the strongest case that could be made for its side (Weiner, Rubin, and Sachse, 1978; Popham and Carlson, 1977).

To assess teacher attitudes, the teams distributed a questionnaire. Its very last item asked the teachers to judge the value of Three-on-Two on the assumption that budgets would not be reduced, implying that no school would have to reduce its staff. Teachers were clearly divided on the choice between using money for the Three-on-Two plan and using it for specialist teachers or for making conventional classes smaller. The responses elicited by that astute question smoothed a path toward compromise. After the adversary teams argued their case before a statewide television audience, it was clear that the data on student achievement did not make a positive case for the program. The responsible officials decided to give schools the option of continuing Three-on-Two or assigning the displaced teachers as reading specialists or to other services. Each side could accept the decision, the evaluation process having disclosed the middle ground between the warring factions. We suspect, however, that the opportunity for negotiation is greater in a nonadversary evaluation than in a confrontation.

### Responses in the Political Community

The public cannot *study* social programs and problems. It can at best catch impressions on the fly, and it usually settles on a simplified version of whatever simplified account or generalization is presented to it. Here, as elsewhere, the specialist's knowledge has to be boiled down for easy recall and communication. Meteorology is vastly more sophisticated today than it was just a few years ago—but the person listening to a complex weather report still wants to know, Shall I carry my umbrella?

*Means and Styles of Communication.* All research strives to reduce reality to a tellable story. But more "tellable" usually means less complete. As Cohen and Weiss (1977) are at pains to point out, thorough study of a social problem makes it seem more complicated. "Increased accuracy [of analysis] is likely to generate political confusion," says Aaron (1978, p. 49). All that becomes clear is how many variables make a difference.

Careful expositions that make the story more complex and more true make the listening harder and the audience smaller. The difficulty is especially acute in evaluation, where much of the information is to be communicated within a short period and to diverse audiences. Evaluation users will give only so much time to communication. They will not watch an eight-hour Warhol movie of the Empire State Building; they might look at a snapshot. Only a few of the users are social scientists. Few of them will work hard to comprehend the technical or the intricate. They will tolerate only so many words of scientific caution before dismissing a report as empty.

Artful presentation is especially important when the understanding of the larger community is wanted. The relevant presentation is only rarely a direct transmission from the evaluator to the members of the PSC. Most of the members hear not the words of the evaluator, but the reverberations of his report. And the PSC thinks less about the program evaluated than about the social endeavor of which the program is illustrative or symbolic.

Evaluators tend naturally to think of their main product as formal, written communications, but these are clearly insufficient. Informal and usually oral statements are potentially far more influential. A legislator cannot take time to burrow through a file of documents, but she can listen to a visitor who offers a quick overview and then responds alertly to pointed questions. At the end of the conversation, the legislator is ready either to dismiss the matter or to invest staff time in following up the visitor's message. Indeed, not many members of the PSC are accustomed to getting their information in writing, however much that may be the preferred mode of communication among scientists. The evaluator's final, formal report is essentially an archival document, not a live communication.

In the light of Caplan's report (Caplan, Morrison, and Stambaugh, 1975; see Chapter Two), Boruch (1975a) suggests that broad and semipopular articles in *Atlantic*, *Fortune*, *Science*, and similar media carry more influence than original accounts of field studies. For one thing, such articles cover more than one study; for another, they sum up and offer a firmer position statement than is customary in "objective" documents. These articles lend themselves to quick reading and, thanks to Xerox, to circulation up, down, and across normal lines of bureaucratic communication.

The results of evaluations ought to be communicated, then, through many media and at several levels of detail and precision. Much evaluative information that could be useful to the PSC is lost because it is inadequately packaged. Imaginative communication devices can help the PSC benefit from evaluation. Evaluators will find untapped possibilities in film clips and sound tapes, as well as in personal appearances before groups ranging from local parent associations to congressional committees (Boruch, in Boruch and Riecken, 1975, p. 102). Communication counts as much toward the contribution of an evaluation as the adequacy of the data collection itself.

The limits of what can be communicated should influence the design of the research. We shall urge comprehensiveness in the next chapter, but comprehensive examination of a program does not necessarily justify an exhaustive report. When the evaluator cuts short his investigation of some matters, after preliminary readings have indicated that in those respects all is proceeding according to plan, he reduces the burdens of field investigation and communication alike.

Many evaluations are reported with self-defeating thoroughness. As an extreme example, one recent report on nonformal education in Latin America ran to 900 pages (single spaced and in English!); perhaps that document found no audience at all. A normal human being will try to assimilate only so many numbers, and not much more prose. When an avalanche of words and tables descends, everyone in its path dodges. The member of the PSC knows that she will never grasp the study fully. If aware that the overview she reads was prepared or censored by a partisan, she will surely hang on to her preconceptions, ignoring equally the superficial summary and the excessively detailed report.

Communication overload is a common fault of routine monitoring systems (Arrow, 1974; Keen and Morton, 1978). Many systems generate masses of results that are interesting, important—and never used. In one Latin American country, for example, an elaborate system for feedback on instructional television was developed. At first, the attitudes of classroom teachers toward each series of lessons were surveyed and reported regularly to television production teams. Just as regularly, any negative report was ignored, although positive reports were not.

Since the producers continued to ignore teachers' criticisms, the supervisors asked evaluators to monitor student accomplishment midway in each six-week unit. After the fourth week of instruction, the student viewers took a brief (televised) test on important topics. Two days after the test, the production team was handed a catalogue of concepts well learned and poorly learned. The team was to prepare a "remedial" broadcast for the sixth week of the unit.

This system did not work badly in its early trials. When it became a regular practice for unit after unit, however, it broke down. Too much professional effort was required. The course embodied eighty units per year. The feedback operation for each unit demanded at least twenty person-days for instrument development, collection and analysis of data, and reporting. Three professionals and seven research assistants could barely manage. The error count did not tell producers why their original lessons missed fire. And, even though the data might have influenced the next year's program, more leisurely feedback would have served that purpose at least as well. Producers simply could not assimilate intensive feedback into their tight delivery schedule. Avoiding dead air at broadcast time was vital to them; pupil learning was secondary. Only the evaluation team seemed to make pupil accomplishment the chief criterion.

*Selective Reception and Counterattack.* Audiences select information from the stream that flows past. Some of the selection is motivated, as when producers in the example above picked out favorable comments for attention. But much selectivity is simply attraction to what is readily assimilated.

An individual has one set of beliefs about the world on awakening in the morning and a different set on falling asleep that night. Her beliefs were adjusted in the light of information that came during the day. But a report inconsistent with prior beliefs is given less credence than a similarly grounded report that fits the beliefs held at daybreak. The literature of psychology and communication research is filled with demonstrations of selectivity—in reception, perception, memory, and reasoning.

Selection reduces incongruent data to an internally consistent whole (Steinbruner, 1974). Two persons who start the day with different beliefs would hold different end-of-day beliefs even if they were wholly rational in attending to the same information. New information is expected to determine belief completely only when the interpreter had no prior opinion.

Evaluative findings cannot alone determine beliefs for another reason: interpretations related to a given program come from other sources at the same time. The personal experience of participants and what their peers say carry weight. Demonstrations and picketing win disproportionate attention for some views. A personalized newspaper story about welfare fraud may outweigh a solid statistical appraisal of the effects of a welfare program.

Among the politically committed, of course, use of the evaluative report is highly selective (Wurzburg, 1979). Out of the flow of evidence and gossip, the political actor scoops up the twigs and straws that fit her building plans. Incidents in which a partisan selects facts to fit her case, and there are many of them, are not to be regarded as perverse. They are characteristic of the system. The theory of trial by adversary rests on the assumption that truth will out when one advocate champions her client unrestrainedly and another drives home every argument that favors the second party.

Many governmental accommodations are worked out in an adversary manner. It has even been suggested that the agency "lets the side down" if it does not commission a summative evaluation with the conscious intention of ultimately making public any good news about the program it manages and suppressing any bad news. We understand this as a truth about bureaucratic warfare as seen from the inside. We regret that investigators are employed in press-agentry, but we acknowledge that partisan service, in its own way, helps the system to function. True as that is, critical machinery is needed to expose *ex parte* evaluations as the opposite of inquiry. The PSC can learn to give greatest weight to balanced information.

House (1974) has told a vivid tale that unfortunately we must compress. His subject was evaluations within colleges and universities, and he documented quite adequately that the evaluator who undertakes appraisal of a program for the eyes of outsiders is proposing "to evaluate a bear trap by sticking [a] leg in it" (p. 621). One study of technologically oriented instruction was put to constructive use as long as the shortcomings of the instruction were reported quietly within the project staff. The project leaders, in fact, said that they had known about these problems all along—but they did make changes. It was when a formal final report was unexpectedly called for that all went wrong, or nearly all. A narrative account of what had been observed (of what had originally been "true but not news") now was censored to eliminate unwelcome content. Though the report was descriptive and not a judgment of success or failure, the project leaders insisted on holding its circulation to a minimum. The few copies that did reach the university administration were passed from hand to hand because, although the report was long, it was a colorful narrative of believable incident. "The last I heard," wrote House, "it was crashing around through the administrative underbrush like a wild beast on the loose in the forest" (p. 624). Even academic man, turned project leader, wants his work to be perceived as wholly admirable. Those who must defend public programs against political rivals have reason to be even more defensive.

We have urged the evaluator to be as active in communication as his contractual understandings allow, so that good use will be made of his work. Coleman (1972, p. 12) has told how the Department of Health, Education, and Welfare (HEW) attempted to reduce the impact of *Equality of Educational Opportunity* and how his independent writing came to make a difference:

> The report was made public in a press interview at HEW at a time [a holiday weekend] that was not designed to draw attention, and the general tone of the interview suggested that the report contained nothing especially new. It lay relatively unnoticed until Senator Ribicoff, having read a set of galley proofs from an article of mine made avail-

able to him by Patrick Moynihan, challenged the
secretary of HEW and the commissioner of education in Senate testimony concerning the contents
of the report. This event brought the report into
the open, but for nearly a year after that the report
remained unavailable from the Government Printing Office, unreprinted after a small initial printing.
It was only after the mass media brought the results
of the report to a wider public view that the government agency which had issued the report, the Department of HEW, paid serious attention to it.

In a recent comment, Coleman (1980, p. 80) stresses that
university-based investigators are the ones who can help the political community get the full benefit of social inquiry: "Nearly
all the examples I know in which policy research has arrived at
results that throw doubt on federal policies and has insisted that
the results be publicly available are cases in which the analyst
was *not* in a contract research organization wholly dependent
on government funds, but was a university faculty member."

The neophyte evaluator who expects objectivity suffers
his greatest shock in discovering that his information is reshaped
for political purposes. Once a report enters a context of accommodation, a participant who does not favor the action that the
evaluation seems to support will capitalize on variables or hypotheses that the evaluation neglected. Experimental instruction
to improve written expression will not persuade an audience of
English teachers if only grammatical accuracy is tested. Some
critic will ask, "Did quality of thought improve or deteriorate?"
—and opponents of the innovation will have found their rallying
cry. Broader studies are in a better position to answer questions
that are raised as afterthoughts, but the evaluator and sponsor
cannot hope to anticipate all critics. Using as ammunition any
evaluative information that will serve one's purpose, while at
the same time trying to minimize or discredit any unwanted
news, is a natural part of the accommodative process.

What is needed if the system is to work well is a debate
either balanced enough to enlighten the uncommitted or private
enough to allow those who are committed to a service to face

having its flaws uncovered. Once we recognize how unlikely it is that political contenders will be silenced by a factual report, we also begin to see how unlikely it is that an evaluator's conclusion will unite all parties behind the same option.

The Head Start evaluation is a particularly well-known example of selective release of information, attack, and counter-attack. Williams (1971, pp. 122–123) saw its reception as typical of the kind received by an impact appraisal that arouses political interest:

> [The history of Head Start evaluation is] a stark illustration of what might be termed the implications of the iron law of absolute evaluation flaws. That is, as a general rule, *the absolute methodological and logistical deficiencies in any evaluation make political infighting a near-certainty when evaluation results threaten a popular program.* In short, "questionable evaluation practices" can always be attacked on methodological grounds for political and bureaucratic purposes.
>
> For the analyst, these deficiencies mean that even a relatively sound evaluation can easily cause severe controversy, and the battle, although expressed in the jargon of the professional statistician, can be nasty (for example, with hints of foul play or at least the claim that the evaluator is insensitive to program needs and problems). As must be clear from the Westinghouse example, tense situations will arise that require great sensitivity, good timing, good judgment, and probably a goodly amount of pure luck in order to survive the political battle. And it is not certain that the analyst will acquire through any formal training or experience the "art" of bureaucratic infighting required to be effective.
>
> If the iron law of absolute evaluation flaws holds, one may well ask from the perspective of various interested parties whether a study such as the Westinghouse evaluation—primarily [summative]—was (and more importantly is) really worth the effort.

When we take up the planning of studies, we shall say more on vulnerability and how to reduce it. For now, let us say only that the "best" of techniques—random assignment, strict sampling, objective measurement, rigorous inference, or whatever—will not provide magic armor for the evaluation. A research worker can make his conclusion invulnerable by limiting it strictly to what the research operations showed and by attaching an index of statistical uncertainty. But members of the PSC will have a larger, less operational question in mind and will use the results to carry on that larger debate. The research cannot expect to settle that question.

In principle, the mass media play a highly significant part in bringing all sides of an issue out into the open. Sometimes a journalist does probe thoroughly into the information available regarding a program, but the media may also contribute to imbalance. Even when they strive for objectivity, the media are not capable of restoring balance if their sources tell only part of the story. The media add biases of their own—biases that arise out of the art and business of journalism.

Liveliness sells papers and therefore vivid, position-taking, corner-cutting pronouncements command space, while balanced and guarded analyses do not. The journalist looks for a "story line" on which to hang facts and interpretations that, while being collected, pointed in many different directions. The journalist reverses the Agatha Christie formula. In a Christie whodunit, each divergent fact is exploited to make the reader attend to a new hypothesis, one that contradicts the hypotheses of earlier pages. But today's journalist wants to tell her audience what to think and so gives primacy to one line of evidence and plays down other viable hypotheses. Selection of the journalistic line is motivated less by partisanship than by the urge to sell papers. "Man Bites Establishment" is news, and it is easy to find instances where ill-supported but iconoclastic views received unwarranted prominence (Cronbach, 1975b).

An example drawn from *Pygmalion in the Classroom* (1968) is pertinent. Rosenthal and Jacobsen conducted two formal experiments with random assignment to demonstrate that giving pupils' mental-test scores to teachers has a bad effect. An experiment in California came out as they expected it to.

But Rosenthal's companion experiment in Ohio showed a statistically significant (!) effect in the direction opposite to his thesis. Immediately upon completion of the studies, Rosenthal described his results to the *New York Times*, which gave the story front-page play ("Study Indicates...," 1967). The evidence of the California and Ohio studies would carry equal weight with a jury free from preconceptions. (The research program had serious flaws, however; see Elashoff and Snow, 1971.)

But the *Times* took Rosenthal's thesis as a story line: pupils' futures are unfairly influenced when mental-test results are given to teachers. Following a dozen paragraphs describing the California study and Rosenthal's "tests-do-harm" interpretation, the reporter "balanced" the account by inserting one paragraph, on the inside-page carry-over of the story, to say that the California result was not duplicated in an Ohio study. The story failed to say that the Ohio results contradicted the others and concluded with several further paragraphs amplifying Rosenthal's thesis.

*Modifying Broad Views and Shaping Fresh Agendas.* Stimulating a discussion that leads to gradual change in prevailing views is very likely the most important effect of evaluation research. The program evaluated may be seen in a new light, but what weighs heavier is the change in social agendas and in the general view of problems and institutions. This contribution of evaluation is essentially the same as the contribution expected of other kinds of historical inquiry. Information even on long-dead institutions and programs can modify thinking about their contemporary counterparts.

Evaluators report to officials whose perspective is continually changing. This is supported by the retrospective accounts we now have of the debates about compensatory education that took place between 1967 and 1972 (Rivlin and Timpane, 1975b; Datta, 1976; Timpane, 1976; Williams, 1971; Haney, 1977). Thought evolved with respect to what the programs were trying to do and how easy those aims would be to accomplish. "Will compensatory education work?" was seen to be a bad question, and it gave way to the idea that some variations or models were better than others. Once they were systematically compared, it was thought, the "right" approach could be written into law.

This view ultimately gave way to a realization (at least at a sophisticated policy level) that in education no model or practice can be imposed from Washington; local professional understandings, restrictions, and habits make the treatment events what they are. Sharp choices among alternative programs were seldom made on the basis of the evaluations. Rather, a kind of course of least resistance was followed. As a result of this change in view, no push was made to scale up expenditures on preschools for the disadvantaged, although appropriations continued. (See Chapter Two.)

The discovery that compensatory education was hard to accomplish altered the strategy of the War on Poverty. If compensatory education was not making a demonstrable impact on root causes of adult poverty, it seemed better to shift the line of attack to income maintenance for families. In its heyday, compensatory education was in repertory on the big White House stage; now it dropped back to the Little Theatre of the education bureaus.

The positive outreach of an evaluation over a long period of time can be illustrated by taking up once again the Eight-Year Study of the Progressive Education Association. This evaluation of new course offerings for high schools, along with new teaching methods, was commissioned about 1933 as a result of the distrust that colleges harbored for the nontraditional high schools (Echols, 1973). The question posed by the sponsor was this: Would the progressive schools, if left free to experiment with new curricula, maintain sound college-preparatory standards?

College records of experimental subjects were compared with those of college classmates who had graduated from traditional high schools. When ultimately reported (Drought and Chamberlain, 1942), the findings—equal grade averages, greater extracurricular participation among experimentals—caused scarcely a ripple. Many of the experimental teaching practices had appeal and had filtered out into high schools generally— long before the "test" was complete. In 1933 the elite colleges that dominated the College Entrance Examination Board (the prime movers for the summative test) shaped their programs to fit graduates of selective Eastern preparatory schools. By 1943, however, these colleges had become interested in attracting students from all regions and from all kinds of schools, although for reasons having nothing to do with the progressive experiment.

This summative quasi-experiment happened to be seriously flawed, though it was an example of 1930s social science at its best. Critics of the report made the point later used in attacking the Head Start evaluation: matching experimentals and controls post hoc probably overstated the success of the experimental group (Chauncey, 1941; Johnson, 1946). The Chauncey critique appeared before the main report was completed, and its authors indicated their reasons for dismissing his objection (Drought and Chamberlain, 1942, p. 34). One limited check that they could make suggested to them that their technique had introduced no bias. The statistical comparison lacked credibility even after the rejoinder was taken into account, according to Johnson's later review. But no one in the world of policy cared, and even in the world of research the conflict of views passed almost unnoticed. No direct and serious consideration was given to the summative statistical findings, simply because the issue was dead. The criticism of the formal, quasi-experimental comparison did not undermine the much looser (and clearly valid) conclusion that school people carried away: "students without the traditional college preparatory curriculum could succeed in college" (Graham, 1967, p. 134). The simplification of the message is painful to perceive. The success of these students was attributable not to the absence of traditional requirements but to the adoption of well-conceived, painstakingly developed alternative curricula. *That* was the program evaluated. Few in the audience thought of the specific program; indeed, the book describing the instructional activities of the experimental schools sold fewer than 1,000 copies (Graham, 1967, p. 133).

Where the Eight-Year Study had its impact was in the ideas about curriculum and educational evaluation that it promulgated. Professional courses down to the mid 1960s reflected the enthusiasm among educators for the concepts and techniques exemplified in the study. These concepts had been in the air for decades, reaching back to John Dewey's popular but rather abstract theory of education. The concrete realization and the prestigious research "brought the concepts home" to practical educators. In planning high school courses, educators shifted the emphasis from "coverage of subject matter" to a concern for what the student would carry away from the course: attitudes, ability to apply principles in unfamiliar contexts, ability to analyze arguments, and so on. Knowledge about polygons, bimetallism, chiaroscuro, and other specifics was only a vehicle; many equally worthy topics could serve just as well. The Deweyan emphasis on advancing problem solving to the highest possible level became a staple of teacher training in English, mathematics, and social studies.

Although the schools included in the study aimed to serve all levels of the population, they had their eyes on grander ambitions than teaching the basic skills of reading and writing. Bringing these basic skills to a usable level among the least able students did not come to be a first priority for high schools until the 1970s. Perhaps high schools were slow to confront these shortcomings just because the study helped to promulgate an emphasis on higher mental processes.

The evaluation methods of the study were themselves a contribution. Converted to a simpler, mass-producible form, some of the techniques of assessing change in students were taken into College Board examinations and into published tests for use in high school instruction. The study's techniques of faculty development were imitated by colleges, and a *Taxonomy of Educational Objectives* (Bloom and others, 1956) grew out of the college projects. The *Taxonomy* in turn became the chief intellectual framework for developing evaluation instruments in education during the 1960s. Its emphasis on analytic skills and other high-level processes is still a potent counterforce to the neobehaviorist view of schooling (which sees instruction as the training of specific acts).

## Reconciling Public Loyalties and Private Obligations

The evaluator takes on a considerable responsibility when he attempts to influence actions that affect the public and the political system. At best, he is caught in the cross fire of political antagonists; at worst, he becomes the corrupt servant of a partisan. Evaluators have not lost their ideals, we insist, but they often find themselves caught in painful conflicts in which one ideal must give way to another. Some commentators scent outright fraud in much current evaluation; for examples, see the critique of evaluation by allies of Ralph Nader (Guttman and Wilner, 1976). While Bernstein (1977) sympathizes with the anomalous position of the scientist whose findings are purchased to "put up a heat shield" for a political figure about to make an unpopular decision, she is blunt in saying that honesty is a prime concern in the world of evaluation contracting.

The late C. Wright Mills (1959) was particularly forceful in reproaching the social scientist who allows himself to be used politically. Mills considered it dangerous for the social scientist to seek to wield power and equally dangerous for him to become a confidential adviser to the powerful. Both roles are antidemocratic. They subvert the accommodative system by offering packaged policies for the public to take or leave, inhibiting rather than facilitating political participation. Add to this the inherently conservative influence of evaluations, and one can understand Mills' recommendation. He would have the social scientist remain far outside the system, speaking out as frequently as his information warrants in a loud voice and in a public forum, not in a whisper to the Princess.

Evaluators cannot follow Mills' advice and remain evaluators. Substantial evaluations are almost always financed by persons in positions of some authority. Any one social scientist can accept Mills' advice to remain an outsider. But even if all qualified social scientists were to accept this advice, evaluations would still be commissioned by the powerful. Responsible officials would find advisers prepared to render what is, after all, an entirely legitimate service. The social science community has a positive responsibility to encourage excellence in evaluations, including those commissioned to further the policies of the Princess. It therefore becomes necessary to examine just how to reconcile the intent to benefit the system with the other commitments of the evaluator—to his sponsor, to his informants, to his political preferences, and to his own economic welfare.

When our examination is finished, the dilemmas will still be dilemmas, but their importance for evaluation should be more evident.

*Ethical Hazards.* Evaluations should not misdirect the course of political action, but they can do so if initiated with partisan intent. And even a well-intended evaluation can be at fault if the planners are insensitive to the political issues at stake. The person interested in political equity should be concerned particularly with three questions:

1. Did the questions selected for investigation, considered as a set, favor one political interest over another?
2. Did the evaluator falsify the data, the analysis, or the report?
3. Did the sponsor withhold politically significant information from the PSC or distort what was transmitted?

Two further ethical questions are different in character:

4. Did the evaluation subject persons who supplied data to risks they would not otherwise have run?
5. Did the evaluator undertake work that promises to have little or no social value?

This list of questions is not exhaustive, but it adequately represents the range of ethical concerns in evaluation.

Among these five questions, only the answer to the second is wholly under the evaluator's control. Some of the events are determined by the agency that commissions the work or by a legislature; still others are the end products of complex negotiations. But even the matters that are not under his control are still matters for which the evaluator must take some responsibility. Where he foresees one or another of the risks mentioned above, he can make an effort to minimize it. For example, he can ask that safeguards be written into the plans, or he can refuse to undertake work where the risk is too great. Where the risks become apparent only in mid investigation he is confronted with other choices. The day may yet come when an evaluator has to go to jail to "protect his sources," as journalists have in the past. Also, on rare occasions, an evaluator has to decide whether he should violate a contract or tacit understanding in order to make public what otherwise would remain hidden.

The fifth question—whether the evaluation promises to have social value—is perhaps not so much a problem in ethics as in self-respect. An evaluator, like any other professional, wants his work to produce social benefits as well as personal income. If he can find assignments that offer both satisfactions, he will surely choose them. But when belt tightening is the only alternative to taking on busywork, he deserves sympathy rather than condemnation.

Still, the evaluator who does not press for productive assignments can be accused of taking the King's shilling for selfish reasons. Bernstein (1977, p. 8) is one of those government officials who expends evaluation funds, and she finds evaluators far too passive in accepting the work as it is offered: "I'd like, just once, to meet an evaluator who states honestly that in his opinion the agency's criteria aren't workable and who subsequently proposes an alternative. Instead, I meet evaluators who say (in confidence) that a particular activity is doomed to failure —but they are submitting a proposal anyway." The dilemma is inevitable in the contract-research industry. The leader of a firm has to keep a staff together, and this implies a necessity, in lean times, to bid for every opportunity.

In this connection it is to be reiterated that the worth of an evaluation is not to be conceived narrowly. An evaluator must, as a scientist, feel a certain self-contempt for an inquiry whose end use will be noninformational. We have pointed out, however, that evaluations do contribute to the functioning of the political system by serving, for example, as symbolic reminders of ideals. A democratically minded evaluator will have respect for an assignment that arises out of a mature political process. If he considers unproductive, for example, a state-mandated educational test that leads only to a quickly forgotten tabulation of district-by-district averages, he could, as a citizen, properly present his objections in a political forum. But he would be wrong to assume that legislators had no reason to establish the program; they may judge that scheduling the test heightens teachers' commitment and sense of accountability.

An investigation worthwhile in itself may jeopardize those providing data. One striking difference between the evaluator and the journalist is that a manipulative social investigation alters the services people receive and so alters their conditions of life. The evaluator's responsibility is in this respect greater than that of the journalist. (The two have quite similar responsibilities regarding the privacy and self-respect of their informants.) The symposium volume of Rivlin and Timpane (1975a) is eloquent testimony to the grave risks sometimes imposed on subjects in social experimentation and to the fact that professional thought on ethical issues is not yet mature. A summary of that volume would not be particularly appropriate here, but we do endorse its concerns.

A novel program can impose risks on those it is tried on, whether or not the trial is evaluated (Schultze, 1975). One example would be an experimental housing allowance. The family accepting the allowance moves out of rent-controlled quarters. Then, if the program is discontinued, the family is worse off than it was originally, since the rent-controlled quarters are no longer available to it. (The family suffers the same penalty if it exercises its option to drop out of the trial. Making families aware of this risk is the evaluator's responsibility under the doctrine of "informed consent.")

The policy maker calling for the trial may judge that serious damage to individuals is rare enough to be accepted as a social cost. The policy maker judges in terms of costs and benefits summed over the entire community. The evaluator, however, takes on a professional obligation to the individuals who cooperate with him, and ought to consider safeguards to forestall foreseeable damage. If the safeguards he considers necessary are not provided, he may feel morally obligated to decline the commission and to oppose the experiment.

Informants may suffer when an evaluator's report exposes individuals to censure or to sanction. The evaluator's responsibilities to respect confidences and to disguise the identity of individuals who figure in anecdotal reports are surely obvious enough to require no elaboration, but the will to be discreet is not enough. Case files of investigators were subpoenaed in the New Jersey negative income tax study (Rossi and Lyall, 1976), and this published incident is not unique. At Stanford, for example, a questionnaire on drug usage was administered in nearby high schools as a baseline against which to evaluate a planned intervention, and law enforcement officials subsequently claimed a right of access to the data. When a subpoena opens data files to expose statements made in confidence, too much can be learned from the evaluation! Increasing thought is therefore being given to encoding or aggregating records so that none of the information in the evaluator's files can be traced back to individual informants (Committee on Federal Agency Evaluation Research, 1975; Baratz and Marvin, 1978; Boruch and Cecil, 1979).

An investigation that does not threaten those who take part may nonetheless carry risks for institutions or for a sector of the community. This too is an ethical concern. Consider a plan for identifying "potential delinquents" by some form of testing at age eleven. Research evaluating the test might convince authorities that the plan makes somewhat valid forecasts. Yet the labeling procedure threatens the rights of young persons who have committed no offense, and the confidence that the research gives officials makes the hazard greater.

We see little likelihood that a professional evaluator will falsify data. To present facts in a palatable manner is not falsification; we consider it appropriate, for example, for him to go out of his way to praise some program features before turning to its shortcomings. We mention the possibilities of self-deception only briefly, though it takes much self-discipline to avoid them. Because of his political influence and because time does not allow for the replications that catch the inadvertent errors of the pure scientist, the evaluator has a special obligation to be self-critical in all that he does. If the evaluator fails to monitor himself closely, or if pressure from a sponsor forces him to make a wrong choice, the best correctives lie in critical review and secondary analysis.

Let us illustrate the pitfalls in everyday evaluation procedures. When, in a distribution of cases, the scores for one case are so far removed from the others as to be suspect, there is a legitimate reason to discard those particular scores. The temptation, however, is to discard the case if its evidence constitutes bad news and to keep it if the result is pleasing. Another temptation is to adopt whatever statistical technique makes a treatment effect appear to be statistically significant, even though a better-justified technique leads to a weaker conclusion. Likewise, though every result in analysis is presumably double-checked, the result that gets triple-checked is the one that contradicts the investigator's preconceptions. Thus a main conclusion of the Coleman report was that the aspirations of peers —the "student body" factor—had a larger effect on achievement than did teacher characteristics or facilities and curriculum. This conclusion was closely in line with Coleman's earlier research. But a later analyst (M. Smith, 1972, p. 272) found that inadvertent "mechanical" errors had exaggerated the student body effect. In the reanalysis it ranked third among the three factors as often as it ranked first.

Strictly honest data collection can generate a misleading picture when questions are not framed with the intent of exposing both the facts useful to partisans of the program and those useful to its critics. An example is the time-honored practice of choosing items for educational tests that about half the students are expected to pass. Such items are more powerful for ranking students than are easy or hard items. The National Assessment of Educational Progress adopted another policy, specifically for the sake of evenhandedness. Its tests for a given age deliberately included items that about 90 percent of the students were expected to pass in order to give warranted support to educators who want to advertise school successes. Items that only a few students were expected to pass were included also, as a way to disclose shortcomings (Finley and Berdie, 1970).

The smallest details of evaluative method can be shaped to disclose or to suppress results. In an evaluation of courses at Stanford University, for example, students were asked whether courses had lived up to their billing. For example: "Did this course lead you to consider value systems other than your own?" (as had been promised in the program plan). Since students are not inclined to rate harshly a professor they have found acceptable, a simple "Yes"/"No" format would have produced a ringing endorsement of the courses. The evaluators, to assist in course improvement, offered four carefully phrased response options, not just two: "Yes"; "Yes, but I hoped for more"; "Somewhat"; "Not at all." This gave the student positive language in which to express reservations. (Almost never did a student check "Not at all," except for an item irrelevant to the course. That option served as a buffer and made "Somewhat" a gentle expression of disaffection.) The typical course piled up a count of 90 percent "Yes" on most items. Against that norm, a buildup of "Yes, but" responses on a few items gave the instructor something to think about. The evaluators had provided a channel whereby students could send a message to the instructor in a kindly but impressive manner.

Evaluators who strive to detect both the admirable and the imperfect foster the communication of subordinates with superiors, of clients with program operators, and of potential clients with those who could reach out to them. To neglect such opportunities is to feed complacency on the one side and to let discontent fester on the other.

*The Evaluator's Loyalties.* Evaluators are much less independent than the typical social scientist, as they typically take their charge from an official. Even when they do not, they incur obligations in obtaining access to program sites. The evaluator's relations to the person studied, the person or agency that commissioned him, and the larger PSC can take many forms. Links with one level of the program hierarchy may be close, while those at another level may be distant. And, as Anderson and Ball (1978, p. 128) point out, organizational and financial independence are distinct and have different consequences. These complications can be reduced, for our purposes, to three kinds of relationship: (1) the evaluator allies himself with the staff or community he observes; (2) the evaluator undertakes to serve a central agency that is making policy for the program "from above"; (3) the evaluator is charged by the sponsor to serve the general interest.

In case (1), the evaluator is in effect a part of the staff. He has agreed to advance the interests of those who engaged him, and he is to that extent a captive. The more he is trusted, the better the information he will get and the more help he can give. But the trust imposes an obligation to be thoroughly discreet; moreover, he is expected to make his reports to and through the staff and not to release information to higher authority or to the public. A slightly different obligation arises when he is engaged by the program staff and the client community together; then both elements have to be represented in the advisory committee that receives his reports. The captive evaluator cannot control the uses made of his report; he signed away his rights in taking the commission. It is for those who commissioned him to decide which observations to release and which to suppress. This decision falls within their responsibility to decide which concerns can be handled constructively by public exposure and which are better handled behind the scenes. The one demand the evaluator can properly make is that no false statements be attributed to him.

Macdonald and Walker (1978), whose evaluations consist of intimate case studies of single schools, hold that the evaluator in case (1) should make no independent judgments about what to release even within the institution. They regard an observer's report as the property of the individual observed; they would not release a description of what was seen even to her colleagues until the individual, after seeing the draft description, consents to the release of some or all of it. A similar rule would apply to observations of a staff collectively.

We do not believe that this is generally the best way for an evaluator to proceed. To give the local parents an uncensored appreciation of the school's practices, for example, is likely to be more helpful than to report to and through the professional staff. Rather than accept Macdonald and Walker's constraint, the evaluator might reasonably negotiate for greater freedom. Thus he might agree to restrict his report to what the school principal or a parent could equally have observed if present at the same time and place. The evaluator then would not disclose statements made to him privately, save in an aggregated form that masks their origin. But he would be free to draw attention to a practice that ought to concern those he reports to, even at the risk of distressing the practitioner in question.

What is required is a common understanding from the outset. The evaluator will sometimes accept restrictions in order to work more intimately with a staff, and in other circumstances he will forgo intimacy for the sake of greater freedom to report. As always, his preference should be for what promises to improve the system.

A conception almost the opposite of Macdonald and Walker's is embodied in the report of the prestigious Carnegie Commission on Children (Keniston and others, 1977, p. 145). This commission was concerned particularly with improving local community services, which requires an informed clientele, it said. But if the evaluator is hired by the service agency, as is now the common practice, his wish to be hired again next year biases him strongly toward giving the agency high marks, or so the commission argued. The commission thus proposed that the clientele for a certain kind of service organize formally into a council and hire an evaluator to make a needs assessment and a "quality audit." As we see it, however, this approach puts a premium on finding fault; the more grounds for complaint that the council's evaluator can turn up, the more likely he is to be hired next year. The *ex parte* evaluation seems likely to generate tensions rather than to foster accommodation. Any narrow alliance of the evaluator with a party has its own distinct problems.

Case (2), where the evaluator is commissioned by an official in an upper echelon, is common in the evaluation of dispersed programs, whereas case (1) applies almost exclusively to small, decentralized evaluations. In the stereotypic concept of evaluation, reports go to the decision maker, and only to her. She is free to ignore the information, to suppress it, or to edit and transmit it selectively. Her evaluator is a confidential consultant; his role is akin to that of the company lawyer, the company financial officer, or the executive's physician. When the object of research is technical, the model rarely breaks down. No one at higher levels in a firm wants to examine the manager's quality control charts—not, that is, until there are complaints from customers or a pollution scandal breaks out. When the manager is trusted, closed-circuit communication is left unchallenged.

Managers have many reasons for wishing to maintain control over evaluative information. (See Kelly, 1977). Releasing information selectively helps the manager to defend a decision once she has committed herself and to conceal the uncertainties she had prior to the moment of choice. Purposive release of information enables her to influence subordinates, clients, and higher officials who make resources available to her.

Withholding information also enables the manager to delay a decision while cross-checking or waiting for events to take clearer shape. It preserves the manager's options. For example, an evaluator may find serious fault with three aspects of the work of a unit. The manager may decide to suppress two criticisms while acting swiftly to remedy the third. She might have various reasons for suppressing a criticism: an attempt to advance on all fronts could be too burdensome; an open criticism might be expected to arouse damaging contention; or perhaps the criticism bears on particular staff members whose morale she does not want to shake. The manager, then, can have excellent reasons for commissioning a private study.

The evaluator can respect all such reasons. They fall within the sphere of management and imply no lack of willingness to take the evaluator's information seriously. As Orlans (1972, p. 94) commented, public disclosure of findings of government-supported research can be no more than a utopian goal: "It can counter inclinations toward excessive secrecy, but taken too seriously it can only attenuate the quality of research by limiting its objectives, data, conclusions, and recommendations to those which can be freely revealed. A degree of confidentiality is as necessary to good government as to good diplomacy, good journalism, good social research, and good human relations."

Appropriate as it may be for a manager to commission a scientist to assemble data for her eyes alone, such cloistered investigation lacks an essential feature of science. Central to the scientific process is a social process of challenge and confirmation. The scientist lays out data and interpretations so that peers can question assumptions, offer competing interpretations, repeat procedures on fresh subjects, or in other ways cross-check the conclusions. In the absence of free exchange, corrective processes cannot function. The investigator working *in camera* will try to proceed, one hopes, as he would under conditions of open communication with peers. And, of course, fellow scientists can conduct a proper collegial review within the agency walls. In the absence of at least that exposure, the investigator is only simulating science, just as Army engineers constructing a pontoon bridge on training maneuvers only simulate what engineers under enemy fire would do.

Evaluations of social programs typically arise where political forces press the agency to extend, reduce, or redirect the program. To sponsor an evaluation can be a move in the political game. The agency is committed to certain aims, policies, or programs, and it wants an evaluative report consistent with that commitment. It is entirely understandable that the agency will wish the report to bring out facts consistent with its good repute and further growth. The agency may, then, decide which issues the evaluator is free to examine and may retain the right to preview the report and require modifications. But even a political official may play by case (3) rules, inviting an open inquiry that will be openly reported. Which stance is adopted depends on the program and the political climate.

The same sponsor may encourage free multipartisan inquiry in one instance and constrain the study to "making a case" in another. This is true of private foundations as well as of governmental sponsors. It is true of agencies that arrange evaluations by members of their own staffs and of those that contract with an outsider. The evaluator who is asked to carry out the will of the agency may, if he chooses, decline the commission. But once commissioned, he has an obligation to abide by the agreement. His ethical problem arises from the possibility that in conforming to such understandings he will not represent the public interest.

## The Evaluator as Public Scientist

If Ralph Nader can identify himself as a "public citizen," the evaluator can in prideful, hopeful moments identify himself as a "public scientist." We have urged him to judge his work by its impact on the total system. He ought, then, to plan activities that will serve the public interest to the limit that the terms of his employment allow. The responsibility to consider the interests of all sectors of the PSC enters at all stages of the investigation, but perhaps especially when the research questions are formulated.

If the evaluator does not try to see the program through the eyes of diverse partisans, the posing of the questions may itself—myopically or intentionally—favor the interests of one agency, one sector of society, or the ideology of the evaluator himself. Some lists of outcomes worth measuring, for example, foredoom the program by asking the impossible of it; other definitions turn the evaluator's eyes away from shortcomings and lead to a positive report on practices that are in fact inadequate. Concrete examples of this point have been scattered throughout our book.

A properly comprehensive plan will entertain questions about the program that arise from all sectors of the PSC. We have advised the evaluator to seek out these questions, consulting with prospective and actual clients of the program, with spokespersons for the disadvantaged and for the taxpayer, with program advocates and program critics, and with scholars who know the problem area. This will produce a list of hopes and fears to be considered in selecting variables and observation sites. How intensively each issue will be investigated is a matter for negotiation and judgment; we devote much of Chapter Four to such decisions. Even when a question is dropped from the list, the evaluator can interpret his study better by knowing what politically significant matters have been neglected. In saying this, we are endorsing the statement of Coleman (1972) that the task of the evaluator is to translate societal interests sensitively and accurately into the investigative plan.

Turning to the evaluator's personal values and political sympathies, we amplify on Coleman (1972) and on Mazure (1973) in defining three distinct roles:

1.  At the outset, in the decision to accept a commission, the evaluator's values should loom large. In particular, we urge that he not attempt to evaluate a program with whose basic aims he is not in sympathy; a pacifist agreeing to conduct an

impartial evaluation of ROTC would find himself torn by conflict after conflict. (That the evaluator will be too sympathetic is not a grave danger; the more he believes that an effective program is socially desirable, the keener his search for possible improvements in it will be.)

2. In collecting data, the evaluator strives for openness and neutrality, shaping his techniques to bring both good and bad news to light. When it comes to interpretation, he tries to be as impartial as possible, not by striving for a value-neutral report but by considering the facts from the relevant, no doubt conflicting, value perspectives. He does press to get the possible value-laden perspectives before all the parties, except as agreements he has made proscribe such active communication.

3. Having done his professional job, he puts off his professional robes and, if he chooses, speaks up for what he as a citizen favors.

The advice in the preceding paragraphs makes the evaluator a political actor, perhaps more so than some members of the profession would consider appropriate. As we said in Chapter One, however, we are not advocating a grab for power; we are only recognizing the evaluator's inescapable political influence. Green (1971) and House (1976) have assigned the evaluator a still more active political role. House adopts Rawls' (1971) conception of social justice and turns it into advice that the evaluator advance the interests of the least privileged members of society. As we understand him, House would have the evaluator seek out the data most likely to support programs that benefit the dispossessed—not in a spirit of misrepresentation but in a spirit of highlighting what the well-to-do overlook. Moreover, House would have the investigator interpret the facts from the standpoint of citizens who are least well-off and would have him try to persuade the entire PSC to do what will best serve that subgroup. The facts reported would be legitimate, honest fruits of research; the partisanship would lie in the emphasis given them.

For our part, we advise the evaluator to be multipartisan, to make the best case he can for each side in turn. The evaluator's values enter his work in three distinct ways; in Green's and House's recommendations, however, his roles as conscientious public servant, impartial inquirer, and member of the electorate become blurred.

The evaluator's personal and professional interest is in providing information that will be taken seriously and will lead to better public services. He loses credibility—and so does the whole professional—if his reports are seen as special pleading for his sponsor or some other partisan. The evaluator can state lofty terms on which he will undertake a simon-pure study, but he will then find himself out of business (Brickell, 1976). Other hands will do the work, on terms acceptable to the sponsor. The evaluator should therefore use his opportunities to negotiate so that he can better serve the public interest.

The crucial issue appears to be freedom to communicate during and after a study, subject to legitimate concerns for privacy, national security, and keeping the agency in question governable. If the study procedures are completely documented and the data files are available for reanalysis, a proper review is possible. It does not matter whether the review is undertaken in the spirit of science, or of the audit profession, or of partisan counterattack; the possibility of review invites the evaluator to do his best and discourages the sponsor from distorting findings in transmitting them.

Extensive discussion of the problem of reconciling scientific ideals with the political milieu has taken place—a discussion that has focused as much on arms limitation and environmental impact as on social programs (Caywood and others, 1971; Dror, 1971; MacRae, 1973; Quade, 1975; Stake, 1976; Brickell, 1976; Ezrahi, in press). There now appears to be widespread, though not unanimous, agreement on these principles (here restated to apply to evaluation):

1. The evaluator should have an explicit written understanding with the sponsor as to their respective rights to release information.

2. Having entered into such an agreement, the evaluator should abide by it, short of tacit complicity in perjury.
3. The evaluator should not undertake to serve an agency unless he is in sympathy with its general mission.
4. In planning and interpreting his work, the evaluator should think in terms of the larger public interest even when that is inconsistent with the parochial interests of the agency.
5. The evaluator should not agree to let an agency alter or withhold his reports if he has reason to believe that in past instances the agency has distorted evaluative information in releasing it.
6. Provision should be made for full scrutiny, by a panel of qualified reviewers who are not aligned with the sponsoring agency, of any politically controversial finding. Such review may be carried out *in camera*, when public disclosure would not be in the public interest.

Two specific comments are called for. Regarding the second point, conscience will in a rare instance impel an evaluator to make public what he has agreed to conceal, even though he will thereby jeopardize his career, damage the firm he works for, and hurt the reception of other evaluators by already jittery agencies (B. Smith, 1977, p. 256). No abstract principle can serve as a guide for eventualities, and it is unlikely that the ethics of a particular action will be viewed in the same way by all detached observers. With regard to the fourth point, we note that some critics would have social scientists refuse to undertake a study intended to provide a supporting brief for a position that the sponsor has already settled on. But selective use of facts is a legitimate part of the political process; an ethical issue arises only if opponents of the position are denied an opportunity to use the underlying corpus of evidence as a basis for making *their* case.

It is not easy for evaluators to take the necessary tough negotiating posture toward employers or sponsors. The individual evaluator has only one card to play, that is, his willingness to turn down a commission. The prospective employee or contractor who negotiates by himself is in a weak position. Appropriate protection of the public interest will become more likely as a strong professional community develops. Communal discussion will clarify issues and evolve norms. Over time, collective action can win increased freedom to live by these norms (MacRae, 1976).

# 4

■■■■■■■■■■■■■■■■

# Allocating Research
# Resources

■■■■■■■■■■■■■■■■■

An evaluative inquiry lights a candle in the darkness, but it never brings dazzling clarity. On the one hand, there are limits to what can be included in an inquiry; on the other, the list of significant questions is almost unlimited. Moreover, the full meaning of even the best study will become apparent only when its findings have been integrated with information developed concurrently by other sources, and even that interpretation will be modified by later experience.

This chapter and the following one take up the innumerable choices made in planning, analyzing, and reporting an evaluation of a program. "Design" of research is far more than laying out $X$'s and $O$'s to represent treatments, rules for assigning units to treatments, and measurements—"tic-tac-toe," as Cooley (1978) calls it. Along with Cook and Campbell (1979, pp. 343 and 384), we reject the view that "design" begins *after* a research question is chosen, as a mere technical process to sharpen the inquiry. Choice of questions and choice of inves-

213

tigative tactics are inseparable. Political considerations, as well
as substantive and technical ones, should influence what the
evaluator does.

The scale and the cost of an evaluation should be in keeping with the usefulness of the information and the attention it is
likely to get. Balance is hard to achieve. The overambitious evaluator can easily commit himself to an impossible task or to
a study so grand that its payoff is sure to disappoint. Awareness
of this hazard encourages modesty in planning. No one should
harbor the illusion that even a massive and masterful study will
end argument about a program.

Firm directives to guide evaluation practice are not to
be hoped for. Given the diversity of programs and possible investigations, advice on planning has to be nonprescriptive and
contingent. The design that suits a program in one political setting will not necessarily fit other settings and programs. Even
for a single study, no one design is ideal in all respects.

Evaluators gain much experience in the course of designing and redesigning a study. Unfortunately, little of that experience is recorded for the benefit of the evaluation community.
Rarely does a research report mention the branching points
where the study took one shape rather than another or explain
why the final plan was preferred. Indeed, most of the choices
that shape the evaluation are made rapidly and by tacit consent
rather than by explicit weighing of options. Methods of evaluation would improve faster if evaluators more often wrote retrospective accounts of design choices. These accounts should
reach well beyond the "tic-tac-toe" aspects of the design to consider how questions were chosen, how resources were deployed,
how quality of data was controlled, and how observations were
assembled for communication.

This chapter sets forth a perspective that was developed
through strenuous discussions among members of the writing
group. In another manuscript one of us discusses the design of
evaluations in more detail and somewhat more technically
(Cronbach, in preparation). The two presentations are in harmony, we think, but they are cousins, not clones.

## Design: A Question of Balance

How to design an evaluation is a lively topic in the current literature, as it should be. But many of the writers, regrettably, seem convinced that there is just one best way to evaluate, and most of them advocate a summative, hypothesis-testing style. In elaborating on the stereotypic concept of evaluation as "appraisal" (see Chapter One), some writers set forth commandments:

1. Thou shalt test the worth of a program whose goals are definite and whose plans have been fully worked out. Otherwise, don't evaluate.
2. Thou shalt compare. Compare the program that is of central interest with almost anything else, but compare!
3. Thou shalt assign. Preferably, distribute subjects or institutions so as to make the comparison groups equivalent.
4. Thou shalt measure goal attainment. Since comparison is possible only when the same measuring stick is applied to all groups, concentrate on the goals that the programs have in common.
5. Thy instruments shall be reliable.
6. Thy procedures shall be objective.

. . . . . . . . . . . . . . . . . . . . . . . . . . . . . . . . . . . . . . . .

10. Thou shalt judge. Tell the client how good or bad the treatment is.

These stern commandments are softened a bit when side remarks acknowledge restrictions on their applicability. The evaluator who accepts the commandments as an ideal will do no more than approximate it in practice, and most writers admit that. Sometimes, indeed, the one who lays down commandments is playing Humpty-Dumpty, not Jehovah. His rules of procedure mean no more than this: "Many styles of research into a program are warranted; *I*, however, choose not to call a study an evaluation unless it is in *this* style."

We are not in accord with these commandments or even with the idea that certain designs are to be preferred over others. The issue is one of spirit more than of substance; we emphasize not form of inquiry but relevance of information. The tasks set before evaluators and the appropriate patterns of inquiry are infinitely variable. Whether the context is one of command or accommodation, the stage of program maturity and the closeness of the evaluator to the probable users should affect the style of the inquiry. Under many circumstances, the emphasis on assessment of outcomes of a supposedly fixed program runs counter to the aims of understanding the problem and rendering better service.

In speaking of commandments, we do not exaggerate. A "checklist" released for comment by the General Accounting Office (GAO) (Comptroller General, 1978) makes this evident. In effect, the document lays down rules for agencies in the executive branch and their contractors—rules whose violation may bring censure by an agent of Congress. The word *must* appears several times on the typical page; these are indeed commandments. A few sentences can indicate the rationalist flavor of the document (Comptroller General, 1978, pp. 13–14): "Before attempting to study the program's impact, the evaluator must also determine that the program has actually been implemented and the intended operations are being accomplished. . . .

"[The] evaluator must be able to identify the program's contribution to any effect measured. The certainty with which this cause and effect relationship can be established is referred to as the study's 'internal validity.' Without some degree of internal validity, the evaluation is useless; when the effects of the program remain confused with those of other programs or of the environment, there is no adequate basis for making decisions. . . .

"Establishing internal validity requires comparison. The most rigorous form of comparison is the experimental method.

"When less certainty is acceptable, other methods are available. . . ."

External validity is acknowledged only as a secondary consideration to be achieved by replicating the internally valid study in diverse settings.

We place our emphasis quite differently. In particular, we do not consider it reasonable to separate the effects of the program from the rest of the client's experience. As Pillemer and Light (1979) demonstrate, an educational program that appears superior when compared with a rival program in isolation may be inferior when each program is embedded in the regular sequence of school experience. Although we criticize the GAO document, our criticism is muted for several reasons. To issue standards in draft form in itself implies readiness to hear counterarguments. The document is generally sophisticated, and we concur with many of its statements. Taken as a whole, it is less positivistic and stereotypic than a similar document would have been five years ago. The final version will be vastly significant.

The commandments conceive of evaluation as confirmatory research. If a hypothesis is to be tested formally, it is sound discipline to fix it at the outset. But confirmatory research properly comes after exploratory research, as statisticians recognize. Exploratory inquiry is the mode of a scientist coming to understand a phenomenon—and that is the evaluator's proper assignment also. An evaluator looking for sensible hypotheses as he goes along cannot adopt the usual statistical logic. Even among writers on evaluation who press for confirmatory proof that Program A has a greater effect than Program B, the sophisticated ones (including the GAO) warn against premature confirmatory testing. A strong test is sensible only after sufficient pilot work has pinned down the definition of each treatment.

Given a developing political situation, an expensive, focused statistical comparison of alternatives may appear worthwhile or it may not. Rivlin (1974) provides a politically sophisticated reflection on comparative trials of complex programs: "[I]nterest in the innovation may have died before it reaches a stable state." Moreover, Rivlin questions whether it is desirable to perfect a design and impose it on several sites so as to test the theoretical model. After the experimenter with his artificial constraint leaves the scene, the operating program is sure to be adapted to local conditions.

How statisticians reason about the use of formal designs is illustrated in the following passage from Gilbert, Mosteller, and Tukey (1976). The first two have written a number of papers advocating tough-minded confirmatory evaluations; hence this passage in another such paper is highly significant:

> Before these confirmatory studies are carried out, extensive preparation must already have gone on, preparation that may be much more difficult and time consuming than carrying out the confirmatory studies. Preliminary information about the process under study, information that leads someone to have insights about the sorts of programs that are needed, is absolutely essential. These insights often come from theory and from good anecdotal evidence—that is, careful case studies—and they may also come from other sorts of qualitative and quantitative investigations. Without such insights leading to programs, there will be no programs to test.
>
> But good ideas are not enough either. After such ideas must come the often tiresome work of developing them into a going program, something very concrete that can be taken to the field and tried out, not in competition with anything, but just to get the bugs out. These steps may be called pilot studies or they may be demonstration studies. And some fields may have other names for them. Sometimes years of work are required to bring ideas to this level of practicality. Thus the aspect of the work we treat in this paper comes after a great deal of solid initial work has gone on. That such initial work is essential must not go without saying, even though the present paper emphasizes a different aspect of program evaluation.
>
> Thus, we need a true partnership between innovation, development, execution, and evaluation, or progress will always falter. To sum up, not only must insight and exploration come before evaluation, but after exploration must come development and feasibility studies.
>
> Equally, confirmation—either positive or negative—has to be the foundation from which the

next generation of insight, perception, and anecdote development climbs to new improvements. A good example is given in Gilbert, Light, [and] Mosteller [1975] where a particular new surgical treatment was found not to be successful, but the investigation that showed this to be so has been the rock upon which the next ten years of successful research in that area was built [pp. 297–298].

A statement with similar implications appears in Riecken and Boruch (1974, pp. 32–33), and Cook and Campbell (1979, p. 345) also warn against "premature experimentation" in evaluation research. The GAO standard seems to make the same point. But if one is to compare two policy proposals, the degree to which operators translate each into the intended field operations may be one of the most important dependent variables; the standard quoted above rules out this variation.

*Multiple Studies Within a Single Frame.* The evaluator observes one program plan or eight, follows subjects for six months or six years, takes events where they are found or arranges them for the sake of investigation. Such choices—the kind with which the commandments are concerned—frame only the outer limits of the research; it is convenient to speak of this set of decisions as defining the "hull" of the study. The plan for the hull generally identifies sites or a sampling plan, one or more treatment plans, and the outcome variables that are to be measured everywhere. Within a hull, substudies are appropriate and sometimes essential. The substudies may take many forms, as Boruch (1975) suggests: small formal experiments within quasi-experiments, quasi-experiments within randomized experiments, and so on. Many questions about a program or problem area arise, in parallel or in succession. Hence an evaluative inquiry ought to launch a small fleet of studies, each with its own plan and time schedule (Saxe and Fine, 1979; Cordray and Lipsey, 1979).

Evaluative inquiry as a program of evolving studies using many methods is particularly well illustrated by Tharp and Gallimore's report (1979) on a developmental effort that has extended over six years in a single site. Only now is the program being disseminated to other schools on a significant scale and undergoing tests in them. At every stage of development, evaluative information played a crucial role; this happy relationship was possible because the evaluators were also the chief developers and because the local sponsor provided continuous support.

Tharp and Gallimore describe how a philanthropic foundation in Hawaii, committed to improving the education of the children of Hawaiian descent and, secondarily, of children in other ethnic groups, established a special school for research and development. The school enrolls about 100 children from kindergarten through grade 3, and new entrants are selected at random each year from a district of Honolulu where families are predominantly disadvantaged and ethnically diverse.

According to Tharp and Gallimore, the program was perceived at the start as a blend of elements that could be independently judged, then revised or eliminated. Some elements (physical education, for example) were not evaluated. Some, such as training teachers to rely heavily on praise, were retained because evaluations consistently supported them. Others were tested and abandoned. For example, a small formal experiment compared teaching letter recognition individually with teaching it in groups; because the group version came out ahead, it survived. A cumulation of observational, correlational, and experimental results, combined with continual tinkering, led the developers to a reading element based on phonics that could be "fixed" for a year of formal trial.

In a quasi-experimental comparison, the trial program did not beat out the normal program of a neighborhood school; achievement was poor in both settings. The program element was replaced with an approach emphasizing comprehension—an approach that had already been under development with a class of recently enrolled children. A one-semester experiment did show superior outcomes from this alternative, but the plan was not considered finished. Rather, intensive observation of students and teachers, together with frequent performance tests and frequent adjustments to the program plan, occupied the next semester. Results at this time were judged by a standardized posttest; finding that the class median matched the 70th percentile of the norms was sufficient reason to stabilize the element.

Now a grand "program evaluation" was run, with one randomly assigned group receiving all the program elements that had evolved from separate developmental cycles and a control group receiving none of them. Favorable though the results were, the evaluators are continuing informal and microexperimental studies to improve the elements. And they continue summative evaluation, if only through regular end-of-year achievement tests.

At any one time in this history, several studies were in progress—some highly controlled and others uncontrolled, some brief and others year long. The balance of the several styles of research shifted as the program matured. Formal research was blended with the experience of teachers and with advice from linguists and anthropologists in producing the current package. The evaluators liken the package to the "climax" stage of a forest—not unchanging, but unlikely to be replaced by a different range of organisms until conditions change drastically.

In evaluating a dispersed program, studies conducted by different teams can capitalize on disparate perspectives and technical skills. Multiple investigations expose complexities and so reduce the urge to generalize grandiosely. The wealth of wisdom that can alleviate a social problem is no lone explorer's cargo; it can be drawn only from a treasure room that many expeditions have stocked.

*Obtaining Adequately Complex Information.* The evaluator is essentially a historian: he helps individuals and organizations to learn from what has happened. The historian prefers to study remote events, after time has diminished passion and provided perspective. The evaluator never has that luxury, but he has a countervailing asset. He can accumulate his own record of events instead of relying exclusively on documents prepared for participants' purposes. Moreover, with strong enough backing, he can shape some of the events so as to make the lessons of experience more telling.

The evaluator, of course, can report only on occurrences at a particular time in a few particular places. This is true even of the formal, large-scale experiment. Recall that the negative income tax experiment was set up in New Jersey specifically because that state had no general welfare plan. The experimenters pitted several benefit plans against one another. But midway in the experimental period New Jersey established an operational welfare plan using state funds. The federal payments were less attractive than the payments from New Jersey for some of the experimental subjects, and selective dropout resulted. To interpret results, the investigators had to take note that data were collected in two historically distinct periods, marked off by the start of welfare payments from state funds.

Natural scientists can acknowledge without distress that a report of a scientific experiment is a history of a time and place. The scientist assumes that the same experiment could be reproduced in other epochs—that is to say, that changes in society and the environment make no difference within the laboratory walls. This assumption is highly plausible in the physical sciences, less so when biologists work with fast-evolving species, and it becomes highly dubious when sophomores read in a textbook about a psychological experiment before *they* become subjects in a replication (Gergen, 1973). Finally, a program evaluation is so dependent on its context that replication of it is only a figure of speech.

To say that the end product of evaluation will be a history does not depreciate quantification, comparison, controlled assignment, and objective measurement. These have their time, place, and function; we ask only that they be introduced as a result of reason and not reflex. Like Campbell (1974) and Weiss and Rein (1969), we see a large place for qualitative data and qualitative interpretation in evaluation. In particular, qualitative case studies may reasonably be completed within a statistical plan; quantitative controls can bolster what is, overall, a case study. And we do not go so far in opposing the quantitative as does the humanistic school of evaluators (see Hamilton and others, 1978).

The possibility of using intensive qualitative studies of local sites is well illustrated by the work of a committee of the National Research Council. The Committee on Evaluation of Employment and Training Programs was established to review the impact and potentialities of the Comprehensive Employment and Training Act (CETA) of 1973. Case studies of local projects dramatized both the variation in experiences and the problems that agencies had in responding to new responsibilities. The studies also documented and made concrete the conclusions from the quantitative national survey, which in a sense was the "main" evaluation (Mirengoff, 1978).

The prevailing view of everday social phenomena, is expressed in common language. The practical aim of social inquiries is to alter this interpretation (Shils, 1977; Campbell, 1975a). Campbell notes that recognizing this function "immediately legitimizes the 'narrative history' portion of most evaluative reports and suggests that this activity be given formal recognition in the planning and execution of the study.... Evaluation studies are uninterpretable without this, and most would be better interpreted with more" (p. 9).

The evaluator will be wise not to declare allegiance to either a quantitative-manipulative-summative methodology or a qualitative-naturalistic-descriptive methodology. He can draw on both styles at appropriate times and in appropriate amounts. Those who advocate an evaluation plan devoid of one kind of information or the other carry the burden of justifying such exclusion.

The hypothesis-testing mode views the program—the treatment—as a fixed and unified stimulus applied to the system. The reaction—the outcome—is measured. But, as Hastings (1966) put it, the evaluator ought to be concerned with "the why of the outcomes." Weiss' classic book (1972b) elaborates admirably on Hastings' theme. Here are a few of her statements with which we fully concur:

> It is important to look at program variations.... [T]hey show the range of elements that are encompassed by the program-that-is. [Also,] the analysis of program variables begins to explain why the program has the effects it does. When we know which aspects of the program are associated with more or less success, we have a basis for recommendations for future modifications [pp. 45–46].
>
> The increase in information [from seeing the single treatment as a collection of diverse realizations] is of two kinds—increase in generalizability of results, and increase in the specification of which

strategy under which conditions has better effects
with different kinds of participants [pp. 78–79].

We try to identify the means and the steps
by which a program is intended to work. . . . The
model [the evaluator constructs] indicates the
kinds of effects that should be investigated. Once
. . . measurements are made, it is possible to see
what happens, what works and what doesn't, for
whom it works and for whom it doesn't [pp.
50–51].

There are many variables that are interesting
to study. . . . But most evaluations have limited resources. . . . After considering the range of possible
variables, the evaluator usually has to make his selection on the basis of scraps of data, the accumu-
lated folk wisdom of practitioners, or the application of theory. Until research provides better
information, these are not negligible sources of
plausible hypotheses [p. 47].

*Choosing Among Questions.* The list of questions relevant
to political actors is almost endless, and it is never complete.
When a program is proposed, each sector of the policy-shaping
community (PSC) will have its own slant on it. Additional questions surface during the tryout. So the list of questions whose
answers might have leverage on action tends to grow as the evaluation moves forward. The resources available for studying
these countless questions are severely limited. Never is there
enough money, staff, and time to do all that seems worth doing.
At best, an agency increases the budget for one evaluation only
by withdrawing funds from another evaluation or from service
to clients.

The most painful constraint on evaluators is that quick
answers are called for. Marris and Rein (1972, p. 3) have commented on "the dilemma of research which hopes to be useful.
The longer it takes, the more thorough the knowledge. But by
then the events it describes are long since past, the context of
decisions may have changed, and its insight is of only historical
interest. And conversely, the more immediately relevant the

comment, the sketchier is the understanding on which it is based. An exact, thorough analysis of a particular event can usually only be made long afterwards, when the knowledge is no longer directly useful. . . . Thus the search for accurate judgment conflicts with the urgency of decisions."

Evaluation cannot possibly give a responsible answer to all the questions that arise about a program. The research plan should give most attention to those uncertainties that have greatest significance for the PSC. Variables of lesser significance can well be given less systematic attention or none at all. Deciding what not to look into is part of design. Planning calls for artful trade-offs in deploying resources.

The trade-offs do not boil down to purely technical decisions. Abt (1978) reported on the evolution of plans for a study of rural schools. Alternative strategies were debated hotly because each strategy challenged certain interests, preconceptions, or political allegiances. The research staff felt that its reputation and future funding depended on the technical strength of the design. The sponsor wanted the program operators to receive formative help even if this would make the data unrepresentative. Anthropologists were at odds with the experimentally minded. Some parties favored dropping the study on the grounds that the "treatment"—extra dollars for each school to use as it pleased—could not possibly yield an explainable, generalizable result. In the end, the arguments were settled by negotiation. Adjustment took place at the margins, as agency policies shifted and personnel changed. Abt's case history makes it clear that designing a large study is a continuing political process.

As in the instance just discussed, most program evaluations are planned partly by an evaluation team under contract and partly by the staff of the sponsoring agency. The sponsor's representative is acting as a member of the evaluation community and ought to view the plan through the eyes of the evaluator in the field. Decisions may be made by one or both of these parties or by a more inclusive group. (With a few obvious exceptions, in Chapters Four and Five the term *evaluator* should be understood to refer to all parties who think through the evaluation plans.)

A reasonable strategy is to think first of the least costly design that might answer a particular question. Envisioning the objections that a critic might make to discredit an unpalatable answer from that limited design will suggest the most important ways to augment it. The aim is not to achieve a watertight design but one sound enough to allow the ship to make port. Bear in mind that it will have to pass through gales of criticism blown up by those distressed by a conclusion. Added controls make the design more likely to weather the critical objections, but it is not practicable to guard against all possible ambiguities and objections. At most one guards against the counterinterpretations that would be credible and that would confuse discussion in the PSC.

Adding a control costs something in dollars, in attention, and perhaps in quality of data. Records routinely collected by the operating units are cheap and unobtrusive sources for the evaluator. Being outside the evaluator's control, however, these records will be of uncertain accuracy. Worse, pretreatment data may not be recorded by the same rules as posttreatment data. The evaluator therefore will almost certainly want to invest in direct observations of his own. But it is far cheaper to use spot checks to find out which routine records provide adequate data than to reject them out of hand. Collecting fresh data on what has been recorded is a necessity only when the records prove to be hopelessly erratic.

A control that fortifies the study in one respect is likely to weaken it in another. Many of the commandments mentioned earlier favor artificiality in the field trial. This is not in itself objectionable; all science relies on artifice to get better evidence. Some controls, however, change the investigation in such a way that it no longer bears on the important questions. Standardizing delivery of the treatment, for example, is often recommended so that the investigator will know just what variable he is drawing a conclusion about. But to do this at the prototype stage of program evolution has a serious cost: one no longer is testing the program under normal operating conditions (Cook and McAnany, 1977).

No matter which way the designer turns, he leaves a flank open to critical attack. The federal watchdog agencies have tended to favor controlled comparative experiments and to attack evaluations that have not been forced into that mold. But they attacked with equal ferocity the plans for one of the most strongly controlled social experiments to date—the Experimental Housing Allowance Program. An operational program of this type would have applied throughout the nation to all needy families. The Office of Management and Budget (OMB) and the General Accounting Office (GAO), between them, raised such questions as these: Could even a ten-year study in a few sites show how landlords and investors would respond to a permanent and universal program? Would data from sites such as South Bend, Indiana—small enough for an affordable experiment—be pertinent to the large urban centers where housing problems are greatest? Can providing benefits to a fraction of the eligible households in a community provide a reasonable picture of the effect of a community-wide intervention on housing supply? Could the strict controls on eligibility built into the experiment be maintained in a national program? If not, what would happen to costs? (Committee on Evaluation Research, 1978). Fears regarding the political consequences of the trial were an additional concern at OMB but not at the GAO (see Chapter Three).

As we have said, when an evaluation is planned, divergent and convergent thinking are both required. It is convenient to speak of both a divergent "phase" in which the widest possible array of questions is entertained and a convergent "phase" in which the list is reduced and resources allocated to study the survivors. In reality, convergence starts very early. And, though divergent thinking tapers off, it should never stop; new questions will come up even after all the data are in.

Four considerations—two external and two internal—enter convergent decision making; we mention them here only as a preliminary to later discussion. The two "external" considerations are prior uncertainty and leverage. First, is the PSC divided in its beliefs about what will happen when the program is introduced? Second, would new information on the point influence subsequent discussion and action? The concern that rates high on both leverage and prior uncertainty becomes a prime candidate for thorough investigation. The two considerations internal to the design are cost and information yield. A given investment will do only so much to reduce uncertainty. Questions of equal importance are likely to differ in the investment required to get reasonably dependable answers to them, and some important questions cannot be answered for a tolerable price. Minor questions are worth looking into if a small investment will yield good information. These four aspects of convergent decision making are considered simultaneously in planning and replanning the study.

*Need for Flexibility*. The reference to replanning introduces another of our recurrent themes. Plans should be kept as open as is practicable. One reason for this is that the leverage of questions changes with time. New uncertainties arise during a study—sometimes out of the evaluator's observations, sometimes out of the movement of public discussion. New voices raise new questions. When prototype operations begin, a program staff is assembed, and someone must now come to grips with operational details. Fieldworkers spot crucial variables that were overlooked earlier. Community members enlisted as guinea pigs for the trial may call attention to processes and effects whose importance no one else had noticed. At the same time, the investigator begins to discover that some matters are harder (or easier) to pin down than he anticipated (Field and Orr, 1975). When cost-yield projections shift, the plan for data collection ought to change in response.

Textbooks on design are silent about flexibility, and many evaluators are insensitive to its importance. Sometimes the evaluative search party continues to snuffle faithfully on the trial of the quarry that policy officials asked them to track down, long after the policy team itself has veered off in another direction.

Properly flexible response is illustrated in a study of instructional television in junior high schools that was set up in El Salvador with funds from U.S. Agency for International Development (USAID). If instructional television was found to outperform traditional schooling in El Salvador, similar broad-casting systems in other countries would be funded by USAID. The evaluators were given a general charge: Appraise the value of instructional television for developing countries. Four years later the evaluation data were in hand—but the policy winds had shifted. USAID no longer wanted to spend money on formal schooling; instead, serving nonelite populations had become its conscious policy. In Washington, junior high school instruction was a dead issue since, in developing countries, the junior high schools serve mostly the well-to-do. Aware of the political change, the evaluators addressed their report to current prior-ities. The entry of television technology, they said, had stimu-lated changes of many kinds in the schools. Could not a fresh technology break up fossilized routines in other equally static institutions? The report went on to emphasize possible benefits to the disadvantaged of a broadcasting system for educational purposes (Mayo, Hornik, and McAnany, 1976). Thus, while the tests and observations in schools were not ignored, the ques-tions asked of the data were not those originally foreseen.

Choice of questions and procedures, then, should be tentative. Budgetary plans should not commit every hour and every dollar to the samples and operations of the initial plan. Quite a bit of time and money should be held in reserve. It is often advisable to arrange for successive waves of investigation that start at different dates in different sites. Even a few months of observation may permit important improvement in the pro-gram (or the research procedures). A surprise result observed casually in the first wave can become a focus of inquiry in a sec-ond wave. Later samples can overrepresent the kinds of cases on which more thorough evidence is wanted. In a later sample one can measure initial characteristics that no one thought to assess systematically in the first one.

The contract for an evaluation too often rigidifies the study. Research whose prospective operations are unspecified or are open to change is uncongenial to the bureaucracy that con-tracts for an evaluation; such research is unpredictable and there-fore risky. Programmatic support has, however, paid off in basic research, where only a general direction of inquiry is foreseen.

The head of the GAO himself so testifies (Staats, 1979). Those who fund and oversee evaluations should think in the same terms.

When the time is ripe for a confirmatory study, certain aspects of the plan do have to be set firmly. But flexibility of evaluation is still in order (Edwards and Cronbach, 1952). Evaluators can keep a free-ranging history of events, can mount structured studies of process variables that emerge as important, and can add outcome measures when new variables come to prominence. None of this spoils the hypothesis test unless the evaluator acts so obtrusively that he modifies the course of events. A study of infant nutrition in Guatemala, for example, had a strong formal design. This did not prevent the investigators from responding to unforeseen events and exploring a whole range of new phenomena (Klein and others, 1979). Nor did the exploration compromise the confirmatory experiment that was the basis of the inquiry.

The original hypothesis for the Guatemala study was that adding protein to the diet would make a critical difference in physical and intellectual growth. Social centers were set up in two villages where expectant mothers and young children were given as much of a protein-rich supplement (*atole*) as they wished. Similar centers were set up in two control villages; the villages were allocated between treatments at random. Mothers and children visiting the control centers received a sweet drink (*fresco*) that provided some calories but no protein. When data from newborns in the cohort began to flow in, growth proved to be associated with number of calories of supplement received, regardless of the type of supplement. With caloric intake held constant, it seemed to make no difference whether the children received *atole* or *fresco*. This led the evaluators to look more closely at the normal native diet. Contrary to what had been anticipated when plans were laid, the normal diet in these villages was not seriously lacking in protein, but it was short on calories. The study thus could neither affirm nor deny the value of a protein supplement for children who *normally* eat little protein. Analyses in Guatemala from that time forward concentrated on caloric intake. Because participation in the program was voluntary, this treatment variable was not under experimental control. Fortunately, however, intake had been recorded, and the extensive records from the four sites provided good correlational evidence on the effect of extra calories. The study was able to relate the effect both to age of ingestion and to background factors that determined who came to the center.

## Extrapolation in Using Conclusions

Writings on experimental design emphasize extrapolation much less than is appropriate for evaluation. Data on a particular set of program operations are collected in specific sites, but the evaluation is intended to answer a much broader question. Logic enables one to generalize formally to the domain from which he sampled, but members of the PSC extrapolate his findings to modified programs and to sites of a kind not studied. The design best for sharpening a limited statistical conclusion may not be the best basis for the broader inferences. "External validity" —validity of inferences that go beyond the data—is the crux in social action, not "internal validity." These terms were made famous by Campbell and his co-workers; see Campbell (1957) and Campbell and Stanley (1963). We give the term *internal validity* a slightly broader sense than these authors did. We retain the original two categories; Cook and Campbell, (1976, 1979) have proposed a four-category system that is more elaborate than our argument requires.

Others have said repeatedly that internal validity is the *sine qua non*, as if one could not have external validity without satisfactory internal validity. All the commandments on evaluation are intended to increase internal validity. But again, we emphasize the trade-off involved: narrowing one's question can tighten the design and increase internal validity to some extent, but relevance is likely to suffer. Writers on evaluation who see this dilemma are sharply divided in their recommendations. On the one hand, Parlett and Hamilton (1972) favor the naturalistic design with few controls: "rarely can 'tidy' results be generalized to an 'untidy' reality" (p. 8). On the other hand, Boruch and Gomez (1979) find distressing untidiness even in the highly structured field experiment and set out to devise additional controls. Either answer, by itself, is too simple to have wide applicability. A balance has to be worked out to fit the evaluation in hand.

An investigator states a question by specifying a treatment, a population, and a measuring procedure. The specifications define domains, not instances; the three respective domains are identified by the symbols $T$, $U$, and $O$. The three together—with a convenient change of order—form a composite domain $UTO$ from which the investigation considers a sample. (In this code, a letter or set of letters may have a singular or plural meaning. Thus we speak of a particular unit $u$ or a sample $u$.) The domains are these:

$U:$ The population of independent units to be studied—communities, schools, clinics, individual pupils or clients, and so on. If treatments are applied independently to individuals, $u$ is the familiar kind of sample, that is, a sample of persons from a defined population. In evaluation, however, it is often more logical to think of the unit as the classroom or other site. The sites studied constitute a sample; many other sites would have been of equal interest.

$T:$ The treatment to be studied, defined as a plan to be carried out. If the program operations are already under way when the study begins, the investigator requires rules for recognizing instances where "the treatment" is being applied. Thus $T$ may be the category "informal teaching in the fourth grade"; the investigator has to decide which teaching styles will count as "informal." Any one instance of the treatment is a $t$, a particular realization; it differs from other instances that also fall within the category $T$. We use $T_A$ and $T_B$ at times to indicate the alternative treatments in a comparative study; for each alternative, there is a sample of realizations.

$O:$ A variable to be measured, described in terms of a universe of admissible observing operations (occasions, observers, test stimuli, and so on). Variables include data on initial status of persons and institutions, on process, and on outcomes. $O$ can refer to one variable or to several indicators collectively. The plan for collecting data chooses a sample

$o$ for each $O$. To appraise spelling skills, the investigator asks the pupil on a given day to write a given list of words; other days and other words would have served just as well.

Every research question can be stated in approximately this form: "What scores on $O$ result when $T$ is applied to $U$?" (Sometimes the question asks about the relation of one $O$ to another). The data are limited, however, to observations $o$, following application of $t$ to $u$. Generalization is thus required. Investigators are well aware that they generalize from $u$ to $U$, and conventional statistical procedures highlight the risks of generalizing from $uto$ to $Uto$. But evaluators and readers often do not realize that a conclusion also generalizes to domain $O$ or $T$.

Failure to recognize that $o$ imperfectly represents whatever $O$ the conclusion mentions has serious consequences. For example, the conclusion that "schooling makes no difference" of Jencks and others (1972) is reversed when the incompleteness of measurement is allowed for (Luecke and McGinn, 1975; for a nontechnical summary, see Aaron, 1978, pp. 81 and 103).

Evaluators who observe a single $t$ or just a few instances of $t$ speak too readily of a generalized $T$, such as "informal teaching." The interpreter with strong self-discipline may confine his statements to the narrow $T$ that the data represent. He may say, for example, that his conclusion applies only to performance contracting as established in his experiment by certain guidelines, contract conditions, and relations of teachers to suppliers of lessons. In other words, he consciously restricts his generalization. Even so, his hearers are apt to disregard these strictures and to think in terms of a broader treatment domain. They think not about $T$ but about what we may call a $T^*$. We use $U^*$, $T^*$, or $O^*$ to symbolize a domain that differs from $U$, $T$, or $O$ respectively. Any question that alters one or more of the domains is a new question, symbolized by $*UTO$. (Read this as "star $UTO$"; the asterisk is placed in front to avoid the suggestion that $U$ and $T$ are combined with $O^*$.)

As policy options are never confined to the operations studied, the PSC is concerned chiefly with inferences to various $*UTO$. Often a finding of the evaluation itself suggests a $T^*$ to replace the original $T$; a judgment as to its probable outcomes then has to be made. A public health campaign, for example, may have little effect on practices in comparatively isolated cultural groups where physical disorders are regarded as acts of God rather than as something to take action against. (The campaign in Nicaragua described below might turn out this way.) Someone may then suggest modifying the campaign to create an identification with this religious belief. The conjecture that the change will work is a judgment about a $T^*$. The inference is supported by substantive beliefs, not by statistical logic. An even longer reach is involved in an inference from a public health study in Nicaragua ($U$) to one in Gambia ($U^*$). But an official in the World Health Organization has to make such leaps if she is to use a finding for all it is worth.

Public discussion of policy is carried on in broad language. Arguments about "compensatory education" or some equally loose category of treatments lose sight of the $UTO$ concretely represented in the investigation. There is a similar free translation with respect to operations and populations served.

The $U^*$ or $T^*$ to which attention turns may be narrower than the original instead of broader. A particular hospital administrator considering the procedure that was evaluated in several other sites has to ask how it will work in *her* hospital. She takes into account the kinds of patients served, the physicians who use the hospital, and the local cost structure in trying to judge whether her results would resemble those that the research reported. Unless convinced that her hospital is very like the typical site in the study, she will attend chiefly to the results in the sites most like hers. Either the data in the study or her own hunches have to tell her which differences among hospitals will affect the success of the innovation.

If an investigator knows just what question will be significant to the PSC, he of course bears down on the $U$, $T$, and $O$ that best match that question. He tries to design a highly replicable study. The larger his sample and the better he controls sampling, delivery of treatment, and quality of outcome measure, the less uncertainty remains when he is finished. When all goes well, everyone finds it plausible that an investigator with the opposite bias would have found the same thing. But it is in the context of command, and especially in the study of familiar technical problems (for example, testing bactericidal effects of drugs), that evaluative questions are likely to be this definite. Then *UTO* is all—or very nearly all—that matters, and focused designs that promise internal validity are fitting.

When the evaluator anticipates that the PSC will want to use his data to reason about a variety of treatment alternatives and sites, a different strategy becomes fitting. The greater the variety of treatment realizations he can study, the greater the diversity of his settings, and the more processes and outcomes he studies, the more likely it is that he can supply evidence pertinent to whatever *\*UTO* the PSC cares about. Diverse data also give him a better chance to explain results, and so to answer "What would happen if. . . ?" questions.

The limitation of broad investigation is, of course, that resources can be spread too thin. The answers offered may be too sketchy to carry weight. Although risks of extrapolation are reduced when a subset of *UTO* is a close match to *\*UTO*, the thinness of the data on the sub-*UTO* leaves much room for dispute. As we proceed, we shall illustrate how evaluators can reason about such polarities as breadth versus depth and realism versus control, but we can offer no ideal solution. As we said earlier, the balance has to be unique to the task at hand.

## Stages of Program Maturity

Chapter Two discussed how information is used at four stages of program maturity: breadboard, superrealization, prototype, and established. This evolutionary cycle, it was noted, is a convenient simplification. A program may skip a stage, and various aspects of a program may be at different stages of maturity. In an established program, some elements will probably go back to the breadboard stage for revision. Even those programs that seem to amount to no more than a distribution of funds, as in plans for income maintenance or housing allowances, require thoughtful tinkering with the innumerable rules about eligibility, reporting requirements, payment levels, re-

Table 4. Information Most Pertinent to Each Type of User

| | User 1. Policy Makers | User 2. Program Administrators | User 3. Operating Personnel in Local Sites | User 4. Illuminators | User 5. Constituencies |
|---|---|---|---|---|---|
| Established program | Outcome information on program success and reasons for it; costs | Monitoring<br><br>Limited studies of modifications | By-product suggestions for change | By-product puzzles, insights, and data | By-product summative impressions |
| Prototype | Estimate of outcomes and costs | Information for redesign of delivery<br><br>Studies of variants and of parameters affecting outcome | By-product suggestions for change | By-product puzzles, insights, and data | Awareness of gross impact on own interests that is likely to follow adoption |
| Super-realization | Estimate of outcomes | Information for quality control | Information for quality control | By-product puzzles, insights, and data | Awareness that possible program is emerging |
| Breadboard | By-product outcome information | Information for redesign | Information to shape role | Awareness of possible program far down the road | Awareness of possible program far down the road |

sponse to household splits, and so on (Hollister, 1975; Field and Orr, 1975). As Field and Orr say, "development of the rules is a process that may extend over several years and continue even after a prototype experiment has been set in motion" (p. 76). We now consider just what service evaluation might reasonably seek to render at each stage, and to whom.

What information is of greatest use varies with the user. The synoptic Table 4 relates the phases of program maturity to roles within the PSC (see Chapter Two). Users in each category will be served to different degrees by an evaluation plan.

Table 4 begins with those who allocate funds or choose broad lines of action. Depending on the political situation, the active "policy makers" may be few or many: legislators, leaders of labor unions, or spokesmen for interested citizens. The program administrator can use information on operations that would be ignored in allocation decisions; we place her in the second column. When operational changes have to be negotiated with staff members or clients, they play a similar role. The third column considers the more normal uses of information by front-line operators and their immediate supervisors. A professional program evaluation is almost never designed to guide nonrecurrent, day-to-day decisions, but it should influence the operator's style and point of view. The illuminators (fourth column) are in a standby role; if an evaluation catches the ear of one of them, she may become a major influence on events. Finally, the constituencies whose goodwill or ill will can affect a program's fate are likely to hear sketchy messages from an evaluation, if they hear any at all. Still, these constituencies are potentially weighty.

In each row in Table 4, boldface type is used to suggest the most prominent user of the evaluation of a program at that stage of development. We shall consider the rows in turn, with emphasis on the prominent users, and then discuss the columns.

*The Task at Each Stage.* When development is in its early stages, nothing is fixed. Evaluation at that point is for the use of those shaping and reshaping the proposed service. The service and delivery system takes shape through trial and error. Whatever is tried first will have to be altered, and sometimes many revisions of the basic plan or its details are required before the operation is judged adequate.

The nascent program or the nascent modification within a program—the breadboard stage—is not the place for formal assessment, as Suchman (1970) noted. It is misleading to assess an immature practice formally before it has found its feet. It is wrong to freeze an improvable program for the sake of an assessment. And, if arrangements change from month to month, a summary assessment becomes uninterpretable.

For the developers and operators, informal evidence ordinarily suffices. The evaluator reports to insiders, not outsiders, except, that is, for his very last report. That report, transmitted by the project chief to higher-ups, bolsters the claim that the plan is now debugged and ready for wider use. The evaluator inevitably becomes something of an insider. He is in effect a staff member given a roving commission to interview, test, comb records, and observe. The evaluator is called in because the program operators are too busy to collate their experience and reflect on it.

Technical skills are of some use, but the evaluator's activities are not predominantly technical. It is true that he will make up questionnaires, draw samples, perhaps even conduct a small quantitative and randomized experiment. He will look at outcomes: What is the average end-of-year test score? How many graduates are employed? How favorably do they rate the program? But the resulting statistic is not interpreted as an "evaluation" of the program idea; it is a benchmark, an indicator of current progress. And, in general, the qualitative notes on recurrent difficulties and dissatisfactions are what the developers find useful. Communication of these impressions is conversational and continuous.

Rivlin (1974), we should note, argues for technical studies at an early stage in planning certain kinds of economic policies that impinge on individuals or households. She sees the New Jersey study of the negative income tax as a useful type of experiment that is quite distinct from the trial of a program. This was a parametric study of the trends in individual behavior that are associated with changes in economic incentives. What makes such a formal, quantitative study feasible is the assumption that units (in this instance households) do not influence one another. Rivlin believes that the evidence helps the planner enough to justify its cost, even though behavior may be quite different when a program is installed community-wide. "The New Jersey experiment, for all its careful design and execution, may tell us nothing about what would happen if all low-income families were eligible for negative income tax benefits" (Rivlin, 1974, p. 347). One can envision quantitative studies of individual response that would help in planning an instructional program also—for example, studies of the parameters of text passages that affect reading comprehension. But Rivlin sees such studies as background research, not as program evaluation; we concur.

The breadboard stage may be followed by a superrealization, that is, by an unrealistic field test of the finished plan. Extra controls and supports are introduced to ensure that clients experience the program as planned. The superrealization may be allowed far more resources—to find out what the scheme can do at its best—than would be available to an operating program. Positive evidence confirms that the program is based on valid concepts; negative evidence challenges the premises. The superrealization is the prime target for controlled, summative experimentation. So say Suchman (1970) and Weiss (1974a), but we have doubts. A comparative design is sometimes worthwhile, sometimes not. This will be argued out in Chapter Five.

Careful appraisal of outcomes is of primary interest when a superrealization is studied; the evaluation is then mostly summative in intent. Summative evidence finds a market because the next move in the game will be made in an echelon above the development staff. Officials decide whether to budget for a field trial under realistic conditions. A larger PSC is unlikely to be aroused unless the new plan threatens to take a prerogative away from some group. "Formative" questions receive little investment at this stage because the developers believe that the plan has been adequately refined.

For a technique of health care, a trial under highly controlled conditions almost always precedes a more realistic field test. An educational or welfare service is much less likely to be installed as a superrealization. Since the theory underlying an educational proposal is not so definite as the biological hypothesis from which a vaccine is derived, there is less interest in what is ideally possible. Also, where biologists have a tradition of patient, step-by-step experimentation, social reformers are impatient. Action moves ahead despite large uncertainties. That being the case, a common recommendation (for example, Riecken and Boruch, 1974, p. 21) is to arrange a realistic "best" treatment in a few sites during the prototype phase.

With or without evidence from pilot work or superrealization, a trial of prototype installations is a prudent step. Suchman writes:

> Most important for prototype programs is that the program be practical and realistic in terms of what can be done on a large scale with available resources. The evaluation design can attempt to approximate the experimental approach and should compare the new prototype program with traditional programs as controls. But, since the prototype and traditional programs must be carried out under normal operating conditions if one is to be able to generalize the findings, rigorous controls over matched experimental and control groups may not be readily obtainable. It is absolutely essential for the prototype program to be evaluated under conditions as similar as possible to the proposed operational program for the results to be applicable to these programs. A research dimension can profitably be added, however, in order to determine how and why the prototype program was a success or failure and to specify what aspects of the program were relatively more successful than others, and among which population subgroups [1970, p. 107].

Weiss (1974a, p. 677) concurs with this and so do we, save as we question the importance of a comparative framework. The task, as Rivlin (1974) says, is one of "monitoring the experience of a series of sites," and statistical comparisons may be impractical, if not wholly beside the point.

The prototype phase is still a developmental phase. At the outset, plans for delivery in ordinary, dispersed institutions have not been carried beyond the breadboard stage. As a consequence, study of how delivery and effects vary from site to site becomes central to the evaluation. To provide a picture of the full range of field problems, the sites for the prototype ought to be reasonably representative of target communities and institutions. Otherwise, the evaluation tells less than it should about what to expect and what to do when the program becomes fully operational.

Writers on summative evaluation assume that a definite treatment is being appraised. That is almost never true of a social innovation. The assumption does apply to technological interventions: a way to treat sewage can be specified so thoroughly that all installations will use the same procedures. The tight New Jersey negative income tax experiment seemed reasonable because a treatment could be specified in a formal payment rule and controlled to the same degree that any operational payment rule would be enforced. But recall that this was *not* a prototype study.

Ordinarily, guidelines for social programs can provide only a loose rein for the actions of those who supervise local offices or interact with clients. Their choices, considered and unconsidered, shape the treatment realizations. In the Follow Through study of compensatory education, unplanned variations of the $t$ from site to site within each of the program alternatives accounted for more variance in outcomes than the planned contrasts among categories of $T$ (Anderson and others, 1978).

The freezing of guidelines would ordinarily be premature even if they could be enforced. The "prototype" trial of the usual social program is set in place long before an operational form for large-scale application has been fully worked out. It would have been foolish to ask the sponsors of a particular $T$ in Follow Through not to improve the instructional materials or the training of teachers during the trial, whenever a source of confusion came to light. No one would have wanted a summative assessment of the inadequate plans that the developers first took into the field. The changes, however, made the study an exploratory one. The comparative design pitted one set of changing procedures against another. Whatever would be recommended for establishment was tested—if at all—only in the last year or two of the long study.

Table 4 suggests that the evaluation of a prototype has two main types of consumers. Officials close to the program are naturally concerned with descriptive and explanatory information that will help them to improve the service rendered during the trial and to put forward the best possible plan for a more permanent program. Often they are so firmly committed to continuing and expanding the service that they care comparatively little about the evidence on its overall effect (Pedersen, 1977). In contrast, the policy official who will decide whether to push for establishment of the program is chiefly interested in estimates of outcomes and costs. As was stressed earlier, however, she must judge the best-bet $T^*$ that emerges from the trial, not the $T$ that entered the trial. The policy official is gatekeeper here, as at the superrealization stage. Once the political spotlight is on the program, persons in other categories may give close attention to the summative report.

The most obvious plan for the prototype study is to start the trial under a carefully reviewed set of guidelines. If all goes well, these guidelines will serve for the later operational program. To report a "treatment effect," the evaluator strikes an average over all the realizations that the guidelines generated. Beyond that, he can keep a sharp eye on the variations in practice that arise, as well as on the concomitant variation in outcomes. This suggests how to amend the guidelines, the supervisory technique, and so on. The evaluation thus encourages adoption of an operational $T^*$ that departs from the prototype $T$.

Instead of passively observing diversity, the evaluator can create it. More specifically, he can propose a plan for diverse interventions that officials can approve and set in place. The plan can pit alternative sets of guidelines against each other. The plan can vary the scale of program expenditure and add or subtract program features that are in question. A few variations can perhaps be built into a strictly balanced design, but not all.

Having passed all shakedown trials and won a measure of trust, the program becomes fully operational. Operating personnel are left to do their jobs; superiors and outsiders take the program on faith. Many elements are under command. Roles have crystallized, and each administrator has authority to settle certain questions. In principle, even procedural decisions about an established program are subject to approval of the PSC; in fact, however, most of the activity rolls along like Old Man River.

The PSC actively attending to operations at this point is a community of insiders, and information useful for the operator's day-to-day choices and for administrative regulation receives most attention. The evaluation design will be not "before and after," as Suchman (1970) noted, but "during-during-during." Where do inefficiencies occur? Is last year's patch still holding? Have clients' needs changed? Answering these questions is within the province of regular monitoring. But information from monitoring has uses that go beyond program regulation (Weiss, 1974a). Not only does it show where activities are drifting off course, but it shows whether the program is for the most part on course. Therefore, to make public a periodic summary maintains trust. Even to report a shortcoming serves that purpose if it appears that a conscientious management is ready to take action. The report to the general constituency is ordinarily routine and minimally informative. Ninety percent of the time, anecdotes, photographs, and a few numbers generated internally meet the demand.

A second, targeted kind of evaluation for the benefit of a user within the program is made on occasion, when an administrator will try a modified procedure and ask that it be closely observed. She seeks a way to cope with a difficulty, perhaps one revealed by the monitoring. One modification after another is tried until a suitable one is found. The trial may be informal, with only a modest investment in evaluation, or the results under new and old procedures may be systematically measured. How much evidence is wanted depends on the seriousness of the difficulty, the cost of the change, and the number of persons who have to be convinced. Unless the modification requires a good deal of money (and so brings higher officials into the discussion) or inconviences a group of clients, the function of evaluation is to guide decisions within the program staff.

A much more comprehensive review is occasionally commissioned, most often by a newly appointed administrator who intends to shake up the established practices. As in the Metropole County story (see Chapter Three), it is the administrator truly in command who has the best chance of capitalizing on this kind of inquiry.

*Requirements of Various Users.* We now turn to the upper left corner of Table 4, where we can begin *seriatim* consideration of the users.

The policy official is charged with monitoring the community or nation in the large to determine what social problems are out of tolerance. This is true both of the planning officer who puts forward a new proposal and of the legislator who must react to it. Therefore, the policy officer's first question is: How great is the need? If the seriousness of a need (or the clamor for attention to it) does not place it high on her agenda, the policy officer is likely to give little thought to the programs currently in place that address the need. Information on the magnitude of needs comes from *problem*-centered social indicators, not from evaluations focused on one or another program. Numerous programs and social conditions have an impact (positive or negative) on almost any aspect of individual and community welfare. An evaluation of a state's mental hospitals is not the way to assess the mental health needs of the population, although a program evaluation may well turn up facts that say something about unmet needs—a useful by-product.

If the problem demands attention, the policy maker reaches a second question: Should there be more service or a different kind of service? She will propose to expand the existing program if it is her impression that it will then reach the neglected clients. An example of this is the action most states took in the 1950s to create additional institutions of higher education. The existing system was in good repute, and policy makers thus saw a need for more of the same. Obviously, summative evaluations can contribute to a good or bad reputation, but the absence of formal evaluations of state universities did not slow down the action of planners and legislators.

In deciding which way to move, the policy maker relies on her understanding of the persons needing help and the nature of their difficulties. Almost anything written on the problem may add to that understanding. Social scientists and other illuminators contribute here. Also, a program evaluation may indicate why some persons do not have access to the existing service or do not make appropriate use of it. An evaluation, however, studies the persons a program reaches more than it studies those outside the program's clientele. The policy maker who wants to know more about the character of unmet needs would do better to set up a sophisticated "needs assessment" rather than a program evaluation.

The policy maker who comes to think that a qualitative change in services is needed reaches a third question: Is the established institution capable of shifting direction? This question is readily answered if the institution has already been conducting relevant pilot work. Otherwise, the very absence of forward-looking efforts gives the policy maker pause. Some qualitative changes are easily accommodated within the traditions, staff qualifications, and structural framework of an existing program. If not satisfied with "changes at the margin," the policy maker usually seeks a new and independent program. Simply knowing the outcomes of existing services is not the key to this third decision. To judge an institution's adaptability, the policy maker needs to know *why* the institution is succeeding or failing with its old mission. Moreover, the decision rests as much on studies of the nature of the problem and of possible new programs as it does on evaluation of the institution now in place.

With regard to the remainder of the first column in Table 4, we need only recapitulate. The policy maker controls allocation as long as a program is not in the political spotlight, and this is usually the case with the prototype and the superrealization. During the breadbroad stage, however, the policy official waits in the wings; only a final, favorable report will nudge her to move the program ahead. As Weiss (1975) says, policy officials need to generalize and so require data from many sites. In contrast, "the local administrator is concerned about *his* program, here and now, and the people it serves. He is not necessarily agog with pleasure at collecting data comparable with that of thirty other programs when the data don't seem germane to the issues at hand. He wants to take into account the very local idiosyncrasies that seem distorting to the high-level policy maker" (p. 241).

Since those directing the program are concerned with evaluation in the same way at each stage, we have already said what there is to say about them, except to point out this very continuity. At all stages but the superrealization, the program administrator is an executive with an executive's responsibility for recognizing shortcomings and making appropriate changes. Consequently, she needs information that can serve as a signal for intensive investigation or as a guide to change in procedure. In addition, low-key passive surveillance is required to send up early warnings before a shortcoming reaches the critical stage. This is not to say, "the more information the better." The energy available to initiate and absorb evaluations and at the same time to take corrective action will be barely sufficient to address critical shortcomings.

During the superrealization, the program administrator is told not to exercise independent judgment and initiative. As her task is to hold the program on course, the only information that she requires is short-term feedback about operations that might drift away from the plan.

Rank-and-file operators (column three) make only slight use of an evaluation from outside. They rely more on what they observe as they monitor their own clients. Moreover, an established program will have its own internal evaluative procedures. Supervisory activities may rely entirely on impressions, with no attempt at systematization, or they may be institutionalized. For example, colleges sometimes institute department-wide or campus-wide systems for collecting student ratings of courses.

Spin-off from an external evaluation can be of use to those directly serving clients. The more uncertain the operating personnel are and the greater the novelty of the service, the more important such feedback can be. Thus, in the breadboard stage, those who deliver service are discovering how to carry out a new assignment, and the evaluator can transmit information about what worked well for others or can help the operator recognize mistakes she is making. The feedback changes from a suggestive to a controlling mode in the superrealization. Operating personnel can learn many things while an evaluation of a prototype or established program proceeds, as was illustrated in Chapter Three, and they can also learn from the final report. In the course of a program evaluation, collecting extra data primarily to serve rank-and-file operators is unlikely to pay off. But incidental observations specific enough to help the practitioner can be fed back as a by-product.

The same remark applies to users in the two remaining categories—illuminators and constituencies. Information for the illuminator and the general public is spin-off. Column four in Table 4 locates the illuminator in the wings rather than on stage. No one can foretell which reports an illuminator will attend to or how she will use them. As the table suggests, evaluations serve the illuminator in the same way no matter what the maturity of the program.

The multiplier effect of an illuminator should not be underestimated. A single illuminator—journalist, statesman, social scientist, or iconoclast—may in the end do more with a finding about an established program than all the responsible officials together. This is not to say that evaluations can be shaped to anticipate the interest of the illuminator. An illuminator's interest may alight on any fact, and that fact may fuel an argument about almost any social need or institution.

Consider an example from the early 1960s. The military draft was then an established program, and it was being evaluated only through low-key monitoring. Almost by chance, the data produced movement on another front. Numerous illiterate or physically unfit draftees were being turned down, and a routine report of this was picked up by the *New York Times*. Daniel P. Moynihan, then holding a research-and-planning post in the Department of Labor, spotted the short article. Shocked by the number of failures, Moynihan called for a tabulation by community of origin. The statistics for the inner cities were acutely depressing. It happened that President Johnson's advisers were beginning to select planks for the 1964 election platform; somewhere down the list came steps to improve conditions within cities. At this point Moynihan, goaded by the figures on draftees, convinced the group to put the highest priority on urban pathologies. The War on Poverty had been declared (Meltsner, 1976, p. 92). In this example, Moynihan counts as illuminator rather than as responsible official. He was commenting on needs far outside his direct responsibility.

From here on, our discussion of design will concentrate on the evaluation of prototypes. Evaluation of prototypes, on which debates about evaluation have centered, contributes at the first two stages. Of course, evaluations of superrealizations are close to the traditions of experimental research in education, medicine, and engineering. Perhaps the trials are comparatively small, the research question is focused, and fewer issues of trade-off arise. As for breadboard evaluations, the questions and the mode of investigation arise out of the immediate circumstances of a project. Fluid pilot inquiries scarcely lend themselves to planning, and so they are not a subject about which to give general advice. Likewise, we shall say almost nothing about how to monitor an established program in which a management-information system is to be designed for a particular context in close collaboration with a knowledgeable manager.

## Envisioning Program Events, Assumptions, and Issues

This section emphasizes the divergent aspects of planning, that is, it emphasizes the broad-ranging search for relevant questions that might deserve direct study. By deferring consideration of the convergent process, we perhaps seem foolishly to advise the investigator to study every question that comes to mind. But we intend to say only that the evaluator should try to become aware of the full reach of investigative possibilities.

*A Field Trial in Nicaragua.* We begin by describing an investigation set in motion by the U.S. Agency for International Development (USAID). The study was somewhat unusual, inasmuch as a client nation was used as a laboratory to obtain information for policy makers in the American agency. The client nation itself, however, stood to benefit from the prototype service.

USAID hoped that broadcast messages advocating practices beneficial to health would be a comparatively inexpensive way to improve the welfare of the population in developing countries. In any country where the technique has been applied, the message has centered on a local problem of some urgency. In Ecuador, iodized salt has been promoted, as has extended breast feeding; in the Philippines, broadcasts have recommended foods for use at the time of weaning. From among these several evaluations we take one in Nicaragua as an example. The objective there was that children with diarrhoea be given Superlimonada as a remedy for dehydration, which can lead to death. Parents could easily prepare Superlimonada at home; the broadcasts encouraged its use and told parents how to prepare it.

We develop the story as a more or less canonical description of projects of a certain kind. Our remarks are not to be taken as either a definitive account or a criticism of the actual Nicaraguan evaluation. Rather, we want to portray the complex, fast-moving thought processes desirable in evaluation. Though present to some extent in every sophisticated evaluation, these seem never to be put on record.

USAID had general questions in mind. As noted, it supported health-related broadcasting campaigns in many places, and information from Nicaragua was to be used to improve judgments about funding further broadcast campaigns elsewhere. The information would presumably serve public health officials in developing countries also, whether or not they turned to USAID for money. Obviously, research on Nicaraguan events would have implications for Nicaraguan planners. If the Superlimonada campaign seemed to work, the messages would continue to be broadcast for a while. Once Superlimonada became widely known, the air time would be turned over to a new campaign. The program that might be "established," then, was not a Superlimonada program ($T$) but a much more general one ($T^*$).

The question before the evaluator was whether the broadcasting scheme was a good way to change adult behavior. Information to improve the Superlimonada broadcasts could be of interest only if it came in early—and inexpensively. How to improve all such campaigns was a much more significant question. In this sense the evaluation was a pilot study. The potential users included policy makers in Nicaragua, in other countries, and in national or international development agencies; they also included whoever made administrative arrangements in Nicaragua. This multiplicity of audiences and this mix of local and generalized concerns are typical of evaluations of broad-aim programs. Although the Nicaraguan campaign had a highly specific aim, it was evaluated as exemplar of a style of intervention that could serve numerous aims.

The Superlimonada broadcasts were a prototype even though this field test was the first systematic trial. An American advertising agency was engaged to prepare a series of spot announcements. The spots were broadcast repeatedly (up to ten times per day) over a period of twelve months or so. Some face-to-face pilot work was done to check the comprehensibility of messages. No one wished to delay the campaign by making thorough local trials and polishing the messages prior to nationwide operation.

The Superlimonada study would not be definitive for distant policy makers. Their $U^*$ includes a wide range of cultures, along with populations quite different in their level of education and modernity. And the $T^*$ for future consideration would not be confined to Superlimonada, to treatments of infants, or even to nutritional remedies. Moreover, the messages broadcast were limited to the style that one advertising agency judged appropriate. To be sure, the companion studies in half a dozen other places greatly strengthen the possibility of generalization —if those studies produce consistent results. Increasing the sample from one to six is an increase, even though the basis for extrapolation to a seventh message in a seventh culture is still weak. This weakness has to be accepted; it would be foolish not to learn from experience recorded as carefully as the costs of research allow.

Knowing this week's score does not tell the coach how to prepare for next week's game. The information that an intervention had satisfactory or unsatisfactory outcomes is of little use by itself; users of the study need to know what led to success or failure. Only with that information can the conditions that worked be replicated or modified sufficiently in the next trial to get better results. "Did the broadcasts succeed in promoting use of Superlimonada among these people?" is just a fraction of what the responsible officials want to know. Their task is to produce future successes. If the Superlimonada broadcasts in Year 1 fail, Nicaraguan administrators will want ideas for a campaign against diarrhoea in Year 2. Those concerned with the program as exemplar will want to know why the broadcasts failed. Is the broadcasting technique hopeless? Or might it work with other messages, with altered arrangements, or under other conditions? Even if the Superlimonada broadcasts succeed, the question remains: Under what circumstances can such a technique be expected to work?

As we are about to amplify these questions, recall what was said earlier in this chapter. An array of questions identifies *possible* investments; not all will be studied. The hull of the inquiry (or the hulls of several smaller concurrent inquiries) will be planned to produce good information on main questions. Many of the questions will be left to casual observation, whose only cost is the effort of jotting down memoranda. Logically, priorities are set after one has envisioned possibilities; in practice, the planner does both at once.

*The Evaluator's Homework.* To begin the search for specific questions, the evaluator should find out what images of the program, its probable working, and its effects are held by those who see the program from different angles. (The sponsor's is just one.) As we said in Chapter Three, the evaluation is to serve the whole PSC. A more substantive point is also to be made, that is, persons in different roles have different experiences and therefore perceive the social need and the services differently. Bush and Gordon (1978, p. 774) speak specifically of research on services for neglected and dependent children. Those working with the children saw their emotional problems as the focus of remediation and therefore of evaluation. The children and their parents, however, attributed the difficulties to such external circumstances as the parents' poverty or the shifting of children from one surrogate home to another. The statement that the problem lies outside the child challenges the premises of the therapeutic service, identifies information for the evaluator to collect, and suggests new goals for intervention.

To locate the relevant questions, the evaluator has to do considerable homework. Thus Cohen and Farrar (1977) developed perspective on the Alum Rock school-voucher demonstration by searching out the philosophies behind Milton Friedman's (1963) initial proposal and the radically different scheme that the Office of Economic Opportunity took into the field. Digging into the history, they learned that New Hampshire had refused to accept funds for a field trial in that state and that the issues in those negotiations had centered on the viability of the voucher policy. The empirical assumptions underlying either the original theories or the political arguments in New Hampshire should have been candidate questions for a field study. In fact, they were; the Alum Rock evaluation carried out by the Rand Corporation (on which Cohen and Farrar drew for their work as illuminators) was sensitive to the political history. Along with facts about enrollment shifts and student achievement—the "obvious" dependent variables for a voucher plan—the Rand evaluators kept a close eye on shifts in power and their consequences for principals, teachers, and parents.

Even more obviously, the evaluator ought to find out what is already known about the program and its clientele. The agency may have data in its archives that reduce uncertainty about many questions. Indeed, the agency may even have a file of past evaluative reports of which current policy makers, because of staff turnover, are unaware. (See Meyers, 1975, on the Peace Corps; also Meltsner, 1976, p. 273.) Because of the fragmentation of services and disciplines, society's "collective memory" has become less and less adequate. Bringing past findings to light may alter the new evaluation or even render it unnecessary.

Homework should include a look at the social theory and research that undergird the program. Planners can state what theory (of poverty, family stability, language acquisition, and so on) they have relied on. The advertising agency on the Super-limonada contract relied on the trade's considerable experience in making spot messages effective and may have been aware of the whole body of research on persuasion and behavioral change. If the planners articulate the prevailing theory or professional folklore on which the program plan relies, their explanation will give the evaluator a good start. Probably, however, the planners have paid little attention to voices that have challenged this accepted wisdom, and it is the evaluator who has to search out the critics. Those contrary opinions may give the best hints as to unwanted side effects whose presence or absence should be determined.

The sand dunes of thought atop which most programs are erected do not really qualify as "theory." But academic analyses and basic research do have a bearing on evaluation plans. Take a homely example. Dozens of quasi-experiments have contrasted classes composed of students of uniform ability with heterogeneous classes. Evaluations of "grouping" policy followed the psychologist's traditional view: mastering content is an individual process, while the group is an influence primarily on morale. The evaluations left pupil-to-pupil interaction uncontrolled and unobserved. A laboratory study by Webb (1978), however, inserted a new note. Small groups of high school students were told to work together so that all would learn the experimental lesson. Both able and weak students retained more in groups of mixed ability than they did when learning individually. (Results for students in the middle range of ability are less easily summarized.) The able students evidently consolidated their thinking when they explained the task to others, and the weak students received considerable help from the explanations. In groups of uniform ability, collaboration did not pay off; weak students could not help each other and strong students did not need help. Even though Webb's study was small, her findings recast the "grouping" problem. They imply that the effects of group composition are entirely different when students work together than when group members work separately. An evaluator of a grouping plan who encounters the Webb report while doing his initial homework receives a strong hint that he had better observe or even instigate student collaboration.

It is productive to dissect a program to trace the links among successive acts and their immediate consequences—consequences that in turn influence later effects (Weiss, 1972a). These acts include the operations that put the program in place, the supplying of the resources, the immediate responses from clients, and the day-to-day operations of delivery (including policies that turn possible clients away). The links connect these actions to the week-by-week changes in the clients and the institutions or communities, as well as to the final outcome. This model sets down the anticipations of the program developers and other informed persons. It embodies their theory as to how the program can produce effects and their awareness of likely departures from the ideal. Thus, for example, the model recognizes that not everyone will accept the treatment offered; the model therefore ought to include a best guess about the fraction of the target population that will accept the program, and about the demographic or other correlates of acceptance. The model for the Superlimonada campaign would recognize, for example, that repeating the persuasive message is expected to increase compliance. That postulated relationship, loose as it is, raises a question for *possible* investigation: Where is the point of diminishing returns? The question goes on the shopping list.

A model of the Superlimonada intervention would start by setting down the "givens": (1) the prevailing conditions with regard to health, sanitation, beliefs of mothers about illnesses, number and range of broadcasting stations, and so on; (2) scientific conclusions about the effects of ingredients of Superlimonada on the body; and (3) the political-administrative system that will be responsible for delivery. The operating plans are then represented as additional, somewhat controlled, variables. The modeler will try to identify the significant connections between actions and forward steps in the process of delivery and cure.

Figures 4 and 5 outline two subsystems to illustrate this kind of reasoning concretely (but incompletely). An arrow connects an influence with a consequence; the implication is that within certain limits an increase in the former will produce a greater amount or quality of the latter—for example, more funds or better writers. The charts could be elaborated by adding elements, by indicating expectations regarding the elements, and by describing each relation in terms of a probability or a trend line.

The planners have expectations regarding each element in the model. They have some idea of the fraction of homes equipped with radios and of the fraction of mothers who regard illness as something to be fought rather than accepted passively or prayerfully. They have some expectation regarding the number of messages and the frequency of transmissions. They may anticipate that 40 percent of the target mothers will hear at least ten announcements under the planned broadcasting schedule. These are the prior beliefs that planners relied on in launching the program. They are used to justify the commitment made.

Our schematic diagrams are intended only to illustrate a habit of thought appropriate to evaluation planning. Models can be considerably more formal than the one these figures sketch out, but for most social programs it would be confusing to try to express the whole story in a diagram or a set of equations. The evaluator may content himself with listing in four columns background conditions, procedural variables, intermediate variables such as amount of service reaching clients, and end states. He carries in his head the "arrows" linking one process to later processes. Figures 4 and 5 suggest how numerous the causal links are; the evaluator can investigate only a chosen few. Such models foster a healthy humility about what a single evaluation can do and in addition they suggest what might be observed.

*Locating Candidate Questions.* Each link identifies a possible inquiry, and absence of a link implies a question not to ask. It makes no sense for an evaluator to compile data on a variable unless he judges that its strength affects consequences in some way. One can ask whether the scientific information is correct; for example, does the Superlimonada formula work under home conditions? Are the broadcast messages consistent with scientific facts about dehydration? But not every link is studied.

Figure 4. Partial Model Describing Events Antecedent
to Treatment Delivery

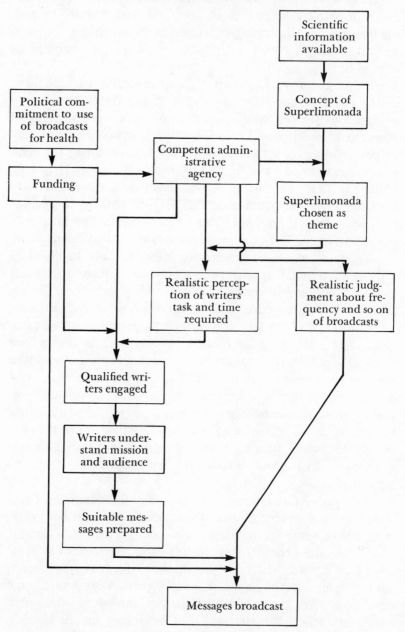

Figure 5. Partial Model Connecting the Planned Intervention
to the Intended Result

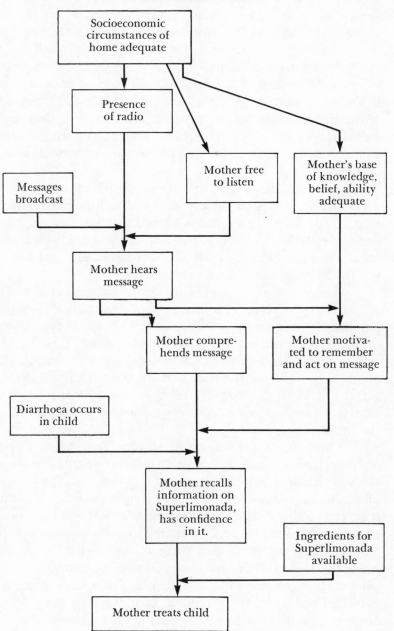

Some arrows are ignored because unchallenged or untestable. Casual reports, or observations in passing, will suffice to confirm some other expectations. The remainder, which are the critical questions, call for some amount of direct evidence.

If planners are wrong in thinking that mothers will understand the messages or in thinking that the ingredients are within reach of the mothers, outcomes will fall short of expectations. If the study checks out links early, the information may improve the program before outcome evidence is collected. If a difficulty—lack of radios, perhaps—is seen as insurmountable, an alert administrator is put in a position to cancel what would be a fruitless trial.

Some questions have to do primarily with the population of Nicaraguan listeners, others with the cultural and political setting. The more the evaluator learns about both sets of questions, the easier it will be to judge what can be expected with other campaigns intended for a different audience and setting or for a Nicaraguan audience in later years.

A service draws a positive response from some citizens and is ignored or rejected by others. Persons who listen to Superlimonada broadcasts are somewhat atypical, and those who act on the message differ from those who do not act. How do they differ? Would those who failed to act respond to messages in another style? Would the style best for the Superlimonada target also work with other targets? Questions of this sort recognize that client characteristics often interact with features of the treatment.

Consider also the context of delivery. To install the Superlimonada project, national officials had to override the objections of health educators committed to more traditional forms of instruction. Recording this fact is of some importance in that it suggests a difficulty to anticipate in other nations. It also suggests that further broadcasting campaigns in Nicaragua may be sabotaged by the permanent party in the Ministry of Health when and if the officials who installed the first campaign are replaced. More generally, special influences that operate during the field trial but would be unlikely to continue once the program becomes routine should be recognized in the interpretation.

The investigator cannot anticipate a particular political conflict or cooperative action so as to write a pointed question about it at the planning stage. But a sense of the flow of events would lead him to entertain some generalized questions about the history: What support was required within the political system, and was it forthcoming? Who stood to lose power as a result of the change, and at what cost were these persons appeased? Such questions are pertinent to virtually any social intervention.

The obvious $T$ for the investigation is some single series of messages. But even in the promotion of Superlimonada, a great variety of message styles, durations of the campaign, and so on might be considered. For example, which broadcast voices serve best—those speaking as authority figures or those of actors who depict villagers? (That alternative is easier to study in a laboratory than in broadcasts.) To maximize the yield of the research, the evaluator will identify factors about which there is some doubt and which it may be possible to vary deliberately.

Questions about institutional arrangements should be raised. Is it possible that local stations would reach the intended audience better than broadcasts emanating from a powerful transmitter in the national capital? Different answers might be given to this question, depending on the audience's listening habits and the credibility of the central government in the time and place of the study. In a similar vein, the evaluator might suggest that village opinion leaders could make a substantial difference in the acceptance of the message, and he might further suggest that this be checked by enlisting their support in a subset of communities. A more generalized question is simply, Where did the logistics break down with appreciable frequency?

Once again, we are illustrating our belief that the evaluator ought to elaborate his original charge by sensing the questions that might interest others. We do not tell him to embellish his basic question—"How well do the broadcasts work?"—with every planned variation that suggests itself. We say only that one of his tasks is to identify subinquiries and side inquiries that some of his clients might find worthwhile if brought to their attention. The evaluator who amplifies the original question offers services that the sponsor did not think to request.

In the same spirit, the evaluator interprets outcomes broadly and envisions possible negative effects as well as the intended positive ones. Certainly the extent to which parents gave Superlimonada to their children is to be determined. Beyond that, however, one might imagine unhealthy effects if the broadcasts are too persuasive. If the view develops that the radio is a trustworthy source of messages about health, hyperbolic commercial messages may also become more credible. The pitch that this or that soft drink provides energy, strength, and beauty might work to the detriment of health. On the positive side, the broadcasts and the curative effects of Superlimonada may generalize into an increased "modernity" of outlook and a greater receptivity to further changes in health practices.

A similarly sophisticated eye should be turned on costs. An accountant's summary of the project budget is pertinent. A breakdown of costs will permit better judgments about the probable costs when the program is operated on a larger scale or otherwise modified. For example, the administrative bureaucracy required by a full-scale program may be considerably more costly than scaling up the administrative costs of the pilot project would imply. In the other direction, some costs will diminish because materials can be reused and because experienced personnel make fewer false starts than those new to their work.

The multifaceted series of questions generated by this divergent process cannot be fully investigated, and no one would listen even if a long-winded, all-inclusive answer could be given. Our aim in elaborating on subquestions is to make evaluators mindful of the buried substructure of policy and planning. Officials do not trace out the whole complex of future possibilities before acting, any more than chess players (or even chess-playing computers) trace out move after move after move. Simon (1957; 1972), who has studied both administrators and chess players, tells us that decision makers attend to whatever threatens to go out of tolerance and to promising openings. On those matters, they dig in as deep as necessary. They pass over whatever in the situation is tolerably good. They respond to the evaluator's results in the same manner. (See also Arrow, 1974.)

With an aspect-by-aspect study, the evaluator learns enough to call attention to risks and opportunities. He can say something about the promise for other settings. He looks at more than he reports. Out of a dozen possible worries that he looks into, he perhaps reports on only one or two. A dismissive reference to the rest is sufficient to imply that they are likely to stay within tolerance.

## Criteria for Design Decisions

So far we have encouraged the evaluator to scan widely; only in passing did we acknowledge that all lines of inquiry are not equally important. How to cut the list of questions down to size is the obvious next topic. Claims for the program that a skeptic or devil's advocate could reasonably challenge are highly important, and so are many matters about which the planners themselves are uncertain. Still, as Lindblom and Cohen say (1979, p. 88), "Judgment about the importance of a problem is a naive and wholly indefensible guide to research priorities." Other factors must be weighed in deciding what to investigate and how intensively.

Design is a spiral process. The investigator lays out a rough plan for fieldwork and envisions the interpretations such a study will warrant, as well as the matters it will leave unsettled. He may decide that some of the latter are too relevant to be left so unsettled, and he shifts resources to reduce these uncertainties (at the cost of increasing uncertainty elsewhere). He continues this process until the plan appears to be adequately balanced. Effort is allocated in accord with the utility of the possible subinvestigations; simultaneous consideration is given to the criteria already mentioned: prior uncertainty, information yield, costs, and leverage (that is, political importance).

*Uncertainty and Information Yield.* The more a study reduces uncertainty, the greater the information yield and, hence, the more useful the research. Almost never does it make sense to study a link in the process model about which members of the PSC hold the same belief. The significant exception arises when the evaluator doubts something that others are confident of. For example, the USAID planners may be entirely confident that Nicaraguan radio stations will broadcast spot announcements in accord with the schedule they have agreed to. The evaluator, mindful of long communication lines and backwoods indifference, will plan to find out exactly what goes on the air and when. But uncertainty in itself, even about an important matter, does not warrant an investigative effort. Indeed, the available social science techniques may not even be capable of reducing uncertainty.

Information yield includes the statistician's technical concept of "power." A study is said to be powerful if replications of fresh samples would give much the same answer about *UTO*. The results, then, are not uncertain. Reduction of uncertainty is a concept in information theory and in Bayesian statistical logic that fits evaluation well. We draw attention to the papers collected by Badia, Haber, and Runyon (1970)—mostly on basic psychological research—and the analysis by Rouanet, Lépine, and Pelnard-Considère (1975) of a comparative evaluation of two methods of teaching mathematics.

Instead of asking a "yes" or "no" question—"Is there a treatment effect?"—the Bayesian asks which values of an effect (in the population) are consistent with the information from the present study and all past experience. Instead of reporting that *40* percent of mothers hear ten broadcasts, the Bayesian would perhaps say, "Any figure from 28 percent to 56 percent is consistent with what we know." The range indicates the uncertainty of the information. Before collecting most of the data, the investigator can estimate the likely uncertainty of any one result. The evaluator and his clients might be satisfied when the plan promises to identify audience size with a 20 percent margin for error. If they decide that the figure must be correct within 10 percent to influence decisions, the plan will not be acceptable.

Past experience—research and everyday observations—is counted as information at hand. "Prior probabilities" express initial beliefs. Each informant has a belief about plausible values for the percentage of listeners in the population of mothers. The range of plausible values is reduced by the field data. But even when all the data are in, no one knows the true figure because the data are from a sample and thus subject to errors. But the "posterior probabilities"—the beliefs reasonable in the light of the evidence—are more definite than the prior probabilities. And if the data are impressive, persons who started with different "priors" will be brought closer together in their beliefs.

The statistical conception of uncertainty refers to a single decision maker. Our political conception extends further. Uncertainty remains after each member of the PSC has reached a firm opinion if the opinions disagree. In the end, then, information yield depends on how plausible the evaluator's report is. A single study of a practical issue is unlikely to be entirely convincing, no matter how excellent its controls and how small its sampling errors. Nunnally (1960) has commented that two ostensibly similar studies by separate investigators, each using 50 cases, are more persuasive than a single study with 100 cases.

The "statistician's conclusion"—an estimate of a number accompanied by its sampling error—is a statement about a strictly operationalist *UTO*. It is a modest statement and by itself answers no theoretical or practical question. The substantive "experimenter's conclusion" (Tukey, 1960) is considerably more daring; the interpretation here goes beyond the reproducible experiment. Any field investigator reports a somewhat generalized conclusion. He speaks of treatments and outcomes that cannot be completely controlled, described, or measured (for example, caloric intake, informal education, health status, reading comprehension). A "statistician's conclusion" can be no more than a precise quantitative summary of events in the situation defined by his procedural controls. Any substantive interpretation is an extrapolation.

Independent investigators who intend to answer the same practical question will operationalize it differently. The *UTO* of one investigator does not match that of the next. Although these differences might be called "systematic errors," they in fact strengthen cumulative research. Dividing resources over several independent hulls thus has an advantage. If several experimenters' conclusions agree, the variety of their specific procedures will generate more confidence than would flow from a highly accurate study under one set of conditions. Dividing

resources can increase uncertainty, of course, if the several findings conflict. But so much the better: the resulting uncertainty
is warranted. Either of the studies, by itself, would have been
misleading. Its apparently solid result was valid only for the procedures the investigator happened to fix on. "Bigger," in evaluation, is not invariably "better."

Taking smaller bites of the apple has a further advantage
if political events are moving slowly enough. When modest
studies can be done successively, each can build on the experience of earlier ones. (For still another virtue of a split attack,
see discussion of the Sanchez study (1976) in Chapter Five.)
Concentrating resources can go too far. The PSC has many uncertainties. Bearing down on one central question leaves fewer
resources for reducing other uncertainties. At some level of investment a result is precise enough; stopping at that level frees
resources for another significant question. Of course, this is
a matter for balance, and one has to forgo many attractive substudies to keep an important investigation powerful.

Our leaning toward multiple, diversified, decentralized
studies is just the opposite of what many current writers advocate. Abt (1979, p. 51), for example, wants to see "fewer research questions investigated with more thoroughness and validity (that is, basically larger cell sizes), larger samples on a smaller
number of questions rather than very small samples on large
numbers of questions."

*Cost.* We place cost in a separate section for the sake of
emphasis only, since we cover the subject in the course of our
remarks on other criteria. Most of our argument on allocation
of research resources to this point can be read as an analysis of
the evaluator's decisions about choices among questions when
the budget available is fixed. How large to make the budget is
an open question, at least until a contract has specified the allot-
ment for the next time period. The projected size of the study
can be based only on a judgment about the relation between
rate of research expenditure and contribution to subsequent
social choices. That relation might be thought of as a kind of
S curve. A very small expenditure may produce little reduction
of uncertainty; information yield arises with expenditure up to
a point; and beyond that point the curve begins to flatten off.

It is perhaps hard to believe that a larger research budget will not produce more results than a smaller one if the budget is allocated wisely. But several considerations—apart from the sheer tightness of money—suggest caution in budgeting. In the first place, the money used to increase the budget for one evaluation must be withdrawn either from services to clients or from other evaluations that might be launched. Second, a massive expenditure in one year will tend to be less productive than a paced series of investigations, simply because later studies in a series will be more sophisticated. Third, the logistical burden in large studies is so great that the senior investigators become preoccupied with meeting schedules, and comparatively little energy is left free for thinking. Deciding on a suitable level of expenditure is therefore one of the subtlest aspects of evaluation planning.

*Leverage.* Prior uncertainty, information yield, cost, and leverage are parts of the same balance sheet, but leverage is the bottom line. Leverage refers to the probability that the information—*if* believed—will change the course of events. This means that the information must bear on aspects of the program that could be altered. It is much easier to change administrative procedures and allocation rules than it is to abandon a program or change its basic thrust. Consequently, even Congress finds more use for process information (especially information on who gets what and on costs per person served) than for reports on effects of services.

For information to have leverage, some fraction of the PSC must care about it or be brought to care. Facts that participants in the political process say they will find useful are presumed to have leverage. Additional variables become politically salient as events progress, and the evaluator tries to recognize this potential leverage as early as possible.

The evaluator is indulging himself if he deliberately invests in information that has little leverage. Social scientists are tempted to study the questions to which their research technology is suited and the questions that have theoretical implications rather than to study what matters most to the client. An evaluation is unlikely to carry much weight if it fails to address questions that have great leverage. But sometimes (as in the obsession with IQ after the Head Start evaluation) it can carry too much weight; the evaluation's emphasis on a largely irrelevant variable can distract the community from the uncertainties that matter.

Furthermore, one can imagine an evaluator looking at questions listed in order of leverage and crossing off the first five after judging that the questions could not be answered definitively with the available techniques. Then, after carefully investigating the runners-up that lend themselves to neat investigation, he offers the results to decision makers. If given weight, the findings turn discussion away from the important variables. But if they are rejected as irrelevant, an evaluation that costs much proved to have little value. Insofar as an evaluation purports to be summative, simple honesty requires that the report make clear what politically significant populations, treatment variants, and outcomes were neglected. And, as we have already said, if it can be seen at the outset that this neglect leaves major uncertainties alive, the evaluator should warn the sponsor that the study is not likely to promote accommodation.

The term *leverage* is to be interpreted broadly. Influence on the fate of the particular program studied is a consideration, but so is leverage on future plans. For USAID, it will be recalled, the important decision had to do with future initiatives in countries other than Nicaragua. Investments that would improve the next year's advertisements of Superlimonada had leverage with Nicaraguan planners, but they were a minor audience compared with international planners and national planners in Gambia, Ecuador, and elsewhere.

One reason for emphasizing the extended use of the evaluative information is that, as was said early in this chapter, decisions about future programs are more open than those about a program already established. Even a prototype can usually be changed only at the margin, whereas a program still on the drawing boards or a new policy line can be thought through afresh. In general, therefore, the questions with greatest leverage are the ones that contribute to insight. Explanatory analysis is relevant to subsequent realizations of the program. The planner shaping the next edition of a program can in principle alter any of the program operations. Evidence that clarifies how the program under investigation worked or failed to work shows where added effort would be helpful. It points toward future savings when it finds that some feature of the trial program seemed to make little difference.

Recognition of this outward reach causes one to see variables as important even though they are fixed in the trial site. A procedure so natural as to be unquestioned in the trial setting may not fit other settings. Then it is imperative to ask how important the element is. For example, in the Nicaraguan study the operations of message preparation, purchase of radio time, and so on were under a unified administrative authority. Governmental practice in another country might call for separating the functions by developing the campaign plan in the Ministry of Health, assigning production to a professional advertising agency, and asking the Ministry of Communication to line up radio time. The evaluator, therefore, could well plan to put on record Nicaraguan incidents in which centralization allowed quick response to a difficulty or made certain adminstrative judgments less expert than they might have been.

The more light a study throws on the social problem and the client population, the more it will have to say when fresh proposals are made. The failure of the campaign to vaccinate the American population against swine flu in 1976 was evident; precise estimates of the frequency with which the vaccine was accepted and the ultimate effect on health could add nothing to policy decisions. Public health planners, however, will face many future decisions about threatened epidemics. Anything that could be learned about the psychology of the public response to the flu vaccine would be likely to help in judging whether to launch a campaign when another epidemic threatens and in determining what tactical errors in the swine flu incident are to be avoided next time round.

A general principle follows from our argument to this point: an evaluation of a particular project has its greatest implications for projects that will be put in place some time in the future. Space engineers never aim a missile carrying scientific instruments straight at Venus; rather, they calculate where Venus will be many months in the future and then aim at that spot. The evaluator deploying his forces has similarly to aim beyond the visible target; he, however, has no way to calculate nicely how social priorities and concerns will shift in the months ahead. Insights applicable to many possible programs are therefore more to be treasured than pinpoint conclusions about a program that will soon pass out of the spotlight.

# 5

■■■■■■■■■■■■■■■■■

# The Shape of the
# Field Study

■■■■■■■■■■■■■■■■■

The preceding chapter demonstrated that the planning of evaluative research is as much concerned with substance and politics as with procedures. Unless, in the context of command, an administrator singles out a narrow question about a fixed program, evaluation research is more exploratory than confirmatory. Innumerable uncertainties are identified at the outset, and additional puzzles come into view as fieldwork proceeds. How to test a well-specified hypothesis under fixed conditions is the subject of the usual technical literature on experimental design. Although he should almost never concentrate on a narrow question, the evaluator has to make similar decisions about the shape of his study. As planning moves along, he has to envision possible frameworks for the study and ultimately construct one or more formal plans or "hulls" to specify what observations will be made. How many experimental sites? How formal a sampling plan? What activity in control sites, if there are any?

    As a preliminary illustration of reasoning about a hull, we speak briefly of a hypothetical literacy program in a developing

269

country. The evaluator's main responsibility is to assess the effect of a proposed new method, but he wants to hold down the cost of outcome measurement so that he can also study process and thereby get ideas for improving the program. A traditional design might assign villages at random: twenty villages to receive the instructional services and twenty to remain undisturbed except for the measuring process.

Organizing the study would be costly, and a good deal of political capital would be spent in obtaining agreement to the randomization. Therefore the evaluator should ask whether a less elaborate design could give a useful answer. For example, he could compare literacy before and after the campaign in the twenty villages actually treated. With no control villages, what could he safely conclude?

Suppose that no change is found. The failure of the treatment would not be denied, and the question of why it failed would become important. The control villages could shed no light on that (unless it is believed that a positive effect was masked by a downward trend over time that was taking place for other reasons, in communities generally). Suppose that a small change is found. Someone might explain away the finding by suggesting that literacy improved spontaneously. But if a change is small enough to be explained away as "spontaneous," no one should care whether the program caused it or not. If, for example, the average literacy rate went from 20 to 22 percent, the program failed.

Suppose that the change observed is sizable, that is, large enough to justify extending the program to other localities. Spontaneous improvement can be ruled out as an explanation; experience in many countries has shown that large improvements in literacy do not happen without intervention. A die-hard skeptic might suggest that other interventions concurrent with the new program produced the gain. But control villages would not be required to dispose of this challenge. Asking a few questions in those villages where improvement was greatest would identify any potent teaching activity that occurred alongside the experimental treatment.

The case is strong, then, for a before-and-after study. The resources saved go into studying why the program worked well where it did and into explaining poor outcomes where they occurred. This mixture of information will almost surely satisfy users of the study. Indeed, twenty villages is probably a larger sample than is needed, unless village-to-village variation in program delivery or client response is large. This suggests the possibility of beginning with development work in a few villages and increasing the sample only after pointed, significant questions arise that a small sample cannot answer.

This example in itself makes it obvious that we are at odds with much recent propaganda for "social experimentation." We quickly acknowledge that the book with that title (Riecken and Boruch, 1974) goes beyond propaganda; it is subtly reasoned and its recommendations are carefully hedged. But many other pronouncements that favor formal, randomized experimentation are neither qualified nor subtle. Even in the Riecken-Boruch book the subtleties and qualifying remarks are lost on those who have not thought deeply about the issues. Many writers impressed by the virtues of strong designs say flatly that the design with random assignment is "the only proper design" or "the most desired design" for an evaluation. That kind of statement we find much too sweeping.

As Anderson and Ball (1978) have said, systematic evaluative research necessarily takes many forms, and each has its advantages and limitations. Numerous technical and ethical dilemmas arise in judging whether to run a formal comparative experiment, as is brought out especially well by Tukey (1977). Writing of medical trials, he has set out the usefulness and limitations of exploratory studies, of systematic case histories without a control group, and of focused studies leading to formal statistical tests.

Balance is still lacking, even though the case for formal experimentation is less overstated today than it was five years ago. Unrealistic expectations are seen in the standards that the General Accounting Office (GAO) has proposed for evaluation (see Chapter Four). Formative research during breadboard and shakedown phases is so little valued that it is dismissed with one sentence. The GAO recommends a stand-alone study to answer a sharp question about "impact" in the sites studied; a design other than the fully controlled experiment is acceptable only "when the evaluative goals do not require avoiding every possible source of confusion" (Comptroller General, 1978, p. 14). Within the GAO itself are staff members who know that a completely controlled design runs the risk of giving a seemingly precise answer to the wrong question. That is to be seen in the criticisms that the GAO made years ago of the unrealism and hence the dubious relevance of the randomized Experimental Housing Allowance Plan (summarized in Committee on Evaluation Research, 1978, app. 5, p. 3). The trade-offs between control and relevance are by no means sufficiently appreciated in the circles that matter most for the future of evaluation.

## Virtues of Systematic Inquiry

It is Campbell who has taken the lead in preaching the virtues of systematic evaluation to both the political and the scientific communities. Though he has said much in favor of strong comparative designs, his current position is closer to ours than to that set forth in the evaluative commandments. This chapter comments on four of his main themes:

1. Deliberate trial. Governments should frequently put social arrangements in place on a trial basis. A carefully observed intervention is the best way to learn what arrangements are truly worth adopting on a large scale.
2. Diversity of evidence. Results are more interpretable when variation is built into the design. A heterogeneous population, scattered over a number of distinct settings, tells us more than a purified sample. Capitalizing on variations in treatment delivery from site to site and measuring any key variable in more than one way are more instructive than restricting the study to a narrow set of operations.

3. Comparison. A positive outcome might arise from some cause other than the benefit conferred by the treatment. The preferred way to judge a proposed operational plan is to try it alongside a "control" arrangement in circumstances that are separate but equivalent. The control treatment should be tailored specifically to reflect a certain influence that seems highly likely to produce spurious evidence for the value of an ineffective treatment. Thus, the placebo given to control patients in a drug trial tests for the power of suggestion. Comparison on equivalent groups is also the suitable basis for judging rival interventions proposed for the same general purpose. Interventions should be judged by a comparative trial.

4. Controlled assignment. In a comparative study, the experimenter should control membership in the groups. Units should be assigned to treatments (perhaps by randomizing), not collected casually.

To each of the foregoing paragraphs, specific page citations from the following sources could be appended: Campbell (1957), Campbell and Fiske (1959), Campbell and Stanley (1963), Campbell (1969a), Campbell (1969b), Campbell (1974), Campbell (1975), and especially Cook and Campbell (1976, 1979). The themes are especially well represented in Cook and Campbell. Most of Campbell's arguments have been couched in terms of basic science rather than evaluation, and hence his stress does not match ours. But Cook and Campbell touch on evaluation, and Campbell was a member of the Riecken and Boruch (1974) writing team.

We may appear to disagree with Campbell and his colleagues when we stress the limitations of strong designs for purposes of evaluation, but we are only restoring a balance that the evaluative commandments overturned. In a revision of their earlier thinking, Cook and Campbell, in their 1979 book, acknowledge the pertinence of our reservations. They indicate that assignment rules are only a limited aspect of research design and that under some of the circumstances arising in evaluation the randomized experiment is less suitable than other techniques (pp. 90–91, 342–345, and 384).

Our reservations about stand-alone experiments echo what Campbell and Stanley said some years ago (1963, p. 173). The same thinking surfaced more recently in Cook and Campbell (1979, p. 80) in what federal officials should see as a call for a major change in their evaluation policies: "[Conducting] many small-scale experiments with local control and choice of measures is in many ways preferable to giant national experiments with a promised standardization that is neither feasible nor even desirable from the standpoint of making irrelevancies heterogeneous [that is, of achieving relevance]."

*Trial of Social Inventions.* The virtues of trying out proposals before making a firm commitment to them are so evident that we have little to say beyond concurring with Campbell (1969b). His call for an "experimenting society" echoes the Deweyan faith that ingenuity can improve human institutions. New social arrangements can serve old purposes better and new purposes well.

Experimentalists do not advocate change out of blithe faith in novelty; they are committed to hardheaded testing of new ideas. Although observing an existing activity is instructive and can suggest improvements, to test a truly fresh idea requires active intervention. Only a fraction of the new ideas will turn out to be well grounded; to put promising ideas through a process of development and test is thus sound policy for a society— Popper (1957) calls this "piecemeal social engineering." The testing of novel ideas is, however, only one of evaluation's significant roles. We have argued that most changes in social institutions come by way of adjustments at the margin. These modifications too can be made tentatively, as trials of ventures to which no one is committed; small manipulations can be experimental in spirit.

But a caution about the term *manipulation* is in order. This term conveniently designates deliberate alterations of arrangements or deliberate installation of a new service. The investigator or the social planner has the opportunity to arrange events to a greater degree than is possible when one merely observes a program that has developed "on its own." But the investigator cannot arbitrarily change institutions and assign individuals as dictated by the logic of a research hypothesis. He will have to negotiate to arrive at a plan others find agreeable; that plan makes the research more collaborative than the word *manipulate* suggests.

*Diversity of Evidence.* The strategy of diversifying the data we endorse heartily. It requires discussion not because it is controversial but because few planners of evaluations recognize its full implications.

As we said in Chapter Four, data lead formally to a statistical conclusion about a particular measure used on a particular population to which one particular treatment plan was applied. (Or to a conclusion about the difference between two treatment plans). The conclusion about the treatment operations actually carried out and observed is restated in broad language about: "voucher plans," "recommendations on health practices broadcast by radio," "community participation," "mental health," "employability." Policy is discussed at this general level. Evidence from one intervention plan realized in a certain number of sites provides only limited support for the generalized conclusion that readers and listeners take from an evaluation.

Users are wrong to assume that what worked in the trial will work in the future. The treatment $T$ will be changed into a $T^*$ when it is applied on a larger scale or under other administrative arrangements; moreover, the PSC (policy-shaping community) will often want to depart from the plan originally tried. Transfer to a new population and setting will also modify results. In view of the fact that interactions abound, change in conditions or procedures can enhance, reduce, or even reverse the effect of a treatment (Campbell, 1974; Cook and Campbell, 1979, pp. 28 and 33–35; Cronbach, 1975; Bronfenbrenner, 1976; Pillemer and Light, 1979). The only way that the PSC can exercise judgment about future programs bearing the same label as the $T$ studied is to understand the process by which the treatment works. Understanding is required to make use of even a well-grounded formal conclusion.

Diversifying the sample—the $t$, $u$, and $o$ of the original investigation—is a tactic capable of justifying a broad conclusion. Of course, diversifying spreads a study thinner because fewer data are then collected on any one variant. But the fact that diversification can go too far does not call the principle of diversity into question. It is one of the matters that the designer has to keep in balance.

Consider first the treatment procedure. In most scientific research, procedure is standardized, not diverse. All units within a treatment category are subjected to the same procedures. Pure chemicals, measured doses, standard conditions of temperature and pressure, sterile glassware—these hallmarks of procedure in the natural sciences have their counterparts in social research.

Some writers recommend similar control in evaluation. "[S]pecifying treatments helps to achieve comparability between different experimental sites or to permit exploitation of necessary variations from site to site for useful learning purposes. In other words, when an experimental treatment is repeated (replicated), it should be kept the same or deliberately and systematically altered, rather than being allowed to vary haphazardly" (Riecken and Boruch, 1974, p. 3). This recommendation seems right for a superrealization, where one wants no inadvertent departures from the best-laid plans.

But Riecken and Boruch also recognize good reasons for not standardizing treatment realizations: "[T]he benefits reaped from a closely controlled 'pure' test may incur some costs that a looser design may not. The latter may be more realistically representative of the actual treatment if and when it is installed as a routine program, and, hence, the effects observed in the looser design will be more generalizable. Informed and expert opinion is not homogeneous in this matter" (p. 33). This statement fits our thinking better than the first. At three places, however, we would replace the pallid "may" with "almost certainly will." (Riecken and Boruch go on in their next sentence to say: "Whichever design is used, it is highly desirable that the treatment be specified in as much detail as possible." But here the meaning of "specify" has changed from "standardize," as in the first quotation, to "document what *actually* happened to subjects." Documentation is indispensable if a study is to have explanatory value.)

For a trial program to be a prototype of a potential social program, its specification has to match the specification that the planners expect to impose later by legislation, formal guidelines, and supervision. Some treatments are little specified; an agency, for example, may simply give schools in a defined category some money to spend. The funding formula, along with the category definition, *is* the program. To get a preview of the operational program, the evaluator would standardize the plan for his study in only those respects. It would be unwise to control in the prototype what would not be controlled in an operational program. For example, suppose that the proponent's plan for allocation of funds leaves room for discretion and thereby allows cities with political clout to get more than their fair share. The evaluator should detect that consequence before the plan is made permanent, but he cannot do so if, for research purposes, he brings the allocation under extra control. Likewise, it makes no sense for him to restrict what local authorities do with the money if the proposal for action leaves such decisions unconstrained. That is to say, he ought to investigate the realizations *t* that, collectively, match the program plan.

For purposes of a prototype study, treatment plan $T$ may be installed in a number of sites. Even so, the realizations are almost certain to vary, if only because the guidelines are interpreted locally. In the Follow Through comparison of "models" of compensatory education, the variation in results across sites supposedly using the same model was ten times the variation across models (Glass, 1979). Allowing natural variation to occur and then appraising its extent makes interpretation comparatively easy. If findings are consistent from site to site, the PSC learns that the treatment has much the same consequences wherever and however it is installed. Insofar as the results differ, something much more important is learned: not all realizations that come under the same general label work the same way, and a plan to establish a uniform program by a centralized decision may be a fantasy (Anderson and others, 1978). A more refined analysis will then become the basis for future planning. If nothing else, a close look at the less successful realizations can suggest guidelines that will make such deviations infrequent. But the findings may also suggest establishing radically different programs in settings that differ (Pillemer and Light, 1979).

In the prototype study the evaluator is able to spot variations in practice at an early date. It is a good idea to study the atypical sites more closely than the others in order to learn the consequences of variations. The same policy holds for a program already in operation. The investigator will define the range of programs that fall within the category of interest (say, "informal instruction in science"), and a survey will identify admissible cases. A strictly representative sample may be less useful than a sample in which the exceptional cases are overrepresented; the unbalanced sample can indicate more clearly what variations matter. Even at the breadboard and superrealization stages, planning for deliberate variation is likely to increase information yield.

*Value of Imbalance.* Many of our recommendations call for distributing resources unevenly over questions and subquestions and then throwing in extra resources as events unfold. Balanced and complete designs are a default option for the evaluator who cannot judge what information will be of most use. But social experimenters are likely to adopt unthinkingly the familiar designs from psychological laboratory research and survey research. In these symmetric and nonsequential designs, equally dense samples (or equal samples) are drawn from all sectors of the parent distribution and the evaluator assigns equal numbers of cases to each treatment. The same measures are collected everywhere and from everyone. Although this symmetry makes calculations easier, the considerations of prior uncertainty and leverage justify imbalance.

With regard to units, strictly representative sampling ensures some diversity, but deliberate imbalance gives better information on some pointed questions. If hopes for a treatment are high but there are doubts about its suitability to a special clientele, trying it on a disproportionate number of those hard cases will confirm or settle the doubts. Unrepresentative sampling allows as firm a statistical inference as does uniform sampling provided that the sampling is systematic. Unbalanced samples are stronger bases for some inferences, weaker bases for others. The key to inference is to draw randomly from within subsets of the population—thickly in some, thinly in others—and to know the density of sampling. Taking successive samples is a good practice. Extra data should be collected where earlier waves of data left the greatest uncertainties.

The analysis of an evaluation frequently throws all data into one "main effect," but it is clearly sensible to separate subpopulations (Boruch, 1975c, pp. 123–132). A plan that gets good results with one ethnic minority may fail with another. A procedure that succeeds in schools with above-average students may work badly in other schools. One may set up separate investigations for subpopulations. Or, with a heterogeneous sample, the statistical analysis can relate outcomes to characteristics of units. The better the extremes are represented, the more firmly the trends will be established. When the treatment is delivered to distinct subclienteles, case studies of the process in each category are helpful.

We follow Campbell again in recommending multiple observing operations. When just one indicator is used for an important outcome, the critic can plausibly ask, "Would a different measure tell the same story?" It is also easy to argue that a poor indicator was used. Using two or three indicators reduces argument—or else turns up discrepant trends that force everyone toward subtler interpretation. Moreover, it costs little more to apply three techniques to partial samples than to obtain full data with just one technique. Where aggregates (schools, communities, and so on) are to be assessed, good data on the group can be obtained with observations too inaccurate to assess each individual well. Matrix-sampling designs (which put different test items before each slice of an informant sample) are cost effective in evaluation (Shoemaker, 1973).

Indicators reinforce each other not only statistically but logically. Any one indicator is sensitive to influences that are irrelevant to the variable one wants to assess, and it is thus to some degree off target. But indicators have different biases, so triangulation tightens interpretation. W. G. Smith (1975, p. 121) gives an illustration of this. A regional treatment center for mental patients was assessed by means of three indicators: average length of stay, ratio of readmissions to discharges, and an adjusted count of patients sent to long-term treatment facilities. A short average stay would seem to indicate that most patients become better quickly. But premature discharges would also produce a favorable length-of-stay index and so would the questionable practice of shunting uncomplicated cases off to long-term treatment. The three indicators together made it possible to weigh such doubts.

Evaluators and decision makers are aware of the usefulness of diverse indicators of an outcome, but they are less aware of the usefulness of multiple indicators of initial characteristics (Campbell and Fiske, 1959; Miller, 1956). Even evaluators accustomed to measuring *distinct* initial variables for use as statistical covariates, are not accustomed to using two or more indicators of the *same* construct to describe the subjects who enter treatment. Recent technical developments show how important this approach can be.

Statistical procedures pioneered by Jöreskog (Jöreskog and Sörbom, 1979) make it possible to relate outcomes to an explanatory construct, once two or more indicators of the construct have been applied. This is an extension of the structural regression methods ("causal models") that economists and sociologists have previously used with purely operational indicators. Adjustment for the incompleteness of any single indicator can change the apparent size of treatment effects and the regression weights for predictive variables. Magidson's (1977) application of the method to the Head Start data illustrates its promise. (His assumption that socioeconomic status was the only background factor that influenced outcome is open to question. Bentler and Woodward, 1978, challenged Magidson's conclusion.)

One rarely can satisfy a critical PSC by measuring just one outcome variable, even when excellent techniques are used. An outcome that is socially worthwhile is likely to have several aspects, and the evaluator who gets a good "fix" on some one variable $O$ leaves room for endless debate about the important $O*$

that he did not observe. The recommendation to check on accomplishment by a spread of techniques applies to virtually any attempt to change knowledge, attitudes, or behavior, as well as to programs that attempt to change the incidence of, say, crime or accidents.

Everyone agrees that an instructional experiment should be appraised by collecting evidence of what students learned. But the usual final test that covers the content taught is open to three challenges. First, learning scores drop off rapidly after instruction stops, and the kind of instruction that produces the best immediate scores may not produce the most lasting effects. Second, test items that stick close to the lessons say little about general competence. Students may learn a great number of answers without improving much in analytic ability. Experimental curricula regularly outperform traditional curricula on test items whose specific topics appeared in the new course of study but not in the old. Competing curricula usually come out even on tests of interpretive ability whose topics match neither set of lessons (Walker and Schaffarzick, 1974). This is especially significant because general skills fade less rapidly than specific information. Third, there are opportunity costs. A curriculum that narrows its efforts to a "few basics" inevitably withdraws time from topics that other educators introduce to broaden the student's horizons.

## When Is Comparison Advisable?

Our recommendation is to study each program on its own terms, as should be evident from our view of the evaluator as historian. But this does not rule out comparison of treatments. The only serious disadvantage of comparison is the division of resources that it entails. Some comparisons can be made at almost no cost, but in other studies spending on the comparison group cuts spending on the first treatment in half. Since a contrast group is sometimes a good investment, sometimes not, the designer should be clear that a *particular* comparison will be profitable—in leverage and reduction of uncertainty—before investing in it.

Those who put forward methodological commandments seem to follow just the opposite logic. They see a significance test on the presence of a "treatment effect" as the goal of an evaluation. Even assessing whether the end state is satisfactory is subordinated to establishing that the intervention was the sole *cause* of that outcome (Rossi, Freeman, and Wright, 1979, pp. 161–163). The evaluator is told that he should have a comparison group; he is presumably to accept that advice before beginning to consider what the comparison treatment could be. This exaltation of comparison for the sake of comparison has led some evaluators to introduce control groups whose treatment no PSC would entertain as a serious proposal (Scriven, 1967, p. 69; Crain and others, 1974b, pp. 91–92).

*Type of Comparative Study.* The importance of comparative data depends on the comparison proposed and on the stage of program maturity. Consideration of just seven of the possible kinds of comparative study will make it clear that the question "to compare or not to compare?" is too sweeping. Table 1 lists the seven designs for ready reference.

We suppose that a treatment $T_A$ is the focus of investigation; it is the proposal to be evaluated. The three main divisions of Table 1 identify distinct kinds of contrast. The first plan considers variants of $T_A$. In the second, $T_A$ is compared with a rival $T_B$, which may be a method already accepted as appropriate for the same purpose as $T_A$ or may be a rival innovation. $T_A$ and $T_B$ are serious policy alternatives. Finally, $T_0$ is a "no-treatment" control. Nothing special is being done to the subjects in that group, except for intrusion to collect data; that is, persons receiving $T_0$ are exposed to whatever mix of already extant services and experiences will continue if no action is taken. In addition, they might be supplied a pseudotreatment that is not a serious policy proposal (a placebo, perhaps).

The second major distinction in Table 5 is between studies in which treatments are installed for purposes of the investigation ("Yes" in second column) and those in which instances of the treatment are located wherever they may exist in the field. The last entry (3b2) in the table identifies the pretest-posttest

Table 5. Types of Comparative Designs
for Studying a Proposed Treatment

| Plan | Variation under Formal Control? | Contrast Examined |
|---|---|---|
| 1a | No | Comparisons entirely among variants of $T_A$ as they occur. |
| 1b | Yes | Alternative versions of $T_A$ are installed and compared. |
| 2a | No | A rival treatment $T_B$, already in place, is compared with instances of $T_A$ where they occur. |
| 2b | Yes | Two groups of units are formed; each unit is assigned to receive one of the rival treatments, $T_A$ or $T_B$. |
| 3a | No | A null treatment $T_0$ is in place in some sites; it is compared with instances of $T_A$ where they occur. |
| 3b1 | Yes | Two groups of units are formed; some units are assigned to receive $T_A$ and the rest have only the baseline experience $T_0$. |
| 3b2 | Yes | A group of units is observed at the end of a baseline period under $T_0$ and then shifted to $T_A$. |

design as a comparative study in which one group experiences $T_0$ and $T_A$ in succession.

We can say at the outset that treatment realizations installed at the behest of the evaluator make a comparison more interpretable than a study of realizations found in place. In other words, one will tend to favor designs 1b, 2b, and 3b1 over their counterparts 1a, 2a, and 3a. The first advantage is that a treatment deliberately installed is likely to come closer to the program plan about which a conclusion is wanted. Second, manipulation can produce a greater variety of treatment realizations —a wider range of expenditure per client, for example—than is likely to be found already in place. And, third, the investigator who installs treatments has a much cleaner contrast than one whose treatment groups differ in unknown ways. But logical, as well as practical, difficulties with manipulative designs will be recognized as we proceed.

Control of assignment is the topic for the next section, but let us state here that satisfactory formal comparison of treatments is impossible when assignment is not controlled. Take the Coleman report on *Equality of Educational Opportunity* (1966), which was a study of type 2a, as an example. The data could adequately describe (1) the mean achievement of children whose school systems have highly trained teachers and (2) the achievement in systems where teachers are poorly trained. These are reports on distinct populations as well as on two sets of treatments. On the whole, abler children, with wealthier parents more concerned about achievement, are found where better teachers are found. These children tend to achieve more. But no manipulation of the data will give a dependable report as to how much of the difference (if any) the better teachers account for (Lord, 1967). When programs reach separate clienteles, one can assess what is happening to the clients in each group. But to say what would happen if the first program were delivered to the second group is at best a plausible inference, at worst a dubious speculation (Meehl, 1970, 1971).

Our stated preference for manipulated designs has to be qualified. Cost is one drawback. Moreover, great effort is required to persuade units to accept a treatment arbitrarily selected for them by the investigator or by an administrator if the treatment requires a substantial change from familiar ways of operating. Yet another drawback is that the institutions prepared to adopt a treatment of the experimenter's choice will almost certainly not be typical of the target population. Particularly cooperative subjects are the ones who enlist for a trial at the breadboard or superrealization stages. That is all to the good, but the results of the trial will probably not provide a valid forecast for the target population. These remarks are not intended as an argument against manipulative studies; they are simply reminders of difficulties to be anticipated.

*Functions of Each Contrast.* We have argued at some length for examining variants of $T_A$ : information on the diverse realizations has to be recorded to establish what the $T_A$ of the study amounted to. Comparisons cost very little, and the additional effort required to manipulate program features is likely to be profitable. If, for example, one wanted to know whether the *number* of Superlimonada broadcasts in the Nicaraguan experiment might make a difference, the way to find out would be to broadcast at different rates in different regions. Natural variation among stations would probably be too slight to display the trend clearly. A study of type 1b has the advantage of throwing strong light on a particular kind of variation, though only a limited number of controlled variations can be studied at once.

The comparison of type 1a or 1b undermines the tendency to think of $T$ as monolithic, as a fixed plan that policy makers must take or leave. When variation in outcomes is associated with variations among the realizations, progress toward a better $T^*$ is made. It was on that basis that parent participation came to be a valued feature of compensatory education for preschoolers. Riecken and Boruch (1974, pp. 17–20) strongly encourage studies of type 1b as "social experiments." Studies of type 1a serve the same function. With less strict control, the interpretation is more equivocal; nevertheless, the opportunity for discovery is greater than in studies where the variants are standardized.

Type 1 comparisons can be made at any stage of program maturity, and they are often run alongside or within a comparison of type 2 or 3. Type 1a comparison belongs, we would say, in any study, though it is least significant in a superrealization. Using a 1b shell to test gross variations in a program plan is most suitable during evaluation of a prototype. Experiments on minor features can be a natural part of pilot testing and of self-renewal in an established program.

The policy maker asking for a comparison of programs or proposals anticipates placing a bet on one or another alternative. A comparative study of type 2a or 2b at first glance seems the obvious basis for the decision. But the simple horse-race question, "Is A better than B?," should be put more subtly: "What does each program return, at each plausible level of effort?" This calls, in effect, for a study of type 1a or (preferably) 1b within each program. The comparison across treatments becomes a comparison of two within-treatment studies, which are not necessarily concurrent.

*Logical Difficulties of Summative Comparison.* Glennan (1972) develops this argument with manpower retraining as an example. He notes that high-level decisions are rarely "go/no-go." For programs already launched, the allocative decision is usually about minor increases in budget for one or another competitor. If $T_A$ outperformed $T_B$ at the levels of expenditure tried in the investigation, is $T_A$ the better choice for the increment? Not necessarily. As an economist, Glennan asks what is the *marginal* benefit from a projected increase in input. That gain is generally not proportional to the benefit per dollar at lower levels. As a retraining program expands, it enrolls more and more hard cases. If $T_A$ is less suited to those cases than $T_B$, any advantage that $T_A$ showed in a low-budget comparison would be a false guide to large-scale planning.

Quantitative comparison of outcomes gives a strong hint for policy when treatments $T_A$ and $T_B$ are aimed toward the same near-term ends. The investigator is likely to ask precisely the same questions about outcomes of two patterns of day care, for example, even though the pertinent questions about process may differ. Comparison becomes far less instructive if the alternative programs have entirely different near-term aims. While instructive studies can then be made within programs, comparison across programs may be impossible. Think, for example, of two programs for undergraduates who are looking toward medical careers—one program providing a more liberal education and the other a more technical one. Many of the important differences would not be expected to appear until after the students had completed medical school; even a comparison of medical school grades would be a dubious basis for a policy choice. (To be sure, a choice could be made if the grades of one group were disastrously low, but *that* kind of evidence would lead to action without a comparison group.)

Policy makers do weigh alternatives that have incommensurable outcomes—reduced crime versus community harmony, say, or children's shoes versus army boots. In such cases, comparable data cannot be developed. At most, the evaluator can describe outcomes observed for each program in turn, making a statement valid only for the type of program and the budget level that was tried out. Outcomes of each program can be set alongside estimates of what the same indicators would register if the program was not adopted. But each program has its own outcome variables.

Comparison is invariably judgmental when programs have multiple and perhaps dissimilar outcomes, and the judgments made are political, not analytic. Somehow, a 5 percent reduction in burglaries has to be judged as more (or less) welcome than a 5 percent reduction in community complaints about police. Some evaluators aspire to make such comparisons a technical matter. But those who employ cost-benefit analysis force disparate outcomes into a single framework. Those who ask clients and constituencies to state their divergent priorities (Edwards, Guttentag, and Snapper, 1975; Mitroff, Emshoff, and Kilmann, 1979) strive to calculate an aggregate judgment after members of the PSC rate the outcome dimensions. This procedure can bring out value conflicts and thus produce an educative discussion. However, when the aggregate calculations are used to forestall negotiation by announcing which program is preferred by the community, the claim is too bold. Nelson (1977, p. 18) warns that "the coin of rational analysis is likely to be devalued by trying to achieve what cannot be bought by rational coin."

No technology for comparing benefits will silence partisan discord. Partisans can always reopen the case for an option that fell behind in the calculations. Economists have encountered so much difficulty with intangible and incommensurable outcomes that they now see the cost-benefit model as a metaphor rather than as an algorithm. The technology is adequate for comparing the *costs* of two alternatives judged reasonably effective for the same purpose (Levin, 1975), but in such an analysis outcomes are not formally compared across programs.

Cook and Campbell (1979, p. 345; emphasis added) warn: "It is rarely desirable to conduct an experiment before preliminary conceptual or empirical work has been done to ensure that the manipulations are *exactly* the ones of interest." A type 2 comparison assumes that both rival programs are ready for test. It makes no sense to compare two treatments formally when one of them is known to need considerable revision. At the breadboard stage, then, it is wise to confine comparison to versions of the focal treatment. Formal comparison across candidate programs has occasional value at the superrealization stage. The most significant judgment at the end of the superrealization is that the program does or does not deserve a prototype test. Only if two or more rivals are simultaneously ready for test—and it is impractical to run prototype trials on both—does a direct comparison of superrealizations seem likely to be cost effective.

The argument for such comparisons is essentially that if $T_A$ comes out best, at whatever level of expenditure policy makers are prepared to contemplate, *it* should be the program carried forward to a prototype test. This conclusion is sound only if the program that works best under highly controlled conditions is also going to work best under field conditions. The reverse may be true when the winning program is highly sensitive to change in conditions and the losing one is not.

Direct comparison of costs and benefits is especially appropriate at the prototype stage provided that outcomes are commensurable. The satisficing kind of decision can be reached, however, by testing a single politically credible program. The cost of comparison trials is not warranted unless there is a sharp division of prior opinion about the merits of the program. If the alternative programs seem *a priori* to be much alike in their prospective benefits, it is unlikely that evidence showing a modest superiority for one of them will override preconceptions and self-interest. Prior beliefs and commitments give one competitor a political head start that is hard to overcome.

Moreover, the program undergoing a prototype test is still being developed, at least with respect to administrative and supervisory arrangements. This means that early returns are not to be taken at face value. The experience with Follow Through Planned Variations carries an additional warning. When variation in outcomes among realizations of the same program is greater than the difference between allegedly different kinds of programs, it is obvious that genuine alternatives have not been tested. "It may never be possible," says Rivlin (1974), "to do 'experiments' on which firm statistical inferences can be based" when the program attempts to alter the political and economic mechanism of large institutions. Her examples are educational vouchers, performance contracting, and health maintenance organizations.

### Selecting Appropriate Contrasts

A further major issue is when to arrange for a null control treatment. Judgment that a program is worthwhile is comparative in the sense that the results are perceived against a frame of reference. Whether formal baseline data on a null treatment are wanted depends first of all on the prior knowledge available. Suppose that, after the broadcast campaign in the Nicaraguan experiment, 14 percent of mothers give Superlimonada whenever a child has diarrhoea. That is gratifying, if it is believed that without the broadcasts 5 percent or fewer would do so. Even if beliefs disagree when the trial is launched, simple before-and-after figures should be adequate for drawing a conclusion. Obviously, if Superlimonada is new to the culture, "after" figures alone would suffice. Only heroic imagination could construct a scenario that attributes appreciable frequency of use to anything but the broadcast.

Prior uncertainty and leverage determine how much the investigator should spend to get a baseline figure. The decision is not all-or-none. A quick field survey in a scattering of sites would perhaps confirm the planner's guesses at little cost. If the quick check challenges prior beliefs, a substantial baseline survey becomes better justified. That is a comparatively inexpensive before-and-after comparison of type 3b2.

Comparing treated and untreated groups carries added costs, including the political and morbidity costs of withholding service in some localities. The value of better comparative information did not outweigh those costs in the Superlimonada study. Evidence on $T_0$ guards only against the speculation that some freak of cultural change would within one year make Superlimonada popular in the absence of the broadcasts. Logically, the loophole is a "threat to validity." But not even a policy maker hoping to divert the broadcasters' funds to another use could advance that counterhypothesis with a straight face. Moreover the remarkable extraneous events—if any—that influenced the mothers would have been recorded by an alert evaluator. They would not have appeared in villages all across Nicaragua, so the internal comparison would be enough to assess the spurious influence.

When a study is being planned, whoever calls for a no-treatment control bears a burden of proof—the burden of making it plausible that practically significant change would occur in the absence of $T_A$. Graduate students are taught that it is improper to draw a conclusion from a confirmatory study that is logically open to counterinterpretation; *every* "threat to validity" must be guarded against, they come to think. Glass (1979, p. 12), wryly recalling his training under Julian C. Stanley, says that students "were taught, first, that there were dozens of things one must do to achieve a valid study, and, second, that they were impossible to do." Inquiry does not guard against all threats to validity, nor does any philosopher of science say that it should.

Inquiry proceeds in real time with real hours of effort and real dollars. Threats to validity are always present; an inquiry guards against one of them when the cost of the defense is considered more bearable than the uncertainty that the control aims to reduce. The negative income tax study in New Jersey was probably correct to assign some persons to receive no income-maintenance payments. Assessing attitudes toward work in an untreated group was a rather inexpensive addition to a study of type 1b and provided a needed baseline. Head Start likewise required a baseline; available norms gave no convincing indication of the scores that a young, disadvantaged, minority, strangely selected population would earn in the absence of treatment.

In looking upon a $T_0$ as an option rather than a requirement, we are aligned with Campbell (1969a, p. 356), who stresses that a control group is constructed to inform (or confirm) a particular counterinterpretation: "[I] t is not failure-to-control in general that bothers us, but only those failures of control which permit *truly plausible* rival hypotheses, laws with a degree of scientific establishment comparable to or exceeding that of the law our experiment is designed to test." Cook and Campbell (1976, p. 318) end their paper on this note: "[I] t is unrealistic to expect to control for all the validity threats we mentioned in a single experiment or in a single set of experiments. So, improving validity should not be confused with naive expectations of creating 'a valid experiment.'"

In studying a particular $T_A$, one can think of many possible $T_0$. Each represents a way in which a given effect could presumably be produced without $T_A$. Each $T_0$ has a different implication. A placebo guards against suggestion and observer bias (and also checks on the effects of concurrent events and growth). Providing a control group that receives only the pretest guards against the contention that practice on the test accounts for the final scores in the treated group. A particular control is warranted if it can be installed at reasonable cost and if, in the absence of that control, a positive effect could persuasively be explained away.

Very often, we have said, a suitable standard of comparison is a baseline measure. This can be collected on the experimental subjects (persons or institutions) just before they begin to experience $T_A$. Or, under other circumstances, the data can come from whatever persons were clients last year of the institution where $T_A$ is to be installed this year. This before-and-after design has received so much adverse comment that a word of defense is in order. Campbell and Stanley (1963, pp. 178 and 241) disparaged the design as "preexperimental" and "unacceptable." An untreated group to control for maturation and concurrent influences was lacking, and the pretest might have created the effects later attributed to the treatment. Campbell's view changed. The earlier characterization of the case study was a "caricature" (1975b, p. 179). He acknowledges (1974) the mutual dependence of qualitative and quantitative information.

Each has its distinctive weaknesses and its own justified plausibility (see also Cook and Campbell, 1979, p. 93). Moreover, the risk that pretesting will distort a finding is slight (Campbell, 1969a, p. 355). Studying $T_A$ by itself and letting the initial performance of its subjects serve as a baseline deserves a better press than it has had. This design is logically of the "interrupted time series" or "repeated measures" form—designs that have long enjoyed a good press.

*Hazards Inherent in "Convincing" Evidence.* The GAO draft guidelines (Comptroller General, 1978, p. 15) sound a familiar note in saying, "To be most useful, the evaluator must provide convincing evidence." Before we discuss assignment rules, which logically are the ideal device for strengthening a formal, circumscribed, causal inference, we wish to plant a seed of doubt. We have already suggested that even fragmentary evidence from a design of type 1a is an important corrective to the tendency to take the average result of treatment $T_A$ as a sufficient summary. More generally, we have emphasized that a complex description of events in the field provides a sensible basis for policy discussions.

Some of those who write on designs advocate formal, quantitative, controlled comparisons of outcomes specifically because they "are convincing." Riecken and Boruch (1974, pp. 22–30) are among those who wield this double-edged argument. Even in a very recent work, Cook and Campbell (1979, p. 55) see drawing a conclusion from an experiment as a "deductive process." Admittedly, a conclusion is impressive when derived by methods that mimic laboratory science. The stronger the controls, the harder it is for a critic to question the study itself. Therefore if a pretentious study arrives at a wrong verdict or merely *seems* to answer a question, it makes an undeservedly strong impression. Indeed, as Perelman and Olbrechts-Tyteca (1969, pp. 26–35) make clear by quoting from an "age-old debate" among the most eminent philosophers, the demand that an argument be "convincing" is nothing more than a rationalist attempt to define a category of conclusions that in no way rest on beliefs and values; in evaluation, it is an attempt to place decisions outside politics by establishing an inescapable conclusion.

To illustrate the limits of conclusions, we shall review two of the prime examples used by those who seek "convincing evidence." One is a comparative study of type 3b1, with nearly equivalent groups; the other is a brilliant quasi-experimental analysis of type 3b2 that compared baseline data to data from $T_A$.

*Performance Contracting Study.* This was a notable approximation to controlled experiment. Riecken and Boruch (1974, p. 29) set up our case without intending to when they hail that study as an admirably designed experiment, "sufficiently conclusive to prevent adoption of such programs in the form tested." The study, however, should have convinced no one.

In each participating district the two schools thought to be the most disadvantaged were identified. The superintendent was to assign $T_A$ to the needier school and to do nothing new for the other. This was only approximately an experiment, especially as it is not at all certain that the $T_0$ schools simply carried on "business as usual." Moreover, the Performance Contracting scheme was not ready for a summative trial. Contracting firms had to install special teaching procedures in the $T_A$ schools, but the contracts for service were signed so late that the firms had no reasonable opportunity to prepare and deliver materials and to explain them to teachers. Some observers suspect that teachers sabotaged the program, which had been imposed on them without negotiation or persuasion. We need not repeat the sad story told by Gramlich and Koshel (1975); all the conditions militated against a fair trial of the scheme. Moreover, the overall average taken as the key result obscured the fact that the experimental/control difference was wildly variable from one contracting firm to another and from town to town.

Very likely, the decision to scrap the policy proposal was determined by the vigorous opposition of national teachers organizations, which was evident very early. Profit-seeking contractors, one thinks, might have fought to keep the scheme alive, but no. They had lost so much money, under the slapdash arrangements of the field trial, that they were ready to take their losses and run. In effect, the political decision to discard Performance Contracting was made before the posttest data were in. The adverse statistical report was a timely torpedo hitting a doomed hulk. Its belated release only lighted up the pose of the Nixon administration as tough minded, unwilling to back a program that was not demonstrably cost effective.

The moral of the story is that a timely historical report of events, with or without the final test data, would have shown that Performance Contracting was not ripe for a prototype test and had not really been given one. The proper verdict *on the plan* was "not proven." The purportedly strict, unbiased, statistical comparison of the proposal with the *status quo* led to a verdict of "guilty." Is it not dangerous when purely formal characteristics of studies lead methodologists to hail these studies as "convincing"? (Acland, 1979, gives some comfort, in detailing how policy makers chose to set aside an allegedly significant treatment effect from an experiment on a scheme to help desegregating schools to adapt to a new clientele. What impresses a research expert obsessed with method may not impress someone who sees the larger picture.)

We hasten to say that the Performance Contracting scheme was not a proposal to our liking. But what about future proposals that are subjected to superficially fair comparative tests and then damned when they do not beat their experienced competitors? Is research that purports to give a "final" answer in the public interest?

*The "Breathalyser" Study.* This famous British experiment (Cook and Campbell, 1976, p. 280; 1979, p. 218) asked whether testing by police for alcohol on the driver's breath would make the roads safer—safer enough, that is, to justify the cost. This kind of policy question is fundamentally comparative. The available data came from records compiled before and after the abrupt introduction—on a fully operational scale—of a chemical test for those suspected of driving while intoxicated. Accidents decreased sharply at that time. Supplementary data dispelled counterhypotheses as convincingly as control groups could have. The breathalyser, as installed in 1967 with its attendant publicity campaign, was effective.

In continued operation, however, the system lost much of its effectiveness (Page, 1977). In recent years the breathalyser was applied to only a small fraction of suspects because police considered burdensome the steps necessary to get enough evidence to win a conviction. As the frequency of testing dropped, British drivers came to realize that the odds on being caught were low. Hence, by 1977, the system was no longer a major deterrent to drunken driving. The effect faded because the treatment faded. To quote Page: "Nobody can blame police patrols for being slow to hand out breathalyser bags when they know that if a motorist's breath turns the crystals green it marks the beginning of a complicated and lengthy sequence— a sequence which is boring and time consuming for the police and which keeps valuable patrol cars and crews off the road when they might be doing far more good out on the patch" (p. 41). (This last sentence describes an opportunity cost that the original study missed.)

This story illustrates the need to go behind outcome figures to understand the workings and potential shortcomings of a program. It also illustrates the need to think of the program that will be realized over the long term rather than of the ideal results or the results during the honeymoon period.

## Controlled Assignment

We turn now to the manipulative study in which treatments are to be formally compared. For ease of presentation we speak of a $T_A/T_0$ contrast. The argument would be almost identical if the second treatment were a $T_B$ or if several treatments were compared. In such a study, the usual advice is to randomize assignments, before or after stratification. To stratify, the investigator classifies units by types and within each type assigns perhaps a random half or third to each treatment.

When such a design is fully realized, controlling assignment strengthens certain inferences; we shall discuss those benefits, the costs of such a control, and the difficulties of approximating the ideal. The stratified-symmetric design just described is only one of many possible patterns of controlled assignment. Hence, a somewhat technical preamble is needed to indicate the range of possibilities and to direct attention to crucial assumptions.

*Asymmetric Assignment Possibilities.* Earlier in this chapter we said that a design need not be symmetric. Alongside 100 experimental sites, it is reasonable to use either 20 control sites or 200, depending on the cost of collecting control data. Costs are not simply the costs of measurement. Any withholding of treatment causes some ethical and political pain. And it costs something to make certain that an administrator did not smuggle $T_A$ or a $T_B$ to the $T_0$ group (Cook and Campbell, 1976, p. 228).

There are only two justifications for equalizing the number of control and experimental units. The first is trivial: statistical calculations are simpler with equal numbers. The second has to do with uncertainty and leverage: symmetry makes sense when, unit for unit, information on $T_0$ or $T_B$ is just as valuable as information on $T_A$. That is likely to be true when novel treatments are being compared; it is not likely to be true when $T_0$ is familiar.

Asymmetric sampling was recommended earlier on the basis that oversampling units of a certain type would indicate more about their response to $T_A$. It is not necessary to oversample $T_0$ in the same way. That decision is to be made separately. Once the experimenter has a roster of units available for assignment, he can sort them into cells. One cell might be "urban schools, in western states, with Hispanic enrollment of 20 percent or more." Then, to control assignment, he draws schools at random from that subroster for $T_A$ and for the contrasting treatment. The numbers drawn need not be equal. Even the matched-pairs design has a valid asymmetric form. Cases can be matched up in quartets (say). Assigning one random member of each quartet to $T_0$ leaves three for $T_A$.

For a strict statistical comparison it is necessary only that the relevant frequencies be recorded. Statistics from an unrepresentative sample can be adjusted to estimate whatever quantities a representative sample would estimate, as long as the imbalance in the sample is controlled imbalance.

An extreme form of asymmetric assignment is the "regression-discontinuity" design (Cook and Campbell, 1976, p. 268; 1979, p. 137). Units are arrayed along a continuum; schools, for

example, might be ordered by percentage of Hispanic enrollment. A cut is made at, say, 20 percent. Treatment A (perhaps
bilingual education) is installed in all schools above that point.
Schools below that point get $T_0$. (Schools close to the border-
line may be distributed randomly between $T_A$ and $T_0$.) The
samples for the two treatments are not similar, but a comparative conclusion can be drawn. School-wide achievement levels
are plotted against percentage of Hispanic enrollment. If the
trend over schools in the 0-to-20-percent range is an extension
of the trend in the 20-percent-and-over range, the treatment evidently made no difference. But if, at the cutoff point, the two
trend lines do not join up, the discontinuity indicates a treatment effect.

Such a comparison of trends can be made with any scheme
of proportional sampling, no matter how fanciful. One might,
for example, sort women by age and number of children under
sixteen and investigate the value of a certain kind of home visitor service to a selected sample. If the original sort allocated
women into forty cells, the experimental sample might draw
forty cases from ten cells, twenty cases from ten cells, and none
from the remainder. All that is strictly required is that cases be
drawn at random from the cell population. The $T_0$ group might
be drawn by another formula.

For a simple interview, an ordinary area sample of wom-
en residents might be most economical. For an expensive procedure (say, a physical examination), the $T_0$ sample would be
drawn in a wholly different manner. One might take twenty
cases at random from those cells where the physical examinations of the $T_A$ group showed high variability and five from the
cells where $T_A$ variability was low. Imaginative approaches can
greatly reduce the dollar cost of a controlled-assignment design,
as was brilliantly demonstrated in the New Jersey negative income tax plan (Rossi and Lyall, 1976).

*Conditions Required for Satisfactory Estimates.* In the
past, randomized or stratified-random designs have been set
apart as the ones able to produce unbiased estimates of treatment effects. We discuss instead the whole broad category of
controlled designs. *All of them* give unbiased estimates when

key assumptions are satisfied. This principle has been "on the books" for at least twenty-five years, but its breadth has only recently been appreciated. (For one of the recent mathematical proofs, see Overall and Woodward, 1977.)

Any general statement rests on assumptions. This is true of simple opinion surveys, as well as of experiments. Almost never, in a field study, is it possible to confirm that these assumptions are strictly valid. The result is to be trusted, then, to the extent that the members of the PSC find the assumptions plausible. The controlled-assignment study that loses no cases is a firm basis for generalization to the *UTO* it represents. Any other study, and any other interpretation of the experiment that reaches beyond *UTO*, invokes assumptions. The estimate of the treatment effect is plausible to the extent that the assumptions are trusted.

Let us be clear as to how the treatment effect is strictly to be conceptualized. Imagine that a person takes the treatment $T_A$ and attains an outcome score. Then the slate is wiped clean. The same person takes $T_0$ and reaches a score on the same measuring instrument. The experience of taking $T_A$ is assumed not to affect the result from $T_0$. The difference in scores ($Y_A - Y_0$) is the "treatment effect" for that person, and the average of such differences describes the treatment effect for the sample. As the group increases in size, the mean approaches the effect for the population. This strict interpretation assumes that the experience of each subject is precisely that specified as $T_A$ or $T_0$. Otherwise, reference to "the treatment" is ambiguous. Moreover, the effect is an effect associated with treatment, population, and setting, not with treatment alone.

Only rarely can a person be exposed to two social programs in succession; besides, carry-over effects would be expected in such a case. Hence, as a substitute for the strict interpretation, the parent population is split into indistinguishable subpopulations, roughly equivalent in all respects at the start of treatment. $T_A$ is applied to one and $T_0$ to the other. The difference in outcome means then is a surrogate for the treatment-population-setting effect originally defined.

An actual study yields scores for a sample that experienced realizations of $T_0$ and the mean for the population can then be estimated. (Adjustment is required if sampling was not uniform over sectors of the population.) In a comparative study, a similar mean for $T_0$ leads to a difference that is to be regarded as an estimate of the treatment effect in the population. The estimate will surely not coincide with the true value. If, over many repetitions of the experiment—with the same treatment specifications applied to fresh samples from the same population—the discrepancies average to zero, the estimate is said to be unbiased. The results from the samples have not systematically overstated or understated how much difference $T_A$ makes.

An unbiased estimate is not necessarily trustworthy, however. Estimates vary from sample to sample, sometimes by a large amount. Ordinarily the investigator has only one sample and can recognize uncertainty only by calculating the likely sampling error. The uncertainty interval ("confidence interval") that acknowledges the error is sometimes wide. If so, any one estimate can be far off target. The evaluator committed to controlled assignment often has to content himself with a fairly small study. Accepting data from cases whose assignment he did not control would greatly enlarge his sample. The study without controlled assignment—having an unknown bias but a small sampling error—may report the treatment effect more accurately than the unbiased but imprecise random experiment.

Evaluators should be mindful of Kendall's (1959) Hiawatha, who shot off hundreds of unbiased arrows. His shots were indeed impartial, neither consistently high nor low, neither right nor left. Their average was right on target, but not a single arrow was close. Other warriors, less fearful of systematic error, released their arrows consistently. The arrows of the efficient archers landed close together, off center but not far from the bull's-eye. Unimpressed by the niceties of unbiased performance, the tribesmen banished Hiawatha,

> Took away his bow and arrows,
> Said that though my Hiawatha
> Was a brilliant statistician
> He was useless as a bowman.
> As for variance components,
> Several of the more outspoken

Made primeval observations
Hurtful to the finer feelings
Even of a statistician.

In a corner of the forest
Dwells alone my Hiawatha
Permanently cogitating
On the normal law of error,
Wondering in idle moments
Whether an increased precision
Might perhaps be rather better,
Even at the risk of bias,
If thereby one, now and then, could
Register upon the target [p. 24].

An initial difference between groups tends to make the final estimate of the treatment effect too high or too low. If a randomized experiment, large or small, is repeated, the error will as likely go in the opposite as in the original direction. In contrast, a nonrandom sample chosen by a partisan of $T_A$ may well be biased. The partisan could allot most of the hard-core cases to $T_0$. The randomized study is impartial, but the difference between the sample mean and the population mean—between estimate and true effect—may still be large.

Haphazard influences even out over *large* random samples. Random samples differ in many ways that can influence response to treatment. Outcome differences also arise, for example, when a regular teacher falls ill and a less-prepared substitute teacher takes over. Randomization on a large scale renders such explanations of an effect implausible.

*The Community as Unit.* The link between sample size and benefit from randomizing is an elementary idea, and the reader may have reacted impatiently to our dwelling on it. Does not the modern comparative study of a widespread program collect data on hundreds of clients? True enough, but the pertinent figures are the number of independent units and the number of independent treatment realizations. A study of twenty classrooms may have data on 500 persons; even so, the effective sample size is twenty. Moreover, if $T_A$ is "performance contracting" and only one firm's instructional materials were used in all twenty classrooms, only one realization $t_a$ was selected from the universe of admissible treatments $T_A$ (see Chapter Four).

The point merits emphasis because, in the propaganda for randomization, an experiment with a sample trivially small for statistical comparison has sometimes been held up as an admirable model. The Guatemala nutrition study described in Chapter Four is a favorite example. The units randomly assigned were four villages—two (!) cases per treatment. This gives only two degrees of freedom for a comparative analysis; a valid statistical inference would almost inevitably accept the null hypothesis. Forget "comparison," and the shell embraces four excellent (largely quantitative) case histories of villages.

Another excellent study with the community as a unit was conducted at Stanford. It was excellent because it did not pretend to be statistically definitive. The research (Farquhar and others, 1977; Maccoby and others, 1977) involved a two-year test of persuasive campaigns to change habits likely to bring on heart disease. Only three communities were studied, for the sake of extensive observation and measurement. The communities chosen were similar; all were centers of agricultural business in northern California. Broadcasts provided the main persuasive treatment, and thus the community as a whole was treated. The design was this:

- $T_0$ Tracy. Modified only by the measuring operations.
- $T_A$ Gilroy. Modified by broadcast campaign, diffuse public relations activities, and measurement.
- $T_B$ Watsonville. Same as Gilroy for most cases. Intensive personal instruction was given to a high-risk subsample.

The assignment of towns to treatments was not random. Initial data showed Tracy to be the healthiest of the three communities; moreover, it was more distant from the other two towns than they were from each other and so less likely to be affected by the campaigns in them. Therefore, it was assigned $T_0$. Random assignment would not have reduced uncertainty because the groups were not equal. For example, on an initial measure of triglycerides, the means were as follows:

|              | Tracy | Gilroy | Watsonville |
|--------------|-------|--------|-------------|
| Baseline     | 116   | 138    | 139         |
| End of Year 1| 133   | 129    | 143         |
| End of Year 2| 125   | 133    | 134         |

Suppose that communities had been assigned at random. The initial difference in means was large enough to mask the treatment effect. No defensible adjustment can be made with just one unit per treatment. (For want of a better solution, each final mean was expressed as a percentage of the baseline mean for the same group.) The only counterhypothesis that random assignment would have guarded against was that someone had assigned his favored treatment to the most cooperative community. In addition, random assignment would have earned a small demerit on ethics since Tracy was healthier than the other two towns at the start. The treatment groups would have been no more equivalent than in the actual study.

"High-risk" subjects in Watsonville were divided at random. There, 272 low-risk subjects and 40 high-risk subjects encountered only messages planted in the media. In addition, intensive counseling was given to another 77 high-risk subjects. A within-Watsonville significance test for the two high-risk groups would have been justified if factors producing attrition were similar for these groups. We draw attention to the asymmetric design in Watsonville and to the attrition rates indicated by these figures in Table 6:

Table 6. Numbers of Cases Assigned and Completing Treatment
in the Watsonville Experiment

|                       | All Subjects   | Low-Risk       | High-Risk     | High-Risk                          |
|-----------------------|----------------|----------------|---------------|------------------------------------|
| Treatment             |                | Media          | Media         | Media plus intensive counseling    |
| Sample invited        | 833            |                |               |                                    |
| Loss                  | (228; 27%)     |                |               |                                    |
| Provided baseline data| 605            | 436            | 56            | 113                                |
| Loss                  | (156; 26%)     | (104; 24%)     | (16; 29%)     | (36; 32%)                          |
| Provided final data   | 449            | 332            | 40            | 77                                 |

The study was made far more valuable by the use of a variety of measures. All experimental groups improved on physiological measures. The intensive treatment seemed to have a large effect on verbal knowledge of risk factors and on smoking, but little added physiological effect. With or without significance tests, the data told a rich story of the strengths and weaknesses of the media campaign and of the value of the high-cost intensive supplementation.

The fact that sampling errors can mask results is used by Gilbert, Light, and Mosteller (1975) as a particular justification for randomizing. Thus their reasoning is almost the reverse of ours. They are thinking particularly of confirmatory tests of medical interventions. Such treatments can be defined clearly, and in good professional hands one realization will be very like another. The difference in effects between two drugs that have survived extensive screening is likely to be small. Then only a large, highly controlled experiment will establish which competitor is best on average. And, with a weak effect, the large experiment is required to show that the physical intervention added to the benefits from rest, attention, and reassurance that accompanied it.

Since social programs that attack long-standing problems have weak effects, all the more one wants a large and unequivocal test before a commitment is made to a new proposal, according to Gilbert, Light, and Mosteller (1974). This experimentalist position is politically conservative in putting a heavy burden of proof on proposals for new services. The chief difficulty with this logic is that social treatments are not "fixed" in the statistician's sense. The treatment may have effects as a superrealization very different from those it will have under field conditions. A superiority detected in one setting can easily be reversed with a change in community climate or administrative detail.

The *Plaza Sésamo* experiment provides a striking example. An elaborate superrealization was tested by a fully controlled experiment in three day care centers. The $T_A$ children watching the educational programs improved impressively more than the $T_0$ children who watched ordinary cartoons. As a more complete field test, a further experiment was operated in twelve day care centers and three rural villages. Random assignment was again used, and almost no benefit of $T_A$ was detected. Retrospectively, the investigators judged that the social conditions that formed part of the treatment accounted for the disparity: in the first study, there were small groups with adult observers closely monitoring the degree of attention; the second study took place in an ordinarily turbulent classroom with far less obtrusive monitoring (Diaz-Guerrero and others, 1976; see also Rossi, Freeman, and Wright, 1979, pp. 47–59 and 186–188). No one would deny that a treatment effect appeared in the first study, but it was not an effect of a plan that could be operated on a practical scale.

*Limits of Random Assignment.* Assigning cases randomly to treatments does not necessarily produce a randomized experiment. Units that supply *final* data have to be comparable. Therefore, attrition must occur randomly or selective factors must operate similarly in both groups. (Selective factors change the character of the population and hence the question under investigation.)

Persons or institutions drop out at every stage of an investigation, some by physically withdrawing and some by failing to return questionnaires or to appear for scheduled tests. Attrition is especially heavy in long-term studies and in studies of migrant, alienated, or unemployed populations. A treatment that makes great demands on the persons treated or on the program staff is especially likely to lose cases.

The controlled-assignment study leads to a fully valid comparison on one outcome only: the probability of completing the treatment as scheduled. The dropouts contribute to that statistic. In any other comparison, there is an unknown degree of bias similar to that arising from uncontrolled initial assignment. This is not an argument against controlled assignment but against the unsophisticated conception of random assignment as a magic bullet that kills off all threats to validity.

Selective attrition starts when assignments are announced. Those clients or program operators who do not find palatable the diet or the curriculum or the social service they are assigned may refuse to participate. Some investigators try to forestall such losses by selecting a sample and then asking each unit to agree to accept a random assignment. They are left with the fraction of the original sample who pledge to conform to the luck of the draw. Having discarded the persons with strong preferences, the investigator has now settled for learning what the treatment does for persons who are mostly indifferent. He divides the survivors into fully comparable groups. Even under this plan, however, a teacher who dislikes the instructional methods she is assigned to use can conveniently discover that a personal circumstance forces her to drop out. (In the study of Harvard Project Physics, after agreement to serve and random assignment, nineteen out of seventy-two teachers were lost from the sample.) It is also possible for the teacher ostensibly to accept a new plan while actually continuing her habitual style of teaching. The investigator close to the scene can detect such a case, but if he drops the teacher from the study he no longer has a true sample.

Loss of cases is not likely to be random. When two manpower programs are applied to equivalent samples, for instance, one of them will inevitably retain a larger fraction of hard-core cases. Comparing employment rates of youths who finished training will then give an adverse impression of the effectiveness of the program that had superior holding power (Katz and others, 1975). Ingenious devices have been invented to reduce loss of cases. In Mexico, for example, an evaluator attuned to the culture arranged a lottery with valuable prizes for subjects of the *Plaza Sésamo* experiment; the lottery tickets were valid only if the family had faithfully supplied data down to the end of the study.

With or without such devices, the evaluator should keep his eye on the cases that did not supply final data. As a minimum, he can compare them with the survivors with respect to their initial characteristics and can make a good guess as to whether their disappearance biased the results upward or downward. A step in this direction is seen in the analysis that St. Pierre and Proper (1978) made of the Follow Through data. In four out of five sites where differential attrition was statistically significant, attrition tended to enhance the final standing of the experimental group because children who scored low at the outset of the study were particularly likely to withdraw from the experimental group. (The analysis perhaps placed inappropriate emphasis on significance tests—nonsignificant biases consistent over many sites would also deserve attention.)

Except when each sample supplying final data is fully representative of the target population, some form of adjustment is required. The adjustments embody their own particular assumptions, strong or weak. In the regression-discontinuity design, for example, it is commonly assumed that the trend under examination is linear within each treatment. The presence or absence of a curvilinear trend is hard to establish. In fact, the chief example given by Cook and Campbell (1976, p. 270) of a significant effect disclosed by a discontinuity design proved to be entirely consistent with a no-effect conclusion when they had the opportunity to analyze the original data for curvilinearity (Cook and Campbell, 1979, p. 140).

In analysis of covariance the adjusted group means are commonly interpreted as if the treatment had the same effect in every part of the initial range. And it is hard to establish from the data whether this is true or not unless one has a great number of units or a powerful theoretical hypothesis to guide the analysis (Cronbach and Snow, 1977; Anderson, 1977).

Corrections or adjustments, though troublesome, are indispensable. In accord with what John Tukey has said in many places, we advise the evaluator to acquaint himself with the logic behind the available procedures and to try several plausible procedures in order to establish a reasonable range of estimates rather than a single figure. A fair summary of present understanding is that the same *kinds* of hazards are present in interpreting naturalistic studies and studies with either strong or weak controls over assignment. Because of the historical sequence by which statistical theory developed (and perhaps because loss of cases is no great problem in agricultural and rat-lab experiments), some assumptions and fallacies are far more widely recognized by investigators than are others.

There was a time when criticisms were leveled only at nonmanipulative studies that collect data on units already receiving $T_A$ or $T_0$. The valid complaint was that matching cases post hoc did not produce equivalent groups. Later, it was seen that adjustment by analysis of covariance has the same fault. Recent theoretical work has greatly clarified the issues, and attention should be drawn particularly to these papers: Meehl, 1970; Cochran and Rubin, 1973; Cronbach and others, 1977; Barnow and Cain, 1977; Bryk, 1978; Heckman, 1979; Reichardt, 1979.

This work corrects misconceptions, but it has at the same time established a discouraging conclusion applicable even to randomized experiments. Whenever an uncontrolled, nonchance factor determines who provides final data on one or both treatments, the difference in observed means is probably not the difference that would have appeared in large, comparable samples. No statistical correction or post hoc formation of supposedly equivalent groups leads to a dependable estimate; the attempt to adjust sometimes makes the estimate worse. With or without adjustment, the true treatment effect may be overestimated or underestimated. The fallacious comparison may work to the advantage of either treatment.

*Practical Problems of Controlling Group Membership.* A genuinely dependable summative evaluation will use controlled assignment and preferably an equivalent-groups design, according to the evaluative commandments. This ideal has taken a firm grasp on the imaginations of many influential figures in social science and in government. But the practical difficulties of obtaining and maintaining consent from the affected communities or institutions, of locking treatment plans in place (recall the evaluator as "snarling watchdog" in Chapter One), and of maintaining contact with the geographically mobile persons who are the targets of most social programs—these are too airily waved away.

The control achieved is much more perfect on paper than in actuality. Program operators supposedly delivering the innovative $T_A$ are prone to slip back into their old habits or to depart from the treatment plan in other ways. Think, for example, of the admirable random-assignment design of the Cambridge-Somerville study. One set of potential delinquents in this community was to receive intensive counseling while a randomly equivalent set received none. The results looked quite unfavorable, inasmuch as the members of the experimental group who received the greatest amount of counseling had the poorest post treatment records. But a close look at the case histories (Witmer, 1952) showed that the counselors, pressed for time, had terminated their contacts with youths whose problems seemed to be minor. Those for whom the prognosis was poorest received the counselor's best effort over a long time.

The wide range of practical difficulties in forming equivalent groups, or, more generally, in making assignments to treatments stick, were fairly described in the Riecken and Boruch (1974) and Boruch and Riecken (1975) volumes. Those presentations leave the reader too sanguine, however. Few evaluative experiments to date have achieved all the following earmarks of internal validity: genuinely randomized assignment; meaningful, describable treatments; samples large enough to give reasonable statistical power; and attrition low enough to maintain the initial equivalence. (These criteria remove from the list of successful formal comparisons the Guatemala study, Harvard Project Physics, Performance Contracting, and the like.)

An adequate reminder of the elusiveness of the perfect social experiment comes from Haney's history (1977) of Follow Through. Follow Through Planned Variations was a comparative study, but schools that volunteered to use one variant were not similar to the units adopting the next variant. Worse, in some sites harassed or well-intentioned teachers transferred the children who were making least progress into Follow Through classes (pp. 134–145). The treatments, moreover, were shaped after the study began. The same experimental "planned variation" generated wildly varying realizations, and many $T_0$ groups received federally supported compensatory education of a nondescript kind rather than "regular instruction." And, though the intent was to study cumulative effects, two thirds of those entering treatment at kindergarten were missing from the final grade 3 data set (p. 303); among those survivors vast numbers—sometimes whole classes—had failed to take the pretests that were needed to make adjustments in the outcome data.

It is scarcely astonishing that the General Accounting Office (GAO) reviewers of the study were highly critical, especially since some fifty million dollars had gone into it. A chief complaint was that failure to assign children randomly to variations had created problems of interpretation that "cannot practicably be overcome" (Comptroller General, 1975, p. 6). True enough; the final heroic statistical twisting of the data to line up treatment contrasts led to murky and unconvincing conclusions. What the GAO did not realize is that, in a nationwide study with a four-year treatment, a *random* experiment would also encounter barriers that "cannot practically be overcome."

Haney (1977) also recounts the painful experience of a randomized experiment that Follow Through did fund. It had the advantage of modest scale and duration. Keeping subjects in place for the duration of the assigned treatments is comparatively easy when the study is brief. Further, when the study is small enough for the evaluator personally to keep in touch with the sites, assignment is more likely to go according to plan, and there is a better chance of knowing what treatment was actually delivered. So the prospects were hopeful when David (1974) set out to compare eleven schools operating under various Follow Through plans.

Since each school had chosen a plan it preferred, equivalence of staffs, neighborhoods, and student bodies was lacking. David proposed to concentrate on a $T_A / T_0$ contrast in each neighborhood. Insofar as each school had a different $T_A$, this reduced the study to one unit (class) per treatment; lumping diverse $T_A$'s and $T_0$'s would have allowed only a very loose question to be addressed. Planning to control what was open to control, David started with each school's applicant pool: children to receive summer training would be picked at random, and the rest would be out of school.

Then reality set in. One project folded. In another, the list of applicants was too short to allow for both an experimental and a control group. In three localities, other agencies scheduled instructional programs into which some of the control subjects flowed. Eleven little Indians; then there were six. Of the six, two were useless because pretests were given after rather than before assignment, and few control children received the full battery of tests. Then there were four. David did her best with the four remaining sites, but discrepancies abounded. Some parents of $T_A$ subjects indicated, on the terminal questionnaire, that their children had not attended any summer program. In one site, large $T_A/T_0$ differences on pretests led David to doubt that the assignment rules had been followed. We need not list all the other sources of trouble that surfaced. But if equivalent groups are so hard to achieve on David's small scale, there is no hope that a mobile population can be assigned to identifiable social programs and held in those assignments for a number of years.

*Comparing Response-Defined Subgroups.* When variations among treatment realizations are built into a plan of type 1b, the contrast is as interpretable as any controlled-assignment contrast. Many treatment variations of considerable importance, however, are selected by the program staff or clients and so are not under experimental control. As one example, the study of a contraceptive pill might pair families (without their knowledge) and provide the pill to a randomly chosen family in each pair. Later interviews would show a subset of these to be diligent, regular users of the pill. But the $T_0$ pairmates of these $T_A$ families would not be strictly comparable to them; if the $T_A$ pairmates had been given the pill, not all would have been diligent in taking it. If no cases were lost, the overall comparison of $T_0$ and $T_A$ conception rates would be valid, but there would be no properly matching control for the diligent subset in the experimental group.

Harvard Project Physics offers another example. The instructional materials provided the teacher many options, especially with regard to use of films, laboratories, and teaching styles. Assignment to $T_A$ (Harvard Project Physics) rather than to $T_0$ (the teacher's "regular" course) had been made at random. But the $T_A$ subset who chose to use films was not necessarily like the subset of $T_A$ teachers (and classes) not using films or like any identifiable subset in the control group. Even if there had been no attrition among participants, the experimental assignment provided an equivalent group only for a comparison of

$T_0$ with Harvard Project teachers on the average. That "treatment" was a composite of diverse realizations.

The fundamental matter, always, is what question one wants to ask. If one wants to check an overall average effect of $T_A$, an excellent design is to sample from a population that probably would adopt $T_A$ if it were available; either their prior record or a random subsample restricted to $T_0$ could be the baseline. If one wants to learn about variations of realizations within $T_A$, the $T_0$ group is next to useless. If one wants an average outcome on the assumption that $T_A$ will be available to the whole population, one can obtain valid use-nonuse statistics from a representative sample, but no control group can disentangle the effect of the treatment from the peculiarities of the self-selected users. Often the best solution to a dilemma of design is to use more than one hull. Boruch (1975b) has illustrated some of the possibilities of using controlled assignment for one comparison while studying other matters naturalistically.

We can add an example in which two hulls were used side by side. Televised teacher education in Colombia had been in place for some years. Hour-long, weekly broadcasts reaching a substantial portion of the country recommended certain teaching methods. Sanchez (1976) set out to evaluate program effectiveness. There were two uncertainties: Did teachers watch the program? And if they watched, did they learn?

To answer both these questions in a single strong design would have been awkward and expensive. It would have been necessary to assign perhaps 100 teachers between $T_A$ and $T_0$. A year-long study would be needed at a minimum to estimate rate of dropout. Assuming that all went well—including adequate measurement of learning—some valid information about effectiveness would have resulted. The cost, however, would have nearly equaled the annual budget for operating the program.

Sanchez decided to carry out two studies. To measure continuance of watching, he sent all the teachers who had originally registered with the program letters with prepaid reply postcards. On the card the respondent was to describe herself as a regular watcher, an irregular watcher, or one who had stopped watching. The respondents could afford to be reason-

ably honest, since neither academic credit nor a salary increase
was offered as a reward for viewing. It was sensible to assume,
however, that respondents reported more watching than they
actually did and that those who did not respond were likely to
be nonviewers. The reported proportion who said they watched
regularly was therefore interpreted as an upper limit on the true
proportion of watchers. The survey was also to supply detailed
information regarding watching habits and reasons why respondents stopped watching. Since interviews were too costly to
use, a full questionnaire was sent to a subsample.

"Did watchers learn?" was handled as a separate question. A field experiment—a kind of superrealization—was designed around ten consecutive broadcasts. One hundred teachers
were chosen in such a way that their mix of backgrounds and
teaching experiences resembled that of the national target population. Teachers near Bogota were used; though not fully representative, such a sample kept the study inexpensive. The teachers
were randomly divided into four subsamples. Two samples were
urged to view, two were not. The evaluator—a person of some
local prestige—visited the two samples of experimental teachers
and strongly encouraged them to watch the program. The experimental and control groups were split so that the $T_A$'s and
half the $T_0$'s had a pretest, while the others did not. (This refine-
ment was probably unnecessary, and the lack of pretests for
half the cases reduced the power of the analysis.) Information
was gathered initially on characteristics likely to be related to
learning and, later, on attitudes and concepts acquired. Few of
the teachers had been exposed to the broadcast previously, and
few control teachers watched any of the ten broadcasts. No
mention of the broadcasts was made to the control groups.

The experiment indicated that the broadcasts had some
impact on the specially encouraged $T_A$ group, and the survey
indicated that few teachers were viewers under natural conditions. These two modest designs together answered, reasonably
well, questions that would have required a very large single experiment. It may even have been advantageous to separate the
two questions. A single naturalistic study, no matter how large,
would have been unable to separate fully the consequences of

watching from the selective factors that determined who watched. And, with normal encouragement of viewers, it would have found little or no effect. The *potential* impact of the broadcasts would not have been detected without the superrealization.

## Plausible Inference in Evaluation

We have tried to put controlled experimentation into perspective. The balanced, manipulative design is well calculated to answer a comparative, summative question about a defined pair of treatments. That kind of question is often prominent at the time of a prototype test, but it is not the only question with leverage. The experimental comparative design does not strengthen the answers to most questions about processes and intermediate outcomes within the innovative treatment. The strong design weakens a prototype study insofar as it (1) draws off resources that could be used to advantage elsewhere or (2) restricts the study artificially (for example, by holding the treatment unnaturally constant or by studying atypical cases). Controlled experiments are sometimes worth their price in an evaluation, sometimes not.

Many writers on evaluation are as cool in their appraisal of formal experimentation for evaluative purposes as we are (see, for example, Weiss and Rein, 1969; Weiss, 1974b; Scriven, 1978b). Even Riecken and Boruch (1974), making the case for social experimentation, hedge their discussion with elaborate advice as to when that tactic is suitable. One of the leaders in the New Jersey negative income tax experiment (Kershaw, 1972, p. 239) goes so far as to say that the controlled experiment is a "last resort" for use when other modes of inquiry have been exhausted. And Elmore (1976, p. 377), having directed the Follow Through research for several years, advises that experimentation be kept small in scale until the proposed treatment is sufficiently well developed and specified to be reproducible.

The influential papers by Campbell (1957), Campbell and Stanley (1963), and Cook and Campbell (1976) suggested that the designer of an investigation should make "internal validity" his goal. An internally valid study is one in which the "statistician's conclusion"—the inference from *uto* to *UTO*—is beyond challenge. That ideal is most surely achieved by a comparative experiment with controlled assignment. Internal validity can claim priority when the investigator addresses a summative and causal question, not otherwise. This is the position of all Campbell's writings on the subject, but it becomes fully explicit only at the end of the very recent Cook and Campbell monograph (1979, p. 343): "Though random assignment is germane to the research goal of assessing whether the treatment caused any observed effects, it is conceptually irrelevant to all other research goals." Internal validity, however, is not of salient importance in an evaluation. What counts in evaluation is external validity, that is, the plausibility of conclusions about one or another *\*UTO* that is significant to the PSC.

Did the intervention $t_A$ cause a change in outcome $o$ in the sample $u$? The study of *that* question is judged by its internal validity. The question contains three elements, each narrowly identified with the operations of the study. Thus, in a study of persuasion, the intervention $t$ consists of *this* message as uttered by *this* speaker to a unit who is in a certain physical and social environment; the outcome is the endorsement of *this* belief statement. Statistical inference can at most extend the conclusion to the $U$, $T$, and $O$ that correspond to the operationally defined categories of which the instances $u$, $t$, and $o$ are representative.

To speak of a specific message regarding prevention of heart disease as "an appeal to fear," for example, is to move far beyond operational language. An "experimenter's conclusion" that speaks of a concept cannot have internal validity (see Chapter Four). Conversely, if the speaker looked the subject in the eye while delivering the message in a live setting, eye contact was part of the treatment even if it was not in the plan. The causal claim is that *something* associated with this instance of the treatment made a difference. A two-group controlled-assignment design says that *something* associated with this instance but *not* associated with the second one made a difference on this occasion. This is a report on a local historical event, not a conclusion about a recurrent relation. Only that limited comment can have internal validity.

Interpreters of evaluations never stop at discreet causal claims about local experience. The interpreter always reaches beyond the data. She thinks in general terms about Harvard Project Physics or Superlimonada broadcasts, not about the particular mix of specific realizations that happened to occur during the field trial. She explains a result in terms (for example) of mothers' lack of trust in a speaker who uses elite diction. She extends the conclusions, judging on the basis of the Superlimonada findings that a broadcast program in Ghana would be successful if the listeners perceived the speaker as humble and unsophisticated.

Social scientists are trained to suppress relationships that do not reach statistical significance. However, no relation that makes sense ought to be discarded. We say this despite the truism that an explanation can be dreamed up to fit any adventitious result. The High Impact crime program functioned in those cities where management of the program was tied closely to the mayor's office. This statement (Chelimsky, 1977a, p. 74) is an after-the-fact story that cannot legitimately be extended by *statistics* into a statement about the population. It makes sense on its face, however, and Chelimsky was able to document just how, in certain cities, nearness to the seat of power produced actions that supported program effects. Persons setting up urban crime control programs would be foolish to ignore the advice implicit in the finding, for all that it lacks a certified $p$ value and that distance between the program and the mayor's office was not randomly varied from city to city.

Any extension of findings into explanatory language or to other conditions can have construct validity or external validity, as Cook and Campbell use the terms, but it cannot have internal validity. Cook and Campbell (1976, pp. 245–246; 1979, pp. 83–85) speak of internal validity as a requirement especially for basic research. According to them, the applied scientist, including the evaluator, is *almost* as much concerned with external and construct validity as with internal validity. We go further: external and construct validity *are what matter*.

The pressure for internal validity in each single study seems to rest on the view that action will be taken on the basis of the study in isolation. But Cook and Campbell (1976, p. 227) themselves are at pains to point out that "we would delude ourselves if we believed that a single experiment, or even a research program of several years' duration, would definitely answer the major questions associated with confidently inferring a causal relationship, naming its parts, and specifying its generalizability." The single evaluation falls far short of being a comprehensive program of inquiry, and policy makers do not examine it in isolation. Rich (1977, p. 200) reports that, in the making of policy, information arising from disparate sources "is used in groups or clusters." What makes a limited inquiry worthwhile should be judged from that point of view.

The conclusion a user reaches is influenced by the evaluation data as they are seen in the light of other observations and commonsense linking statements (Campbell, 1974). The whole argument is at best plausible, not logically established. Even the narrow conclusion for which *internal* validity is claimed rests in part on plausible assumptions; for example, "attrition was nearly enough random for us to consider the groups equal," or "the groups were large enough to wash out random differences in uncontrolled influences." The tiniest step toward explanation requires additional appeals to plausibility, such as this assertion: "Knowing that they were in an experiment did not affect responses of the control subjects." Again, Sanchez' (1976) experimental contrast is interpretable as assessing the effect of broadcasts only to the extent that he is able to assert that the teachers who were nonviewers were treated by the prestige figure just as were the viewers, except for his references to the broadcasts.

Human affairs, all of them, are steered by plausible reasoning (Campbell, 1974; Aaron, 1978, pp. 165–167). Without an evaluation, members of the PSC would make plausible inferences from their personal experience, from the laudatory reports released by the program, and from the unfavorable anecdotes relayed by critics. Especially when political interests are at stake, links plausible to one person are likely to be unacceptable to others. A long span of plausible argument is open to more challenges than a short one.

"For practical purposes, knowledge is what the scientist can persuade his audience to accept as such." So writes Mayntz (1977, p. 57). She cites Ziman (1968, pp. 9–11) to show that the statement is relevant to natural as well as to social science. Aaron (1978, p. 166) draws attention to the words of David Hume regarding reports that contradict established beliefs: "No Testimony is sufficient to establish a Miracle, unless the Testimony be of such a Kind, that its Falsehood would be more miraculous than the Fact, which it endeavors to establish." These are the realities that the evaluator must face.

Campbell (1975a, p. 5) notes the gap between the complexity of social issues and the capabilities of the evaluator and comments that "a full account of our difficulties, including the problem of getting our skills used in ways we can condone, is bound to be discouraging. We cannot yet promise a set of professional skills guaranteed to make an important difference." Our analysis has demonstrated the difficulties and they are indeed sobering. The actions that decision makers contemplate as future policy invariably differ from the actions that generated the evaluator's data. Dozens of questions will be asked about the realizations of the plan that were directly studied, but only a fraction can be answered with hard data. Conjecture enters whenever the data are extended to illuminate other proposals.

As House says (1977, pp. 5–6), evaluations "can be no more than acts of persuasion. . . . Expecting evaluation to provide compelling and necessary conclusions is to expect more than evaluation can deliver. Especially in a pluralistic society, evaluation cannot produce necessary propositions. But if it cannot produce the necessary, it can provide. . . 'the credible, the plausible, and the probable' (Perelman and Olbrechts-Tyteca, 1969)." Data coming from diverse settings and types of subjects require less extension than data collected in a homogeneous situation in predicting to new conditions. A study that observes with care and reports enough about settings observed to discourage overgeneralization is a better basis for plausible reasoning than gossip borne by the winds.

Cook and Campbell (1979, p. 78) endorse this "model of heterogeneous instances" as the most useful way to establish external validity. Their immediately following sentences stress that external validity is "a matter of replication," and thus echo the GAO guidelines quoted in Chapter Four. The term *replication* ordinarily refers to the repetition of a study after its completion. This interpretation would throw the weight back on internal validity. It is therefore to be emphasized that Cook and Campbell, as well as the GAO statement, intend "replication" to include the use of heterogeneous instances within any single study and the repetition of a study under new conditions rather than an attempt to duplicate the original.

If, as noted earlier, the difficulties that surround evaluation are sobering, they do not in themselves warrant discouragement. Given a reasonable time to study a program, the evaluator can usually find a way to get information, on some scale and with some degree of precision, about questions that have or should have leverage. One bit of information may simply be that a particular element seemed not to be a source of difficulty; at least, no complaints or other indications of trouble were encountered. That is important information, within a total survey of program history, because it removes a doubt. Other bits of information may lead the investigator or some later illuminator to a wholly fresh perspective on an old problem (Rein and Schon, 1977). One such breakthrough offsets the cost of a dozen workaday studies that improved services or public confidence just a little.

Disillusion is the bitter aftertaste of saccharine illusion. It is self-defeating to aspire to deliver an evaluative conclusion as precise and as safely beyond dispute as an operational-language conclusion from the laboratory. It is unrealistic to hope to tell the PSC all it needs to know. When the evaluator aspires only to provide clarification that would not otherwise be available, he has chosen a task he can manage and one that does have social benefits.

# 6

■■■■■■■■■■■■■■■■

# Improving
# the Evaluation
# Enterprise

■■■■■■■■■■■■■■■■

The evaluation enterprise is a sprawling, loosely connected set
of organizations and individuals. Ten years ago, most of those
now involved in evaluation were doing something else. Organizations heavily engaged in conducting evaluations today did
not exist ten years ago or were concentrating on other tasks.
Today, an important share of the national investment in social
inquiry goes into evaluation.

Evaluation is an aggregate that resembles foreign trade
rather than an industry. Foreign trade transactions require
organizations for buying, selling, brokering, and shipping, as
well as individual specialists of many kinds. Agencies, firms, and
individuals engaged in foreign trade act and interact in many
ways. One participant knows personally only a few of the
others, and no one person knows directly of most transactions.
Yet participants in foreign trade are subject to common forces

of supply and demand, of currency fluctuation, of government policy, and so on. Their own actions produce these forces, which in turn press on each actor individually. The boundary separating those involved in foreign trade from the rest of us is barely perceptible; in some sense, everyone who buys a pound of coffee is "in foreign trade." Similarly, by the broadest criterion, everyone who reads a news story on the success of a prison reform is "in the evaluation enterprise."

Despite the sprawl, the blurred boundaries, and the confusing crowd of actors, the evaluation enterprise falls into definite, even rigid, patterns. Today's patterns have not arisen from the internal logic of evaluative activities or from the self-disciplining actions of the evaluation community. Rather, they are haphazard assemblages of fragments from older institutional forms.

The structural arrangements for evaluation make it difficult to carry on the kinds of evaluation that we consider most useful. Decentralizing authority over evaluation and opening the debate about its implications to more segments of the policy-shaping community (PSC) are advisable. A more open evaluation community can better serve the pluralistic accommodative process. That community should develop a professional spirit that will enable it to bring evaluation nearer to its best uses. We will lead up to concrete proposals for change by describing arrangements as they now are.

## Evaluation on an Industrial Scale

To understand institutions, and so to change them, it is necessary to perceive sympathetically the pressures on participants. We shall be especially concerned with those who head up evaluation teams, their superiors who direct the firms that offer evaluation services, and the officials who speak for one or another sponsoring agency. Here, as elsewhere, our attention is primarily on contexts of accommodation and on broad programs, where the inquiry should not be aimed to serve a decision maker. Our remarks are not directed to the evaluation that a manager requests from an in-house technical staff. That close coupling of research consumer to research producer permits quick correction, whenever the activity is unproductive.

*Contracting Processes.* The typical program evaluation is conducted by a firm. The firm may be a large profit-making or not-for-profit corporation—Abt Associates, for example, or Systems Development Corporation or Educational Testing Service. An institute within a university, usually operating in part on outside funds, can play a similar role. The Survey Research Center at Michigan and the Center for Instructional Research and Curriculum Evaluation (CIRCE) at Illinois are examples. The firm may be a small squad of full-time evaluators competing for a tiny share of the action, or it may be no more than a convenient base for the moonlighting of two or three professors. Although we shall emphasize the larger firm, both large and small firms have a place. We agree with Rossi (1979, p. 27) that the tasks given to small firms are often a waste of effort, but tasks given to large firms often involve a much greater waste of effort. Where Rossi would like to see most of the small firms go out of business, we would like to see firms of all sizes given more suitable commissions.

Evaluation comes in response to funding, most often from the federal government. For evaluations performed by representative firms in the San Francisco area, 85 percent of the funds come directly or indirectly from a few federal agencies (Rubin, personal communication). The percentage is especially high in larger firms, those with twenty or more professionals. Evaluations are also supported by foundations, state agencies, municipalities, local education authorities, and so on, but few of these commission evaluations on the scale of the federal ones.

Some fraction of the federal impetus takes the form of abrupt congressional mandates. In 1964, for example, Congress called for a report on equality of educational opportunity by 1966. It was a great achievement for social scientists to fill this ill-defined order with a substantial study. But the results were equivocal, partly because of haste and partly because the questions reached beyond the state of the research art. The consequence was the ten years of controversy over the Coleman Report to which we have previously referred.

A second example comes from Title I of the Elementary
and Secondary Education Act (ESEA), which required evaluation of the education provided for "neglected and delinquent"
children. Evaluation experts in the Office of Education judged
that no worthwhile study could be performed, and we agree
(see Hess and others, 1977). The institutions for these children
are necessarily heterogeneous and disorganized. Children move
in and out of the institutions; few stay long enough for even the
best conceivable instruction to have a measurable effect. Moreover, the children range so widely in educational level and needs
that the instruction is not at all standard, and thus standard testing gives a poor indication of what is accomplished. Nonetheless,
the experts' superiors in the Department of Health, Education,
and Welfare (HEW) said that the will of Congress could not be
set aside, and the evaluation went forward. In this case as with
the equality survey, Congress expected too much from social
inquiry.

A more heartening example occurred in the period 1975–
1978, as Congress moved to consider renewal of ESEA. Political
support for this funding of schools was so strong that renewal
on at least the same level was predictable, as much as any action
four years away can be. Congress properly asked for research
that would bear on proposed changes in the ground rules, and
directed the National Institute of Education (NIE) to make or
procure such field studies. This is to be praised first as foresight;
Congress looked well beyond the next election. Second comes
praise for the formative rather than summative questions that
were asked. Beyond this point, credit is to be shared between
NIE and Congress. The NIE staff member asked to manage the
task, Paul Hill, was freed to move outside channels and work
directly with members of the House Education and Labor Committee and their staff. Conversations over a long period identified questions with leverage and sorted out those that could be
examined usefully by research. The research was shaped in
a multipartisan manner. Concerns of the party in the minority
and of individual legislators were treated seriously alongside
proposals favored by the majority party or the executive branch.
Hill's work was in the tradition of the British civil service, which

tries to develop information useful to all political parties—useful even if power changes hands while the study is in progress.

Most federally sponsored evaluations are initiated and funded by some executive office rather than by direct congressional action. Most are stand-alone studies, put out for competitive bid by means of a request for proposals (RFP). The *Commerce Business Daily* carries a brief statement on the size and character of a task, and potential contractors are invited to write for more complete specifications. The time allowed for preparing contract proposals is never generous. It is not unusual to find only thirty days allowed for developing proposals for an evaluation that will require at least five person-years of work. Moreover, thirty days between *issuance* of the RFP in Washington and the closing date is said to be "adequate proposal preparation time." (For example, see "Evaluation of the Nutrition. . . ," 1979.)

The timing proposed is like that described in Chapter One: brief planning, a long period of executing the agreed-upon plan, and a completion date that leaves almost no time for a concluding analysis and interpretation. A final document delivered to the sponsoring agency is the main output, though the sponsor usually keeps an eye on preliminary indications and may receive substantial interim reports.

Sometimes planning is carried almost to completion by members of the agency staff before the request for proposals is issued. Sometimes outsiders develop the plan under contract. The planning contract allows time for thinking and for consultation but not ordinarily for pilot runs of the research procedure. Once the plan is submitted, the agency may decide to issue a request for proposals or not to proceed with the study. (The planning firm often captures the eventual contract for operations, but that is not assured; indeed, the planning contract may bar the planning firm from becoming the evaluation contractor.)

The extent to which the contracting process, along with the philosophy of the contracting agencies, shapes the evaluation is brought out in the following comments by K. Baker (1975), who was a social analyst in the Office of the Assistant Secretary of Planning and Evaluation in HEW when he wrote

the article and who has seen the process from inside several
agencies:

> Many applied research administrators push
> for such a detailed specification of the problem
> and research design that the only important ques-
> tion left for the contractor is how much it will cost
> to carry out the agency's plan. The agency, know-
> ing what it wants done and how it wants it done, is
> looking for a skilled staff to carry out its needs,
> not somebody else's desires. . . .
>
> The agency's desire to maximize control
> over the research, to make sure its problems get
> addressed the way the agency thinks [they] should
> be addressed, is precisely the reason why it uses
> contracts rather than grants. The important feature
> of a contract is that it maximizes the agency's con-
> trol [p. 210].
>
> The RFP is very important in the research
> process. It fixes the outline and many of the details
> of the study's methodology as well as specifying
> the problem to be studied. The RFP will generally
> define the population to be studied, sample sizes,
> and whether the study will be experimental, post
> hoc interviews, or pre- and post-field observations.
> The RFP may even specify the instruments to be
> used and the type of statistical analysis to be em-
> ployed. In general, the two areas where the RFP
> leaves greatest discretion to the proposer is in the
> instrument content (the specific items) and data
> analysis. Note again that the RFP is prepared by
> the agency. The people who ultimately do the work
> have no involvement in many of the basic decisions
> of the research process [pp. 213–214].

Although elaborate specification—indeed, overspecifica-
tion—seems to be the rule, underspecification is not unknown.
Where the agency staff is rushed or unsophisticated, the policy
alternatives and open questions may be so little defined that applicants must "second-guess" the intent of the study (Commit-

tee on Evaluation Research, 1978, p. 52). Sometimes, however, a vague task definition bespeaks reality. As one agency official said to us, "The RFP mechanism is fine when you know what you want, but when you are trying to explore an area no one has a good fix on, it is hard to use."

The request for proposals, for all its concreteness, is not the final word. There is room for negotiation and for introducing ideas from the evaluator as the final contract is shaped up. Indeed, says K. Baker, "the real design of the project comes in the days immediately following the award of the contract" (1975, p. 214). The wording placed in the contract is close to final; departures from the plan require specific approval. The agency designates a contract officer who remains in close contact as the work is done. At any time the evaluator may propose changes in the research plan and the contract officer passes on these. The sponsor, responding to a new political wind, sometimes turns the study onto a new course in midpassage (Elmore, 1975; W. P. Abt, 1978).

These cumbersome options provide insufficient flexibility. C. C. Abt (1979, pp. 46–47) speaks from his experience as head of a firm: "Most evaluative research *must* be incompletely defined at the start, because one simply does not know exactly what will be done and needs to be done until the research is under way. Specifically, early definition is limited by a short design period and inaccessibility of descriptive data, which is the most important input into design. All research should be sequential, yet government wants it to proceed in the fashion in which articles are written in a textbook approach: problem-method-results-conclusion. Interim findings produce new questions and the need for applying new analyses and techniques. Yet the entire contracting process works against the flexibility which that situation requires, and the contract administration system works against the need for frequent technical redirection."

*Work Overloads.* An overriding fact of life on the operating end is that everyone is exceedingly busy. A difficult task is undertaken. The work schedule would require prodigious effort even if all went well, and misadventures put the work behind schedule more often than not. These statements are as true for the sponsoring office as for the contractor. Each agency has more projects than it can comfortably manage; each firm is engaged with more projects or bids than its staff has time for. To produce reports on schedule requires a genius for logistics. The calendar set at the beginning of the study dominates the effort, even though the information from an evaluation is typically not used at a foreseeable moment to make a single, long-anticipated choice.

Unfortunately, governmental habits result in a "rush and halt" movement rather than a steady pace. One procedural step has to be complete before the next can begin. An agency staff must think hard (and fast) about a particular evaluation before it issues the request for proposals; during that period, those who might bid on the task can work only on other projects. Once the request for proposals sees print, would-be contractors "rev up" to spin out proposals. The time that can be allotted to any step is bounded by deadlines—deadlines for committing the funds of a fiscal year, deadlines for submitting bids, deadlines for coming up with "answers." When the data are in and the calculations complete, equally stylized exchanges are required before the report can be released. The halts in this process can be lengthy if some central officer finds unwelcome news in the draft report.

More hands would not make the work light. Evaluators or contract officers fresh from their training, or coming fresh to evaluation from other lines of work, require seasoning. Planning, analysis, interpretation, and reporting call for subtle judgments by experienced persons. And the work handed to evaluators seems to have expanded faster than has the cadre qualified for leadership.

Evaluation contracts are being increased in size, and whole programs of investigation are now packed into as few task orders as possible. For the agency staff, this reduces the number of contractors and the number of requests for proposals that the person on point duty has to deal with. For the contractor with many mouths to feed, the single large contract is a victory worth the effort it takes to win, whereas bidding on dozens of small contracts and dealing with many sponsors eats into profits and exhausts the professional staff.

Tying many strands into a single knot, however, is rarely the way to get excellent investigation and excellent use of information. Evaluation activities are regulated almost entirely on a project-by-project basis at the point where contractor and sponsor make contact. The result is an unplanned, structurally weak network. Policy research is chopped into tasks that match the responsibilities of agencies or their subunits, even though problem boundaries do not correspond to agency jurisdictions. Bilingual education, for example, is separated managerially from education of migrants; yet for educators dealing with migrants the two are inseparable. The end result of the structure is that each evaluation analyzes a spoonful dipped from a sea of uncertainties.

Independently the agencies push out tentacles, brandishing separate RFPs. Firms on the other side of the chasm send out tentacles in response and, at various points, contact is made. Each of these junctions is a node in the network, a point of limited centralization. Concerns of officials and legislators are passed down through agency channels to the contracting officer. The instructions she writes for the investigating team are a selection and compression of those many views. When the firm sets to work on its side of the chasm, the thinking of its specialists on the costs and appropriateness of research procedures, as well as their field observations, are passed up through its hierarchy. A compressed version of what the evaluators know is passed across to the agency by the representative who negotiates and delivers reports.

A dozen nodes may regulate separate inquiries into essentially the same subject. Any one representative takes her view of the subject from conversations within her agency; not much of what is being said within other agencies comes to her ear. Likewise, findings from contract work feed in through separate agencies, with reduction and simplification at each step. Only a fraction of what is known about the topic in the large filters through to any one policy maker. On the evaluators' side the work is similarly fragmented.

## Pressures on Contracting Parties

Life in the contracting firm is dominated by the scramble for contracts. At every turn new money must be won to keep a staff in place. However, only large and experienced organizations can successfully solicit and manage large evaluations. A stack of blue chips is required merely to enter the bidding. The competitor must have a sophisticated business office for preparing proposals and keeping track of expenses. A public relations staff stands by, ready to protect the flanks of a politically sensitive study. Computer facilities have to be extensive and up-to-date. Professional managers are needed to keep activities on schedule. And behind the scenes the firm's Washington representative keeps in touch with those who will be commissioning evaluations. Abert (quoted in Biderman and Sharp, 1972, p. 49) commented cynically that good research directors are far less necessary to a firm's success than are intelligence agents able to pick up early word on bidding opportunities. But the firm does what it can to maintain a staff of professionals qualified to plan, collect, and interpret data.

Some firms offer services of many kinds in many different program areas. Once well established, a diversified firm can take the ups and downs of fortune more easily than a specialized firm. But even the largest firm shivers during a budget freeze, and it goes into a spasm of readjustment when it wins an unusually large contract. A narrow specialty makes an organization highly sensitive to the funding priorities of agencies. Over and over the same tale is told. A firm waxes as federal interest in its specialty grows. It welds together a team with complementary skills. The team accumulates special knowledge of the social problem. Then support disappears, the team splits up, and a capable organization is lost (Abt, 1979, p. 50).

As a specific example, consider RSA, a smallish firm in San Francisco. (Our information comes from a case study by David Rubin; RSA is an alias.) RSA was formed in 1971 on the ruins of a branch office of a large national firm. The branch had collected regional data for evaluations of Model Cities programs. Those programs shrank in the mid 1960s, and consequently the parent firm had no reason to maintain the regional office. When the office closed, some of the staff joined with persons from other San Francisco firms to form RSA. Scraps from the Model Cities table supported RSA for two years. When that work ran out, RSA survived on subcontracts from larger firms, responding to requests for proposals in the hope of generating independent income. RSA limped along with about eight professionals from 1973 to 1976; then several of its proposals were accepted. Along with smaller contracts RSA won two big ones: to study how construction of the Alaskan pipeline was affecting small villages (for the Department of the Interior) and to evaluate programs for reducing child abuse (for HEW). The professional staff quickly expanded to forty. Less than two years later, however, the number was down to fifteen. Interior did not need additional studies of the kind RSA had gained experience in. The reverse, ironically, was true with child abuse. HEW increased its budget for such research; large, experienced firms came in to bid, and RSA could not compete.

*How Firms Survive.* Good work is not what keeps a firm alive. The key to survival is "a superbly competent marketing capability" (Abt, 1979, p. 50). Much effort is invested in writing proposals. In the early 1970s, the average number of proposals for a single award was as high as thirty-seven when the competition was open and around ten when the agency limited bids to favored firms (Biderman and Sharp, 1972). With nine or more losers to every winner, the large firm naturally bids early and often.

Reputation does count; contract awards are not determined by the dollar amount of the bid. The firm whose reports are finished on time and receive no loud condemnation comes to be recognized as reliable. Further, a firm attuned to the concerns of a particular agency gains special opportunities.

A firm reaches into new areas as old areas dry up. Driven by necessity, the firm promises services that its current staff cannot deliver. That is part of the game. Keith Baker (1975, p. 215) pointedly advised the would-be contractor: "Don't be overly modest in describing your staff's capability." Tooling up can wait until the contract is signed. The firm commonly assigns its best-qualified professionals to write proposals but it is less-experienced staff members who do the research, down to writing the final report. This occurs even when the reputation of those signing the proposal helped win the contract.

An ordinary scientific research grant is directed, from proposal to final interpretation, by the same chief investigator. But if personal responsibility is the norm in scientific research, it is a rarity in evaluation. In evaluation contracts, a firm is responsible for finding qualified persons to perform specified tasks as they come up. Often this works out well. If field evaluators become interchangeable parts, however, they are reduced to technicians who exercise skills for a purpose someone else has chosen. They lack the perspective, the power, and the incentive to turn out the best possible evaluation.

Repeated reassignment to new tasks is discouraging for the research worker, deprives him of the pleasure of seeing his work reach fruition, and fails to capitalize on his expertise. Let us quote Abt again (1979, p. 52): "The employment insecurity of the researchers associated with these costs tends to limit the attractiveness of the field for some of the best minds, because the best minds generally have many other options. If the evaluation research career option is highly unstable, unpredictable, and risky, we will lose some of our best people from it. The apparent lack of concern by many government sponsors for the maintaining of evaluation research institutional capabilities, wherever they may be, over the long term also works in the direction of employment insecurity and the reduction in the quality of the working lives and the working output of the evaluation researchers."

Names on the letterhead help. Half a dozen names of faculty members provide an impressive roster of talent for a small firm, and the reputation of their university can add glamor to the team's proposals. In the end, of course, the project will be given part-time direction by one or two of those listed on the letterhead, while hired hands do most of the work. Other firms spice up their proposals with names of eminent consultants. When actual work starts, however, the consultants may rarely or never appear on the scene, and any comments they make may or may not carry weight.

Tensions between the investigative outlook and the procedural outlook are found within contracting agencies as well as between agency and contractor. Many commissioning officials are seasoned evaluators, perhaps having worked in a firm or a university before coming to a government post. They become part of a team whose other members know a great deal about government rules, regulations, and standard procedures but little about the conduct of investigations. The contest usually does not end with the evaluation-wise civil servant in the saddle. Crises of expansion and contraction plague the contracting agency as they do the contractor, though they take other forms. According to a National Research Council survey (Study Project on Social Research and Development, 1978, p. 48), "Agencies supporting social knowledge production and application [including evaluation research] frequently are subject to highly uncertain and unstable funding. Erratic and excessive increases and decreases in funding levels distort research management and decision making and jeopardize the coherence and quality of programs. . . . We found that the quality and usefulness of research activities suffer if budget resources exceed the capacity of an agency staff to manage them carefully. Because of the inevitable emphasis on spending money before spending authority is lost [with the end of the fiscal year], decisions concerning [agendas and investigators] are made with insufficient care. If staff resources are inadequate, management and monitoring . . . suffer." The pains and adjustments that accompany a sudden reduction of funds can be left to the reader's imagination.

*Chain Reactions.* Agencies put pressure on evaluators because pressures are put on them. Legislators or administrative superiors demand evaluations by a certain date, regardless of whether an adequate job can be done by then. The task is to get definite information quickly and at minimum cost, or at least that is how they see it. Hence agency representatives are likely to be impatient with pleas for more exploration of a problem and more reflective interpretation. They are impatient with reports that emphasize complexity and uncertainty when a simple question was asked originally. The officers overseeing the project amplify this impatience and relay it to the fieldworkers.

The commissioner is vulnerable to criticism and knows it. An evaluation embarrassing to a program makes no friends for the office that sponsored the evaluation or for the individual who approved its details. The credibility of the sponsor in all its many affairs can be undermined by a magazine columnist's attack on one piece of its work. Criticism from the General Accounting Office (GAO), the National Academy of Sciences, or some other visible overseer can be even more devastating. Criticisms cause more than transient pain; commissioners' jobs, budgets, working conditions, and influence all depend on the esteem in which political onlookers hold them.

Wanting to escape criticism, the commissioner may care more that the evaluator's report be ready on schedule than that it be instructive. Typically, she prefers to specify in detail the work to be performed, so that the work is easy to keep track of and unlikely to wander into political quicksands. When previous evaluations have been faulted for one particular shortcoming, the next request for proposals dodges *that* criticism no matter what else is sacrificed. Unfortunately, criticism in recent years has been predominantly scientistic. Only a numerical index of a "treatment effect" that has been tested for "significance" is seen as a worthy end product. This view of what an evaluation offers is distressingly limited, and with respect to some programs and contexts it is wholly inappropriate. Scientistic commandments for evaluation oversimplify. Control and precision are easier to write into a contract than are the elements of planning that call upon art and judgment.

Bureaucratic requirements at times become so unwieldy that evaluators have to bypass them, and a project officer with a sense of humor winks at the violation. Ball (1974) tells of his experience when Educational Testing Service was preparing to evaluate "Sesame Street." Funds from three foundations and the Office of Education (OE) were to be pooled under a single steering committee. Data collection was to start when the first year of broadcasts began. Not only the large aspects of the plan but also the specific wording of every questionnaire required approval from Washington. Here is Ball's story:

> In the first year of our operations before "Sesame Street" was telecast, the OE . . . took an active monitoring role. . . . [I] t . . . was during this period that proposals were written. OE required that the measuring instruments, data collection procedures, sampling and sites, and data analysis be specified beforehand. But, in our first year, we were unable to specify any of these much in advance because we were proceeding on all fronts at once. It was, after all, a new evaluational enterprise. Our tests and questionnaires had to be reviewed by local groups before we could use them. Thus, although we knew we had the job of conducting the evaluation, the actual contract was not signed until after the proposal was written in great detail and that was not done until data were actually collected. It was a source of frustration to us but it would have been a joy to Lewis Carroll that we were writing down for approval or disapproval details that, by that time, were irreversible [1974, p. 26].

The review procedure, incidentally, is an example of legislative pressures bearing down on commissioners, not of bureaucratic zeal. Back in the 1950s businessmen angered by numerous, redundant, and pointless government surveys persuaded Congress to mandate central clearance of every reporting form. Congress may not have meant to place restrictions on contract research unrelated to business, but agencies supporting research applied the rule across the board so as not to risk a congressional reprimand. Relaxation of these onerous rules—which created "a living nightmare," in Abt's words (1979, p. 48)—is only now in prospect, after two decades of complaint.

### Alternative Arrangements for Sponsorship

Sponsorship arrangements should be devised that allow for flexibility and open an evaluation to multiple influences.

One alternative to the prespecified design is "managed social research." By this device, policy-making officials at HEW are trying in some projects to establish cooperation between agency and evaluation staff; the aim is promising despite the somewhat ominous label. A collegial relation has successful precedents in the earlier collaboration between the Rand Corporation and the air force and in the collaboration of several contracting firms in the New Jersey negative income tax experiment with one another and with the sponsor, the Office of Economic Opportunity. The policy makers in HEW recognize that questions initially stated become politically obsolescent and that fieldwork often turns up factual leads that would justify changing a research plan—just what we have been saying. In normal contracting, policy makers who set a study in motion have little to do until the contractor's reports flow back. The HEW proposal calls for a marriage, or at least a liaison of modest duration, between the policy team and a suitable evaluation shop.

Representatives of the policy agency become something like coinvestigators, exchanging views frequently with the leaders of the evaluation team. They acquire up-to-date information, including impressions much too preliminary to be dignified as reportable conclusions, and they bring to proposed changes of plan a wisdom that compliance officers lack. On their part, evaluators can hope for a substantive rather than a bureaucratic response to ideas they generate, and they acquire current information about political concerns that should affect what they do.

The one-to-one relation of agency to evaluator is admirably suited to the context of command, where it may be appropriate to delimit the inquiry to what concerns the manager. Even in a context of accommodation, captive evaluations can help a program manager to anticipate and forestall problems or to defend the program. But evaluations limited to the immediate concerns of one official or one agency are unlikely to be searching and comprehensive. The sponsoring agency is most conscious of those aspects of a project that it can act on, just as it is most aware of the political interests that constitute or threaten its power base. Agencies concerned with the same problem but acting along other lines can broaden the planning for an evaluation. Program operators should also be enlisted both to improve the plans and to gain their respect for the evaluation results.

Coleman and others (1979, p. 18) suggest that the commissioning official could play the role of ombudsman for the many interested agencies and parties. The commissioner would, in this proposal, be freed of responsibility to a single agency and asked instead to weigh the interests of the whole PSC and to review the existing knowledge base before issuing a request for proposals.

The Study Project on Social Research and Development (1978, p. 75) recommended that research be sponsored jointly by the mission-oriented agencies to which a particular problem is relevant. This is highly advisable for major evaluations. Evaluation of a major effort in early childhood education, for example, might be sponsored by the Office of Education and the National Institute of Child Health and Development. Funds from one or more private foundations could serve as a leavening agent. The "Sesame Street" evaluation was a notable example of such collaborative sponsorship.

Joint sponsorship brings an accommodative element into evaluation planning. The team of sponsors could consider questions that do not match any agency's jurisdiction and absorb the pressures (for example, to make a program look good) that bear on the captive evaluator. Since obstacles to collaboration arise from the territorial imperatives and priorities of the agencies, cooperation is most likely if encouraged by officials well up in the executive branch and by bodies such as the House Education and Labor Committee. These reflections lead to what amounts to a separate recommendation; namely, that evaluation be conducted under simultaneous legislative and executive guidance. Shared parentage seems likely to provide a ready audience for the evaluation, as was true of the studies made in anticipation of the extension of ESEA.

Like many other commentators, we have serious reservations about the blockbuster evaluations so dear to federal officials and managers of large contracting firms. Huge evaluations are not necessarily better than smaller ones; we are tempted to assert that smaller total expenditures would generate more insight. Without going that far, we can condemn the eggs-in-one-basket strategy. In this section we consider ways of bringing flexibility into even stand-alone evaluations. Later we shall consider the fact that even the evaluation of one program does *not* stand alone and should not be planned as if it could. It is properly to be seen as part of the movement of social thought on a broad front. Substantial managerial changes are required to enable research to perform that broad function properly.

Decentralizing much evaluation to the state level would be a healthy development. National programs can be evaluated by state-managed studies. Services having the same purpose and carried out under the same federal appropriation nevertheless differ in form from state to state; evaluations of the variants might reasonably adopt somewhat different procedures. Should the several evaluations agree, the reports would be more persuasive than a single centralized study. If the independent studies reached conflicting conclusions, they would dramatize warranted uncertainty in a way that a monolithic national study probably could not.

Decentralization in one sense provides an opportunity for closer coordination, since agencies within a state are closer to each other and to the local sites than a federal sponsor is. Also, a resident evaluator is better attuned to local conditions than is a firm operating from a distant head office. The state evaluation is more likely to see things whole and to balance attention between federal concerns and information that could improve state and local operations.

If states cannot put much money into evaluations, federal grants are justified. Much support for social programs now comes through federal grants to states, as an accommodation to divergent state concerns and powers. It would be entirely consistent with this practice for the federal government to send evaluation funds downstream along with the operating funds. Requiring the state to put up a fraction of the evaluation funds would be desirable, since state officials are more likely to be attentive to procedures and results if they are footing part of the bill.

For questions unrelated to state jurisdictions, it would often be desirable to set two or three evaluation teams to work more or less in parallel, each with its own cohort of sites, its own treatment realizations, and its own instruments. This suggestion has been put forward by Coleman (1972) and Cook and Campbell (1979). Each team would have substantive and methodological preoccupations. We also anticipate that each team would assign priorities differently to interests among the program operators and program clients, would introduce different assumptions into statistical analyses, and would put a different coloration on the conclusions. An evaluation carried out by a single team is one sample from a universe of possible realizations of the task, just as the treatment delivered in a site is only one realization of the program plan. The combined result of two evaluations would not represent the average of all reasonable evaluations, but a proper sense of uncertainty would be gained.

Contradictions between sets of data would arouse tension, but this tension would itself serve the purpose of attracting more interest to the research. Rechecking would naturally follow. If the projects disagreed regarding client satisfaction, for example, a small side study might show that differences in the phrasing of questions produced the discrepancy. Similarly, if the teams adopted different statistical techniques, discrepancies would expose weaknesses in an argument that one or the other team would otherwise have put forward confidently.

Rossi (1979, p. 30) goes further. Committed to summative evaluation, he favors assigning one team of evaluators known to be partisans of the program to make the best possible case for it and another team of known opponents to assemble evidence that the program is a failure. We do not call for such adversary investigations. We would prefer to see evaluation teams mimicking the spirit of two scientific laboratories, each doing its damnedest with its intellectual resources. The two (or more) teams should be in regular communication, not to prevent the two studies from diverging but to help each team with its month-to-month decisions.

Dividing an investigation adds some costs. The agency has to monitor more contracts. Expenditures for instrument development and similar tasks may be doubled—this is not "duplication," however, because distinct instruments will emerge. The gain in quality of information and interpretation and, hence, in the respect that the cross-checked findings will command should be worth the extra cost. This is particularly the case because the added expenditures are mostly buying added thought—two teams designing counterpart instruments, two teams deciding on statistical procedures, two teams deciding what conclusion to draw. The costs of routine field operations would not increase by much, since each team would cover only a fraction of the sites that a single team would. Thus costs that are proportional to the number of sites or number of subjects would be almost the same with a dual or triple organization. Scriven (1978a, p. 21) argues that splitting up the large evaluation would actually buy more evaluation per dollar because smaller tasks could be handled by small firms. Since their overhead rates are lower than those of the large firm, the cost per unit of investigation would go down. More contracts to small firms would also build up additional evaluation resources.

Simultaneous parallel analysis, which is less expensive than dual investigation, has many of the same virtues. "Secondary analysis"—warming over of data taken from cold storage— is recognized as an inexpensive way to benefit more from expensive fieldwork (Bryant and Wortman, 1978). Anyone in the social science community can apply alternative analytic techniques to data archives or trace neglected relationships. Reanalyses such as those made of the Westinghouse Head Start data have obviously contributed to sounder evaluation methodology. Secondary analysis illuminates the social problem when the reanalysis contradicts the original analysis. These postmortems come too late, however, arriving long after the original, questionable report. The second opinion can do more good if it is simultaneous with the primary contractor's analysis (Cook and Gruder, 1978).

Parallel analysis violates the tradition of pure science. The traditional scientist "owns" his data down to the point where he has capitalized on his time and effort by drawing his own conclusions. It would be wrong to rush the scientist into premature disclosure. His patient examination of the data should not be threatened by the intrusion of an impatient fellow scientist who wants a quick finding and is willing to dig it out of the data himself. Science has plenty of time; investigators who might detect in the data something the first investigator missed will get their turn.

In evaluative research, however, time presses. The public has a proper interest in dependable interpretations that are up-to-the-quadrennium if not up-to-the-minute. The reward systems of evaluation and basic science, their support and planning systems, and their audiences are different. Evaluative data can reasonably be regarded as public property. They are not owned by those who collected them (except in a command context).

A contracting agency has been known to issue a separate RFP for analysis and interpretation, once the field team has gathered in the data. The firm that did the fieldwork may or may not be the contractor for the analysis. To propose simultaneous first-phase analyses simply envisions the further step of providing identical computer tapes to two or three analytic teams.

Qualitative data probably could not be transferred adequately to a second team, and this suggests a significant limitation on dual analysis. Lacking the direct field experience of the team that collected the data, the statistical analyst can take the numbers only at face value. Knowledge of events in the field cannot enrich the interpretation. But many an evaluation conducted by a single team suffers in this way. A firm working toward a quantitative report may use a two-platoon system. One squad spends its time in the field and gets to know people and events at first hand. When the contract clock calls "Time!" on fieldwork, the scene shifts to the computer facility. There, a new squad manipulates whatever marks-on-paper the first squad handed them. Superior interpretations of evaluations can be expected from interpreters who know the field events *and* the rationale for the statistical work-up. An outside analysis simply cannot do as well. But wherever purely statistical work-ups are

made, the advantage lies in having more than one analysis completed before a "main" report goes out to the PSC.

## Educating Evaluators

The education of evaluators, before and during their professional careers, surely can be improved. Better formal instruction can also improve the knowledge and sophistication of those
who commission evaluations and those who look to evaluation
for information and guidance. More sophisticated professional
work will do little good unless there is also a more informed and
thoughtful audience.

Many universities have no recognizable program to train
evaluators, and some of the training programs that exist are
parochial. Evaluation training is too often the stepchild of
a department or school engaged chiefly in training academicians
or providers of service. If evaluative work is seen as an ignoble
form of, say, psychological or sociological research, no significant training for evaluation will be added to the discipline-oriented doctoral program. If it is thought that anyone who can
make cost-benefit calculations is an adequate evaluator, a modest
competence in economics is being asked to go a long way.

As we see it, evaluation involves far more than routine
application of one or more traditional techniques. It can capitalize on many modes of inquiry and couple these with insight into
political and administrative contexts and the special requirements of policy research. Beyond that, of course, the better the
evaluator understands the service he evaluates and the theory
relevant to it, the better he can perform.

We do not expect all evaluators to be fully trained and
would not ask that the newcomers master all these elements before entering the profession. As they have done in the past,
leaders in evaluation will continue to drift into the field after
some years in basic research or service activities. This source of
talent should not be cut off by certification rules, but it should
be made easy for these latecomers to become familiar with what
their original training neglected.

We shall describe a somewhat idealized program of training for entry—a program intended for those who aspire to even-

tual leadership of the profession and who hope to direct evaluations early in their careers. Tasks in evaluation vary. Some demand only skills of elementary data processing; some demand the mature wisdom of a senior designer, a creative critic, or an official capable of judging when the time for evaluation has come. There is a place for master's programs in evaluation and for a minor within a graduate program in social welfare, public policy, or communication. A single intensive course will provide significant in-service training for persons whose main responsibilities lie outside evaluation. We note also the innovative seminars and short courses that have sprung up in Washington and in state capitals to give elected officials, legislative staff, policy executives, and program managers a better sense of what evaluation can do. Though we shall lay out a plan to prepare a kind of evaluator-for-all-seasons, we also favor a steady effort to improve training for narrower responsibilities.

Our ideal program for educating professional evaluators of social programs would have four major components: (1) disciplinary preparation—at the doctoral level—in a social science; (2) participation in dozens of interdisciplinary seminar sessions that examine evaluations; (3) an apprenticeship to practicing evaluators; and (4) an internship in an agency where policy is formulated.

These demands are not light; many students would require unusually long predoctoral work or a postdoctoral extension. We do not expect this kind of training to become the norm in the foreseeable future. Even if all other conditions were right, such training programs could be developed only piecemeal, not on a scale that would supply the present demand for evaluators. We have not managed to arrange at Stanford for most of our would-be evaluators to receive the full program that we advocate. Our intent here is to describe an ideal that more and more persons can experience more and more completely. From the way our ideal has evolved, moreover, we know that the ideal will change with experience and that faculties will extend it in idiosyncratic but sensible directions.

*Disciplinary Preparation.* Our call for basic training in a social science requires amplification. Of all the social sciences, anthropology, psychology, and sociology place greatest weight on the collection of field data and their interpretation; hence these fields are fully suitable for evaluators. But economics or statistics could be an equally appropriate base if the instruction went deeper into the collection of primary data than is usual. Rigorous disciplinary training can be given within a professional school rather than within a traditional department. Stanford has had good experience with training to the doctoral level in psychology or some other social science within its schools of business and education, and its department of communication. For some health-related programs, the appropriate social research training can be given in a school of medicine. The possibilities are by no means exhausted by these examples.

We do remain cool to a training that touches on diverse research skills relevant to a kind of social service but concentrates on no one discipline. At Stanford, for example, we have chosen to subordinate "educational measurement," whereas some universities make that the principal field of specialization for evaluators. We expect better results in general from making training in measurement part of training as an educational psychologist, an educational statistician, and so on. Training "in measurement" can too readily become centered upon skills and even upon the subset of skills currently in demand; the broader fields link techniques more closely to substantive questions and through them to a comparatively mature conceptualization of human affairs. A sense of how a body of knowledge evolves may be more necessary for the evaluator than for most research workers, if only because so much of his career will be spent on ad hoc investigations that seem to have no ancestors. But having explained our preference, we shall not insist on it. If a program labeled "educational measurement" or the like has the qualities we are stressing, we would not quarrel with its label. We do not insist that the program center on a discipline, as long as it is rigorous. It is possible to train an investigator of mathematics education or a student of penal institutions as an evaluator; such fields have a history and a critical tradition.

Our proposal for concentrated training departs from the pattern that the new schools of "public policy" have developed during the past decade, and that departure requires comment.

These schools prepare policy analysts for service in government and in research firms that contract with government, and we do not quarrel with their curricular principles. For evaluators, however, we propose a somewhat different strategy.

The premise behind separate graduate programs in public policy is that analytic work will be woven into the day-to-day exercise of authority by the analyst's executive and legislative colleagues. Fluency in shifting styles of thought and sources of concepts counts for more than mastery of one discipline. Instruction by a multidisciplinary faculty (primarily from economics and political science) is the heart of the policy-training programs. How to distill results from completed social research and evaluation is emphasized, not how to conduct fieldwork. The training accustoms students to meeting early deadlines and to assembling recommendations on the basis of fragmentary information. The cases on which lessons are based come from a wide variety of foreign and domestic agendas.

The attitudes, skills, and coping strategies developed in policy schools are cousins to the outcomes we desire for professional evaluators. We think, however, that in the future a chief evaluator should be less tolerant of the time constraints and political bounds that circumscribe the career policy analyst, should be resistant to the call for instant expertise on whatever topic reaches the in-basket, and should be rooted in the community of scholars in social science. This advice follows from recognition that the chief benefits of evaluation are not in immediate answers delivered to a key customer concerned with a specific program, but in growth of understanding. If conceptual uses are what count, evaluators should be trained to link facts to conceptual schemes and to criticize conceptualizations, as a social scientist does.

We know that some of those trained as "analysts" come to see themselves as evaluators; training in the first role does not incapacitate one for the second, or vice versa. The distinction between graduates of policy schools and evaluators is more like the indefinite boundary between neighborhoods in the same community than like the border between nations. Indeed, as we shall explain, graduate training in public policy on a campus may provide a base on which an excellent arrangement for training evaluators can be established.

Now let us return to first principles. There are two chief reasons for advocating doctoral training in a social science. First, an evaluation is likely to be better if those who conduct it have specialized qualifications and bring a mature set of concepts and skills to bear. An evaluator who has pursued applied statistics as a doctoral specialty, for example, asks more penetrating questions than the one whose statistical preparation was incidental to a degree in some other field. The specialist in a discipline does not ask the same kinds of questions or approach a field problem from the same angles as a person who has only general training or comes from another discipline. The psychologist is sensitive to the perceptions and motivations of operators and clients. The sociologist asks about structural constraints on behavior. And the economist, instead of viewing the program as a test of a discrete hypothesis, asks how production varies as inputs are varied over a continuous range.

Doctoral training in a discipline can be counted on to emphasize competence in research design, data analysis, procedures for collecting data, and tough-minded interpretation. Whatever coloration a particular discipline gives to these topics, thorough training gives a critical perspective that is invaluable in looking at plans and results of evaluations. Training in design of evaluations should go further, however, and focus on designs for specific situations (with much critical reexamination of specimen studies).

Second, the social scientist whose qualifications are not limited to evaluation has a healthy range of career options. The market for evaluators has been capricious and probably will remain so. Moreover, with its logistical and political requirements, evaluation can be so strenuous that many persons prefer not to make it a steady, lifelong occupation.

Versatility has an unselfish value. The more confident the evaluator is that he is qualified to win positions outside evaluation, the more easily he can resist the temptation to grab for a contract that has no redeeming social importance or to acquiesce in a report that does not represent his best professional judgment. Evaluators feel confident enough to bargain individually and collectively for appropriate assignments when leaving the field is a real option.

How evaluations can contribute to a social system should be a theme in many courses, if not the subject of a course in itself. The motives and demands associated with each distinctive role in the PSC should be examined in even the briefest instruction about evaluation. That emphasis will help to erase the misconception that evaluation is primarily a technology, with mysteries and benefits accessible only to the highly trained social scientist. This prescription may seem modest, but it is not. Many instructors in evaluation are not interested in social decision making, and many know little about the utilization of evaluation. If those who teach evaluators consider seriously the major themes presented in this book, that will in itself upgrade instruction.

Admittedly, not much training in politics can be accomplished on a campus, but readings can communicate something of life in government. Allison's *Essence of Decision* (1971), Meltsner's *Policy Analysts in the Bureaucracy* (1976), and Menges' "Knowledge and Action" (1978) are examples of useful works. We have been well satisfied with a course given at Stanford on the interaction of investigation and policy making, and we recommend the idea to others. But a nodding acquaintance with governmental realities is insufficient, and that is why we favor internships.

*Interdisciplinary Seminars.* Even though the mode of thought of his home discipline should be ingrained in the evaluator, his awareness ought to range more widely. The student of psychology cannot become a statistician's statistician and an anthropologist's anthropologist. He is badly handicapped as an evaluator, however, if he knows experimental psychology and the related statistics but nothing of structural regression analysis or the ethnographic approach. When he begins to conduct evaluations, he will have to take account of the questions others are prone to ask, the procedures they use, the results they get, and the interpretive concepts they rely on. He thus requires an understanding of their rationale and its blind spots.

A departmental faculty is not the place to get interdisciplinary preparation; inevitably, it has greater enthusiasm and respect for its own traditions than for those of others. Nor can the student hope to get what he needs by sampling one course in economics, one in epidemiology, and so on around the campus. That might be possible if the economics department, for example, were to design a course for outsiders along the lines of "what the economist can offer an evaluation team." Since a menu of such courses is unlikely to develop, however, we are led to think favorably of an interdisciplinary minor taught by faculty members from many departments for students from many departments.

The primary vehicle for this minor would be a case seminar. The seminar would function best if it included a reasonable admixture of postdoctoral participants: faculty members, postdoctoral fellows, and professionals currently engaged in evaluation. The seminar would set out to scrutinize, one by one, radically diverse evaluative studies. How well the style and plan chosen by the evaluator matched the character of the program and its services ought to be considered along with the more obvious questions about technical excellence. It would be asked whether the style, the choice of variables, and the timing of the evaluation matched the political realities surrounding the program. The seminar should examine why the evaluation occurred when it did, how a particular evaluator came to be chosen, and how the evaluation was managed. Informants who know a study at first hand should visit the seminar to tell the story that did not reach print. Written evaluation reports give little perspective on the decisions that investigators and commissioners made and on the political significance that the work had, or could have had, or was foredoomed not to have. The goal of the discussion would be to weigh up the evaluation's net contribution to the system. This critique would carry the seminar to the level of thought that has been missing from the education of evaluators.

The seminar could trace, for example, how a specific evaluation used statistics to serve the needs of the PSC or how it misused them. An unwarranted pretense to precision, the interment of important results in statistical tables, the successful use of simple tabulations—these are prime exhibits for the seminar. Professional evaluators should tell the seminar about ethical choices and problems of human relations they have had to face. The complex responsibilities of the evaluator will thereby become evident to the student.

Because it would cover diverse cases, the seminar would have special value for those who take research degrees in an applied field such as education or social service administration. As we have said, where the relevant faculty is active in research, such a degree can provide rigorous preparation. The applied-research student becomes familiar with the substantive issues in his chosen field and the value systems of its practitioners—a familiarity that helps him as an evaluator. In the best training programs, he goes deeply into the relevant methodologies. What he does not get is a broad view across kinds of social service. The student of educational evaluation, for example, encounters innumerable evaluations of instruction but is unlikely to explore evaluations of community mental health, welfare, law enforcement, or even manpower programs.

The several social services ought not to be the terrain of separate professions developing their own traditions and techniques of evaluation. The fields differ somewhat with respect to the kinds of data they have learned to use and the difficulties of interpretation that they are most conscious of. Each could profitably import further techniques and criteria. Ecumenism across substantive fields is as important for evaluation as is communication across disciplinary lines.

Practicing evaluators need the broadening experience that the seminar described above would provide for the trainee. Three-day workshops have their place, and so do conventions; but such instruction is thin or narrow or both. The Social Science Research Council has had great success with summer institutes or seminars of about six weeks' duration. In these seminars a few dozen persons who have already cut their permanent teeth as investigators and users of research come together under senior leadership to look at emerging techniques and ideas. We have some knowledge of one series of such institutes, run first at Stanford and then outside the United States, from 1964 to

1972. The institutes were designed to cover instructional research and development of several kinds; evaluation was a concern of perhaps one fourth of the participants in each institute. Having observed the subsequent work of the participants—several of whom are now highly visible as evaluators—we enthusiastically recommend further ventures of the same kind, with evaluation at the center. Postdoctoral institutes of the right kind do change career trajectories.

*Apprenticeships.* The tasks handed professionals call for discretion and autonomy and require that abstract knowledge work in harness with lessons from experience (Dornbusch and Scott, 1975). Apprenticeships play an important role. In clinical practice, the medical student learns to fit general knowledge to the specific case and to cope when stored-up knowledge is remote from the case at hand. Each patient in a hospital is different, yet from a succession of patients the embryonic physician carries away some general standards for treatment. Similarly, the junior evaluator has much to learn from each evaluation in which he takes part, especially if he works shoulder to shoulder with a reflective senior investigator.

Evaluators should have both intensive and extensive practice. Intensive participation carries the young evaluator deeply into the several activities of the evaluation. It is from the inside that one learns how the parts support each other and how, if ill-matched to the task, they generate futility or even chaos. But the trainee should extend his experience over far more evaluations then he can know intimately. Diversity of field experience is wanted: diversity of topic, of political and administrative context, and of scale. Participating in a single large evaluation introduces the novice to logistics and management. It takes a project on another scale to acquaint him with the stresses that beset evaluators who meet frequently with the operators whose service is being evaluated. Organizations that serve different clienteles have different things to teach. As far as possible, the student should see these differences from the inside.

On-line responsibility will drive home the value of effective communication. Students should see successive drafts of evaluation reports; better, they should participate in rewriting them. The student should listen in when results are being communicated orally. Observing which messages "take" and which do not is a first step toward acquiring skill in communication. Further along, the student should prepare critiques of evaluation reports, assist in drafting proposals to conduct evaluations, and draft interpretations of data.

Much fieldwork consists in handling dirty details: persuading local units to participate, developing instruments, interviewing clients and nonclients, eliciting facts and cooperation from an operating staff, coding records. The student who does these things begins to see what can go wrong with representativeness and data quality. Ethical questions also acquire flesh and blood vividness in these contexts.

*Political Internships.* Ten years ago, evaluators spoke of politics as an alien intrusion into their work. Even today, the literature describing the interface between research and politics consists mostly of horror stories: political villainy thwarts the scientist-hero-evaluator down to the final page, and no *deus ex machina* saves the day. Sophisticated evaluators, however, have begun to realize that the legislator and the bureaucrat are professionals. The political process has a life-style and morality of its own—a life-style and morality that evaluators have to respect if they are to be of use (Lindblom and Cohen, 1979).

Understanding should grow if a student serves even briefly in the office of a manager to whom evaluations are directed. He will be disheartened to see how hastily the reports are skimmed and how expeditiously they are filed away. Yet this is part of the reality. So is the keen questioning that ensues when a report does strike a chord. One good place for a political internship is the office of a senior legislator (state or federal) who serves on an appropriations committee. The coordinating agency for higher education of a state with many colleges and universities is another good bet, and so is the office of state superintendent of public instruction. Likewise, the student affiliated with the governing agency of a large city would have the opportunity to observe under what circumstances evaluation receives attention.

*Obstacles to Change.* Our enthusiasm in proposing reforms is matched by the sober realization that they will be difficult to bring about. Our suggested reforms would extend training by a year or two. Faculty members would have to collaborate across school and departmental lines. Practicing evaluators and policy makers would have to accept interns and donate time and attention to them. A considerable adminstrative effort would go into locating opportunities for internship and into keeping a seminar on the move.

The first requisite is faculty and staff time. With the current tight budgets in American higher education, these resources will not come easily. But foundations can help, and university departments that see an opportunity to be seized will somehow scrape funds together. Their motivation for doing so is likely to be enhancement of their ability to place graduates. Hence no information is more critical than up-to-date facts on the job market for those with strong credentials in evaluation.

While the structure for evaluation training probably should cross school and departmental lines, no program is likely to emerge unless evaluation has an institutional advocate. The unit chosen to foster training activity would not do all the training; it would be a catalyst to mobilize resources. One of its roles would be to attract students from various graduate programs into evaluation as a specialty. The agency would also organize the nondepartmental aspects of the training: the interdisciplinary seminar, the apprenticeships, and the internships. Its form would depend on the particular structure of the campus and on faculty interests. A graduate program already oriented to research on policy issues and the preparation of students for public service would probably be attuned to needs in evaluation. In many places a graduate program in public policy and public administration would therefore be a proper seedbed for an interdisciplinary effort toward training in evaluation.

The experience of the Stanford Evaluation Consortium from 1974 to date has been instructive. Although we have had mixed results in mounting doctoral training for evaluators, nothing that we experienced leads us to doubt the validity of the principles suggested here. In general, we increased our appreciation of the practical difficulties involved, as well as of the enormous influence of idiosyncratic features of a training institution.

Student enthusiasm for evaluation training was keen from the start. To some extent students had the job market in mind; an "evaluation minor" is an extra credential with which to dazzle a prospective employer. But students were also truly eager to range into a broader field and to collaborate with faculty and other graduate students in applied research. It was possible to add a course on evaluation and policy making and a seminar that looked at a variety of evaluations, thanks in significant part to a foundation grant that partly supported one faculty member. A loose coalition of professors with experience in evaluation drew together, each of them prepared to trade yarns with peers for the benefit of the seminar. And it was easy to identify courses at Stanford relevant to the practice of evaluation.

As long as the consortium's training program stayed close to the walls of the university, all was well; but the attempt to merge academic and practical training proved frustrating. Allocating time was one significant problem. Stanford signs students into regular time commitments over a quarter; not many hours are free for next week's unanticipated demand from a field project. The need for concentrated effort arises suddenly. The choice of neglecting scheduled commitments or passing up a valuable field experience placed students in many dilemmas.

Evaluation firms and policy makers had concerns other than training. Firms and officials did take on students for short-run, limited tasks, but these scarcely provided a diverse and comprehensive apprenticeship. Perhaps the practitioners could have been persuaded to broaden the experiences available, but we had neither a ready model to offer them nor the staff to coordinate a plan. We had hoped that faculty supervisors could broaden the field experiences and point up their lessons. But regular duties left faculty members little opportunity to supervise or comment on students' outside work. Faculty and students both were busier than we had anticipated. In the end, the best prepared and most experienced students found apprenticeship opportunities, while the students who most needed the experience were left at the starting gate.

Our recommendations for the education of evaluators call for commitment from faculty, students, practicing evaluators, and policy makers. A persuasive case can be made that the additional effort is in the self-interest of each group. But the dough will not rise without yeast from all of them. Truly outstanding evaluation training needs direction in which the views of faculty, practicing evaluators, and policy makers are all represented. The central leadership, the disciplinary training, and the interdisciplinary seminar are the responsibility of the university. The practicing evaluators and policy makers must accept the purposes of the training program and must be ready to furnish the necessary training off campus. The best site for such a program would be a major research university located near a cluster of firms that provide evaluation services and near a concentration of government offices that receive evaluative information. Our advice does not apply fully everywhere. Still, the potential does exist to create several outstanding centers for the education of evaluators in the United States.

## The *Sine Qua Non*: A Stronger Profession

This report is jammed with suggestions for doing better evaluations. But evaluators, commissioners of evaluations, and users of the results cannot simply act on one of our suggestions that happens to have that strong appeal. Suppose that evaluators were persuaded, for example, that in evaluating a social program a no-treatment control group is rarely cost effective. They could not drop the practice unilaterally. Hard-line methodologists would reiterate the arguments for rigor. The writers of requests for proposals would continue to call for no-treatment control groups even in studies where the argument for such controls is weak. The GAO would continue to tell congressional committees not to trust findings whose "internal validity" is uncertain; Congress could be expected to write a control group into the next mandate for an evaluation. In short, the rest of the community must share the viewpoint of evaluators if it is to affect practice.

Individual evaluators campaigning for sensible allocation of their energies fight a lonely uphill battle. The more the questions touch political and organizational nerves, the harder the battles. It is inconceivable that evaluators will win these battles if they remain mutually unacquainted, insensitive to their common interests, and intellectually fractionated. Evaluators form a small and relatively powerless group. Their main hope lies in making the potential contribution of evaluative work so clear that those who want excellent programs will join the battle on their side.

Coalition starts at home. Before allies can be enlisted, evaluators have to thrash out their own main ideas and become clear about priorities in their own minds and hearts. No two evaluators will or should agree about everything. But only after evaluators know what, by and large, they do agree on can they coordinate their actions. If the ideals expressed in this volume are to be realized, the evaluators who understand their rationale will have to work together. That demands both professional morale and professional machinery for exerting influence. Part of that influence will be directed toward members of the profession, part toward outsiders.

A strong profession develops internal agreement on the marks of good practice. It tries to eliminate meretricious projects and, where it has the power, expels those who do shoddy or inept work. It encourages sound interpretation of its practices. (The legal profession, for example, works hard at generating public understanding of the system of appeals that would otherwise be seen only as "the law's delays.") A profession presses its customers to seek services that are truly beneficial and not to request services that use the profession poorly.

Legislatures must be educated, on the one hand, not to ask for what cannot be delivered and, on the other, not to tolerate suppression or distortion of results. Other protracted struggles will be required to improve contracting and administrative practices. Finally, universities will have to be persuaded to make a place for training in evaluation as a distinctive practical art, one that cannot be compressed within present disciplinary traditions.

A strong profession can influence the institutional structure in which evaluators operate, as it informs and influences everyone interested in making the system work. Evaluators,

united, might hope to influence those who commission evaluations, for example, to put up enough dollars to make a specific
study fruitful or otherwise not commission it at all. If what
evaluators have to say is important and their influence on the
planning, conduct, and use of evaluations is to be felt, it will be
necessary to build an organization that can speak for them.

A powerful profession could conceivably make evaluations worse rather than better. A badly led profession serves its
members rather than its clientele. To identify one's field of
work as a "profession" is, in part, a bid for status. To justify
elite status, the would-be profession typically makes restrictive
moves (Hughes, 1965). Prerequisites to professional training are
multiplied, course work is prolonged, internships of some duration are called for, and the price of entry is thereby raised. Moreover, ideals prominent in the professional rhetoric may not affect practice. Many medical practitioners do not live by the pro-
fessed ideals of that field, according to the evidence of Freidson
(1970). "All professions are conspiracies against the laity," said
George Bernard Shaw. To professionalize evaluation, then,
carries risks. The social costs are offset only by integrity in
shaping standards to fit the public interest and by vigor in en-
forcing them.

To create a cohesive profession is to build an institution.
Historical examples of successful institution building indicate
that it requires inspiring ideas about what is to be accomplished
(an ideology, if you prefer), leadership, enormous quantities of
hard work, and a bit of luck. Those who understand what evaluation can do—and that means a small cadre of evaluators and
others intimately involved with evaluation—have to supply the
moving force. We dare not lay out a *plan* for building the profession of evaluation; much depends on circumstances and
events. Even the few steps that we have suggested are major
undertakings. Progress will begin slowly, but it can be continuous and cumulative.

*A National Evaluation Federation.* The time-honored
voice for a profession, as well as its conscience, is the professional association. Until very recently, evaluation had no such
groups. Now we have the broad Evaluation Research Society

and a Policy Studies Organization, along with more restricted groups such as the Evaluation Network (identified with research on schools). The long-standing professional organizations—the American Psychological Association, for example—have put evaluation on their agendas. Perhaps a dozen organizations have thus provided some degree of moral support and advice for attempts to prepare a professional code for evaluators.

The firms that compete for contracts have begun to work together, particularly through the Council for Applied Social Research. On the one hand, these firms sometimes work in concert to encourage changes in a sponsor's administrative practices that have caused trouble for more than one of them. And, on the other, the council each year publicly honors an official whose planning and contracting performance the members admire. The council thus serves to express industry views on matters of common interest. If it becomes strong enough and remains conscientious, this representation will be able to head off potential disasters for evaluations.

Unfortunately, as matters stand at this writing, few organizations aspire to represent the interests of the entire evaluation community, and none of them has strong ties across the whole spectrum of evaluation specialties or a sizable and diversified membership. None of them, therefore, provides the needed "public meeting" of the evaluation community. In our judgment, a new umbrella organization is needed, something like a "national evaluation federation" that would encompass evaluation of social programs of all kinds.

The federation that we envision would be a central council linking the many membership groups that evaluators join, not a body competing with them for enrollments. Specialties and roles should have properly balanced representation on its council. The first goal of the federation would be to increase communication among evaluators of social programs, their parochial organizations, and training institutions. The larger goal, further down the line, would be to discover, articulate, and advance the recommendations that evaluators can agree upon. An existing association such as the Evaluation Research Society could evolve into such a federation. Indeed, the steps under way to merge that society with one or more of the other organizations may have borne fruit by the time this book appears.

We arrived at the idea of a federation because the group it should speak to and for is exceedingly diverse. Most members are already rooted in a specialized subset of the evaluation community or in a profession for which evaluation is only one outlet. A federation with lines of communication to the many centers of evaluation interest could serve far better than a group whose members chose it as their primary organization.

We have no explicit program or structure to propose for such a federation. Obviously, it would cope with the same range of topics as other modern professional associations: training, ethics, employment, legislature watching, technical standards, and so on. We hope that it would have a limited but worthwhile publication program—not one that would increase the flood of printed chatter about evaluation but one that would help everyone recognize the important trends and issues, as well as the exemplars that go beyond the state of the art.

Should our proposed federation have membership meetings? A national convention with participants numbering in the thousands would, we judge, fill a much-needed gap. We do see promise in regional and local-area meetings under the federation's auspices. Traveling workshops or an analogue of the Sigma Xi lectureship could be a good investment. Any appealing local offering would help to overcome the academic isolation that prevents one evaluator from meeting the evaluator next door. (That is not exaggeration. The Stanford Evaluation Consortium began when several professors in the same small department discovered that they had all been conducting or advising evaluations "on the side" and that each had experience to offer his neighbor's students.)

*Surveying Evaluation Resources.* There is a need to keep track of the evaluation enterprise. Too little is known about the evaluation industry and the supply of evaluators. In describing the kinds of agencies and individuals now carrying evaluation responsibilities, we have had to rely on impressions because there are no solid bodies of data. There is no substantial survey of the evaluation industry, and even routine tabulations of the training and experience of evaluators are lacking. The problems of evaluation are much the same in all social service fields, and evaluators and firms cross from one program area to another. This means that surveys of evaluators, of evaluations, and of training should be comprehensive instead of being carried out separately in education, law enforcement, and other specialties.

Various sources could contribute to an emerging picture of the evaluation enterprise. Membership lists of associations of evaluators could be of use, even though the information in them is incomplete. Scholarly studies of the contracting process such as Biderman and Sharp (1972) pioneered should be encouraged. We also encourage further intimate accounts of particular evaluations—their origins, the planning decisions, the operating choices forced by circumstances, and the history of interpretation, counterinterpretation, and influence or noninfluence. Among the valuable recent examples are Gramlich and Koshel (1975) and Rossi and Lyall (1976). Beyond these, a more comprehensive analysis of evaluation resources and structures is badly needed.

Biderman and Sharp (personal communication, 1979) have undertaken a survey within education that can and should be broadened. The American Register of Research Organizations in Education (ARROE) was sponsored by the National Institute of Education; its computer file of 5000 or more organizations questioned in 1977 can and will be readily updated. Contracting firms and research units in school systems and universities are listed. Part of the information is to be printed as a directory and analytic studies are also projected, mostly in the form of cross-tabulations of the size of evaluations, their sources of funds, and the tasks they undertook.

It should be possible to organize a survey of evaluators in all social areas. (It would not have to cover all research and development as ARROE does.) The survey could be an activity of the "national evaluation federation" if that comes into being, but it could also be done under other auspices. It would require an advisory group of greater breadth than the representatives of educational institutions and selected professional associations

on whom Biderman and Sharp relied. It might be well to bring
in, say, the American Society for Public Administrators and the
National Conference of State Legislators, and, of course, persons
informed about research on health, crime, and so on. The thinking of consumer advocates, Chambers of Commerce, program
clients, and program operators should be accessible to those
who plan analyses. Such wide-ranging inputs would make the
questions asked by evaluations more searching and the findings
more broadly acceptable. The survey would examine a firm
with respect to the size and subject matter of its typical contract, the characteristics of its staff, the style of its evaluations,
and so on. Even the simple frequencies that Biderman and
Sharp plan to report in their survey will tell much about firms
that is now only guessed at.

A companion survey of agencies that sponsor evaluations
would be equally valuable. Agencies with similar missions, we
suspect, differ in the size of the evaluations they commission.
They also interact differently with the field evaluators: this
surely affects design, quality of data, and the use of findings. It
may be that evaluations have more payoff when a foundation
foots the bill than when an agency with a mission is the sponsor.
This may also be true when the topic is health rather than crime.
All such correlations say something about how to deploy evaluation resources and how to match the management of evaluations to the public interest.

Another kind of correlation would relate the social impact of evaluation studies both to their technical characteristics
and to the expertise of the evaluators. This would shed light on
the issues of design discussed in Chapter Five and on the alternatives open for training evaluators. One illustrative subquestion
is this: On what topics and in what agency settings do cost-
effectiveness or cost-benefit analyses prove useful? The evidence
would enable the profession to judge which evaluators should
have training in those techniques.

Analytic studies of the evaluation enterprise have been
rare indeed. Probably the closest approximation is Bernstein
and Freeman's (1975) correlation of the style of evaluations
with their institutional origins. Better work, they concluded, is

done by university investigators than by contracting firms. But their criteria tilted toward academic values rather than toward excellence in governance, according to critics of the book (Gray and Weiner, 1976; Windle, 1978).

Penetrating, balanced, extensive inquiry regarding the evaluation enterprise is what we recommend. Detachment—or at least balance of partisanship—is of the essence. The world can do without business-seeking propaganda from the firms or from a discipline that wants jobs for its graduates; a slashing attack on current practices is equally dispensable. (The Guttman and Wilner book (1976) passed almost unnoticed, perhaps because it was unrealistic and unconstructive.)

## Providing for Peer Criticism

There is a great need for mechanisms of criticism and appreciation within the evaluation community itself. Oversight of the evaluators' work by their peers is the most promising means of upholding professional standards and of precipitating debate about strategy and tactics. As the Committee on Evaluation Research says (1978, p. 55), "If researchers and sponsors realize that their work will be subject to public and peer scrutiny and that this scrutiny may influence their personal careers, then they are likely to perform better." Reports are typically printed in small quantities and given limited circulation; the committee recommends wider dissemination as the solution, but that is not enough. Only if public review becomes a regular practice will the prospect of good or bad publicity be a strong incentive for the evaluator to put his most self-critical effort into each new project.

Professional reviews of evaluations are sporadic and normally come too late to help either the target evaluation or those who use its findings. Reviews in the professional literature are hardly ever made from the perspective of users in the PSC; reviews are normally of, by, for, and even about evaluators. Just about the opposite is true of reviews by the GAO or the Office of Management and Budget (OMB). These do take the perspective of a client, but typically the client is thought of as a lone

decision maker operating in a context of command. Although
the reviews frequently come early—even during the planning
stage—we do not find anyone saying that such reviews have had
constructive influence on the evaluations in question. Since the
reviews by these agencies are not fed into the professional literature, they do not influence professional thought outside Washington. Restricted circulation also cuts off the kind of professional reaction to the reviews that could reorient the oversight
agency.

A review should consider whether the task set for a particular evaluation made good use of the energies of evaluators,
commenting even on the wisdom of setting up an evaluation of
that program at that time. That is to say, critics should review
what commissioners do as well as what evaluators do. A contract
that overspecifies the work, or a process of transmission that
muffles the findings, is an abuse. Abuses deserve exposure. Criticisms should appreciate any difficulties that evaluator and
sponsor encountered and overcame; beyond that, it is proper
to complain about difficulties unresolved. But a review is likely
to concentrate on alleged faults. Reviewers want their keenness
to be admired, and sometimes they aim to tear down findings
they dislike. We want evaluations to be reviewed in a collegial
rather than an adversary spirit.

When a conclusion supports one side in a political contest,
the other side properly looks hard at the research. Partisans
who attack a finding play a necessary role. In the time-honored
theory of adversary processes, challenge is the key to justice.
The advocate does not undertake to be fair minded: she presents
a weak case as if it were the strongest ever heard. And if the
weakness in the case is not exposed by her adversary on the opposite side of the table, justice has been hoodwinked.

Advocacy is selective and slanted argument, deliberately
so. Although it is contrary to the scientific norms from which
the evaluator inherits an important part of his tradition, legal
and political tradition gives it a positive ethical value. This poses
a peculiar dilemma for evaluators, similar to that faced by scientific experts appearing as court witnesses. When they take opposite sides regarding the research itself, they cast doubt either on

the adequacy of their science or on the competence of its practitioners.

In the Hawaii Three-on-Two evaluation (see Chapter Three), for example, the evaluators agreed on the measures of achievement and attitudes that were to be the primary data of the study *before* the coin flip that determined who would be program advocate. In the end, required to uphold the program before a television audience and in the face of discouraging data, the chief advocate felt compelled to attack the validity of the tests that he had earlier agreed to. This, even though some of the tests had been constructed under his own direction!

Critics do not all share the same point of view, which is surely good on balance. A multiplicity of critical views promotes reflection and encourages evolution of technique. If every overseer applied the same standards, the results would surely be stereotypic evaluations. Any one review is likely to be myopic; for example, it may stress evaluative commandments inappropriate to the political context within which the evaluation was conducted. Yet multiple reviews of an evaluation are rare, and it is even rarer for conflicting comments to reach the same audience. Especially when conflicting criteria are applied by different reviewers, the widest possible discussion within the evaluation community is desirable. Then warranted implications for future evaluation practice can be reached.

Professional oversight is a scholarly function. The review of an evaluation is comparable to the law-review article that points up conflicts among decisions of courts in different circuits or to the alternative explanation a second scientist offers for the first one's results. Serious reviews—as distinct from partisan retorts—are still initiated mostly by individuals and published in professional journals or conference papers. This long-standing practice and its potential benefits are illustrated by the Chauncey (1941) and Johnson (1946) criticisms of the Eight-Year Study (see Chapter Three) and by the Campbell and Erlebacher (1970) critique of Head Start. All three questioned the comparison of nonequivalent groups. The first two received no attention, but the third (because it appealed to prevailing political sentiments?) stimulated intensive scrutiny by statisticians of the adjustments commonly recommended. The conclusion that has now emerged (see Chapter Five) has implications for the trustworthiness of *any* comparative study. Thus the art has been advanced.

To leave reviewing to the initiative of individuals will not do. The hit-and-miss character of reviewing is the source of both the inadequacies described above and the consequent failure of the evaluation community to get a clear picture of its function. Moves to stimulate reviewing are therefore very much to be encouraged, and a few "public interest" institutions have already taken such initiatives.

Thus the Ford Foundation commissioned four scholars to write a critique of the Follow Through evaluation (House and others, 1978). The report was enhanced by rejoinders (Anderson and others, 1978; Hodges, 1978; Wisler, Burns, and Iwamoto, 1978). The Russell Sage Foundation has sponsored and published major studies of the New Jersey negative income tax experiment (Rossi and Lyall, 1976) and evaluations of "Sesame Street" (Cook and others, 1975). These thorough studies enlightened all evaluators by tracing the logical and political processes that shaped the original work and the conclusions.

As part of a further exploration of innovations, the Russell Sage Foundation also commissioned Hess and others (1977) to write a brief review of a request for proposals to explore whether criticism of such plans could advance thinking. The foundation underwrote the cost of extra pages in *Evaluation Magazine* to carry both the review and a rejoinder from the contracting agency.

Far more frequent reviews of evaluations are needed, and reviews from diverse perspectives should be brought together in the same forum. Valuable though open disagreement is, chaos is not the proper end state. The reader who struggles with the various arguments on Follow Through cited earlier will be unable to resolve them if she is as qualified technically as the best of the reviewers. As a minimum, she would have to go back to the massive original reports and to other sources cited by the reviewers in order to decide what the findings add up to. Arguments must be far better resolved if they are to help the PSC.

As a minimum, evaluations should be reviewed the same way books are. An evaluation-review editor could be appointed not only by a "trade" journal like *Evaluation and Program Planning* but also by *Contemporary Psychology* and the *American Educational Research Journal.* The editor would obtain evaluation reports at the moment of release and enlist a reviewer (or, perhaps, two or three reviewers with disparate orientations). Another minimal step would be to arrange symposia at professional conventions in which designs or preliminary reports would be presented, then criticized by speakers given advance copies of the presentation, and eventually put into perspective by round-table discussions. Beyond this, we hope that one of the evaluation journals would make reviews, counterreviews, and syntheses of reviews a major part of its offerings; a ready outlet would itself encourage reviewing.

More ambitiously, we urge that some organization obtain foundation funds wherewith to commission several panels every year that would each review one major evaluation as expeditiously as possible. This is not, we think, an idle dream. The National Academy of Education was given funds to commission reviews of scholarly works in education with a special concern for works bearing on educational policy. (For an example, see Ross and Cronbach, 1976.) Reviews under the auspices of our proposed federation would have to be sophisticated and responsible to maintain the respect of affiliated organizations; consequently, this kind of national federation could do more to advance critical standards than any lesser body.

Substantial reviews backed by a representative professional group—but not "speaking for" the group—are indispensable to the health of the evaluation enterprise. Otherwise the increasingly vigorous reviewing program of the GAO is likely to preempt the field and to set standards that should be emerging from the profession as a whole. We do not speak out of paranoia or out of disdain for the GAO's motivation and competence. It is no more fallible than other single agencies or academic groups like our consortium. The persons in the GAO now concerned with evaluation are competent and reasonable and are collaborating with evaluators (or at least a select subset) in developing their rules. But the GAO stands in a unique position in the political system, and it will not be good for the system if evaluation is dominated by views from it or from any other government bureau. The danger is already a cloud considerably larger than a man's hand.

A danger lurks in strong machinery for oversight. Standards frozen prematurely could lock evaluation into unproductive practices and impede the intellectual growth of the enterprise. The best safeguard is multiple, independent sources of criticism. Differences in values and orientations of overseers connected to various institutions are not only inevitable but are to be cherished. As long as the conflicting perceptions are expressed with equal force, the tensions will promote understanding and discourage any tendency to fit all evaluations into a single mold. The profession has to become much stronger before *it* can exercise oversight of the GAO's work in evaluation. The way to reconcile evaluators and the GAO is to make it a part of the evaluation community. But to harmonize the expectations of the GAO with what evaluators expect of themselves, each must hear the other.

### Need for a Collegial Mechanism

We have been speaking of the value of improving the single study and its interpretation, but a more crucial question is how information is to be pulled together for the reliable education of the interested public. Ideally, the community will update its view of social needs and services as new information comes in. That information comes from many sources, as we have said, and no evaluation standing by itself should be decisive in reshaping or confirming beliefs. Traditional practices in commissioning, reporting, and reviewing evaluations were not developed with the "conceptual uses" of evaluation in mind; for that reason, if no other, practices should change. One partial solution is increased reliance on what we shall call "social problem study groups." Each of these groups would be asked to weigh and consolidate knowledge and to play a significant part in directing future inquiry.

It will do no harm to review what has been said about the inadequacies of social inquiry and the difficulties that impair its usefulness. It is for these inadequacies and difficulties that the study groups are to compensate.

*Inadequacies of Information to Guide Policy.* A statement that Joseph Califano made to a Senate subcommittee on
evaluation and planning (Special Subcommittee on Evaluation
and Planning of Social Programs, 1970) is representative of
laments heard year in and year out from those who hope for
more from systematic inquiry: "The disturbing truth is that the
basis of recommendations by an American cabinet officer on
whether to begin, eliminate, or expand vast social programs
more nearly resembles the intuitive judgment of a benevolent
tribal chief in remote Africa than the elaborate, sophisticated
data with which the secretary of defense supports a major new
weapons system" (p. 204).

Congressional aide Donald Elisburg relayed forceful complaints about just where evaluators are going wrong. Among the
perceptions in the halls of Congress are

> That the assumed posture of objectivity
> among program evaluators often masks subtle but
> important biases and hidden agendas;
> That there persists an inability or unwilling-
> ness to merge the contours of various impact eval-
> uation studies so that common patterns of findings
> can be codified and differences in findings high-
> lighted;
> That interpretations of findings are cast in
> terms far in excess of their value and far overstated
> to listening audiences; and
> That the conduct and packaging of evalua-
> tive research supports first the publication interests
> of the investigators and too often relegates the
> needs of clients and sponsors to second place [Elis-
> burg, 1977, p. 68].

Evaluators have not yet come round to the view, well
accepted in philosophy of science, that even the most "objective" studies are based on preconceptions and value judgments.
Aaron (1978, p. 156), in his review of shortcomings of recent
social research, argues that the very attempt at elegance in research may obscure biases: "All science imposes certain rules of
discourse. They are intended to foster detachment and a will-

ingness to follow where findings lead, to report findings whether or not they agree with one's preferences or prior expectations and hopes. Full achievement of these goals is impossible but the very existence of the standards imposes a powerful discipline. Still, the intellectual standards of the social sciences may camouflage distortions, selective reporting of results, or more subtle violations of objectivity. Outsiders may be lulled into thinking that issues are being debated with scholarly impartiality, when in fact more basic passions are parading before the reader clad in the jargon of academic debate. Untrained readers are most easily misled, but properly guarded prose may delude trained researchers or even the analyst himself."

We illustrate Aaron's point with a report on the effects of day care on infants (Ricciuti, 1977). Policy recommendations appear at the end of this lengthy summary of research, and the naive reader would assume that the recommendations rest on the research. The recommendations reflect humane judgment—judgment we would agree with on the whole—but they did not derive from the literature reviewed. No one can make policy recommendations without going beyond the empirical evidence. Yet if the social scientist imbeds armchair recommendations in what appears to be a factual analysis, he distorts. He invites the reader to see merit in them because of their supposed scientific origins. When members of the PSC penetrate the disguise, the social science community is discredited.

The fractionation of problems and the fragmentation of communication of which Elisburg complained have arisen at least partly from the disciplinary loyalties and habits of social scientists. Attempting to emulate the formal elegance that physical science has laboriously achieved, the typical social scientist seeks simple and elegant answers to questions that cannot be given definite answers (Aaron, 1978; Lindblom and Cohen, 1979).

Typically, the investigator isolates problem elements that he can manipulate and measure under controlled conditions. A variable that cannot be easily coded is ignored. Computer-compatible data are collected on the assumption that masses of uniform data will lead to an unequivocal choice between competing views. But this is true only when the views are fully reducible to alternative predictions about just those variables. The data, perhaps considered alongside available theory and other research, produce the interpretation. No wonder that many talented social scientists never raise their eyes above minutiae and no wonder they assert that the political scene should not and does not influence them. Apprenticed in a technology of research, they little understand that the substance of their work is political. Though we are supposed to have a *social* science, too many social scientists shun fieldwork, and their theories are not required to describe or predict everyday events.

Social scientists live within disciplinary circles. Papers are exchanged and problems are discussed with colleagues in the same discipline far more than with scholars having other affiliations. Consequently, the view of the investigator is artificially limited. Divorce, child abuse, and child custody, for example, are foci of policy. Esoteric variables generated from, say, Piaget's theory of moral development are not.

Research is necessarily difficult to interpret. Alternative analyses lead to divergent conclusions, and findings can be explained in many ways. An early interpretation, not necessarily sound, lodges in the public mind; criticisms and counterinterpretations appear months or years later, but not alongside the first report. Some of the criticisms confuse or distort issues, and even the best trained and motivated readers lack the time to disentangle the threads of a dispute and trace the line from data to warranted conclusion. Even if fully balanced information were promptly available, few persons in the PSC could study it— and yet the PSC ought to have a sound, nonsimplistic summary of the relevant knowledge.

In fact, what the public gets is hasty, uncritical, fragmented reporting of evaluations. Little time intervenes between collection of the last sample data and release of the report to the press. That report may itself be stripped of content inconsistent with the aims of the sponsoring agency. The public hears the conclusions before it hears any external review, whether collegial or partisan. Long before a qualified appreciation has been made, persons who care about the program have begun to capitalize on the findings or to tear down the report.

The complexity of social problems and the timing of action make it hard to use even excellent fieldwork. Analysts have little to say when the client needs an answer in a hurry on a major social issue, according to Meltsner (1976). Ideas about policies are always in flux. New options for action are introduced, and new criticisms of existing institutions are voiced. As we have illustrated repeatedly, an evaluator who conducts an extensive study on which a decision about a program could be based is likely to find, when the study is done, that interest in the political community has shifted. The then-current question of the PSC is likely to profit more from ideas about the social problem under discussion than from exact data about a particular program whose star has passed its zenith.

Half-understood results, overdramatized in the reporting, distort political debate. This is exhibited in the contrast between what the media say about crime and its impact on the elderly and the testimony that scholars gave at a recent House subcommittee hearing on crime. The elderly are victimized less often than others, according to four out of five scholars who drew on large sample surveys designed to assess crime. The media, nonetheless, continue to suggest that crime against the elderly is a particularly virulent contemporary pathology. As Cook (1978, p. 2) says, "The nation badly needs a credible body [rather, bodies] that can quickly compile and evaluate the relevant data whenever pressures arise to place a particular issue —like crimes against the elderly—on the national agenda. The reports of such a body will not always influence the profile of a social issue or suggest the limits of its applicability—and in our democratic society they *should* not. But they may well help to inform the policy debate with the most accurate information available, however partial or flawed."

*Collegial Process in Science and in Policy Research.* Such a mechanism as Cook calls for is indeed required if the nation is to move from stand-alone reports, sometimes misleading in themselves and often ignored or misunderstood, to appropriate social learning from evaluation. Timely updates of what is known about particular problems are required. Continual discussion is needed to identify the research most worth pursuing.

But it will take much thought and ingenuity to find the variety of alternative arrangements needed to speak to current debates in a pluralistic world (Lindblom and Cohen, 1979).

In scientific work, studies do not stand alone. Studies cumulate, results conflict or coincide, false assumptions are exposed, narrow questions are shaped into broader ones, and overly broad questions are broken into more focused ones. Collegial review relies on concentrated attention from a limited circle of specialists, a so-called invisible college. Comparatively few criticisms are public; the college communicates privately, by correspondence, in seminars, or, less often, in symposia open to interested professionals. The process goes on quietly for whatever period of time is required to generate a conception that most of the informed persons can accept in its major outlines. It may take a generation or more to reach consensus on a puzzling matter; if so, scientists are allowed to puzzle away in private. Only rarely do ill-supported and conflicting views come before the public (unless, of course, some entrepreneur rushes ahead with a technology to exploit a debatable idea).

Vigorous mutual criticism is a defining feature of scientific work. The scientist reports to a prepared audience, and within that audience the members who have a special concern with his topic decide—by informal collective judgment—whether to accept his conclusion. The process is active. When editorial referees find an analytic technique to be at fault, the author has to correct it before the study sees print. When a theoretical interpretation fits the present data but not the results others have reported, someone will speak sharply about the discrepancy. Even if no evidence to date contradicts the interpretation offered, some scientist may mistrust it. If so, and his time permits, he will set out to gather data that the suspect interpretation cannot live with.

The very existence of colleagues who believe that challenge is central to science exercises a quiet discipline. The individual scientist may not be a fully disinterested seeker after truth, but even in the midst of a quest for glory he is well aware that one who is not self-critical risks looking foolish later. Not all work is properly evaluated; errors are missed for a time and unfashionable ideas are unfairly attacked. Despite these aberrations, most scientific work is judged by disciplinary standards that investigators know well. Professional control thus operates not merely through criticism but through standards that investigators internalize.

The critical process generates new research. It discredits a certain number of ill-justified conclusions and, on the positive side, reinforces the accumulation of knowledge. Despite occasional notorious rivalries and shouting matches, much of the critical process is cooperative and intellectual. Investigators genuinely assist each other by their criticisms and cross-checks. Collective judgment coalesces. It becomes possible to say, for example, "Here is the accepted concept of the causes of earthquakes at this time, and here are the matters on which we cannot agree."

When research is to bear on current decisions of social or technological importance, however, the leisurely process of the invisible college does not suffice. Physical and biological scientists are only slowly coming to terms with the need to offer responsible guidance for public decisions, especially when information is seriously incomplete. In the same way, incomplete and controversial observations by social scientists must be weighed into current decisions; to say otherwise is to argue that decisions should rest only on folk wisdom, personal anecdotes, and vintage ideas long ago accepted by the academy. The question of this section then becomes: How can social interpretations be filtered, blended, and brought into balance through a comparatively fast-moving collegial interchange? If an answer is found, the public will remain dependent neither on dated ideas nor on the limited insight of whoever is prepared to turn illuminator.

Review of evaluative studies by specialists in statistics, in the program area, or in public management moves along about as slowly as in basic science. That is slow indeed in comparison to the pace with which thinking in the PSC moves. The specialist reviews are fragmentary and are reported at scattered times and places. When comments on a report conflict, no dialogue leading to comprehensive reinterpretation ensues. Likewise, independent studies that bear on a single social problem are reported in isolation. Occasionally but only occasionally, some individual does weigh up the consistencies and contradictions in the several reports. A synthesis that develops a collective view of even a single project is rare, and a synthesis that puts a single social investigation into a broad substantive or intellectual context is almost never requested (Study Project on Social Research and Development, 1978, p. 43).

Many writers have suggested special devices to bring collegial wisdom into social research. Some favor broader research, centered on current problems, while others stress better synthesis of ideas. One recent statement grew out of an analysis of the federal investment in knowledge of social problems. The study, which was made for the National Academy of Sciences, found underutilization of policy research a principal shortcoming and recommended greater effort toward synthesis and communication (Study Project on Social Research and Development, 1978, pp. 5–6).

State-of-the-art documents or a few meetings of selected authorities are not sufficient. A single author or a congenial committee seeks consensus. They concentrate on what is settled or least controversial, not on what is unsettled; they rarely look across disciplinary, political, and philosophical boundaries. Hurriedly arranged conferences can put current views on record, but they are not likely to raise thinking to a new level.

More radical institutional innovations are needed. The Study Project on Social Research and Development (1978) recommended a number of substantial efforts, particularly with respect to problems so broad that they cannot be handled by any one agency. Among other recommendations, the report called for creation of independent temporary commissions: "The purpose of such commissions would be to review and synthesize knowledge in broad problem areas, to set priorities for future research in those areas, and to explore points of intervention for framing remedial policies and programs. They would be able to mobilize unusual expertise for one or several years to enlarge understanding of a broad problem area and stimulate problem-exploring research" (p. 75). Similar ideas appeared earlier. "Social problem institutes" were proposed to the National Science Board in 1969; these would make knowledge readily available to individuals responsible for social policy; ad hoc councils were suggested by Cellarius and Platt (1972) to advise the scientific community, public group, and policy makers on urgent issues.

Caplan (1977, p. 196) sees the need for a group capable of "[1] making realistic and rational appraisals of the relative merit of the enormous amount of diversified information that abounds in the social sciences; [2] making appropriate reproductions of information from the universities to the policy setting so as to overcome problems of translation; [3] recasting policy issues into researchable terms; [4] recognizing and distinguishing between scientific and extrascientific knowledge needs; [5] dealing with the value issues and bureaucratic factors that influence the production and use of scientific knowledge; and finally [6] gaining the trust of policy makers as well as sufficient knowledge of the policy-making process to substantially introduce social science knowledge in usable form into the policy-making process at the key points where it will most likely be used." To outline a group's function does not accomplish the harder task of actually making the group perform well, as Caplan warns; only experiment with different types of groups will generate long-range institutional plans. We agree fully with his remarks and, in what follows, attempt to build upon them.

## Social Problem Study Groups

To provide an equivalent of the scientists' invisible college, it will be necessary to organize a forum far more energetic than ordinary academic communication and far more responsible than ordinary partisan debate. To digest knowledge from diverse sources, including program evaluations, requires diverse talents; the task is not one to be assigned to a single individual or a small group. We shall return to questions of form, but function is far more important.

The "social problem study groups" would study problems in the broadest possible way. That is to say, the groups would look beyond any one program, agency, or piece of research. We envision groups that would remain in business for a considerable period to allow time for the growth and ripening of new ideas. We are mindful of what Merton (quoted in French, 1952, pp. 7–8) said a long while back regarding an ambitious proposal for evaluative studies of social work: "There is one danger that needs special attention in an affair of this kind: that of overstating the claims regarding what social research will do for social work. This takes one form above all others, and that is not having an adequate time perspective. I have the impression that this undertaking is being considered with the idea that, in the space of a few years, five perhaps, there will be a very notable impact of social research on practice. . . . I think this is very unlikely."

The task of the individual study group would be, first and foremost, to make the best possible sense of what informants say. The group would hear from those who conduct evaluations, preferably as their work progresses rather than at the very end; it would hear from those doing relevant academic research; it would hear from those who deal with the problem in service agencies; and it would hear from those who have ideas about new policies and interventions. The study group would have to decide on the soundness of any observation or summary conclusion before deciding what weight to give it, and this implies that some of its members would have to be excellent methodologists. Meanings derive from theories and from past as well as present observations, so substantive expertise would be crucial. The discussions of the group would produce a far more comprehensive and dependable interpretation than emerges when an investigator draws implications from his single study or a lone critic attacks the investigator's conclusion.

Interpretation is more than a process of arriving at best answers. As Cohen and Weiss (1977, p. 394) emphasized, properly comprehensive social inquiry "usually tends to produce a greater sense of complexity. . . . It leads . . . to a more complicated view of problems and solutions." As Moynihan (1970) remarked, more careful investigation is likely to disturb complacency by contradicting prevailing beliefs, and this can only undermine confidence in self and others. But then he added, with measured optimism, "I believe there is an answer to this. We must develop new journalism, and political leadership, capable of handling information and of translating it into valid terms of political debate. But this will not be easy. I cannot imagine it happening inside a generation" (p. 96).

The social problem study groups would continually be reformulating the questions worthy of study and recasting the key terms that define stated problems. They would thus be in an excellent position both to suggest needed investigations and to note additional variables that deserve attention in current studies. We would hope that when any major evaluation is mounted in a study group's area of concern, the evaluator would have a standing invitation to discuss his plans and perplexities, and later his observations, with the group or a suitable subset of it. Both parties would then be in touch with emerging ideas.

*Functions.* Basically, the study group would be a device for educating its members, with much of the process being mutual education *by* the members. The character and timing of efforts would obviously vary with the problem. For some problems, the first priority would be to collate, analyze, and interpret studies already completed, leaving further research for another day. For other problems, exploratory surveys or observations would be required at the outset, and in still other instances analyses of extant data would be the first move. Where research has been extensive, a group with a relatively short projected life-span can concentrate on synopsis. More commonly, we suggest, multiple-track investigations will run parallel to the continuous interpretative work of the study group, as sketched out in Chapter One. Ideas from the study group would be available to investigators, but the groups would "direct" only a small fraction of the primary investigations, if any at all.

A particularly important function of the social problem study groups would be to put research into proper time perspective. The policy maker's illusion that quick and partial studies will resolve her dilemmas leads to excessive investment in superficial appraisal of immature program ventures. As the Study Project on Social Research and Development (1978, p. 59) complains, "The current participants in the policy process, whose predecessors did not leave them with a firm base of information, are understandably preoccupied with their immediate information needs rather than with laying a firmer base for their successors. The farther in the future the results of research, the smaller its current constituency. Policy making is concerned with current issues and problems. Policy makers with short time horizons would rather commit resources to obtain immediate help than invest in an uncertain future in which they may play no part. . . . Better policies and institutional arrangements are needed to balance the inherently political, event-forced, short-run perspectives of the policy process with a research process that needs political support, the effective deployment of a scarce resource, and time." The social problem study groups, by projecting the significance of research undertakings against a more distant horizon, would encourage appropriate distribution of resources among studies with contrasting techniques and delivery dates.

Our proposed study groups differ from the usual blue-ribbon panel or commission in one important respect. These groups, like the invisible college, would issue few reports. In view of the pluralistic character of the PSC, the groups should not be constrained to agree or to offer an "answer" on a set date. Similarly, the groups should not stifle public debate or preempt decisions. At times, of course, they might respond to a request for an advisory opinion or initiate a release on their own. The statement, which might include multiple and even adversary opinions, ought to be of an educative sort; that is, it should make information available and suggest matters to consider without trying to preempt decisions. Any statement ought to be available to all sectors of the PSC. Obviously, a policy official wanting expert advice for her ears only could engage a private expert.

If the proper spirit prevails, the study groups would be judicious in what they do and do not say, trying always to win a respectful hearing in all political quarters. Making public pronouncements would not be their main function, however, any more than a continuing seminar of scientists studying earthquakes is primarily a generator of press releases. The groups would function best in the eye of the storm, as an area of calm where members can sort out what their fellow investigators and interpreters have to offer at a given moment. The more they reflect, the better informed will be their individual writings and actions.

The members of a study group would have much to say to the larger research community, to policy officials, to program participants, and to the public. These listeners need to know the range of credible views on a topic, along with the critical open questions. The way to recognize plural values and honest intellectual disagreement is to urge individuals to speak out. The member of a social problem study group would be as free as any citizen to make a public statement. The topics before a group would have political significance, and the members would have political affiliations. No one should expect a member not to communicate to allies. Indeed, outreach would be positively desired to make social research power equalizing. Freedom of speech would be constrained only by respect for what group is told off the record. In the same spirit, the existence of the study groups would not preclude any nonmember from issuing a report on the group's topic at any time. There are risks in openness. Half-baked ideas invite attack, yet the group would have to hear ideas as they are taking shape. The risk must be run, we believe, if we are to break away from a system where evaluators are too often pressed to assist those currently in power.

A study group would not be an arena for working out political accommodations; rather it would be a place for putting observations and uncertainties into perspective. Such a group would be qualified to say what is known and what questions are salient, not what action should be taken.

*Precedents.* The social problem study group would simply be an adaptation of a collegial activity that has appeared in other forms. The counterparts described below differ from the study groups that we recommend in their policy on reporting, or their duration, or their role in directing research. But individual study groups would also differ from one another.

Two of our three examples come from the work of the National Academy of Sciences, whose "operating arm," the National Research Council, was set up precisely to make scientific knowledge available to government. Until recently, the academy and its council were predominantly concerned with physical and biological science, and few of their projects focused on social programs. Even so, their experience in putting research at the service of the PSC should be invaluable in reshaping the conduct and use of social investigations. At the same time, we do not mean to imply that all social problem study groups should have such distinctive sponsorship or even a home in Washington; on the contrary, we would welcome decentralization in this as in other aspects of evaluation.

The risks of nuclear power plants are one of the pressing uncertainties of the time. The National Academy of Sciences asked qualified scientists and engineers to form a panel to sum up what is known on the subject. Some of the members favored construction of more nuclear power plants and some were active opponents; the majority had, as individuals, taken no public position. Hot though the issue is, the committee was able to produce a report that all members were willing to sign. The report (National Academy of Sciences, 1979) does not tell the PSC "what to do." Indeed, it says that a policy should be framed only after completion of similar cost-benefit analysis of alternative energy technologies. Specific technologies carry specific risks; no technology is safer than the next on all counts. Thus the committee denied that fossil-fuel technologies are demonstrably safer than nuclear energy, and vice versa.

The report weighed the available research on the many projected nuclear hazards; the committee agreed to dismiss some estimates while relying heavily on others. Some facts were agreed on; in other cases, the committee emphasized the uncertainty of present estimates. Moreover, the committee refused to see nuclear power as a fixed object. Consequences of changes in reactor design, handling of wastes, and so on were projected; the report was to this degree "formative." The evidence went well beyond the history of existing reactors and their safety records; the analyses called upon biomedical and geological knowledge in addition. Thus the assessments of risk were based on the best available theories and counterhypotheses. The report paints a variegated picture, contradicting all easy generalizations.

It remains to be seen how policy makers and the public will be led to appreciate this warranted complexity. The report was never expected to eliminate debate or to bypass political reconciliation. It may channel discussion toward genuine dilemmas, including some that policy makers were not aware of when the study began. And it may help to discourage clamor about prophesied disasters that have only an infinitesimal probability of occurrence and place proper stress on other hazards.

A second example is the Family Impact Seminar, which was set up to consider how feasible it is to assess the effects of government policies and programs on families. According to the head of the seminar ("Family Impact Analyses. . . ," 1977, p. 9), it is uncertain how such programs can use research; "[W] hile the knowledge base for such work is 'deep in psychology, sociology, anthropology' and other fields, not enough has been done to synthesize existing knowledge, particularly in relation to policy" (Johnson, 1977, p. 9). The group, which includes both social scientists and policy officials, will look into such policy areas as foster care, income taxes, and the government as employer. The preliminary results will be shared with a broad range of organizations and individuals. Johnson is not interested in pushing for action but in "slowing down the instinctive political reaction to families as 'hot'—let's do something" (p. 9). As in the previous example, the chief result of the work may be to expose complications and uncertainties.

Our third example is the National Research Council's Committee on Child Development and Public Policy. This is probably closer to the kind of study group that we envision than the previous examples. The twenty-odd members of the committee include psychologists, sociologists, an economist, a lawyer, a pediatrician, a social worker, a statistician, and two former HEW subcabinet officers. Social problems affecting children are identified by the committee or by outsiders; seed money from a foundation facilitates this problem-setting activity. Task forces are set up to dig into specific issues; the committee seeks funds for these targeted projects, enlists participants largely from outside its own membership, and turns the task force loose. Meanwhile, it carries on its own interpretive and issue-defining work.

The primary purpose of our proposed study groups would be to improve the quality and use of social knowledge. Their activity would generate timely, argumentative, and integrated information to illuminate the warranted complexity of their chosen problems for scholars, evaluators, policy makers, program staffs, and the public. All manner of organizational questions have to be faced, but it is not necessary to settle any of them here. Indeed, we do not want to discuss them with any specificity, lest debate over details distract from the main idea. In suggesting some operating principles, we offer no master plan. We expect the character of the problems undertaken to affect the form of the study groups, and we expect the first trials of the idea to modify the initial conception.

*Membership.* This is the heart of the matter. Members would have to be willing and able to think hard about the specified problems. We suggest that two thirds of a study group be social scientists or members of such neighboring disciplines as systems analysis and epidemiology. They should be drawn from corporations engaged in social research and from government, as well as from academe. Some should be well acquainted with the group's topic; others should come fresh to it and have no territory to defend. It would be important to include operating personnel of relevant programs; their closeness to the field should keep discussion from drifting off into abstractions. For example, the program operator who works with policy makers might insist that aspirations be cut to fit the cloth. "An attempt to serve nearly all children implies something less than ideal day care for many," she might say, which comes down to asking what can best be sacrificed. We would also include a few policy analysts from pertinent agencies to gain the benefit of their knowledge of the political and bureaucratic scene.

Diversity of political sympathies would be required as well as diversity of expertise. Attempting to ignore political sympathies in making appointments would open the door to inadvertent imbalance. The membership should not be a reflection of the party in power (as the Council of Economic Advisers has come to be) or of any other political position.

Because we seek detachment, we would not enroll officials responsible for policy, legislators, or representatives of interest groups and constituencies. A policy official, for example, cannot reasonably be asked to make a detached judgment about activities her agency has to regulate and defend. A reasonable device would be to invite a number of persons in administrative and political roles to meetings as visitors, perhaps with the privilege of the floor; this is an established means of interagency coordination in government. One could also appoint some retired legislators and officials as members and thus have the advantage of their experience.

In seeking political diversity, we depart from the preference some might have for a purely scientific review body, but we agree with them that members should not represent partisans. A member who represents a political interest is almost forced to be a spokesperson instead of speaking her own mind. And yet, if these study groups are not to be perceived as manipulated by the Establishment, their thinking must be accessible to the least powerful sectors of the relevant PSC. Our best suggestion is to reach out for members who, in their own right, would be entirely worthy of membership in a study group *and* who are visibly identified with outgroups. Dissent would be proper in a member and so would the member's interaction with political activists outside the group meeting.

A critical impediment is the enormous number of problems to which social research should be relevant, and the limited amount of time that group members could siphon off from commitments to research, program administration, and civic activity. The difficulty cannot be evaded by assigning broader topics to fewer groups; a group concerned with "education," for example, would necessarily break down into subgroups. A topic such as "instruction in basic skills" or "education of the handicapped" is also unreasonably broad. Perhaps a task of that order can be managed by deciding that inquiry into reading, for example, deserves primacy, whereas writing can wait. We do not consider it necessary for us to cut social problems into bits of the right size. An actual study group will pare its tasks to manageable size.

Size of group and size of topic are intimately related, but we think of a social problem study group of thirty members as a reasonable possibility. This would be small enough for vigorous plenary sessions, large enough for diversity. It would permit formation of strong subgroups. If too few members of a study group have the specialized competence to cope with a pertinent technical issue, outsiders can be added to a task force.

Insofar as one aim of a study group would be to educate those who influence the PSC, thirty is a painfully small number. In addition, innumerable individuals will want to belong to each study group, as membership would carry genuine advantages. Even in the microcosm, information is power. The member of a study group would be brought up to the minute on both evidence and opinion. That is a marketable asset, and so would be the prestige of membership. For this and other reasons it would be wise to rotate members after, say, three years, and to recruit persons not serving on other social problem study groups. A further restraint is the expectation that members will give a significant number of working days each year to the task without receiving a lavish stipend. These devices have worked well for study sections in the National Institutes of Health.

Funds for a study group could come from various sources: private foundations, government, and corporations. Joint sponsorship is to be preferred. But the important matter is not where the money comes from. Whatever the source, a charter that guarantees autonomy and stability would be essential. Freedom, diversity of opinion, and social responsibility must be maintained when study group members begin to challenge some idea that a sponsoring organization is committed to.

A study group might find an institutional home in many places. It might perhaps be advisory to some body, as long as its findings are available to outsiders also. Alternatively, work could be undertaken through a long-standing institution such as Brookings provided that persons not on the permanent staff of the institution played a substantial role.

The budget for a study group would have to be on the order of magnitude of that for a study section or a committee of the National Research Council, adjusted upward because of the larger membership. At current cost levels, the budget should come in well under $500,000 per year—a figure that is shocking only at first glance. The funds would support a small staff, provide travel expenses and modest stipends for members, and allow for a few inexpensive studies.

We are optimistic that reports of social inquiries, properly studied and placed in context, can make a practical contribution to society. But we are also aware of the limits of analytic and investigative techniques—and of the elitism in any hint that the social scientist can tell the PSC what to do. Given the speed with which a modern culture changes in its tangible aspects, as well as in personal values and aspirations, findings about programs and institutions can describe only a passing scene. Lasting ideas of great power can emerge from inquiry, but even first-order findings do not provide long-term answers.

This character of social knowledge implies that the evaluators are not called to describe last year's program and its early consequences. These are of transient interest at best. The calling of evaluators is to augment other ways of learning about human affairs, whether personal encounters, journalistic snapshots, literary representations, routine social statistics, or discipline-oriented social research.

The evaluator is set apart from some of these approaches by his commitment to offer a balanced view and, to the extent possible, an objective view. He is set apart from others by his commitment to see things whole, raising questions those married to a theory or line of action are unlikely to raise. He is set apart from still others by his commitment to help the system function in the short run as well as the long. Evaluation is not as timely as journalism, not as detached as philosophy. It does not produce knowledge for the sake of knowledge, yet it contributes to the evolution of understanding. It is not of itself sufficient to produce policy, yet without it the democratic political process can easily lead to shortsighted policies.

Most important—and this has been the message of our book—a professional, sophisticated evaluation community, free to do its best work, will educate all sectors of the political community. Out of that understanding will come more realistic demands for social services, more stable policies, and services that merit the trust placed in them.

# References

Aaron, H. J. *Politics and the Professors: The Great Society in Perspective*. Washington, D.C.: Brookings Institution, 1978.

Abert, J. B., and Kamrass, M. (Eds.). *Social Programs and Social Program Evaluation*. Cambridge, Mass.: Ballinger, 1974.

Abramson, M. A. *The Funding of Social Knowledge Production and Application: A Survey of Federal Agencies*. Washington, D.C.: National Academy of Sciences, 1978.

Abt, C. C. (Ed.). *The Evaluation of Social Programs*. Beverly Hills, Calif.: Sage, 1976.

Abt, C. C. "Government Constraints on Evaluation Quality." In L. -E. Datta and R. Perloff (Eds.), *Improving Evaluations*. Beverly Hills, Calif.: Sage, 1979.

Abt, W. P. "Design Issues in Policy Research: A Controversy." *Policy Analysis*, 1978, *4*, 91–122.

Acland, H. "Are Randomized Experiments the Cadillacs of Design?" *Policy Analysis*, 1979, *5*, 223–241.

Advisory Committee on Government Programs in the Behavioral Sciences. *The Behavioral Sciences and the Federal Government*. Washington, D.C.: National Academy of Sciences, 1968.

Alkin, M. C., Daillah, R., and White, P. *Using Evaluations: Does Evaluation Make a Difference?* Beverly Hills, Calif.: Sage, 1979.

Allen, H. M., Jr., and Sears, D. O. "Against Them or For Me: Community Impact Evaluation." In L. -E. Datta and R. Perloff (Eds.), *Improving Evaluations*. Beverly Hills, Calif.: Sage, 1979.

Allison, D. *The R & D Game*. Cambridge, Mass.: M. I. T. Press, 1971.

Allison, G. *Essence of Decision: Explaining the Cuban Missile Crisis*. Boston: Little, Brown, 1971.

Almond, G. A. *The American People and Foreign Policy*. New York: Praeger, 1950.

Anderson, N. "Weak Inference with Linear Models." *Psychological Bulletin*, 1977, *84*, 1155–1170.

Anderson, R. B., and others. "Pardon Us, but What Was the Question Again? A Response to the Critique of the Follow Through Evaluation." *Harvard Educational Review*, 1978, *48*, 161–170.

Anderson, S. B., and Ball, S. *The Profession and Practice of Program Evaluation*. San Francisco: Jossey-Bass, 1978.

Archibald, K. A. "Three Views of the Expert's Role in Policy Making: Systems Analysis, Incrementalism, and the Clinical Approach." *Policy Sciences*, 1970, *1*, 73–86.

Arnold, M. *Reports on Elementary Schools, 1852–1882*. (F. Marvin, Ed.) London: His Majesty's Stationery Office, 1908.

Arrow, K. *The Limits of Organization*. New York: Norton, 1974.

Atkin, J. M. "Some Evaluation Problems in a Course Content Improvement Project." *Journal of Research in Science Teaching*, 1963, *1*, 129–132.

Attkisson, C. C., and others (Eds.). *Evaluation of Human Service Programs*. New York: Academic Press, 1978.

Ayres, L. *Laggards in Our Schools*. New York: Russell Sage Foundation, 1908.

Badia, P., Haber, A., and Runyon, R. P. (Eds.). *Research Problems in Psychology*. Reading, Mass.: Addison-Wesley, 1970.

Baker, F. B. "Experimental Design Considerations Associated with Large-Scale Research Projects." In J. C. Stanley (Ed.), *Improving Experimental Design and Statistical Analysis*. Chicago: Rand McNally, 1967.

Baker, K. "A New Grantsmanship." *American Sociologist*, 1975, *10*, 206–219.

Baker, K. M. *Condorcet: From Natural Philosophy to Social Mathematics*. Chicago: University of Chicago Press, 1975.

Ball, S. "'Sesame Street': A Case Study of an Evaluation." In J. G. Abert and M. Kamrass (Eds.), *Social Experiments and Social Program Evaluation*. Cambridge, Mass.: Ballinger, 1974.

Ball, S., and Bogatz, G. A. *The First Year of Sesame Street: An Evaluation*. Princeton, N. J.: Educational Testing Service, 1970.

Baratz, S. S., and Marvin, K. E. "Resolving Privacy, Access, and Other Problems in the Audit and Reanalysis of Social Research for Policy." *Evaluation and Change*, 1978, pp. 31–35.

Bardach, E. "Policy Termination as a Political Process." *Policy Sciences*, 1976, *7*, 123–131.

Barnow, B. S., and Cain, G. G. "A Reanalysis of the Effect of Head Start on Cognitive Development: Methodology and Empirical Findings." *Journal of Human Resources*, 1977, *12*, 177–197.

Beckman, N. (Ed.). "Policy Analysis in Government: Alternatives to 'Muddling Through.'" *Public Administration Review*, 1977, *37*, 221–263.

Behavioral and Social Sciences Survey Committee. *The Behavioral and Social Sciences: Outlook and Needs*. Englewood Cliffs, N.J.: Prentice-Hall, 1969.

Behn, R. D. "The False Dawn of the Sunset Laws." *The Public Interest*, 1977, No. 49, pp. 103–136.

Behn, R. D. "How to Terminate a Public Policy: A Dozen Hints for the Would-Be Terminator." *Policy Analysis*, 1978, *4*, 393–413.

Bentler, P. M., and Woodward, J. A. "A Head Start Reevaluation: Positive Results Are Not Yet Demonstrable." *Evaluation Comment*, 1978, *5* (4), 6–7.

Bentler, P. M., and Woodward, J. A. "Nonexperimental Evaluation Research: Contributions of Causal Modeling." In L. -E. Datta and R. Perloff (Eds.), *Improving Evaluations*. Beverly Hills, Calif.: Sage, 1979.

Bernstein, A. "Evaluating the Evaluators." *Change*, 1977, *9*, (6), 8.

Bernstein, I. N., and Freeman, H. E. *Academic and Entrepreneurial Research.* New York: Russell Sage Foundation, 1975.

Best, M., and Connolly, W. E. "Market Images and Corporate Power." In K. M. Dolbeare (Ed.), *Public Policy Evaluation.* Beverly Hills, Calif.: Sage, 1975.

Biderman, A. D. "Information, Intelligence, and Enlightened Public Policy: Functions and Organizatons of Societal Feedback." *Policy Sciences,* 1970, *1,* 217–230.

Biderman, A. D., and Sharp, L. M. *The Competitive Evaluation Research Industry.* Washington, D. C.: Bureau of Social Science Research, 1972.

Bloom, B. S., and others (Eds.). *Taxonomy of Educational Objectives.* Handbook 1: *Cognitive Domain.* New York: Longmans, 1956.

Blumer, H. "Social Problems as Collective Behavior." *Social Problems,* 1972, *18,* 298–306.

Bolt, R. *State of Revolution.* London: Heinemann, 1977.

Boruch, R. F. "A Discussion on Issues in Managing Experiments." In R. F. Boruch and H. W. Riecken (Eds.), *Experimental Testing of Social Policy.* Boulder, Colo.: Westview Press, 1975a.

Boruch, R. F. "Coupling Randomized Experiments and Approximations to Experiments in Social Program Evaluation." *Sociological Methods and Research,* 1975b, *4,* 31–53.

Boruch, R. F. "On Common Contentions about Randomized Field Experiments." In R. F. Boruch and H. W. Riecken (Eds.), *Experimental Tests of Public Policy.* Boulder, Colo.: Westview Press, 1975c.

Boruch, R. F., and Cecil, J. S. *Assuring the Confidentiality of Social Research Data.* Philadelphia: University of Pennsylvania Press, 1979.

Boruch, R. F., and Gomez, H. "Measuring Impact: Power in Social Program Evaluation." In L. -E. Datta and R. Perloff (Eds.), *Improving Evaluations.* Beverly Hills, Calif.: Sage, 1979.

Boruch, R. F., and Riecken, H. W. (Eds.). *Experimental Testing of Social Policy.* Boulder, Colo.: Westview Press, 1975.

Boyce, D. E., Day, N. D., and McDonald, C. *Metropolitan Plan*

*Making*. Philadelphia: Regional Science Research Institute, 1970.

Braybrooke, D., and Lindblom, C. E. *A Strategy of Decision: Policy Evaluation as a Social Process.* New York: Free Press, 1963.

Brickell, H. M. "The Influence of External Political Factors on the Role and Methodology of Evaluation." *Evaluation Comment*, 1976, *5* (2), 1–6.

Bronfenbrenner, U. "The Experimental Ecology of Education." *Teachers College Record*, 1976, *78*, 157–204.

Bryant, F. B., and Wortman, P. M. "Secondary Analysis: The Case for Data Archives." *American Psychologist*, 1978, *33*, 381–387.

Bryk, A. S. "Evaluating Program Impact: A Time to Cast Away Stones, a Time to Gather Stones Together." In S. B. Anderson and C. Coles (Eds.), *New Directions for Program Evaluation: Exploring Purposes and Dimensions*, no. 1. San Francisco: Jossey-Bass, 1978.

Bureau of Education for the Handicapped. *Progress Toward a Free Appropriate Public Education: An Interim Report to Congress. . . .* Washington, D.C.: Department of Health, Education, and Welfare, 1978.

Burke, E. *Reflections on the Revolution in France.* (2nd Ed.) London: J. Dodsley, 1790.

Bush, M., and Gordon, A. C. "Utilization, Knowledge-Building, and Institutionalization: Three Criteria by Which Evaluation Research Can Be Evaluated." In T. D. Cook and others (Eds.), *Evaluation Studies Review Annual*, 1978, *3*, 767–783.

Butler, N. M. "Remarks. . . ." In *Public Schools and their Administration*. Chicago: Merchants Club, 1906.

Callahan, R. E. *Education and the Cult of Efficiency.* Chicago: University of Chicago Press, 1962.

Campbell, D. T. "Factors Relevant to the Validity of Experiments in Social Settings." *Psychological Bulletin*, 1957, *54*, 297–312.

Campbell, D. T. "Prospective: Artifact and Control." In R. Rosenthal and R. L. Rosnow (Eds.), *Artifact in Behavioral Research*. New York: Academic Press, 1969a.

Campbell, D. T. "Reforms as Experiments." *American Psychologist*, 1969b, *24*, 409–429.

Campbell, D. T. "Qualitative Knowing in Action Research." Occasional Paper, Stanford Evaluation Consortium, Stanford University, 1974.

Campbell, D. T. "Assessing the Impact of Planned Social Change." In G. M. Lyons (Ed.), *Social Research and Public Policies*. Hanover, N. H.: Public Affairs Center, Dartmouth College, 1975a.

Campbell, D. T. "Degrees of Freedom and the Case Study." *Comparative Political Studies*, 1975b, *2*, 178–193.

Campbell, D. T., and Erlebacher, A. E. "How Regression Artifacts in Quasi-Experimental Evaluations Can Mistakenly Make Compensatory Education Look Harmful." In J. Hellmuth (Ed.), *The Disadvantaged Child*. Vol. 3. New York: Brunner/Mazel, 1970.

Campbell, D. T., and Fiske, D. W. "Convergent and Discriminant Validation by the Multitrait-Multimethod Matrix." *Psychological Bulletin*, 1959, *56*, 81–105.

Campbell, D. T., and Stanley, J. C. "Experimental and Quasi-Experimental Designs for Research on Teaching." In N. L. Gage (Ed.), *Handbook of Research on Teaching*. Chicago: Rand McNally, 1963.

Caplan, N. "A Minimal Set of Conditions Necessary for the Utilization of Social Science Knowledge in Policy Formulation at the National Level." In C. H. Weiss (Ed.), *Using Social Research in Public Policy Making*. Lexington, Mass.: Lexington Books, 1977.

Caplan, N., Morrison, A., and Stambaugh, R. J. *The Use of Social Science Knowledge in Policy Decisions at the National Level*. Ann Arbor, Mich.: Survey Research Center, 1975.

Caywood, T. E., and others. "Guidelines for the Practice of Operations Research." *Operations Research*, 1971, *19*, 1123–1258.

Cellarius, R. A., and Platt, J. "Councils of Urgent Studies." *Science*, 1972, *177*, 670–676.

Chadwin, M. L. "The Nature of Legislative Program Evaluation." *Evaluation*, 1975, *2* (2), 45–49.

Chase, W. G., and Simon, H. A. "The Mind's Eye in Chess." In W. G. Chase (Ed.), *Visual Information Processing*. New York: Academic Press, 1972.

Chauncey, H. "Some Observations on Evaluation in the Eight-Year Study." *North Central Association Quarterly*, 1941, *15*, 237–264.

Chelimsky, E. *A Symposium on the Use of Evaluations by Federal Agencies*. Vol. 1. McLean, Va.: Mitre Corporation, 1977a.

Chelimsky, E. *A Symposium on the Use of Evaluations by Federal Agencies*. Vol. 2. McLean, Va.: Mitre Corporation, 1977b.

Christakes, G. *Albion W. Small*. Boston: Hall, 1978.

Clarke, R. V. G., and Cornish, D. B. *The Controlled Trial in Institutional Research—Paradigm or Pitfall for Penal Evaluators?* Home Office Research Studies, No. 15. London: Her Majesty's Stationery Office, 1972.

Cochran, W. G., and Rubin, D. B. "Controlling Bias in Observational Studies: A Review." *Sankhya-A*, 1973, *35*, 417–446.

Cohen, D. K., and Farrar, E. "Power to the Parents?—The Story of Education Vouchers." *The Public Interest*, 1977, No. 48, pp. 72–97.

Cohen, D. K., and Weiss, J. A. "Social Science and Social Policy: Schools and Race." *Educational Forum*, 1977, *41*, 393–413.

Coleman, J. S. *Policy Research in the Social Sciences*. Morristown, N.J.: General Learning Press, 1972.

Coleman, J. S. "Policy, Research, and Political Theory." *University of Chicago Record*, 1980, *14* (2), 78–80.

Coleman, J. S., and others. *Equality of Educational Opportunity*. Washington, D.C.: U.S. Government Printing Office, 1966.

Coleman, J. S., and others. *Policy Issues and Research Design*. Chicago: National Opinion Research Center, 1979.

Committee on Evaluation of Employment and Training Programs. *The Comprehensive Employment and Training Act, The Early Years*. Washington, D.C.: National Academy of Sciences, 1978.

Committee on Evaluation Research, Social Science Research Council. *Audits and Social Experiments*. Washington, D.C.: General Accounting Office, 1978.

Committee on Federal Agency Evaluation Research. *Protecting*

*Individual Privacy in Evaluation Research.* Washington, D.C.: National Academy of Sciences, 1975.

Comptroller General. *Follow Through: Lessons Learned from Its Evaluation and Need to Improve Its Administration.* Washington, D.C.: U.S. Government Printing Office, 1975.

Comptroller General. *Problems and Needed Improvements in Evaluating Office of Education Programs.* Washington, D.C.: U.S. Government Printing Office, 1977.

Comptroller General. *Assessing Social Program Impact Evaluations: A Checklist Approach.* Washington, D.C.: General Accounting Office, 1978.

Cook, T. D. "'Sesame Street' and the Medical and Tailored Models of Summative Evaluation Research." In J. G. Abert and M. Kamrass (Eds.), *Social Experiments and Social Program Evaluation.* Cambridge, Mass.: Ballinger, 1974.

Cook, T. D. "Speaking for the Data." *APA Monitor,* 1978, *9* (3), 1–2.

Cook, T. D., and Campbell, D. T. "The Design and Conduct of Quasi-Experiments and True Experiments in Field Settings." In M. D. Dunnette (Ed.), *Handbook of Industrial and Organizational Psychology.* Chicago: Rand McNally, 1976.

Cook, T. D., and Campbell, D. T. *Quasi-Experimentation: Design and Analysis Issues for Field Settings.* Chicago: Rand McNally, 1979.

Cook, T. D., and Gruder, C. L. "Meta-Evaluation Research." *Evaluation Quarterly,* 1978, *2,* 5–52.

Cook, T. D., and McAnany, E. G. "Some Recent U.S. Experiments with Evaluation Research and Their Implications for Latin America." Paper for Conference on the Measurement of the Impact of Nutrition. . . . Panama City, Panama, August 1977.

Cook, T. D., and others. *Sesame Street Revisited.* New York: Russell Sage Foundation, 1975.

Cook, T. D., and others. *An Evaluation Model for Assessing The Effects of Peace Corps Programs in Health and Agriculture.* Washington, D.C.: Practical Concepts Incorporated, 1977.

Cooley, W. W. "Explanatory Observational Studies." *Educational Researcher,* 1978, *7* (9), 9–15.

Cordray, D. S., and Lipsey, M. W. "Using Patterns of Evidence in Social Program Evaluation: An Overview and Elaboration." Paper presented at the annual meeting of the Evaluation Research Society, Minneapolis, Minn., October 1979.

Crain, R. L., and others. *Design for a National Longitudinal Study of School Desegregation.* Vol. 1. Santa Monica, Calif.: Rand Corporation, 1974a.

Crain, R. L., and others. *Design for a National Longitudinal Study of School Desegregation.* Vol. 2. Santa Monica, Calif.: Rand Corporation, 1974b.

Cronbach, L. J. "Evaluation for Course Improvement." In R. W. Heath (Ed.), *New Curricula.* New York: Harper & Row, 1963.

Cronbach, L. J. "Beyond the Two Disciplines of Scientific Psychology." *American Psychologist*, 1975a, *30*, 116-127.

Cronbach, L. J. "Five Decades of Public Controversy Over Mental Testing." *American Psychologist*, 1975b, *30*, 1-13.

Cronbach, L. J. "Designing Educational Evaluations." Occasional Paper, Stanford Evaluation Consortium, Stanford University, 1978.

Cronbach, L. J. "The Armed Services Vocational Aptitude Battery—A Test Battery in Transition." *Personnel and Guidance Journal*, 1979, *58*, 232-237.

Cronbach, L. J., and Snow, R. E. *Aptitudes and Instructional Methods.* New York: Irvington, 1977.

Cronbach, L. J., and Suppes, P. (Eds.). *Research for Tomorrow's Schools: Disciplined Inquiry for Education.* New York: Macmillan, 1969.

Cronbach, L. J., and others. "Analysis of Covariance in Nonrandomized Experiments: Parameters Affecting Bias." Occasional Paper, Stanford Evaluation Consortium, Stanford University, 1977.

Cullen, M. J. *The Statistical Movement in Early Victorian Britain.* Hassocks, Sussex, England: Harvester, 1975.

Cushing, J. G. N. "Committee on Evaluation of Psychoanalytic Therapy." *Bulletin of the American Psychoanalytic Association*, 1952, *8*, 44-50.

Cyert, R. M., and March, J. G. *Behavioral Theory of the Firm.* Englewood Cliffs, N.J.: Prentice-Hall, 1963.

Dahl, R. A. *Pluralist Democracy in the United States: Conflict and Consent.* Chicago: Rand McNally, 1967.

Dahlgren, J., and Lindkvist, L. *Program-Oriented Evaluation (Programorienterad Utvärdering).* Lund, Sweden: Foundation for Information about Economic Research, 1976.

Dasgupta, P., Sen, A., and Marglin, S. *Guidelines for Project Evaluation.* New York: United Nations, 1972.

Datta, L. -E. "The Impact of the Westinghouse/Ohio Evaluation on the Development of Project Headstart." In. C. C. Abt (Ed.), *The Evaluation of Social Programs,* Beverly Hills, Calif.: Sage, 1976.

David, J. "Summer Study: A Two-Part Investigation of the Impact of Exposure to Schooling on Achievement Growth." Unpublished doctoral dissertation, Harvard University, 1974.

Davis, H. R., and Salasin, S. E. "The Utilization of Evaluation." In E. L. Struening and M. Guttentag (Eds.), *Handbook of Evaluation Research.* Vol. I. Beverly Hills, Calif.: Sage, 1975.

Delbecq, A. L., and Gill, S. L. "Political Decision Making and Program Development." In R. F. Rich (Ed.), *Translating Evaluation into Policy.* Beverly Hills, Calif.: Sage, 1979.

Deutsch, M. "Introduction." In M. Deutsch and H. A. Hornstein (Eds.), *Applying Social Psychology.* New York: Wiley, 1975.

Deutscher, I. "Toward Avoiding the Goal-Trap in Evaluation Research." In C. C. Abt (Ed.), *The Evaluation of Social Programs.* Beverly Hills, Calif.: Sage, 1976.

Diaz-Guerrero, R., and others. *"Plaza Sésamo* in Mexico: An Evaluation." *Journal of Communication,* 1976, *26,* 145–154.

Dornbusch, S. M., and Scott, W. R. *Evaluation and the Exercise of Authority: A Theory of Control Applied to Diverse Organizations.* San Francisco: Jossey-Bass, 1975.

Downs, A. *The Issue-Attention Cycle and Improving Our Environment.* Chicago: Real Estate Research Corporation, 1971.

Dror, Y. *Designs for Policy Sciences.* New York: American Elsevier, 1971.

Drought, N. E., and Chamberlain, C. D. *Did They Succeed in College?* New York: Harper & Row, 1942.

Duke, C. "Robert Lowe: A Reappraisal." *British Journal of Educational Studies,* 1965, *14* (1), 19–35.

Echols, J. P. "The Rise of the Evaluation Movement: 1920–1942." Unpublished doctoral dissertation, Stanford University, 1973.

Edelman, M. *The Symbolic Uses of Politics*. Urbana: University of Illinois Press,1964.

Edwards, A. L., and Cronbach, L. J. "Experimental Design for Research in Psychotherapy." *Journal of Clinical Psychology*, 1952, *8*, 51–59.

Edwards, W., Guttentag, M., and Snapper, K. "A Decision-Theoretic Approach to Evaluation Research." In E. L. Struening and M. Guttentag (Eds.), *Handbook of Evaluation Research*. Vol I. Beverly Hills, Calif.: Sage, 1975.

Elashoff, J. D., and Snow, R. E. *Pygmalion Reconsidered*. Worthington, Ohio: C. A. Jones, 1971.

Elisburg, D. "A Congressional View of Program Evaluation." In E. Chelimsky (Ed.), *A Symposium on the Use of Evaluations by Federal Agencies*. Vol 1. McLean, Va.: Mitre Corporation, 1977.

Elmore, R. F. "Design of the Follow Through Experiment." In A. M. Rivlin and P. M. Timpane (Eds.), *Planned Variation in Education*. Washington, D.C.: Brookings Institution, 1975a.

Elmore, R. F. "Lessons from Follow Through." *Policy Analysis*, 1975b, *1*, 459–484.

Elmore, R. F. "Follow Through: Decision Making in a Large-Scale Social Experiment." Unpublished doctoral dissertation, Harvard University, 1976.

Encyclopedia Britannica. Vol. 12. (3rd ed.) Edinburgh, Scotland: Encyclopedia Brittanica, 1797.

Etzioni, A. "Two Approaches to Organizational Analysis: A Critique and a Suggestion." *Administrative Science Quarterly*, 1960, *5*, 257–258.

"Evaluation of the Nutrition Education and Training Program." *Commerce Business Daily*, March 7, 1979, p. 2.

Ezrahi, Y. "Political Contexts of Science Indicators." In Y. Elkana and others (Eds.), *Toward a Metric of Science*. New York: Wiley-Interscience, 1978.

Ezrahi, Y. "From Utopian to Pragmatic Rationalism: A Comparative Study in the Political Context of Scientific Advice,"

*Minerva*, in press.

"Family Impact Analysis—A Novel Policy Experiment." *APA Monitor*, 1977, *8*, 9.

Farquhar, J. W., and others. "Community Education for Cardiovascular Health." *Lancet*, 1977, No. 1, 1192–1195.

Field, C. G., and Orr, L. L. "Organizations for Social Experimentation." In R. F. Boruch and H. W. Riecken (Eds.), *Experimental Testing of Social Policy*. Boulder, Colo.: Westview Press, 1975.

Finley, C. J., and Berdie, F. E. *The National Assessment Approach to Exercise Development*. Ann Arbor, Mich.: National Assessment of Educational Progress, 1970.

Finney, D. J. "The Statistician and the Planning of Field Experiments." *Journal of the Royal Statistical Society*, 1956, *119*, 1–27.

Fisher, R. A. *The Design of Experiments*. Edinburgh, Scotland: Oliver and Boyd, 1925.

Fisher, R. A. *Statistical Methods and Scientific Inference*. (2nd Ed.) Edinburgh, Scotland: Oliver and Boyd, 1959.

Floden, R. "Counterfactuals: The Logic of Statistical Adjustment." Unpublished doctoral dissertation, Stanford University, 1979.

Frankel, C. (Ed.). *Controversies and Decisions: The Social Sciences and Public Policy*. New York: Russell Sage Foundation, 1976.

Freeman, H. E. "Conceptual Approaches to Assessing Impacts of Large-Scale Intervention Programs." *Proceedings, American Statistical Association* (Social Statistics Section), 1964, pp. 192–198.

Freidson, E. *The Profession of Medicine*. New York: Dodd, Mead, 1970.

French, D. G. *An Approach to Measuring Results in Social Work*. New York: Columbia University Press, 1952.

Friedman, M. "The Role of Government in Education." In C. S. Benson (Ed.), *Perspectives in the Economics of Education*. Boston: Houghton Mifflin, 1963.

Gardner, E. A. "Responsibilities and Rights of the Evaluator in the Evaluation of Alcohol, Drug Abuse, and Mental Health

Programs." In J. Zusman and C. R. Wurster (Eds.), *Program Evaluation*. Lexington, Mass.: Lexington Books, 1975.

Gergen, K. J. "Social Psychology as History." *Journal of Personality and Social Psychology,* 1973, *26*, 309–320.

Gilbert, J. P., Light, R. J., and Mosteller, F. "Assessing Social Innovations: An Empirical Base for Policy." In C. A. Bennett and A. A. Lumsdaine (Eds.), *Evaluation and Experiment*. New York: Academic Press, 1975.

Gilbert, J. P., Mosteller, F., and Tukey, J. "Steady Social Progress Requires Quantitative Evaluation to be Searching." In C. C. Abt (Ed.), *The Evaluation of Social Programs*, Beverly Hills, Calif.: Sage, 1976.

Glass, G. V. "Policy for the Unpredictable (Uncertainty Research and Policy)." *Educational Researcher*, 1979, *8* (9), 12–14.

Glennan, T. K., Jr. "Evaluating Federal Manpower Programs: Notes and Observations." In P. H. Rossi and W. Williams (Eds.), *Evaluating Social Programs: Theory, Practice, and Politics*. New York: Seminar Press, 1972.

Glueck, E. T. *Evaluation Research in Social Work*. New York: Columbia University Press, 1936.

Graham, O. L., Jr. *Toward a Planned Society: From Roosevelt to Nixon*. New York: Oxford University Press, 1976.

Graham, P. A. *Progressive Education: From Arcady to Academe*. New York: Teachers College Press, 1967.

Gramlich, E. M., and Koshel, P. P. *Educational Performance Contracting*. Washington, D.C.: Brookings Institution, 1975.

Graubard, S. R. (Ed.). "Limits of Scientific Inquiry." *Daedalus*, 1978, *107* (2), whole number.

Gray, L. E., and Weiner, S. S. "Review of *Academic and Entrepreneurial Research*." Occasional Paper, Stanford Evaluation Consortium, Stanford University, 1976.

Green, P. "The Obligations of American Social Scientists." *Annals of the American Academy of Political and Social Science*, 1971, *394*, 13–27.

Greenbaum, W., Garet, M. S., and Solomon, E. R. *Measuring Educational Achievement: A Study of the National Assessment*. New York: McGraw-Hill, 1977.

Grinder, R., and others. "Symposium: Joseph Mayer Rice

(1857-1934): Pioneer in Progressive Education, Educational Research, and Educational Measurement." *Journal of Educational Measurement*, 1966, *3*, 127-145.

Guttentag, M., and Struening, E. L. (Eds.). *Handbook of Evaluation Research*. Vol. 1. Beverly Hills, Calif.: Sage, 1975a.

Guttentag, M., and Struening, E. L. (Eds.). *Handbook of Evaluation Research*. Vol. 2. Beverly Hills, Calif.: Sage, 1975b.

Guttman, D., and Wilner, B. *The Shadow Government: The Government's Multi-Billion-Dollar Giveaway of Its Decision-Making Powers to Private Management Consultants, "Experts," and Think Tanks*. New York: Pantheon, 1976.

Halberstam, D. *The Best and the Brightest*. New York: Random House, 1972.

Hamilton, D. *Curriculum Evaluation*. London: Open Books, 1976.

Hamilton, D., and others (Eds.). *Beyond the Numbers Game*. Berkeley, Calif.: McCutchan, 1978.

Haney, W. *A Technical History of the National Follow Through Evaluation*. Cambridge, Mass.: Huron Institute, 1977.

Hastings, J. T. "The Why of the Outcomes." *Journal of Educational Measurement*, 1966, *3*, 27-32.

Heckman, J. J. "Sample Selection Bias as a Specification Error." *Econometrica*, 1979, *47*, 153-161.

Herzog, E. *Some Guide Lines for Evaluating Research*. Children's Bureau Publication, No. 375. Washington, D.C.: Department of Health, Education, and Welfare, 1959.

Hess, R. D., and others. "An RFP for Evaluation of Title I Programs: Will OE Learn What It Wants to Know?" *Evaluation*, 1977, *4*, 152-156.

Hobbs, N. *The Futures of Children: Recommendations of the Project on Classification of Exceptional Children*. San Francisco: Jossey-Bass, 1975.

Hodges, W. L. "The Worth of the Follow Through Experience." *Harvard Educational Review*, 1978, *48*, 186-192.

Hofstadter, R. *The Age of Reform: From Bryan to F. D. R.* New York: Knopf, 1955.

Hollister, R. "The Role of Experimentation in Policy Decision-Making." In R. F. Boruch and H. W. Riecken (Eds.), *Experimental Testing of Social Policy*. Boulder, Colo.: Westview

Press, 1975.

Horst, P., and others. "Program Management and the Federal Evaluator." *Public Administration Review*, 1974, *34*, 300–308.

House, E. R. "The Politics of Evaluation in Higher Education." *Journal of Higher Education*, 1974, *45*, 618–627.

House, E. R. "Evaluation as Justice." In G. V. Glass (Ed.), *Evaluation Studies Review Annual*, 1976, *1*, 75–100.

House, E. R. *The Logic of Evaluation Argument*. CSE Monograph Series in Evaluation, No. 7. Los Angeles: Center for the Study of Evaluation, University of California, 1977.

House, E. R., and others. "No Simple Answer: Critique of the 'Follow Through' Evaluation." *Harvard Educational Review*, 1978, *48*, 128–160.

Hughes, E. C. "Professions." In K. S. Lynn (Ed.), *The Professions in America*. Boston: Houghton Mifflin, 1965.

Inkeles, A. "Rising Expectations: Revolution, Evolution, or Devolution?" In H. R. Bowen (Ed.), *Freedom and Control in a Democratic Society*. New York: American Council of Life Insurance, 1976.

Jencks, C., and others. *Inequality: A Reassessment of the Effect of Family and Schooling in America*. New York: Basic Books, 1972.

Johnson, Harry G. "Scholars as Public Adversaries: The Case of Economics." In C. Frankel (Ed.), *Controversies and Decisions: The Social Sciences and Public Policy*. New York: Russell Sage Foundation, 1976.

Johnson, Helmer G. "Weakness in the Eight-Year Study." *School and Society*, 1946, *63*, 417–418.

Jöreskog, K. G., and Sörbom, D. *Advances in Factor Analysis and Structural Equation Models*. Cambridge, Mass.: Abt Books, 1979.

Jouvenel, B. de. *The Pure Theory of Politics*. Cambridge, England: Cambridge University Press, 1963.

Katz, D., and others. *Bureaucratic Encounters: A Pilot Study in the Evaluation of Government Services*. Ann Arbor, Mich.: Survey Research Center, 1975.

Kaufman, H. *The Forest Ranger: A Study of Administrative Be-*

*havior*. Baltimore: Johns Hopkins University Press, 1960.

Kaufman, H. *Are Government Organizations Immortal?* Washington, D.C.: Brookings Institution, 1976.

Keen, P. G. W., and Gerson, E. M. "The Politics of Software Engineering." *Datamation*, 1977, *23* (11), 80–86.

Keen, P. G. W., and Morton, M. S. S. *Decision Support Systems: An Organizational Perspective*. Reading, Mass.: Addison-Wesley, 1978.

Keeney, R. L., and Raiffa, H. *Decisions with Multiple Objectives: Preferences and Value Trade-Offs*. New York: Wiley, 1976.

Kelly, T. E. "Economic Development." In E. Chelimsky (Ed.), *Proceedings of a Symposium on the Use of Evaluation by Federal Agencies*. Vol. 1. McLean, Va.: Mitre Corporation, 1977.

Kendall, M. G. "Hiawatha Designs an Experiment." *American Statistician*, 1959, *13* (5), 23–24.

Keniston, K., and others. *All Our Children*. New York: Harcourt Brace Jovanovich, 1977.

Kershaw, D. N. "Issues in Income Maintenance Experimentation." In P. H. Rossi and W. Williams (Eds.), *Evaluating Social Programs: Theory, Practice, and Politics*. New York: Seminar Press, 1972.

Kershaw, D. N., and Small, J. C. "Data Confidentiality and Privacy: Lessons from the New Jersey Negative Income Tax Experiment." *Public Policy*, 1972, *20*, 257–280.

Kirst, M. "Short- and Long-Range Consequences [of Proposition 13]. *California School Board Journal*, 1978, *37* (6), 27–30.

Klein, R. E., and others. "Malnutrition and Mental Development in Rural Guatemala." In N. Warren (Ed.), *Advances in Cross-Cultural Psychology*. New York: Academic Press, 1977.

Kuhn, T. S. *The Structure of Scientific Revolutions*. Chicago: University of Chicago Press, 1962.

Lasch, C. *The New Radicalism in America*. New York: Random House, 1967.

Levin, H. M. "Cost-Effectiveness Analysis in Evaluation Research. In M. Guttentag and E. L. Struening (Eds.), *Hand-*

*book of Evaluation Research.* Vol. 2. Beverly Hills, Calif.: Sage, 1975.

Lichfield, N., Kettle, P., and Whitbread, M. *Evaluation in the Planning Process.* Oxford, England: Pergamon Press, 1975.

Lindblom, C. E. *The Intelligence of Democracy: Decision Making Through Mutual Adjustment.* New York: Free Press, 1965.

Lindblom, C. E. *The Policy-Making Process.* Englewood Cliffs, N.J.: Prentice-Hall, 1968.

Lindblom, C. E. *Strategies for Decision Making.* Urbana: Department of Political Science, University of Illinois, 1972.

Lindblom, C. E. *Politics and Markets: The World's Political-Economic Systems.* New York: Basic Books, 1977.

Lindblom, C. E., and Cohen, D. K. *Usable Knowledge.* New Haven, Conn.: Yale University Press, 1979.

Lipset, S. M., and Dobson, R. B. "The Intellectual as Critic and Rebel, with Special Reference to the United States and the Soviet Union." *Daedalus,* 1972, *101* (3), 137–198.

Lord, F. M. "A Paradox in the Interpretation of Group Comparisons." *Psychological Bulletin,* 1967, *68,* 304–305.

Luecke, K. F., and McGinn, N. F. "Regression Analyses and Education Production Functions: Can They Be Trusted?" *Harvard Educational Review,* 1975, *45,* 325–350.

Lynd, R. S. *Knowledge for What? The Place of Social Science in American Culture.* Princeton, N.J.: Princeton University Press, 1939.

Lynn, L. E., Jr. "A Decade of Policy Developments in the Income-Maintenance System." In. R. H. Havemann (Ed.), *A Decade of Federal Anti-Poverty Programs: Achievements, Failures, and Lessons.* New York: Academic Press, 1977.

Lyons, G. M. *The Uneasy Partnership.* New York: Russell Sage Foundation, 1969.

Maccoby, N., and others. "Reducing the Risk of Cardiovascular Disease." *Journal of Community Health,* 1977, *3,* 100–114.

MacDonald, B., and Parlett, M. "Rethinking Evaluation: Notes from the Cambridge Conference." *Cambridge Journal of Education,* 1973, *3,* 74–82.

MacDonald, B., and Walker, R. "Case-Study and the Social Philosophy of Educational Research." In D. Hamilton and others (Eds.), *Beyond the Numbers Game*. Berkeley, Calif.: McCutchan, 1978.

McLaughlin, M. W. *Evaluation and Reform: The Elementary and Secondary Education Act of 1965*. Cambridge, Mass.: Ballinger, 1975.

MacRae, D., Jr. "Science and the Formation of Policy in a Democracy." *Minerva*, 1973, *11*, 228–242.

MacRae, D., Jr. *The Social Function of Social Science*. New Haven, Conn.: Yale University Press, 1976.

Magidson, J. "Toward a Causal Model Approach for Adjusting for Preexisting Differences in the Nonequivalent Control Group Situation: A General Alternative to ANCOVA." *Evaluation Quarterly*, 1977, *1*, 399–420.

March, J. G., and Olsen, J. P. *Ambiguity and Choice in Organizations*. Bergen, Norway: Harald Lyche, 1976.

March, J. G., and Simon, H. W. *Organizations*. New York: Wiley, 1958.

Marris, P., and Rein, M. *Dilemmas of Social Reform*. Chicago: Aldine, 1973.

Marvin, K. E. "Issues in Managing Applied Social Research." Paper presented at annual meeting of Council for Applied Social Research, Washington, D.C., March 3, 1977.

Marvin, K. E., and Hedrick, J. L. "GAO Helps Congress Evaluate Programs." *Public Administration Review*, 1974, *34*, 327–333.

Mayntz, E. R. "Sociology, Value Freedom, and the Problems of Political Counseling." In C. H. Weiss (Ed.), *Using Social Research in Public Policy Making*. Lexington, Mass.: Lexington, 1977.

Mayo, J. K., Hornik, R. C., and McAnany, E. G. *Educational Reform with Television: The El Salvador Experience*. Stanford, Calif.: Stanford University Press, 1976.

Mazur, A. "Disputes Between Experts." *Minerva*, 1973, *11*, 243–262.

Meehl, P. E. "Nuisance Variables and the *Ex Post Facto* Design."

In M. Radner and S. Winokur (Eds.), *Minnesota Studies in the Philosophy of Science*. Vol. 4. Minneapolis: University of Minnesota Press, 1970.

Meehl, P. E. "High School Yearbooks: A Reply to Schwartz." *Journal of Abnormal Psychology*, 1971, *77*, 143–148.

Meltsner, A. J. *Policy Analysts in the Bureaucracy*. Berkeley: University of California Press, 1976.

Meltsner, A. J. "Don't Slight Communication: Some Problems of Analytic Practice." *Policy Analysis*, 1979, *5*, 367–392.

Menges, C. C. "Knowledge and Action: The Use of Social Science Evaluation in Decisions on Equal Educational Opportunity, 1970–1973." Washington, D.C.: National Institute of Education, 1978. (ERIC DOCUMENT NO. ED159 286.)

Merton, R. K., and Lerner, D. "Social Scientists and Research Policy." In D. Lerner and H. Lasswell (Eds.), *The Policy Sciences*. Stanford, Calif.: Stanford University Press, 1951.

Meyers, W. B. "The Politics of Evaluation Research: The Peace Corps." *Journal of Applied Behavioral Science*, 1975, *11*, 261–280.

Miller, N. E. "Effects of Drugs on Motivation: The Value of Using a Variety of Measures." *Annals of the New York Academy of Sciences*, 1956, *65*, 318–333.

Mills, C. W. *The Sociological Imagination*. New York: Oxford University Press, 1959.

Mirengoff, W. (Ed.). *Employment and Training Programs: The Local View*. Washington, D.C.: National Academy of Sciences, 1978.

Mitroff, I. I., Emshoff, J. R., and Kilmann, R. H. "Assumptional Analysis: A Methodology for Strategic Problem Solving." In L. -E. Datta and R. Perloff (Eds.), *Improving Evaluations*. Beverly Hills, Calif.: Sage, 1979.

Mosher, F. C. *American Public Administration: Past, Present, Future*. University: University of Alabama Press, 1975.

Mosteller, F., and Moynihan, D. P. (Eds.). *On Equality of Educational Opportunity*. New York: Random House, 1972.

Moynihan, D. P. "Policy vs. Program in the '70s." *The Public Interest*, 1970, No. 20, pp. 90–100.

Munro, R. G. *Innovation: Success or Failure*. London: Hodder and Stoughton, 1977.

Nagel, S. S. (Ed.). *Policy Studies and the Social Sciences*. Lexington, Mass.: Lexington, 1975.

National Academy of Sciences. *Risks Associated with Nuclear Power: Summary and Synthesis Chapter*. Washington, D.C.: National Academy of Sciences, 1979.

National Assessment. *Three National Assessments of Science. Changes in Achievement, 1969–1977*. Denver, Colo.: National Assessment of Educational Progress, 1978.

National Science Board, Special Commission on the Social Sciences. *Knowledge into Action: Improving the Nation's Use of the Social Sciences*. Washington, D.C.: National Science Foundation, 1969.

Nelson, R. R. *The Moon and the Ghetto*. New York: Norton, 1977.

Nienaber, J., and Wildavsky, A. *The Budgeting and Evaluation of Federal Recreation Programs or Money Doesn't Grow on Trees*. New York: Basic Books, 1973.

Nisbet, R. "Knowledge Dethroned." *New York Times Magazine*, Sept. 28, 1975, pp. 34–41, 46.

Nunnally, J. "The Place of Statistics in Psychology." *Educational and Psychological Measurement*, 1969, *20*, 641–650.

Orlans, H. *The Nonprofit Research Institute*. New York: McGraw-Hill, 1972.

Orlans, H. "Comments on J. Coleman's 'Principles Governing Policy Research.'" *Evaluation*, 1973, *1* (3), 20.

Overall, J. E., and Woodward, J. A. "Nonrandom Assignment and the Analysis of Covariance." *Psychological Bulletin*, 1977, *84*, 588–594.

Page, F. "Stemming the Drunken Tide." *The Observer* (London), December 11, 1977, p. 41.

Parlett, M., and Hamilton, D. "Evaluation and Illumination: A New Approach to the Study of Innovatory Programmes." In D. Hamilton and others (Eds.), *Beyond the Numbers Game*. Berkeley, Calif.: McCutchan, 1978.

Patton, M. Q., and others. "In Search of Impact: An Analysis of the Utilization of Federal Health Evaluation Research." In C. H. Weiss (Ed.), *Using Social Research in Public Policy*

*Making*. Lexington, Mass.: Lexington Books, 1977.

Pearson, K. *The Life, Letters, and Labours of Francis Galton*. Vol. 2. Cambridge, England: Cambridge University Press, 1924.

Pedersen, K. M. "A Proposed Model for Evaluation Studies." *Administrative Science Quarterly*, 1977, *22*, 306–317.

Pedersen, K. M. *Theory of Social Evaluation (Social Evalueringssteori)*. In preparation, Odense University, Denmark.

Perelman, C., and Olbrechts-Tyteca, L. *The New Rhetoric: A Treatise on Argumentation*. Notre Dame, Ind.: University of Notre Dame Press, 1969.

Pillemer, D. E., and Light, R. J. "Using the Results of Randomized Experiments to Construct Social Programs: Three Caveats." In L. Sechrest and others (Eds.), *Evaluation Studies Review Annual*, 1979, *4*, 717–726.

Popham, J. W., and Carlson, D. "Deep Dark Deficits of the Adversary Evaluation Model." *Educational Researcher*, 1977, *6* (6), 3–6.

Popper, K. R. *The Poverty of Historicism*. London: Routledge & Kegan Paul, 1957.

Popper, K. R. *The Open Society and Its Enemies*. 2 vols. (5th Ed.) London: Routledge & Kegan Paul, 1966.

Pressman, J. L., and Wildavsky, A. B. *Implementation: How Great Expectations in Washington Are Dashed in Oakland: or Why It's Amazing That Federal Programs Work at All, This Being a Saga of the Economic Development Administration as Told by Two Sympathetic Observers Who Seek to Build Morale on a Foundation of Ruined Hope*. Berkeley: University of California Press, 1973.

Quade, E. S. *Analysis for Public Decisions*. New York: American Elsevier, 1975.

Quarton, G. C. "Evaluating New Science Materials: Thoughts on Methods and Goals." In W. Martin and D. Pinck (Eds.), *Curriculum Improvement and Innovation*. Cambridge, Mass.: Bentley, 1966.

Rawls, J. *A Theory of Justice*. Cambridge, Mass.: Harvard University Press, 1971.

Reichardt, C. S. "The Statistical Analysis of Data from Non-

equivalent Group Designs." In T. D. Cook and D. T. Campbell (Eds.), *Quasi-Experimentation: Design and Analysis
Issues for Field Settings*. Chicago: Rand-McNally, 1979.

Rein, M. *Social Science and Public Policy*. New York: Penguin
Books, 1976.

Rein, M., and Schon, D. A. "Problem Setting in Policy Research." In C. H. Weiss (Ed.), *Using Social Research in Public
Policy Making*. Lexington, Mass.: Lexington Books, 1977.

Rein, M., and White, S. "Belief and Doubt in Policy Research."
*Policy Analysis*, 1977, *3*, 239–272.

Ricciuti, H. "Effects of Infant Day Care Experience on Behavior and Development: Research and Implications for Social
Policy." Unpublished manuscript, Cornell University, 1977.

Riecken, H. W., and Boruch, R. F. (Eds.). *Social Experimentation*. New York: Academic Press, 1974.

Rivlin, A. M. *Systematic Thinking for Social Action*. Washington, D.C.: Brookings Institution, 1971.

Rivlin, A. M. "Allocating Resources for Policy Research: How
Can Experiments Be More Useful?" *American Economic Review*, 1974, *64*, 346–354.

Rivlin, A. M., and Timpane, P. M. (Eds.). *Ethical and Legal Issues in Social Experimentation*. Washington, D.C.: Brookings
Institution, 1975a.

Rivlin, A. M., and Timpane, P. M. (Eds.). *Planned Variation in
Education*. Washington, D.C.: Brookings Institution, 1975b.

Roethlisberger, F., and Dickson, W. J. *Management and the
Worker*. Cambridge, Mass.: Harvard University Press, 1939.

Rosenthal, R., and Jacobson, L. *Pygmalion in the Classroom*.
New York: Holt, Rinehart and Winston, 1968.

Ross, L., and Cronbach, L. J. (Eds.). "Review of *The Handbook
of Evaluation Research*." *Proceedings of the National Academy of Education*, 1976, *3*, 81–107.

Rossi, P. H. "Past, Present, and Future Prospects of Evaluation
Research." In L. –E. Datta and R. Perloff (Eds.), *Improving
Evaluations*. Beverly Hills, Calif.: Sage, 1979.

Rossi, P. H., Freeman, H. E., and Wright, S. R. *Evaluation:
A Systematic Approach*. Beverly Hills, Calif.: Sage, 1979.

Rossi, P. H., and Lyall, K. C. *Reforming Public Welfare: A Cri-*

*tique of the Negative Income Tax Experiment.* New York: Russell Sage Foundation, 1976.

Rossi, P. H., and Williams, W. *Evaluating Social Programs: Theory, Practice, and Politics.* New York: Academic Press, 1972.

Rouanet, H., Lépine, D., and Pelnard-Considère, J. "Bayes-Fiducial Procedures as Practical Substitutes for Misplaced Significant Testing: An Application to Educational Data." In D. N. M. De Gruijter and L. J. T. Van Der Kamp (Eds.), *Advances in Psychological and Educational Measurement.* New York: Wiley, 1976.

Said, K. E. "A Policy-Selection/Goal-Formulation Model for Public Systems." *Policy Sciences,* 1974, *5,* 89–100.

St. Pierre, R. G., and Proper, E. C. "Attrition: Identification and Exploration in the National Follow Through Evaluation." *Evaluation Quarterly,* 1978, *2,* 153–166.

Salasin, S., and Kivens, L. "Fostering Federal Program Evaluation: A Current OMB Initiative." *Evaluation,* 1975, *2* (2), 37–41.

Sanchez, J. E. "Informe sobre la Evaluación del Programa 'Educadores de Hombres Nuevos' en Colombia." Unpublished paper, Institute for Communication Research, Stanford University, 1976.

Sanford, R. N. "Whatever Happened to Action Research?" *Journal of Social Issues,* 1970, *26* (4), 3–23.

Saxe, L., and Fine, M. "Expanding Our View of Control Groups in Evaluations." In L. -E. Datta and R. Perloff, (Eds.), *Improving Evaluations.* Beverly Hills, Calif.: Sage, 1979.

Schick, A. "Beyond Analysis." *Public Administration Review,* 1977, *37,* 258–263.

Schultze, C. *The Politics and Economics of Public Spending.* Washington, D.C.: Brookings Institution, 1968.

Schultze, C. "Social Programs and Social Experiments." In A. M. Rivlin and P. M. Timpane (Eds.), *Ethical and Legal Issues in Social Experimentation.* Washington, D.C.: Brookings Institution, 1975.

Scriven, M. "The Methodology of Evaluation." In R. E. Stake and others (Eds.), *Perspectives on Curriculum Evaluation.* AERA Monograph Series on Curriculum Evaluation, No. 1.

Chicago: Rand McNally, 1967.

Scriven, M. "Prose and Cons About Goal-Free Evaluation." *Evaluation Comment*, 1972, *3*, 1-4.

Scriven, M. "Thoughts on Reading an Issue of *Health Grants and Contracts Weekly.*" *Evaluation News*, 1978a, No. 6, pp. 21-22.

Scriven, M. "Two Main Approaches to Evaluation." In R. M. Bossone (Ed.), *Proceedings, Second National Conference on Testing.* New York: Center for Advanced Study in Education, City University of New York, 1978b.

Self, P. *Econocrats and the Policy Process.* London: Macmillan, 1975.

Shils, E. "Social Science as Public Opinion." *Minerva*, 1977, *15*, 273-285.

Shoemaker, D. M. *Principles and Procedures of Multiple-Matrix Sampling.* Cambridge, Mass.: Ballinger, 1973.

Simon, B. "Classification and Streaming: A Study of Grouping in English Schools, 1860-1960." In P. Nash (Ed.), *History and Education.* New York: Random House, 1970.

Simon, H. A. *Models of Man: Social and Rational.* New York: Wiley, 1957.

Simon, H. A. *The New Science of Management Decision.* New York: Harper & Row, 1960.

Smith, E. R., and Tyler, R. W. *Appraising and Recording Educational Progress.* New York: Harper & Row, 1942.

Smith, M. S. "Equality of Educational Opportunity: The Basic Findings Reconsidered." In F. Mosteller and D. P. Moynihan (Eds.), *On Equality of Educational Opportunity.* New York: Random House, 1972.

Smith, W. G. "The Ideal and the Real: Practical Approaches and Techniques in Evaluation." In J. Zusman and C. R. Wurster (Eds.), *Program Evaluation.* Lexington, Mass.: Lexington Books, 1975.

"Social Science: The Public Disenchantment: A Symposium." *American Scholar*, 1976, *45*, 335-360.

Sorensen, T. C. *Decision Making in the White House.* New York: Columbia University Press, 1963.

Special Subcommittee on Evaluation and Planning of Social

Programs, Senate Committee on Labor and Public Welfare. *Hearings.* Washington, D.C.: U.S. Government Printing Office, 1970.

Spengler, J. J. "Economics: Its Direct and Indirect Impact in America, 1776-1976." In C. M. Bonjean, L. Schneider, and R. L. Lineberry (Eds.), *Social Science in America: The First Two Hundred Years.* Austin: University of Texas Press, 1976.

Sproull, L., and Larkey, P. "Managerial Behavior and Evaluator Effectiveness." In *The Evaluator and Management.* Beverly Hills, Calif.: Sage, 1979.

Staats, E. "Federal Research Grants." *Science,* 1979, *205,* 18-20.

Stake, R. E. "Program Evaluation, Particularly Responsive Evaluation." Unpublished manuscript, Center for Instructional Research and Curriculum Evaluation, University of Illinois, Urbana, 1974.

Stake, R. E. *Evaluating Educational Programmes: The Need and the Response.* Paris: Organization for Economic Cooperation and Development, 1976.

Stanton, A. H., and Schwartz, M. S. *The Mental Hospital; A Study of Institutional Participation in Psychiatric Illness and Treatment.* New York: Basic Books, 1954.

Stebbins, L. B., and others. *Education as Experimentation: A Planned Variation Model.* Vol. 4-A. Cambridge, Mass.: Abt Books, 1977.

Steinbruner, J. D. *The Cybernetic Theory of Decision: New Dimensions of Political Analysis.* Princeton, N.J.: Princeton University Press, 1974.

Stone, A. B., and Stone, D. C. "Early Development of Education in Public Administation." In F. C. Mosher (Ed.), *American Public Administration: Past, Present, and Future.* University: University of Alabama Press, 1975.

"Study Indicates Pupils Do Well When Teacher is Told They Will." *New York Times,* August 8, 1967, pp. 1 and 20.

Study Project on Social Research and Development. *The Federal Investment in Knowledge of Social Problems.* Washington, D.C.: National Academy of Sciences, 1978.

Subcommittee on Elementary, Secondary, and Vocational Education, Committee on Education and Labor, House of Representatives. *Hearings on H.R. 15, pt. 3.* Washington, D.C.: U.S. Government Printing Office, 1977.

Subcommittee on Intergovernmental Relations, Senate Committee on Governmental Affairs. *Hearings.* Washington, D.C. U.S. Government Printing Office, 1977.

Suchman, E. A. "Evaluating Educational Programs." *Urban Review,* 1969, *3* (4), 15–17.

Suchman, E. A. "Action for What? A Critique of Evaluative Research." In R. O'Toole (Ed.), *The Organization, Management, and Tactics of Social Research.* Cambridge, Mass.: Schenkman, 1970.

"Support Your Local Detector." *Newsweek,* August 28, 1978, p. 17.

Tallmadge, G. K., and Wood, C. T. *The User's Guide: ESEA Title I Evaluation and Reporting System.* Mountain View, Calif.: RMC Research Corporation, 1978.

Talmon, J. L. *Romantic Messianism.* London: Secker and Warburg, 1960.

Tharp, R. G., and Gallimore, R. "The Ecology of Program Research and Evaluation: A Model of Evaluation Succession." In L. B. Sechrest and others (Eds.), *Evaluation Studies Review Annual,* 1979, *4,* 39–60.

Thompson, C. W., and Harper, J. K. "Student Attrition at the Five Federal Service Academies." In E. Chelimsky (Ed.), *A Symposium on the Use of Evaluations by Federal Agencies.* Vol. 1. McLean, Va.: Mitre Corporation, 1977.

Thompson, J. D., and Tuden, A. "Strategies, Structures, and Processes in Organizational Decision." In *Comparative Studies in Administration.* Pittsburgh: University of Pittsburgh Press, 1959.

Thompson, M. *Evaluation for Decisions in Social Programs.* Lexington, Mass.: Lexington Books, 1975.

Timpane, P. M. "Evaluating Title I Again?" In C. C. Abt (Ed.), *The Evaluation of Social Programs.* Beverly Hills, Calif.: Sage, 1976.

Tocqueville, A. de. *Democracy in America*. Vol 1. (P. Bradley, Ed.) New York: Knopf, 1945. (Originally published 1835.)

Tukey, J. W. "Conclusions vs. Decisions." *Technometrics*, 1960, *2*, 423–433.

Tukey, J. W. "Some Thoughts on Clinical Trials, Especially Problems of Multiplicity." *Science*, 1977, *198*, 679–684.

Tyack, D. *The One Best System: A History of the American Urban Experience*. Cambridge, Mass.: Harvard University Press, 1974.

Tyler, R. W., and others. "The Florida Accountability Program: An Evaluation of its Educational Soundness and Implementation." Washington, D.C.: National Educational Association, 1978.

van de Vall, M. "Utilization and Methodology of Applied Social Research: Four Complementary Models." *Journal of Applied Behavioral Science*, 1975, *11*, 14–38.

von Neumann, J., and Morganstern, O. *The Theory of Games and Economic Behavior*. (3rd Ed.) Princeton, N.J.: Princeton University Press, 1953.

Walker, D. F., and Schaffarzick, J. "Comparing Curricula." *Review of Educational Research*, 1974, *44*, 83–111.

Webb, N. "Learning in Individual and Small-Group Settings." Unpublished doctoral dissertation, Stanford University, 1978.

Weikart, D. P., and Banet, B. A. "Model Design Problems in Follow-Through." In A. M. Rivlin and P. M. Timpane (Eds.), *Planned Variation in Education*. Washington, D.C.: Brookings Institution, 1975.

Weiner, S. S. "Participation, Deadlines, and Choice." In J. G. March and J. P. Olsen (Eds.), *Ambiguity and Choice in Organizations*. Bergen, Norway: Universitetsforlaget, 1976.

Weiner, S. S., Rubin, D. P., and Sachse, T. "Pathology in Institutional Structures for Evaluation and a Possible Cure." Unpublished manuscript, Stanford University, 1978.

Weiss, C. H. *Evaluation Research*. Englewood Cliffs, N.J.: Prentice-Hall, 1972a.

Weiss, C. H. (Ed.). *Evaluating Action Programs: Readings in Social Action and Education*. Boston: Allyn and Bacon, 1972b.

Weiss, C. H. "Alternative Models of Program Evaluation." *Social Work*, 1974a, *19*, 675–681.

Weiss, C. H. "Evaluation in Relation to Policy and Administration." Paper presented at National Conference on Evaluation in Alcoholism, Washington, D.C., April 1, 1974b.

Weiss, C. H. "Evaluation in Relation to Policy and Administration." In J. Zusman and C. R. Wurster (Eds.), *Program Evaluation*. Lexington, Mass.: Lexington Books, 1975.

Weiss, C. H. (Ed.). *Using Social Research in Public Policy Making*. Lexington, Mass.: Lexington Books, 1977.

Weiss, C. H., and Bucuvalas, M. J. "The Challenge of Social Research to Decision Making." In C. H. Weiss (Ed.), *Using Social Research in Public Policy Making*. Lexington, Mass.: Lexington Books, 1977.

Weiss, R. S., and Rein, M. "The Evaluation of Broad-Aim Programs: A Cautionary Case and a Moral." *Annals of the American Academy of Political and Social Science,* 1969, *385*, 133–142.

White, S. O., and Krislov, S. (Eds.). *Understanding Crime: An Evaluation of the National Institute of Law Enforcement and Criminal Justice*. Washington, D.C.: National Academy of Sciences, 1977.

Wholey, J. S. "Scholarship in the Evaluation of Federal Programs." Unpublished paper, 1973.

Wholey, J. S. "Evaluability Assessment." In L. Rutman (Ed.), *Evaluation Research Methods: A Basic Guide*. Beverly Hills, Calif.: Sage, 1977.

Wholey, J. S., and others. *Federal Evaluation Policy*. Washington, D.C.: Urban Institute, 1970.

Wiles, P. "Crisis Prediction." *Annals of the American Academy of Political and Social Science*, 1971, *393*, 32–39.

Williams, W. *Social Policy Research and Analysis: The Experience in the Federal Social Agencies*. New York: American Elsevier, 1971.

Williams, W. "Implementation Analysis and Assessment." *Policy Analysis*, 1975, *1*, 531–566.

Williams, W., and Evans, J. W. "The Politics of Evaluation: The Case of Head Start." *Annals of the American Academy of*

*Political and Social Science*, 1969, *385*, 118–132.

Windle, C. "Review of *Academic and Entrepreneurial Research.*" *Evaluation and Program Planning*, 1978, *1*, 87–88.

Wisler, C. E., Burns, G. P., Jr., and Iwamoto, D. "Follow Through Redux: A Response to the Critique By House, Glass, McLean, and Walker." *Harvard Educational Review*, 1978, *48*, 171–185.

Witmer, H. L. "Analysis of Methodology." In D. G. French and associates, *An Approach to Measuring Results in Social Work.* New York: Columbia University Press, 1952.

Worthen, B., and Sanders, J. R. *Educational Evaluation: Theory and Practice*. Worthington, Ohio: C. A. Jones, 1973.

Wurzburg, G. "What Limits the Impact of Evaluations on Federal Policy?" In L. –E. Datta and R. Perloff (Eds.), *Improving Evaluations*. Beverly Hills, Calif.: Sage, 1979.

Ziman, J. M. *Public Knowledge: The Social Dimension of Science*. Cambridge, England: Cambridge University Press, 1968.

# Name Index

413

# Subject Index

sign, 232–235; comparative studies of, 281–313; defining groups by response to, 310–313; delivery process, 226, 254–261; diversified concepts of, 223–224, 275–278, 285; generalization of, 249–251; in null control studies, 282–283, 289–291, 293, 295–301; during prototype phase, 241–242; setting and conditions of, 303–304; standardizing of, 226. *See also* Assignment to treatments; Comparative studies; Controls; Superrealization stage
Trial studies, 42; of social programs. 272, 274–275, 277–278

# U

Uncertainty: and balance of evidence, 278; and baseline data costs, 289; and comparison of treatments, 281–282; in evaluative design, 227–228, 261–264; and information yield, 261–264; interval, 299; and team evaluation, 337
Unemployment issues, and social values, 91–93
United States: evaluation concepts in, 14–15; social sciences in, 26–35. *See also* Congress; Federal agencies; General Accounting Office (GAO); Government programs; Legislators
U.S. Agency for International Development: health broadcasts in Nicaragua, 248–262, 266–267; instructional television project, 228–229
U.S. Civil Rights Commission, 168–169
U.S. Department of Commerce, 141
U.S. Department of Defense, 30
U.S. Department of Health, Education and Welfare: busing study, 77–83; and Coleman report, 189–190; goal specification by,

131; Office of Education, 33, 131, 322, 332–333; Office of Planning and Evaluation, 323–324; relations with evaluators, 334; research expenditures of, 41
U.S. Department of Housing and Urban Development: housing allowance trial, 164–165; research expenditures of, 41
U.S. Department of Justice: in busing controversy, 81–83; research expenditures of, 41
U.S. Forest Service: command and accommodation within, 86–88, 105, 134; policy studies in, 143–145
U.S. Office of Economic Opportunity, New Jersey negative income tax study, 164, 334 (*See also* New Jersey negative income tax study); school voucher study, 252
U.S. Office of Management and Budget (OMB), 141; design criticisms of, 227; review perspectives of, 359–360
U.S. Postal Service, 146
Units (U): cell divisions of, 296–297; choice of, 232–235, 239; community as, 300–304; extrapolation from studies, 250–251; populations and subpopulations of, 298–300; post hoc assignment of, 306–307; unrepresentative sampling of, 278–279
UTO model: extrapolation from conclusions, 232–235; and inferences of study, 314
*UTO (star-UTO): and conclusions of study, 314; as policy concern, 232–235. *See also* Extrapolation; External validity

# V

Validity: construct validity, 315; and random assignment, 304; threats to, 290–291. *See also*